From the Fulda Gap to Kuwait

U.S. Army, Europe
and
the Gulf War

by

Stephen P. Gehring

DEPARTMENT OF THE ARMY
WASHINGTON, D.C., 1998

Library of Congress Cataloging-in-Publication Data

Gehring, Stephen P., 1945–
   From the Fulda Gap to Kuwait : U.S. Army, Europe, and the Gulf War
/ Stephen P. Gehring.
     p. cm.
   Includes bibliographical references and index.
   1. Persian Gulf War, 1991—Regimental histories. 2. United
States. Army. Europe and Seventh Army—History—20th century.
I. Title.
DS79.724.U6G44 1998   97–39460
956.7044'242—dc21   CIP

CMH Pub 70–56

First Printing

For sale by the U.S. Government Printing Office
Superintendent of Documents, Mail Stop: SSOP, Washington, DC 20402-9328
ISBN 0-16-049385-4

Foreword

Iraq's aggression against the oil-rich emirate of Kuwait in August 1990 sparked an international crisis in a part of the world vital to the West but where the United States and its allies maintained few land-based forces. As a result, the United States faced a significant test of its ability to project decisive military power to the Persian Gulf region in a timely and effective manner and to employ those forces as the cutting edge of the international coalition.

The United States Army contributed the bulk of the manpower and much of the equipment that this nation dedicated to the coalition's triumph. While airborne soldiers based in the United States were the first ground troops to deploy to Saudi Arabia in response to the crisis, U.S. Army, Europe (USAREUR), ultimately sent a heavy armored corps and thousands of support troops and equipment that provided the critical mass to the coalition, contributing immeasurably to the historic 100-hour land victory over Iraq. In this book we will examine the efforts made by USAREUR to deploy the substantial land forces that proved so critical to the success of coalition operations in the Persian Gulf.

At the time of the crisis in the Gulf, U.S. forces had been stationed in Western Europe for over forty years, protecting American vital interests from the powerful armies of the Soviet Union and its Warsaw Pact allies. In 1989 and 1990, however, the threat environment in Europe underwent a profound change. Cold War tensions diminished substantially as a result of the cutbacks in military forces undertaken by Mikhail Gorbachev and his government's acquiescence to the collapse of Communist regimes across Eastern Europe. These sea changes in the threat enabled a substantial portion of the American forces based in Europe to expand their focus to events in the Gulf.

Prior to the Gulf crisis, the U.S. government's reaction to the political changes in Eastern Europe was marked by a prompt but careful reevaluation of America's international responsibilities and associated military requirements. At the direction of Headquarters, Department of the Army, leaders of U.S. Army, Europe, drew up plans for a smaller but more versatile force on the Continent—a force that could rapidly respond to crises throughout the region. As early as 1989, USAREUR began to introduce significant alterations in unit equipment, and it broadened its training focus appropriate to an expanded range of mission requirements. USAREUR also planned to begin substantial reductions in its aggregate force levels beginning in late 1990. Through this period, NATO headquarters, the Department of Defense, and the joint commanders in Europe were actively involved in the planning process.

When the war in the Gulf erupted, USAREUR's reduction plans were temporarily put on hold. But the expansion in the focus of USAREUR training had resulted in Army forces well prepared for military action and mobile warfare in a theater as remote as Kuwait. The training revolution begun in the Army in the early 1980s had come to full fruition by the end of the decade—Army war-fighting doctrine in USAREUR was understood and practiced; training was executed to an exacting standard. USAREUR units, as part of the finest Army our nation has ever fielded, were trained and ready.

By the autumn of 1990, USAREUR had obtained the world's most modern equipment for armored land warfare, ranging from superior tanks, armored personnel carriers, and artillery vehicles to sophisticated attack helicopters and exceptionally rugged and reliable tactical wheeled vehicles. USAREUR troops were among the very best our nation had to offer. They spent five months of each year in a field training environment, mastering the tactics, techniques, and procedures that would undergird victory in battle. It was to these well-prepared and well-led troops in Europe that the Pentagon turned to provide the heavy armored corps that would anchor the American land attack in the Gulf and defeat Iraq's most formidable military formations.

This book describes how U.S. Army, Europe, assembled, prepared, and deployed the powerful forces it contributed to the coalition effort in the Gulf and how USAREUR accomplished these challenging missions while maintaining its continuing security responsibilities on the Continent and preparing to execute its program of force reductions. The book discusses the complicated planning for the deployment and the rapid-fire implementation of those plans, the troops sent to the Gulf and the equipment they employed, and the contributions of the nondeploying troops to the support of family members left at home in Europe. This study also examines how, in the aftermath of our victory in the Gulf, USAREUR redeployed its forces and immediately returned to the tasks of reorganization and reduction developed before the war.

The versatility, deployability, and lethality that USAREUR forces demonstrated in the Gulf War provide an eloquent and powerful statement on the value derived by this nation from a trained and ready Army. As we look ahead to a new era of challenge and change, the historic accomplishments of USAREUR represent a model for those now charged with shaping the Army for the next century—an Army that must retain its ability to protect and advance vital American interests any place, any time.

JOHN W. MOUNTCASTLE
Brigadier General, USA
Chief of Military History

CARL E. VUONO
General, USA (Retired)
Chief of Staff, U.S. Army
(1987–1991)

Washington, D.C.
18 December 1997

The Author

Stephen P. Gehring served as an enlisted man in Army combat service support units in central South Vietnam and in the 82d Airborne Division at Fort Bragg, North Carolina. He earned a B.A. degree in history *magna cum laude* from the University of Wisconsin at Eau Claire and an M.A. degree in that field from the University of North Carolina at Chapel Hill. He taught briefly with the University of Maryland's program in Europe. He has worked since 1976 for Headquarters, United States Army, Europe, serving as chief of its publications division, as a management analyst, and since 1987 as a historian. He is currently writing a history of the reduction and restructuring undertaken by the U.S. Army in Europe during the period 1988–1995.

Preface

This study describes how the United States Army, Europe (USAREUR), under the command of General Crosbie E. Saint, supported the armed response of the United States and the United Nations to Iraq's August 1990 invasion of Kuwait at the very time it was managing a fundamental transition in its fifty-year history of defending Central Europe.

This study was initially drafted in 1991 and 1992. Even after recent revisions, it is still imbued with certain attitudes then broadly shared by both military and civilian personnel throughout USAREUR headquarters. Primary among these was the satisfaction of headquarters personnel who felt they had contributed to two historic American victories—the collapse of the Berlin Wall and the Warsaw Pact, marking the end of the Cold War, and the defeat of Saddam Hussein's armies in the Gulf War. Present also were the concern and nostalgia felt by many of these personnel as they helped dismantle the larger part of a very successful army at the outset of a new and unpredictable era.

It is the responsibility of historians, including historians employed by the U.S. Army, to overcome narrow prejudices in order to describe and explain as accurately as possible the subject at hand. The revival of interest in this subject after a lapse of several years gave the author the opportunity to review the content and conclusions of this study in the light of another day. The facts, story, and conclusions still are valid. The study describes how U.S. Army leaders in Europe used the unique opportunities presented by a reduced threat in their theater of operations to make a major contribution to resolving a crisis in another theater. The lessons taught by this history about how military assets can be effectively applied in scenarios that were not anticipated, even by commands undergoing significant reorganization and reorientation, remain directly applicable to the myriad challenges faced by today's Army.

Historians need access to accurate and complete information. General Saint opened his door to the author during sensitive meetings in his office, and his excellent team of generals in the Command Group and headquarters staff offices shared information freely in oral history interviews, provided copies of important documents, and encouraged their subordinates to do the same. In the Office of the Deputy Chief of Staff,

Operations, Darrell Pflaster, Virginia Jay, and other members of Pflaster's Conventional Forces Europe Division always took time from their hectic schedules to share information. Historians require this sort of support in order to tell the story fully and objectively.

The author and the reader are indebted to Dr. Charles D. Hendricks of the U.S. Army Center of Military History for devoting his time, knowledge, and exceptional writing and editing talents to making the draft more readable, more precise, and often more persuasive. He challenged and rewrote the fuzziest sentences and paragraphs, and he contributed much of the description and analysis of the war in the Gulf at the end of chapter 6, when the author's nerve failed to produce a coherent synopsis.

I would like to thank Brig. Gen. John W. Mountcastle, Chief of Military History, and Dr. John T. Greenwood, Chief of Field Programs and Historical Services Division of the U.S. Army Center of Military History, for restoring work on the study; Bruce H. Siemon, USAREUR Historian, for giving me time, guidance, and support; and my colleagues Warner Stark and Dr. Bruce D. Saunders for listening to me, advising me, and often covering the phone and other everyday duties that I should have shared more fully. My sincere appreciation goes as well to Anne Waller, who edited and formatted early drafts before returning to the United States; to Peter Curtiss and Catherine Heerin, who edited the final product; to Diane Arms and Dr. Andrew Birtle, who developed and refined the index; and to Beth MacKenzie, who prepared the maps and formatted the entire book. This study owes its publication to the support and cooperation of many, and to all who assisted the author is most grateful. Nevertheless, the author remains responsible for interpretations and conclusions, as well as for any errors that may appear.

Heidelberg, Germany   STEPHEN P. GEHRING
18 December 1997   USAREUR Military History Office

Contents

Appendixes

Tables

Maps

Illustrations

Illustrations courtesy of the following sources: pp. 37, 47, 61, 70, 77, 102, 111, 123, 139, 167, 174, 179, 184, 249 (*left* and *right*), and 260, *Stars and Stripes*, European edition; pp. 103, 122, 178, 182, 215, 219, 221, and 225, *Heidelberg Herald Post;* p. 217, Kurdirektion des Berchtesgadener Landes. All other illustrations from the files of the Department of Defense.

FROM THE FULDA GAP TO KUWAIT

Chapter 1

Introduction

The participation of the United States Army, Europe (USAREUR), in Operations DESERT SHIELD, the defense of Saudi Arabia, and DESERT STORM, the liberation of Kuwait, in 1990 and 1991 presents three stories, only one of which can be told fully here. The first is the story of how the Commander in Chief, U.S. Army, Europe (CINCUSAREUR), General Crosbie E. Saint, began to transform USAREUR from a basically static, heavy force focused on deterring or repelling invasion across the borders of Eastern Europe to a smaller, mobile, heavy force capable of either winning critical early engagements with Soviet and Warsaw Pact forces or deploying quickly for contingency operations elsewhere. This fascinating story, which made possible and shaped the entire USAREUR contribution to DESERT SHIELD and DESERT STORM, can be only summarized below. Its detailed exposition must await another study.

The second is the story of how USAREUR personnel deployed USAREUR units, their soldiers and equipment, and USAREUR war reserves to the Persian Gulf or Southwest Asia region to stop and reverse Iraqi aggression against its neighbors. This deployment of USAREUR soldiers and equipment would provide the decisive armored units and firepower in DESERT STORM, as well as massive logistical support to the Southwest Asia theater. At the same time, the USAREUR soldiers, civilians, and families who remained in Europe maintained a credible residual force and a secure and stable community thousands of miles from home. Both elements of this story will be covered in depth below, including planning, three phases of deployment and logistic support, the USAREUR home front, and redeployment to Europe.

The third is the story of the success of USAREUR soldiers and forces on the battlefield, where they made a critical contribution to the success of DESERT STORM. This story has been and will continue to be told elsewhere; VII Corps' successful campaign is an important part of the growing historical literature on the Persian Gulf War.[1] This study will include only a brief summary of VII Corps' battlefield actions.

The Defense of Saudi Arabia

On 8 August 1990, as President George Bush announced that the United States would resist Iraq's invasion of Kuwait and any further aggression on the Arabian Peninsula, 82d Airborne Division troops were already on their way to Saudi Arabia from Fort Bragg, North Carolina. Although they were initially vulnerable and poorly supported, these troops made America's presence felt and demonstrated its commitment to defend the area against further Iraqi aggression. Through August and September and into October, General Edwin H. Burba, Jr., the commander in chief of U.S. Army Forces Command, and the XVIII Airborne Corps commander, Lt. Gen. Gary Luck, continued the deployment of their Army forces from the United States to Saudi Arabia. Burba and Luck, along with General H. Norman Schwarzkopf, the commander in chief of the United States Central Command (USCENTCOM), which was responsible for U.S. military matters on the Arabian Peninsula, and Lt. Gen. John J. Yeosock, commander of the U.S. Third Army and USCENTCOM's Army Central Command (ARCENT), expected it to take about three months to build up an adequate defensive force. Their Army units included the 24th Infantry Division (Mechanized) and the 101st Airborne Division (Air Assault), in addition to the 82d Airborne Division. At the same time, USCENTCOM, a joint service headquarters, began to receive air and naval units, including the Ninth Air Force and the 1st Marine Expeditionary Force. It also began planning the reception of military units from the broad international coalition that joined the United States in defending the area.[2] During this period, USAREUR provided to USCENTCOM selected units and personnel as well as expanding quantities of equipment and sustainment supplies that were not available from the United States.

As USCENTCOM built up these defensive forces, leaders and planners at Headquarters, Department of the Army (HQDA), in the Pentagon and at USCENTCOM recognized that the defensive measures against Iraq might be required for many months or even years. They began to reexamine the type of force that was needed and how to maintain it. In early September they began planning for a long-term defense using units that would rotate in and out of Saudi Arabia from the United States and Europe.[3] Headquarters, United States Army, Europe, and Seventh Army (HQ USAREUR/7A), initiated planning to rotate its armored divisions and armored cavalry regiments between Europe and Saudi Arabia.

USCENTCOM also began in September to develop plans for a possible offensive campaign to dislodge forcibly Iraq's substantial military forces from Kuwait. General Schwarzkopf's staff presented on 10–11

October a plan for an attack that would rely on the single corps thus far committed to his command, but that plan was poorly received in Washington. About this time, HQDA asked HQ USAREUR/7A if it could provide a heavy division, an armored cavalry regiment, an artillery brigade, aviation elements, and a corps support command for an "enhanced" USCENTCOM force. In discussions with General Carl E. Vuono, the Army Chief of Staff, General Saint offered to deploy a full, European-based American corps. On 15 October, General Schwarzkopf, encouraged by his superiors in Washington, told his planners to develop a two-corps alternative for a flanking attack, even though "it would require the largest maneuver of armor in the desert in U.S. military history . . ."[4] Such a force and strategy would, four months later, lead the international coalition to a decisive victory over Iraq in and around Kuwait. One of the two maneuvering American corps, the armored main attack force, came from USAREUR.

A New CINCUSAREUR and an Old Cold War

USAREUR's ability to contribute as it did to winning a war in Southwest Asia in 1991 could not have been predicted when General Crosbie E. Saint became CINCUSAREUR on 24 June 1988. After the intervening years of fundamental international political and military change, it has become difficult to remember that prior to mid-1988 there had been virtually no observable change in the Cold War military balance of power on the ground in Europe. The major planning and operational problem then confronting USAREUR was an old one with a new twist: how to employ U.S. Army forces to defend Western Europe against the overwhelming numerical superiority of Warsaw Pact forces after the withdrawal of a key deterrent and equalizer—intermediate-range nuclear forces.

The man who assumed responsibility for facing that challenge, General Saint, was a Vietnam veteran who, like many other veterans of that war, sought to revive the fighting spirit of the U.S. Army. In the command and staff positions he held during his career, he worked to restore the initiative to the soldier, the battlefield commander, and the U.S. Army. Saint believed in the traditional warfighting values expressed in the U.S. Army's AirLand Battle doctrine, and he applied these values to USAREUR through all the dramatic changes he confronted after becoming its commander.[5]

As CINCUSAREUR, General Saint welcomed the opportunity to try to implement his vision of AirLand Battle doctrine in USAREUR, where it had been challenged by North Atlantic Treaty Organization (NATO) concepts of active defense and nuclear deterrence and by contrary European public opinion. Training and modernization were his highest priorities, and USAREUR made significant progress in 1989 and 1990 in modernizing its training and equipment. Saint was devoted to maintaining the highest possible training standards, personnel strength, and readiness levels, so as to be able to field a credible warfighting force at all times. Whatever shortfalls and difficulties he faced, Saint struggled to maintain training levels, if at all possible, and refused to create hollow, understrength forces in any case. Saint's success in achieving these traditional goals in a period of tumultuous change paid off in the warfighting effectiveness of USAREUR units in Iraq and Kuwait.

Despite his traditional military values, General Saint sensed the winds of change from both Europe and America when he became CIN-CUSAREUR. He felt that either the coming international conference on reducing conventional forces or unilateral U.S. military budget cuts would end business as usual for U.S. ground forces in Europe, and he was certain that the structure and nature of USAREUR would have to change during his tenure. Saint thus launched USAREUR on a restructuring planning track that would keep it abreast of the basic political and military changes of the next three years. Within six weeks of his arrival, he began examining possible major changes and developing some options for managing and staying ahead of developments. By early 1989 Saint had assembled a team of planners and had begun to develop a vision of where he and USAREUR were headed. This vision and planning, coupled with a commitment to having at least one corps ready to fight at all times, made it possible for USAREUR to deploy VII Corps to Saudi Arabia in 1990, despite a significant reduction in his funds and well-advanced plans to reduce his personnel and restructure his command.

Europe in Transition

Although General Saint proved exceptionally capable of dealing with change, neither he nor USAREUR intelligence analysts or planners anticipated the fundamental political changes that swept through Eastern Europe and the Soviet Union from 1989 through 1991. By the end of 1991, the Warsaw Pact dissolved, the Soviet Union disbanded, Eastern Europe was "free," Germany was unified, and the need for a large U.S. military force in Europe was seriously questioned. Even by the middle of 1990, virtually every aspect of USAREUR's interrelationship with its host nations, allies, NATO, and its old antagonists had changed. In many areas, the shape of things to come was unclear; the only certainty was that everything had been altered. USAREUR's swift adaptation to fundamental change in the European military and political environment made USAREUR's decisive contribution to Operations DESERT SHIELD and DESERT STORM possible.

USAREUR on Two Tracks

One cannot understand how USAREUR, a massive military organization, could adapt so quickly and contribute so fruitfully to a war in the Persian Gulf region without reviewing the major developments in the Army in Europe from 1988 through 1990. That army inevitably moved on two tracks in this period, one continuing to build on the past and the other planning and preparing for change. U.S. Army, Europe, continued to improve its high state of military readiness and the quality of life of its soldiers while, at the same time, beginning to plan and implement concepts for restructuring to a smaller force appropriate for the new political and military environments. The massive contribution of U.S. Army, Europe, to Operations DESERT SHIELD and DESERT STORM was possible only during this "interlude," this warp in history between the end of the Cold War and the subsequent readjustment of U.S. armed forces to the post–Cold War world.

"Conventional Forces Europe" Planning

The signing in December 1987 by President Ronald Reagan and Soviet leader Mikhail Gorbachev of a U.S.-Soviet treaty to eliminate all of their nations' intermediate-range missiles, many of which had been deployed in Europe with nuclear warheads, heightened expectations that discussions to reduce conventional weapons in Europe would also succeed. Shortly after he assumed command of USAREUR, General Saint gathered together a small group of planners to initiate studies and plans on how to reduce USAREUR forces if required by any agreement that might be negotiated between NATO and Warsaw Pact nations at a forum that would convene in Vienna in March 1989 called the Conventional Forces Europe (CFE) negotiations, or if necessitated by further congressional budget cuts. In late 1988 and early 1989, this small group of CFE planners, following Saint's vision of future mobile, armored combat, gathered data and devised drawdown scenarios, force structures, and treaty compliance schemes that kept USAREUR ready to adapt to political and diplomatic developments and demands of higher headquarters. USAREUR's CFE planners developed a prioritized list of installations that could be returned to the German government and a tentative schedule of such returns. These planners also began to compile a data base of USAREUR equipment that would probably be limited under a CFE treaty. They anticipated that excess "treaty-limited equipment" would have to be removed from Europe or destroyed when the treaty was signed. By the fall of 1989, plans to make a corps the minimum combat force of a smaller "residual" or "end-state" USAREUR were fairly firm, though the total future strength of USAREUR remained undetermined.

Capable Corps Concept

In discussions concerning the employment of this end-state corps, General Saint and his staff uncovered problems with current doctrine that led to a reexamination of how to make a reduced force an effective defense against and a deterrent to potential Warsaw Pact aggression. This reworking of AirLand Battle doctrine led Saint, his CFE planners, and a small group of School of Advanced Military Studies graduates in the operations office of HQ USAREUR/7A to develop a concept of a heavy, armored, "capable" corps and to make plans for its employment. The "capable corps" concept stressed huge areas of operations, long and fast marches, maneuver skills, meeting engagements, and massed firepower. The combination of new doctrinal concepts and employment plans and CFE organizational planning provided the conceptual groundwork and data base for the decisions relating to force structure, training, and equipment modernization that made possible USAREUR's successful deployment to the Persian Gulf area, or elsewhere if necessary, of USAREUR's V or VII Corps, other units, and massive logistical support.

Training for the Capable Corps

In the fall of 1989 and early 1990, the V and VII Corps commanders, Lt. Gen. George A. Joulwan and Lt. Gen. Frederick M. Franks, Jr., began to insert training requirements for the redesigned capable corps into exercises and other training of their corps, divisions, armored cavalry regiments, and support units. In the January 1990 annual Return of Forces to Germany (REFORGER) exercise, VII Corps practiced, in the course of one long march, capable corps maneuvers that would prove to be useful in VII

Corps' campaign in DESERT STORM. In the spring of 1990 the corps dropped some of its NATO General Defense Plan missions, including border patrols, and permanently revised its training standards to meet the requirements of mobile, fluid warfare under the capable corps concept. Commanders of USAREUR elements studied and discussed AirLand Battle doctrine and capable corps concepts at periodic commanders' training sessions. Saint and his staff presented training seminars that introduced the capable corps to VII Corps unit commanders, their staffs, and other key personnel in March 1990 and to other USAREUR commands throughout 1990. The maneuvers and skills practiced under the capable corps concept kept USAREUR ready to respond to European requirements with a single corps, if required, and poised to contribute to military contingencies or war elsewhere, including desert warfare in Iraq and Kuwait.

War Reserves

At the same time, the U.S. Army reassessed the need for and budgetary implications of retaining the substantial war reserve stocks maintained in Europe. USAREUR's anticipated wartime mission had been to help NATO forces disrupt and repel a massive attack from the East until reinforcements could arrive from the United States and elsewhere. As the corps employment concept and threat assessment changed through 1989 and 1990, the staff of HQ USAREUR/7A studied and revised plans for units from the United States to reinforce NATO after a Soviet attack. That staff also studied the need to pre-position for these reinforcing units supplies and equipment, called POMCUS (pre-positioned organizational materiel configured in unit sets) stocks, and to maintain theater reserve stocks for use by USAREUR units in the first weeks of war. Although USAREUR had to store and maintain POMCUS and theater reserve equipment stocks, Department of the Army headquarters in Washington tightly controlled the size and use of POMCUS. In 1989 General Saint began to reduce the size of his theater reserve stocks, based on the reduced threat, his vision of the future force structure, and an inability to pay the huge storage costs. For the same reasons, Saint also proposed a reduction in the number of division sets in POMCUS, which HQDA was slow to approve. In 1990, the ability to reduce war reserve requirements, as well as the growing likelihood of a CFE treaty, resulted in a unique set of circumstances which would make it possible for USAREUR to provide a large amount of war materiel to United States Central Command (USCENTCOM) and Operations DESERT SHIELD and DESERT STORM when it was called upon to do so.

future deployments. Through late September and October, requests for personnel, units, and material began to have a significant impact on USAREUR and its POMCUS and theater reserve stocks. HQ USAREUR/7A geared up to meet these demands. The size and activity of the HQ USAREUR/7A Crisis Action Team in the Office of the Deputy Chief of Staff, Operations, were increased. The Operations and Intelligence (O&I) briefings were expanded from twice weekly meetings of the deputy chief of staff, operations, and the deputy chief of staff, intelligence, and their staffs, to a twice-daily briefing and decision session that included the Command Group and all staff office heads. Gradually the procedures for requesting and approving USAREUR personnel, units, and sustainment for Operation DESERT SHIELD were formalized. Through August, September, and October, USAREUR provided specialized units and substantial equipment and supplies and acquired many traditional functions of a communications zone.

Planning USAREUR's Reinforcement Role

At the same time, General Saint and his CFE planners, who now formed a division of the Office of the Deputy Chief of Staff, Operations, began planning for a major USAREUR deployment to the Gulf region. At first they planned to send battalions or brigades as replacements for units from the United States already in Saudi Arabia. Then they planned to rotate USAREUR brigades or divisions between Europe and the Gulf theater. In October, as rotation plans and one-time requests for units, personnel, and equipment reached nearly corps-size proportions, General Saint and Army Chief of Staff Vuono discussed the possibility of USAREUR's sending a complete corps. Saint then told a few of his closest staff advisers from USAREUR's Office of the Deputy Chief of Staff, Operations, and Office of the Deputy Chief of Staff, Logistics, to look at sending a complete and capable corps. The day after General Saint returned from a trip to HQDA late on 26 October, he directed his corps commanders and key staff to begin planning deployment of the corps in line with a request from the Joint Chiefs of Staff. At the HQ USAREUR/7A level, the basic tasks, and therefore key themes, of this phase were deciding on a force structure and units to deploy and preparing and supporting a movement plan. When Washington announced the deployment of VII Corps on 8 November 1990, HQ USAREUR/7A was far along in planning the deployment.

VII Corps Deployment

USAREUR logisticians and personnel managers were the first HQ USAREUR/7A staff to confront fully the realities and uncertainties of deploying a corps from Europe to another theater in less than ninety days, a challenge that began when the 2d Armored Cavalry Regiment started moving less than one week after the deployment announcement. Key deployment issues included determining the order of deployment, modernizing and fully equipping deploying units, filling personnel authorizations in deploying units through cross-leveling and other personnel management procedures, preparing personnel for overseas movement, predeployment training, and moving personnel and equipment to ports of embarkation. Personnel from USAREUR units that were not deploying operated marshaling yards in Germany and acted as stevedores at ports in Europe. Members of USAREUR's 1st Infantry Division (Forward) deployed from the state of Baden-Wuerttemberg in southwestern Germany to ports in Saudi Arabia to set up reception areas, unload ships, and help units arriving from USAREUR to conduct onward movement from the port facilities. Well over one-third of USAREUR's personnel, critical supplies, and equipment deployed to Southwest Asia in this phase. The deployment of this force to port in forty-two days was an exceptional accomplishment in the annals of U.S. Army history and an important contribution to victory in the Gulf.

Additional Deployments and Sustainment Support

Overlapping the beginning of the deployment of the corps and continuing through the ground war at the end of February, USAREUR received additional requests for units and personnel including crew and individual deployments and replacements; for the rapid deployment of Patriot air defense missiles and crews to Israel and Turkey; and for massive logistical support, including most of USAREUR's ammunition stocks. In its own way, the story of the ammunition support highlights the types of actions necessary for all USAREUR materiel support. Stocks were identified among pre-positioned supplies and war reserves. Procedures were established to protect minimum levels of USAREUR's reserve stocks. General Saint reviewed and approved critical reserve stock decisions to balance his commitment to totally support USCENTCOM with the need to maintain a ready force in Europe. Host nations supported the effort based on long-term partnership relationships and understandings, and the 21st Theater Army Area Command (21st TAACOM) oversaw effi-

cient movement to ports. During this final support phase, which included the air and ground war, USAREUR would also act as the theater's
medical communications zone and provide other support to the
USCENTCOM.

The Home Front

Another important USAREUR story in this period is that of the residual
force rebuilding and maintaining its readiness, while caring for the family members of those deployed to Southwest Asia. The command undertook to prepare anew a combat-ready force in Europe robust enough to
send another division to Southwest Asia or to another contingency elsewhere, if required. But the task of restoring and maintaining the readiness of a USAREUR corps during the Persian Gulf deployment was difficult. It required restructuring V Corps, cross-leveling personnel, and
filling critical positions in USAREUR with Army Reserve and National
Guard personnel. Medical support measures were carefully examined,
including the replacement of deployed medical personnel and the implementation of improved and expanded casualty reporting systems. At the
same time, General Saint tried to keep drawdown on track as much as
he could and to remain poised to resume full implementation of drawdown plans as soon as possible after the return of his deployed forces.

USAREUR soldiers, civilians, and family members came together to
maintain a stable and supportive environment thousands of miles from
the United States. USAREUR commands, communities, and individuals
established or reinforced structures and services to support family members while their sponsors were deployed. As units and communities
pulled together during the deployment, only a small percentage of
USAREUR family members chose to return to the United States. This
experience was a unique and successful demonstration of the adaptabil-
ity and community spirit of Army people—families and communities
confronting together the difficult demands of providing security and
solving individual problems during wartime in a foreign country. Related
to this success was USAREUR's implementation of antiterrorist security
measures.

Redeployment

After the successful conclusion of Operation DESERT STORM, many in
USAREUR headquarters initially predicted that the redeployment of

USAREUR forces to Europe would make their deployment to Southwest Asia look like a picnic. In expressing this view, staff members showed that they were already downplaying the total commitment and intense work that had been necessary to get VII Corps to the battlefield in time, as well as their earlier fear that many soldiers would not return. But the statement accurately underscored the difficulties of redeployment.

The participation of USAREUR units in the Gulf War complicated force reduction plans and intensified the turmoil of many who were part both of the victory and of the drawdown. Deployed units and personnel would return to USAREUR with a variety of statuses: "fastmover" units then scheduled for inactivation would return without equipment and without more of a mission than general training and drawing down. Others returned without equipment but then drew upon the equipment of units that had not deployed and were inactivating. Units returning with equipment might draw down later or become part of the residual force. HQDA added a category of units redeploying to Germany, then moving to the United States to join an enhanced contingency force there. Their equipment would be shipped from Southwest Asia directly to the United States. Further expanding USAREUR's post–Cold War role and complicating redeployment, USAREUR provided residual forces in Kuwait and substantial personnel and assets to Operation PROVIDE COMFORT's humanitarian relief efforts assisting the Iraqi Kurds and to other post–Gulf War contingency operations.

The USAREUR to which the deployed soldiers returned had changed substantially. Army Reserve and National Guard personnel who had replaced some deployed soldiers still occupied some of their facilities. Installations and facilities were starting to close. Some units were gone and others reassigned. USAREUR had been irrevocably launched on a new phase in its history.

Conclusion

The DESERT SHIELD and DESERT STORM experience highlighted the importance of having available in the U.S. Army the type of leadership, well-trained soldiers, equipment, and supplies that USAREUR provided to the Southwest Asia theater during these operations. The achievements both of the USAREUR units and soldiers that deployed to the battlefield and of the residual force and family members that maintained the American home front in Europe should reassure those who believe that a continued U.S. Army presence in Europe is useful in the post–Cold War world. The huge deployment of USAREUR soldiers and equipment and their important contributions in the Persian Gulf war demonstrated the potential effectiveness of forward-deployed forces and pre-positioned stocks in one of the types of contingency missions that the U.S. Army appears most likely to face in the future. USAREUR's large-scale participation in these operations represented an important stage in the command's reorientation from defending the front lines of Western Europe during the Cold War to making contingency forces available to maintain or restore peace anywhere in the world after the Cold War ended. The flexibility and creativity demonstrated by General Saint, the USAREUR staff, and the entire USAREUR community in these unforeseen circumstances enabled the command to make this significant contribution.

Chapter 2

Background

USAREUR History

The organization known as U.S. Army, Europe, traced its origins to the establishment of the European Theater of Operations, U.S. Army, in 1942, during the war against Nazi Germany. USAREUR had, by 1990, focused for forty years on deterring aggression and defending Western Europe against threats emanating from the Soviet Union and its Communist allies in Eastern Europe. Through those decades USAREUR strength and force structure had been repeatedly built up or reduced in response to the military and political crises and detentes of the Cold War between the United States and the Soviet Union.

After the drastic reduction of Army personnel in Europe from almost 2 million in 1945 to 86,000 in 1950, the United States quickly built up U.S. Army personnel strength in Western Europe to over 250,000 in 1952 in response to Communist threats and a new NATO strategy for the defense of the region. Personnel strength then dropped slightly through the mid- and late 1950s, but rose again to a peak of 277,000 in 1961 in response to the building of the Berlin Wall. Through the Vietnam War years of the late 1960s, USAREUR personnel strength fell, reaching a low of about 169,000 in 1970. As new weapons systems were introduced in the 1970s and 1980s, strength grew again to about 200,000 and remained there.[1] Nevertheless through these four decades, whatever USAREUR's strength, whatever the perception of the Soviet threat, and whatever changes occurred in U.S. foreign and military policy outside Europe, the U.S. commitment to maintain the freedom of its allies in Western Europe remained steadfast.

During this period USAREUR was the backbone of the NATO defense of Central Europe. Since the early 1950s, the CINCUSAREUR served simultaneously as the commander of the Central Army Group of

NATO's Allied Forces, Central Europe. From 1952 to 1968 USAREUR forces included two corps and a total of five divisions. With the return of the majority of one of these divisions to the United States in 1968, the USAREUR force structure had then settled on two corps, each including an armored division, a mechanized infantry division, an armored cavalry regiment, corps artillery, a corps support command, and various supporting units. In the mid-1970s, USAREUR received the 3d Brigade of the 2d Armored Division, known popularly as the 2d Armored Division (Forward). During the 1980s, V Corps included the 3d Armored Division, 8th Infantry Division, and 11th Armored Cavalry. The VII Corps included the 1st Armored Division, 3d Infantry Division, 1st Infantry Division (Forward), and 2d Armored Cavalry. The separate 2d Armored Division (Forward) was stationed in northern Germany. These forces were arrayed, in line with the NATO General Defense Plan, in an essentially static forward defense of the traditional, critical eastern approaches to Western Europe. Their mission was to hold off an attack from the East until reinforcements could arrive from the United States. Against the increasing numerical superiority of Soviet and other Warsaw Pact forces, USAREUR concentrated its energy on improving its equipment and training, refining reinforcement plans, building up prepositioned and war reserve stocks, and increasing interoperability with other NATO forces.

Past Deployments

Through the Cold War years USAREUR had made many small deployments of medical and other personnel, supplies, and equipment to help with international disaster relief or other emergencies, but it had little experience with large unit deployments. In 1980, for example, USAREUR's United States Army Southern European Task Force, headquartered at Vicenza, Italy, sent helicopters and a C–12 aircraft, trucks, and soldiers to provide medical and other support to earthquake victims in southern Italy.[2] This support was typical of many USAREUR disaster relief missions through the decades.

Large deployments were a different matter. The largest deployment of U.S. forces from Europe in the forty years after World War II was to Lebanon in 1958. At the request of the president of Lebanon, Camille Chamoun, the United States intervened there to maintain stability in the face of serious internal and external threats. The United States deployed 13,740 ground troops to Lebanon, including 8,509 Army personnel, most of whom were members of USAREUR's Army Task Force 201. The lessons derived from this deployment would be remembered for over three decades. USAREUR leaders at the time concluded that diversions of forces to the Middle East or the maintenance of airborne troops for deployment there would unacceptably weaken USAREUR's ability to defend Western Europe along the Iron Curtain.[3] Large-scale deployments would not be considered possible after that time without the consent of NATO, and after 1961 USAREUR was pinned down in the forward defense of West Germany's borders with East Germany and Czechoslovakia.

A Decade and a Half of Modernization

From the mid-1970s through the 1980s USAREUR made significant improvements in its capability to deter war and to defend Europe against a potential enemy with substantially more personnel and improved equipment. As noted above, USAREUR was able to add in this period a forward brigade of a third U.S.-based corps to increase the credibility of NATO's planned defense on the plains of Northern Germany. President Jimmy Carter and NATO leaders agreed to deploy in Europe a new generation of intermediate-range nuclear missiles, including Pershing II missiles provided to USAREUR and ground-launched cruise missiles assigned to the United States Air Forces in Europe (USAFE). These force enhancements, which occurred while the West sought a balanced, negotiated reduction of nuclear forces, increased the credibility of NATO's deterrence.

A massive force modernization program sponsored by the administration of President Ronald Reagan in the 1980s substantially improved USAREUR's equipment and enabled USAREUR to train personnel to operate the new weaponry. The new equipment, generally thought to be equal or superior to Soviet and Warsaw Pact military hardware, included the M1 tank and the Bradley fighting vehicle armored personnel carrier. New aircraft, principally the Apache combat (AH–64), Kiowa Warrior scout (OH–58D), and Black Hawk utility (UH–60) helicopters, were deployed. USAREUR also received the multiple-launch rocket system and the Patriot ground-to-air defensive missile system. Existing training facilities were upgraded, and construction was started on a new Combat Maneuver and Training Center at the Hohenfels Training Area. Drawing on lessons learned at the National Training Center in California, the new facility at Hohenfels was designed to allow USAREUR units to conduct realistic periodic training. REFORGER exercises grew in size and realism, so that they could truly test reinforcement capabilities.

The revision of Army doctrine from the framework of "active defense" to AirLand Battle in the early 1980s gave USAREUR commanders added offensive options, which might allow them to cope at least briefly with the larger and apparently superior Soviet and Warsaw Pact forces. But basically, NATO and USAREUR stuck with an essentially static forward-defense strategy, because of the inertia of existing plans and the apparent pacifism of European public opinion. Nevertheless, hindsight indicates that the improvements made in the defense of Western Europe in the 1980s, together with the challenge to Soviet strategic offensive capabilities implied by America's Strategic Defense Initiative, contributed substantially to the conclusion reached by Soviet leaders that they could no longer keep pace, as they had done for three decades, in the Cold War between the superpowers.

Arms Control and Reduction Initiatives

In 1986 and 1987, USAREUR leaders began to adjust to a new era of international cooperation in the arms control arena. After Mikhail S. Gorbachev acceded to the post of general secretary of the Communist party of the Soviet Union in 1985, the Soviets had shown a new flexibility in collective security and arms control discussions that had been deadlocked for many years. President Reagan and his NATO partners quickly grasped the opportunity. In the September 1986 Stockholm Agreement, the thirty-five nation Conference on Confidence- and Security-Building Measures and Disarmament in Europe expanded the 1975 Helsinki Final Act, in which the same participants had promised to give prior notification of large military exercises. In the 1986 document European nations, including the Soviet Union, mutually agreed for the first time to involuntary inspections on their territory. A 1986 Warsaw Pact offer to discuss broad, new European arms reduction proposals led both alliances to agree the following year to new negotiations among the twenty-three NATO and Warsaw Pact nations on conventional arms limitations. Bilateral agreement between the United States and the Federal Republic of Germany also was reached in 1986 for the removal of U.S. chemical weapons from Germany by the end of 1992, a deadline that was later moved forward to 1990. In a summit meeting in Reykjavik, Iceland, in October 1986, President Reagan and General Secretary Gorbachev came to an agreement in principle on the limitation of certain intermediate-range missiles worldwide, and in 1987 they agreed for the first time to eliminate totally a whole class of weapons—all intermediate-range missiles. These included USAREUR's Pershing II missiles and

USAFE's ground-launched cruise missiles, both of which carried nuclear warheads. These initiatives indicated that the Cold War was changing, but the shape of the new era remained unknown.

As the details of the intermediate-range nuclear forces treaty were worked out in Geneva, Switzerland, in 1987, General Glenn K. Otis, Commander in Chief, United States Army, Europe, and a small group of his planners began to adjust USAREUR's forces to the elimination of these nuclear weapons and to the possibility of broad conventional arms reductions. In March 1987, General Otis asked his planners to begin looking at alternatives to USAREUR's Pershing II missiles, which were capable of reaching major Russian cities from Central Europe. Otis and his planners were particularly concerned that eliminating Pershing II missiles would reduce the effectiveness of NATO deterrence while increasing the importance of what Otis saw as the Warsaw Pact's most significant advantage over NATO forces, the superior range and numbers of its conventional field artillery. Otis' planners first proposed retaining shorter-range Pershing missiles. As it became clear that this was unacceptable, they developed a proposal to replace the missiles and the 5,700 troops in Pershing II units of the 56th Field Artillery Command with additional multiple-launch rocket system artillery, Apache attack helicopters, and special forces units as well as needed combat service personnel.[4]

As they learned about the arms control process, General Otis and his planners tried to ensure that negotiators considered USAREUR objectives. In the spring and summer of 1987, HQ USAREUR/7A asked to attend negotiating sessions in Geneva on the elimination of intermediate-range missiles and invited negotiators to visit HQ USAREUR/7A and a Pershing site in Germany. On 19 and 20 August, Ambassador Maynard W. Glitman, chief U.S. negotiator at the intermediate-range nuclear forces talks; Brig. Gen. Frank A. Partlow, Jr., the Joint Chiefs of Staff's representative at those negotiations; and other key members of the U.S. delegation visited HQ USAREUR/7A in Heidelberg and a Pershing site near Heilbronn, Germany. General Partlow's briefings during the visit convinced USAREUR participants of the virtual certainty that an intermediate-range nuclear forces treaty would be concluded soon. It also allowed USAREUR participants to show U.S. negotiators the Pershing II weapons system and to help ascertain what support facilities would and would not need to be destroyed.[5]

This visit and periodic visits by USAREUR staff officers to the Geneva negotiations thereafter convinced General Otis and his planners that USAREUR needed to be involved as much as possible in future conventional arms control and reduction negotiations. They also observed that the anticipated loss of Pershing missiles meant that Army planners and

A Pershing II missile on its erector-launcher at a U.S. missile site in Germany, prior to its elimination under the Intermediate-Range Nuclear Forces Treaty

conventional arms negotiators needed to reexamine the entire force structure, a process which indeed was already under way. In September 1987, reacting to word that the Soviets were expected to offer large reductions of artillery and tanks in exchange for smaller reductions of similar U.S. arms, General Otis asked his planners to tell him whether there was any reason he should not favor such a reduction.[6]

On 8 December 1987, in Washington, D.C., President Reagan and General Secretary Gorbachev signed the Intermediate-Range Nuclear Forces Treaty, and it was ratified by the U.S. Senate on 27 May 1988. The treaty called for the withdrawal of warheads and the destruction of missiles and certain associated equipment. Soviet inspectors would make their first visit to a USAREUR Pershing II site on the Fourth of July weekend. The first Pershing II unit would be inactivated in early September 1988.[7]

Budget Reductions and Uncertainties

At the end of 1987 and early in 1988, however, Soviet decline was not obvious, and USAREUR faced difficult problems and an uncertain future.

The most immediate problem was budgetary. USAREUR's basic operating budget, its Operation and Maintenance, Army, funds, had peaked at $4.4 billion in fiscal year 1987 (1 October 1986–30 September 1987), but even this sum was seriously eroded by the declining value of the dollar, which produced an increasingly unfavorable exchange rate with the German *Deutsche Mark* during the year. In fiscal year 1988, USAREUR's Operation and Maintenance, Army, budget took its first unquestionable drop in the decade, falling below $4.0 billion. For fiscal year 1989 and subsequent budgets, Congress demanded more burden-sharing from America's NATO allies and more often than not reduced USAREUR's budget even further. The dimensions of the reductions are easier to understand when USAREUR's operation and maintenance budgets for 1986 through 1992 are converted to constant 1995 dollars as shown in *Table 1*.[8] The 17.5 percent decline in inflation-adjusted operating funds between 1986 and 1988, imposed without a corresponding reduction in mission and personnel, required USAREUR leaders to rethink every aspect of USAREUR's budget, organization, and functions.

TABLE 1—USAREUR's OPERATION AND MAINTENANCE BUDGET, 1986–1992
(billions converted to constant 1995 dollars)

1986	6.33
1987	6.19
1988	5.22
1989	5.29
1990	5.07
1991	4.81
1992	3.35

Source: Memo, Office of the Deputy Chief of Staff, Resource Management, HQ USAREUR/7A, AEAGS-X, for USAREUR Historian, 18 Oct 95, no subject.

The budgetary reductions threatened to affect virtually every aspect of USAREUR planning, readiness, and quality of life. New construction funds were virtually eliminated after 1987, and already approved funds were restricted or reduced. The future promised further reductions and "fencing" of approved funds to restrict interfund transfers within USAREUR. As early as 1987, USAREUR had to fight to ensure that military budget cuts would not undermine the completion of its fielding of modernized equipment or, more likely, the funding for training and facilities to support new equipment fieldings. In addition, budgetary prospects made it unlikely that USAREUR would receive the additional POMCUS or theater reserve stocks on which it had planned or that serious deficiencies in the capability of U.S.-based units to reinforce NATO would be corrected. USAREUR also faced increasing difficulties in receiving local support and land use options from host nations, particularly the Federal Republic of Germany, where, for example, USAREUR remained unable to station Apache helicopters as planned despite two years of negotiation.[9]

A New CINCUSAREUR

On 24 June 1988, General Saint became the new CINCUSAREUR, and commander of the Central Army Group of NATO's Allied Forces, Central Europe, replacing General Otis who had served in the positions since April 1983. General Saint brought to the position experience in commanding armored units, in training and doctrine, and in USAREUR. He had commanded 1st Squadron, 1st Cavalry, 23d Infantry Division, in Vietnam; V Corps' 11th Armored Cavalry Regiment, which was responsible for plugging the Fulda Gap and for patrolling the East German border in the mid-1970s; and VII Corps' 1st Armored Division in the mid-1980s. As chief of the Exercise Division in the Office of the Deputy Chief of Staff, Operations, HQ USAREUR/7A, he was responsible for staff supervision of REFORGER 78, REFORGER 79, and other exercises stressing interoperability with allied forces. The REFORGER exercises stressed deployment and reception of reinforcements from the United States and their integration into maneuvers with USAREUR and allied NATO forces. He commanded USAREUR's Seventh Army Training Command from May 1979 to June 1981, stressing combined arms training and implementation of the Battalion Training Management System. Saint also served as the Deputy Commandant, United States Army Command and General Staff College, in 1981–1983, an exceptionally productive period in establishing, refining, publishing, and teaching AirLand Battle doctrine.

Immediately before assignment as Commander in Chief, USAREUR, Saint commanded III Corps at Fort Hood, Texas, where he tested and implemented many of his operational concepts for a mobile armored corps. He also deployed practically the entire corps to Europe for REFORGER 87. This was the largest deployment of U.S. Army forces from the United States to Europe in an exercise. A total of 30,496 soldiers based in the United States were deployed to Europe on 4 ships and 115 aircraft. REFORGER 87 produced a number of other "firsts." It was the first time an American officer did not command the tactical exercise, which deployed III Corps to defend northern Germany under the British commander of NATO's Northern Army Group. But the plains of northern Germany offered Saint an excellent testing ground for the aggressive, mobile, armored style of warfare that he had planned, taught, and advocated. In this REFORGER III Corps employed the first Apache helicopters. It was the first REFORGER in which the French participated, and also the first which nonaligned and Warsaw Pact countries observed under provisions of the 1975 Helsinki Final Act and the 1986 Stockholm Agreement.[10]

REFORGER 87 provided Saint with valuable deployment experience. During the massive logistical movement of VII Corps from Germany to Saudi Arabia, General Saint would be able to claim that he was the only commander in the Army who had already moved a corps between continents. Many other USAREUR and Army leaders during the Kuwait crisis, including

General Saint

Maj. Gen. William G. Pagonis who would command the theater support command in Saudi Arabia, also had experience with REFORGER exercises, which would provide the model for the DESERT SHIELD deployment plan.[11]

As commander of III Corps, General Saint expanded his role and reputation as an Army leader in the refinement, teaching, and exercise of AirLand Battle doctrine. He preached the fundamentals of this doctrine in Army conferences and military literature, and he proposed realistic and practical concepts to implement it in III Corps and USAREUR operations plans and training. Saint trained his units for quick deployments, long and rapid marches, fluid maneuvers, massed fires, and meeting engagements of unprecedented violence.[12] He also worked with Air Force leaders in examining the complex problems of integrating air and land forces in AirLand Battle operations, including the employment of Apache attack helicopters in night operations.[13]

In a series of articles in leading military journals, Saint, sometimes joined by coauthors, presented his proposals for the employment of modernized equipment in support of the mobile armored corps. He proposed concepts for attack helicopter employment in deep and rear operations.[14] He suggested revised guidance for the employment of fire support for mobile armored warfare to focus combat power on critical points at critical times.[15] He advanced a concept for destroying Soviet forward detachments in case of war in Europe.[16] Overall, Saint was recognized as a leading and candid contributor to Army-wide discussions of refinements to AirLand Battle doctrine in the future.[17]

It is necessary at this point to take stock of what General Saint could and could not have foreseen of future political and military developments in Europe when he became CINCUSAREUR and commander of NATO's Central Army Group. General Saint, like almost all observers of the European scene, did not in 1988 foresee the cataclysmic military and political events of the next several years. General Secretary Gorbachev announced at the United Nations on 7 December 1988 the unilateral withdrawal of 50,000 Soviet troops from Eastern Europe by 1991. In 1989 the Eastern European borders with Western Europe opened, many Communist governments in Eastern Europe collapsed, and the Berlin Wall was unsealed. Democratically elected governments would be established in most Eastern European countries between 1990 and 1992, and East and West Germany would be united with Allied cooperation in October 1990. The Warsaw Pact dissolved in July 1991, and the Union of Soviet Socialist Republics disbanded in December 1991. On 7 November 1991, NATO leaders at a summit in Rome, observing that the immediate threat of invasion of Western Europe by the Soviet Bloc had disappeared but that heightened political instability in Eastern Europe posed new threats to peace, announced a new NATO strategic concept based on smaller, more mobile NATO forces.

Although he did not foresee this upheaval or the end of the Cold War when he became CINCUSAREUR in June 1988, General Saint did foresee that either budget reductions or arms-limitation treaties would likely lead to a smaller and altered USAREUR.[18] Saint viewed this as an opportunity to restructure USAREUR forces and revise doctrinal concepts for the defense of Central Europe in line with his approach toward combined arms fighting the AirLand Battle. He saw himself primarily as a warfighting commander of a warfighting command, and he had a vision of how to fight the next war. Knowing USAREUR as well as anyone, General Saint may have been one of the few Army commanders who could see in force reductions the opportunity to test and implement his concept of a modern, mobile, offensive army.

Early Conventional Forces Europe Reduction Planning

When General Saint became CINCUSAREUR, Soviet and American conventional arms negotiators were still addressing the mechanics of international arms reduction discussions. This included questions like what nations would be included in the negotiations, what was the relationship between Conventional Forces Europe and Confidence- and Security-Building Measures negotiations, and how to address dual-capable weapons, that is, weapons with both conventional and nuclear capabilities.[19] General Secretary Gorbachev would make his first promise of unilateral withdrawal of 50,000 Soviet forces from Eastern Europe in December 1988. The mandate for Conventional Forces Europe negotiations, which would settle what was going to be negotiated and how, was not signed until January 1989, and the actual negotiations on limiting conventional weapons among the twenty-three NATO and Warsaw Pact nations would begin in Vienna only on 19 March 1989.

By August 1988 General Saint was asking his staff to begin planning potential base closures, a personnel strength drawdown, and force restructuring in response to future conventional arms reduction negotiations and budgetary trends. The USAREUR Deputy Commander in Chief, Lt. Gen. George R. Stotser, meanwhile, was preparing to attend as an observer a conventional arms reduction conference in Budapest at the end of August. On 2 August 1988, General Saint asked his deputy chief of staff, operations, and his political adviser to brief him on the lowest level to which USAREUR and NATO could go and still assure a credible defense. A small conventional arms reduction planning group was formed to learn everything possible about the coming negotiations. The group was headed by Mr. Darrell Pflaster, the chief of USAREUR's small Arms Reduction Cell, who had been responsible for much of the planning and implementing of the Intermediate-Range Nuclear Forces Treaty in USAREUR. Pflaster's group briefed General Stotser before his trip to Budapest. Saint had already mentioned to these planners the possibility of major reductions.[20]

At a 31 August briefing, attended by General Saint and key operations and intelligence office personnel, Pflaster stressed that the U.S. objective in conventional arms reduction negotiations was NATO parity with Warsaw Pact forces, not any specific numbers, although he also underscored that the central region would be the major "billpayer." Pflaster suggested that the NATO mission would stay the same, but NATO strategy might have to change. He also outlined proposals for how to make reductions and how to coordinate with negotiators and higher headquarters. Finally Pflaster proposed the creation of a formal conventional forces planning cell or task force in USAREUR's Office of the Deputy Chief of Staff, Operations, which General Saint approved.[21]

In the 31 August meeting, General Saint said he wanted to confront the future rather than react to it. He wanted a single command position and end-state plan, including consideration of the Air Force and allied armies. He was looking for an end-state force that would be highly mobile, would be able to accept quick deployments, and would maintain POMCUS only of infantry and armor items. The end-state force must be capable of fitting into the NATO strategy of forward defense and flexible response, which he anticipated would not change.[22] In this meeting, just two months after becoming CINCUSAREUR, General Saint reoriented a small group at HQ USAREUR/7A from looking at abstract CFE negotiating-mandate issues to analyzing specific impacts of reductions and planning the future USAREUR force.

In the following months, Saint and Stotser made use of the new CFE cell to begin planning a smaller, more flexible USAREUR force structure. First, they looked at the impact of, and began planning for, small USAREUR force reductions of 10,000 or 20,000 troops. The CINCUSAREUR soon decided, however, that this small-scale planning was inadequate, and he asked his planners to "pick up the stick at the other end." He wanted them to determine the smallest possible force capable of performing USAREUR's mission in the future and then to work backwards to design the structure of that force, which they called the "end-state" force. General Saint also foresaw that any sizable reduction would affect the structure of military communities in Europe, in fact every facet of how business was done by the Army in Europe, and he saw an opportunity to correct some of the ills that had afflicted USAREUR for many years.[23]

Under tight security, General Saint began to work out a far-reaching restructuring plan with the small cell and key advisers, who together formed a small planning task force. At various times, depending on what topic was considered and who was available, the task force included the deputy commander in chief; the chief of staff; the commander in chief's executive officer; the political adviser; the deputy chief of staff, operations, his deputy, and a few members of his Plans Division, the CFE cell, which developed the force structure, operations, and stationing plans; and the deputy chief of staff, intelligence, and a few of his intelligence analysts. Early in 1989 an operational research and systems analyst joined the group. In November 1988 and May 1989 General Saint and the task force formally briefed General John R. Galvin, United States Commander in Chief, Europe (USCINCEUR), and Supreme Allied Commander, Europe, on the organization, methodology, and progress of their plans. Access to specific plans was often limited to the USAREUR Command Group; the deputy chief of staff, operations; and the three-man core CFE planning cell in the Plans Division in his operations office.

By the middle of 1989, without any direction from higher headquarters, General Saint and his three-man CFE planning cell had worked out a far-reaching plan for the future USAREUR force. First, they decid-ed that the minimum U.S. Army force that would maintain a credible commitment in Europe and have a significant influence in NATO was a corps.[24] The corps would have to be structured to defend the same terri-tory as in the past with half the force. To do this, the corps would have to have those very capabilities that Saint had previously determined to be integral to modern warfare: quick deployments, long marches, maneuverability and flexibility, realistic training, modern equipment, and massive and lethal firepower. To meet these requirements, they put together a force structure for a corps that would have two divisions, both heavy on armor; two armored cavalry regiments; and two aviation brigades. It would be implemented in conjunction with an initiative to reorganize engineers, called E-Force, to make them more mobile and capable of assisting combat brigade commanders.[25] The corps would be equipped with a new generation of tanks, Bradley fighting vehicles, attack and utility helicopters, updated communications equipment, and multiple-launch rocket systems equipped with the Army tactical missile system, as well as other equipment and capabilities that would make the corps more flexible and mobile.[26] At an in-process review on 29 March 1989, General Saint agreed that reductions to this size might lead to a change of mission; forward defense might no longer be possible.[27] This end-state plan, which with some force structure modifications remained essentially unchanged through the tumultuous military and political events of the following three years, allowed USAREUR to take these events and further budgetary reductions in stride and had a major impact on USAREUR support of Operations Desert Shield and Desert Storm.

Beginning in the spring of 1989, the CFE cell researched and dis-cussed stationing the new force with the assistance of planners in the Office of the Deputy Chief of Staff, Engineer. General Saint saw any drawdown as a chance to fix some of the most glaring deficiencies in USAREUR facilities, including "lousy barracks," other inadequate or poorly situated facilities or installations, and lack of cooperation from some host nation authorities. In spring 1989 Saint asked his V and VII Corps commanders for a list of the worst installations used by their bat-talions and brigades. Based on these lists and Saint's guidance, every installation in USAREUR was analyzed and rated on eleven criteria, including accessibility and adequacy of facilities, tactical position, train-ing areas, congestion of the local area, and friendliness of the local gov-ernment.[28] Following this analysis, the CFE cell put together a prioritized list of installations that could be closed when appropriate. In addition, by June 1989 General Saint, who realized from the start that reductions would necessitate a change in the military community structure in USAREUR, was beginning to talk about establishing area support groups, organized under existing Army tables of organization and equipment, that would be responsible for performing existing community functions and for manning POMCUS and theater reserve storage sites and would become the nucleus of combat service support units with wartime missions.[29]

At the fortieth anniversary NATO summit in Brussels near the end of May 1989, President Bush made the first U.S. proposal that involved reducing the American military presence in Europe and added consideration of limiting combat aircraft and helicopters to the CFE negotiations. The presidential proposal was in response to General Secretary Gorbachev's unilateral announcement in December 1988 that he would withdraw troops and equipment from Eastern Europe. Under Bush's plan, U.S. strength in the Atlantic-to-the-Urals area covered by the CFE treaty negotiations would be limited to about 275,000. The U.S. Army's share of this force would be about 195,000, a reduction of approximately 20,000 from existing strength.[30]

General Saint and the CFE cell quickly selected units for this small drawdown and continued their analysis to determine which units would be part of the end state and which units would be eliminated. General Saint and two of his CFE staff, Pflaster and Lt. Col. John Graham, a School of Advanced Military Studies graduate who handled policy and force structure issues, had already carefully worked out the methodology for such drawdown decisions. A presidential tasking at this time required that, in a matter of hours, they identify units to be eliminated having a total of 21,500 soldiers. In order to do so, they looked at brigades and their locations and considered how each brigade fit into the planned end-state force structure for the single corps. They looked at the location of the brigades in terms of the prioritized list of installations with an eye to limiting as much as possible the restationing of units around Europe, which they knew would be disruptive as well as expensive. They tried to determine which brigades were most deficient in terms of equipment, facilities, and locations and in doing so began to look at the battalions within the brigades.[31]

Saint and his planners were aided in this assessment of battalions by work they had already begun in preparation for a CFE treaty. In late 1988 and early 1989 the CFE cell began to put together an inventory by unit of USAREUR's combat equipment that could be limited by a CFE treaty. Eventually this treaty-limited equipment included tanks, armored personnel carriers, attack helicopters, artillery, and combat aircraft (which applied only to the Air Force). Counting this equipment helped them to assess brigade and battalion modernization and to recommend to General Saint, who made the final determination, which units to keep and which to stand down, as well as to report treaty-limited equipment numbers to higher headquarters and CFE negotiators.

Capable Corps

By the summer of 1989 the essential methodology for reduction/restructuring planning had been worked out. The pace of arms reduction negotiations had quickened, political instability in Eastern Europe was expanding, and calls for a "peace dividend" from the American public were becoming more insistent. General Saint had a good idea where USAREUR was headed, based on his vision and planning with the CFE cell. The hastening revolution in European political relationships called for beginning the implementation of these changes.

As they had done many times before, General Saint and his CFE planners sat at the conference table in his office around a one-meter by two-meter terrain map of Germany and its neighbors. It immediately highlighted the vulnerability of the traditional avenues of attack from the East. The map exercise made it obvious that reduced U.S. and NATO forces in Central Europe would be spread too thin to continue the essentially static, forward defense of West Germany's eastern borders.[32] General Saint concluded that he needed a specific concept of how to configure and employ his reduced force in a potential conflict. He also needed to convince higher headquarters and, for that matter, his subordinates, of the viability of his vision and plan. Above all, in his own view, he needed to fight off higher headquarters' consideration of simply thinning USAREUR forces rather than restructuring the residual force.[33] For some time, the Army Staff had been wrestling with reducing strength in Europe because of U.S.-Soviet arms reduction talks, and throughout the Army because of budget reductions, but from a USAREUR point of view it seemed to look at these issues purely in abstract numbers, in budget- or treaty-driven terms, without a vision of the shape and requirements of the future battlefield.[34]

To put together the doctrinal concepts and briefings to support his vision of USAREUR and the potential battlefield of the future, Saint called on the Doctrine, Concepts, and Analysis Division of his Office of the Deputy Chief of Staff, Operations. The division had been created by his predecessor, General Otis, and was headed by Col. Kenneth G. Carlson, a former School of Advanced Military Studies teacher at Fort Leavenworth, Kansas. He was aided by a staff of three or four graduates of that school, including Lt. Col. Kenneth Sharpe, who came to HQ USAREUR/7A from the headquarters of VII Corps, where he had completed his training with an internship in planning. Shortly after becoming CINCUSAREUR, General Saint asked Colonel Carlson and his staff to calculate how long a corps could fight against the potential enemy forces that confronted it, in the process of which they put together a data base and framework for future discussions of the role and structure of the corps.[35]

In mid-July 1989 General Saint called Colonel Carlson into his office and told him that they had to find a new way to defend the same terrain in Central Europe with half the American troops. General Saint said he envisioned armies fluidly moving about the battlefield seeking each other out for a decisive battle, somewhat as in Napoleon's time. Saint told Carlson to go back to his office, to think about it, and to work with Lt. Gen. John M. Shalikashvili, who would replace General Stotser as deputy commander in chief on 10 August, and with Brig. Gen. Ronald H. Griffith, who was temporarily a member of the headquarters and would soon become the commander of the 1st Armored Division, to put together three briefings that would answer the following questions: Why were U.S. forces needed in Europe when the threat was diminishing? How many soldiers and what size of force was necessary? How would that force be employed? Saint told Carlson that the briefings would be used to explain USAREUR's proposed residual force to HQDA.[36]

Colonel Carlson and his staff put together these briefings during late summer 1989, and they and General Saint presented them in the fall to the Chief of Staff of the Army, General Vuono, and other members of the Army Staff. The briefings closely followed the structural and warfighting concepts that had been discussed and planned by Saint, the CFE cell, and other USAREUR staff through the previous year, but they filled in many details, particularly in the warfighting area. The first briefing addressed whether a U.S. Army presence was required in Europe. The briefing argued that some level of U.S. presence was necessary to show the nation's commitment to European peace and to make a difference on the battlefield, which in the summer and early fall of 1989 was still anticipated to mean a defensive engagement against a potential invasion of Western Europe by the Warsaw Pact. This briefing pointed out that providing American support of NATO forces solely with U.S. forces from the United States would be too slow and too complicated to make a difference in early battles.[37]

The second briefing proposed a size of the U.S. force in Europe. Carlson and his team divided what they saw as the continuing mission into seven functions and looked at what size and structure of organization could accomplish these functions. The seven functions were deterring aggression; maintaining U.S. influence in the alliance and assuring U.S. allies of the nation's commitment to Europe; providing strategic intelligence, threat analysis, and warning; providing a capability to conduct follow-on-forces attack; providing a capability to receive and move reinforcements forward; providing a capability to integrate those reinforcements into U.S. Army and NATO forces; and providing a capability to deal with regional contingencies. In the latter point, Saint and his planners recognized but did not stress at this early planning stage that USAREUR's future would probably increase the importance of quick deployments to deal with regional contingencies.

The USAREUR briefers started their analysis by looking at the capabilities of the corps, the largest self-sustaining force in U.S. Army doctrine. In NATO, the corps commander was one of the lowest level key decision makers; division or lower level commanders were integrated into a corps. This corps, which they began to call the "capable corps," had a structure very similar to that which Saint had asked his CFE planners to consider earlier. It would have a corps headquarters, two heavy divisions, two armored cavalry regiments, and extra aviation and field artillery assets. Ultimately, Carlson and his associates justified this capable corps on its ability to fight on a future European battlefield and, because of this, on its ability to deter war.

The briefers argued that the corps was the lowest level that could perform USAREUR's warfighting functions, but it would need help in fulfilling other roles. The briefers added to the proposed USAREUR structure the minimal echelon-above-corps organizations and strength to fulfill the seven mission functions, including reinforcement and onward movement and theater-level intelligence.[38]

The third briefing explained how the capable corps could fight in the new European environment. U.S. and NATO forces would be smaller but would be required to defend as much territory as earlier. The new force would not be positioned statically forward. The capable corps would use superior mobility to seek out the enemy, to gain positions of advantage, and to attack with massed firepower. In employing the capable corps, USAREUR would position armored cavalry regiments as "picket lines" up front, responsible for stopping anything but the main attack and for directing fire support at the main attack. These forces would be responsible for covering a huge territory from 100 kilometers along the front to more than 60 kilometers in depth. The heavy "linebacker" forces, the armored brigades, would be positioned well behind the picket lines, but they had to be capable of moving 250 kilometers in twenty-four hours and covering a corps area that was 240 kilometers deep and 200 kilometers wide. The USAREUR briefers argued that the capable corps needed the most advanced command, control, and communication systems and had to carry air defense and sustainment along with it. The capable corps also would have to carry its logistical base and base support with it.[39]

General Saint briefed or otherwise promoted the capable corps concept several times a month in late 1989 and early 1990. He briefed it to General Vuono; the Army's Vice Chief of Staff, General Robert W. RisCassi; the Army's Deputy Chief of Staff, Operations and Plans, Lt. Gen. Gordon R. Sullivan; and the Commander, U.S. Army Training and Doctrine Command, General John W. Foss; and at the Army Commanders' and the Major Leader Training Conferences. He engaged in a long correspondence with General Foss about applying many of these same concepts to Army-wide AirLand Battle doctrine that would result in AirLand Battle Future, Nonlinear.[40] At the same time, General Saint explained the capable corps concept to his corps and division commanders, who, in turn, briefed their armored cavalry regiment commanders and other key commanders and staff, who, with General Saint and HQ USAREUR/7A, began to incorporate capable corps concepts and required maneuvers and skills into USAREUR training.

Training and Exercises

Since the mid-1980s USAREUR had been modernizing the training infrastructure which General Saint and his commanders now used to train their units and soldiers in the operations and skills necessary to gain proficiency in the highly mobile, combined arms operations required of the capable corps. This training modernization included building a Combat Maneuver and Training Center at Hohenfels, Germany, that would allow realistic battalion- or task-force-size combat maneuver training. A full instrumentation package to allow automated after action reports or feedback to units, enhance data collection, and improve communications was planned for completion in 1991. In 1989 twenty-nine maneuver battalion task forces were able to train at the still incomplete Combat Maneuver and Training Center. Shortly after arriving in USAREUR in 1988, General Saint pushed up the opening of the Combat Maneuver and Training Center at Hohenfels to September 1989. The opening of the Hohenfels training center would allow fifty-two maneuver battalions to conduct realistic live-fire training each year. In November and December 1989 the USAREUR Leader Training Program was tested and implemented at the training center. Instrumentation was completed in February 1990. This allowed USAREUR and USAFE to integrate computer-simulated air assets into training, which gave USAREUR ground commanders experience in the use of air power.[41] Completion of the Combat Maneuver and Training Center allowed units later deployed to Southwest Asia to conduct realistic live-fire maneuvers in 1990.

From 1988 through 1991 USAREUR also established a full range of simulated battlefield capabilities. In addition to the Hohenfels center, the joint USAREUR and USAFE Warrior Preparation Center located near Ramstein Air Base in West Germany provided fully computerized exercises for joint commanders and staffs at the operational level of war. In January 1989 General Saint decided to build, as well, a battalion/task force simulator network at Grafenwoehr, Germany. This facility would provide realistic all-arms training and battlefield development for battalions and task forces, including exercises involving tactics, force structure, and tactical air maneuvers; an engineer work station with mining and countermining capabilities; and many other realistic options. Training began in mid-1990, although the Grafenwoehr simulator network was not fully operational until 1991. Using these various training facilities, USAREUR corps and divisions were able to launch a Battle Command Training Program in the second half of that year.[42]

The incorporation of many of General Saint's concepts into REFORGER 90 and other USAREUR training in 1989 and 1990 played a significant role in the success of VII Corps and other USAREUR units in DESERT STORM. General Saint began inserting training exercises of the sort he had stressed in III Corps into USAREUR training exercises in the year after he took command of USAREUR, even before CFE plans or capable corps concepts were firm. In January 1989, for example, the 240th Supply and Service Company, 71st Maintenance Battalion, 7th Support Group, and 2d Corps Support Command conducted a Refuel on the Move exercise, which was a first for these units.[43]

In the fall of 1989 General Saint and Colonel Carlson and his team presented the capable corps concept to the corps commanders and selected corps staff. General Franks, commander of VII Corps, was enthusiastic. Franks incorporated these concepts and associated skills whenever possible in Battalion Command Training Program exercises, training at Hohenfels and Grafenwoehr, and road marching. In the road marches, corps units practiced bringing everything with them, including fuel, food, fire support, and air defense. The 3d Brigade, 3d Infantry Division, for example, which would later be deployed to Southwest Asia as part of the 1st Armored Division, was practicing long marches over previously unthinkable distances at the very moment Iraq invaded Kuwait.[44]

The Barge Dynamica *transporting* REFORGER *90 equipment from Antwerp, Belgium, to Mannheim, Germany*

Enhancement Plan, which combined REFORGER 89 and 90, restored corps-versus-corps field training exercises, which had been deleted from early plans for both exercises to save money. It allowed V and VII Corps to operate largely in a simulation mode, while crews, squads, and platoons trained in live-fire exercises at the Combat Maneuver and Training Center. The two corps synchronized deep, rear, and close operations through the Warrior Preparation Center, while deploying a brigade to participate in a computer-assisted command post exercise on the northern flank.[47] Units of V Corps undertook the same kind of training as did VII Corps units. The 3d Armored Division and V Corps, for example, conducted their Battalion Command Training Program WARFIGHTER exercises in May 1990 involving over 2,500 personnel.[48]

Modernization Status in 1990

Training was important, not only to learn to fight with the capable corps but also to hone skills in unit operations using and integrating modernized equipment. The fielding of the M1A1 tank in USAREUR was basically completed in 1989. USAREUR was surely more modernized overall than were units in the United States, but the fielding of other modernized equipment and the completion of new equipment training varied within USAREUR.

In January 1990 the 1st Armored Division was the first USAREUR unit to receive the most up-to-date High Survivable M2A2 and M3A2 Bradley fighting vehicles with 600-horsepower (hp) engines. The division trained with the new equipment through the year. When a moratorium was placed on shipping the remaining 1st Armored Division Bradleys to USAREUR in the summer of 1990, General Saint decided to continue modernizing the division using assets internal to USAREUR. In July 1990 Mainz Army Depot began upgrading 3d Infantry Division Bradleys from 500 hp to 600 hp, and the upgraded engines would later be diverted to units headed for Southwest Asia. The fielding of heavy expanded-mobility tactical trucks and even high-mobility multipurpose wheeled vehicles in USAREUR was also under way. The same was true of the fielding of Apache attack helicopters and Black Hawk utility helicopters. By the end of 1990, eight of ten attack helicopter battalions planned for USAREUR were fielded, including those for 1st Armored Division, 3d Armored Division, and VII Corps' 11th Aviation Brigade.

The modernization picture in USAREUR became even cloudier in late summer. In August all Black Hawk helicopter fieldings to USAREUR were canceled because of the deployment of U.S. forces to Saudi Arabia. Mobile Subscriber Equipment communications modernization was completed only in the 3d Armored Division and 2d Armored Division (Forward). Many other vital, recently developed systems and types of equipment, including launchers suitable to multiple-launch rocket systems equipped with the Army tactical missile system, helicopter-borne air-to-air Stinger missiles, M9 Armored Combat Earthmovers, and improved high-frequency radios were only partially fielded by August 1990. Similar challenges were posed when fifty Refuel-on-the-Move kits, capable of simultaneously refueling eight vehicles, were fielded to supply units in USAREUR during 1990.[49] The partial or very recent fielding of modernized systems meant that many USAREUR soldiers had not received training on the new equipment. The diverse status of the fielding of this equipment, as well as many other less visible modernized equipment items, would pose major problems for Generals Saint and Franks and their planners and logisticians when decisions had to be made about who would deploy to Southwest Asia and how they could take the most modernized and effective equipment to war.

Personnel Status in 1990

In 1990 the Army manned USAREUR overall at just over 95 percent of authorized strength, with even lower strength levels in some critical military occupational specialties and nondivisional units.[50] Typically, strength and authorized levels of organization were kept high in combat units while they were allowed to drop lower in combat support and combat service support units. General Saint gave strong command emphasis to maintaining a high level of training and a reasonable authorized level of organization and strength in USAREUR. He surely had drawn some internal line below which, he believed, training, strength, and, for that matter, end-state force structure could not fall. General Saint recalled his experiences in the hollow force that was USAREUR during the Vietnam War and vowed that would not happen again on his watch.[51]

Military and Political Developments Through 1990

Through late 1989 and 1990, all USAREUR watched the disintegration of the Soviet Bloc, the popular revolutions in Eastern Europe, the reunification of Germany, and the growing unpredictability and instability of European political and military affairs. Negotiations on conventional arms reduction in Europe moved rapidly toward a treaty that would be signed by NATO and Warsaw Pact leaders in November 1990. Responding to treaty developments, to U.S. and Soviet announcements of unilateral European troop reductions, and to the likelihood of additional budget constraints, the USAREUR commander and his staff put together final inactivation schedules and procedures. General Saint and his commanders and staff tried to cope and find money to finance the drawdown, training and exercises, planned modernization, and other ingredients designed to produce a high state of readiness and a reasonable quality of life for the residual military community.

USAREUR was entering a new era in which virtually nothing was business as usual. It was clear that the United States and the Army would be on a completely new footing—or no footing at all—in Berlin. Bilateral and "2 + 4" (the two Germanys plus the United States, Britain, France, and the Soviet Union) talks in 1990 would lead to agreement in September 1990 on prompt German reunification, followed by the departure of the four powers from Berlin by September 1994. The Germans began to talk about revisions to the Status of Forces Agreement (SOFA) and the Stationing Agreement, which had been the foundation of host nation relations since the formal establishment of the Federal Republic of Germany in 1955. Underscoring the seriousness of these expectations, the Germans were sensitive to any indication that they were not fully sovereign or were in any way an occupied country.[52] These trends and the uncertainty of USAREUR's future status and role touched nearly every aspect of USAREUR in 1990.

At the same time, the strictly military position of USAREUR was uncertain. The responsible U.S. civilian secretaries and senior uniformed Army staff officers made no decisions on the future or structure of USAREUR through the summer of 1990. Other allied governments, including those of West Germany and Great Britain, announced reductions of their troop levels in Europe and a reshaping of their entire military forces. New questions were raised about the purpose and future structure of NATO. The basic mission of USAREUR to defend Western Europe from attack, a mission it had performed successfully for over forty years, seemed less necessary. At the same time, it was clear that the political and military situation in Europe, while less immediately threatening and less lethal, was probably also less stable than it had been in several decades. Emerging civil war in the former Yugoslavia, political instability in the Soviet Union, economic disintegration and despair elsewhere in Eastern Europe, and a resurgence of nationalistic hatreds underscored this instability.

Intermediate-Range Nuclear Forces Treaty Implementation

The emerging post–Cold War environment was illustrated in two exceptional USAREUR accomplishments in 1990. The implementation of the Intermediate-Range Nuclear Forces Treaty continued without major incident and with many lessons learned. The last of the Pershing II missiles were scheduled to be withdrawn from Germany and sent to the United States for destruction in March 1991. Between July 1988 and March 1991, Soviet inspection teams continued to inspect USAREUR Pershing facilities and witness the destruction of associated equipment.[53]

Operation STEEL BOX

The year 1990 also saw the withdrawal of all U.S. chemical weapons from Europe. General Saint and Maj. Gen. Klaus D. Naumann, chairman of the German Chemical Weapons Inter-Ministerial Commission, jointly headed a U.S.-German task force that moved over 100,000 old

A U.S. Army chemical munitions storage cage near Clausen, Germany

and deteriorating nerve agent artillery shells from the U.S. storage site at Clausen, Germany (near Pirmasens), to the port of Nordenham, Germany, for shipment to Johnston Atoll in the Pacific. General Shalikashvili ran the operation. A total of 23,000 USAREUR personnel were involved in moving thirty-nine tons of chemical munitions from Clausen to Nordenham between 26 June and 22 September 1990. Two ships carrying the chemical weapons arrived at their destination in November 1990. The highly sensitive operation, which was completed ahead of schedule, required faultless planning, tight oversight, and flawless execution. HQ USAREUR/7A arranged double and triple back-up for personnel, equipment, transportation, and security resources and systems to ensure that operators could respond to unexpected breakdowns or other exigencies.[54] General Shalikashvili; Lt. Gen. William S. Flynn, Commander, 21st TAACOM; Brig. Gen. Dennis L. Benschoff, Commander, 59th Ordnance Brigade; and HQ USAREUR/7A staff members, Maj. Gen. John C. Heldstab, Deputy Chief of Staff, Operations; Maj. Gen. Joseph S. Laposata, Deputy Chief of Staff, Logistics; Maj. Gen. Cloyd H. Pfister, Deputy Chief of Staff, Intelligence; and Brig. Gen. Salvatore P. Chidichimo, Provost Marshal, were devoting much time and energy to this operation when Iraq invaded Kuwait. But the operation provided excellent experience in planning and carrying out a difficult "zero defects" operation, and it taught lessons that were later applied to the deployment of VII Corps to the Persian Gulf.

USAREUR Moving on Two Tracks

Confronting the old exigencies of training, deterrence, defense, and maintenance of the largest overseas organization in the U.S. Army on the one hand, while facing the instability and uncertainty of a new world order, a major drawdown, and budget reductions on the other, USAREUR seemed to be traveling on two tracks through 1989 and 1990. Knowledge of and participation in planning drawdown and restructuring were limited to a small number of personnel, ranging from under 10 in 1988 and early 1989 to perhaps 200 personnel by the summer of 1990. Hundreds of thousands of other personnel were not aware of these plans, although they knew that times were changing and little or nothing in USAREUR would remain business as usual. Nevertheless they went ahead performing the basic USAREUR functions of training and improving the readiness of USAREUR units and maintaining and enhancing the quality of life in USAREUR communities.

General Saint realized that there was a cost in doing business this way. Full benefits would not be realized in the future from some of the actions taken and money spent at this time to maintain the "old" USAREUR designed to deter and fight the Cold War, while a "new," restructured USAREUR was being created to perform new missions in post–Cold War Europe. Saint believed this double track was necessary to maintain USAREUR readiness, which was still his primary mission. He also thought that the inevitable excursions, twists, mistakes, and dead ends of planning for an unstable and uncertain future would cost more in terms of morale and readiness if done openly than if done secretly. Therefore, he strictly limited access to information on drawdown and restructuring planning to a trusted agent list, and he closely monitored and shaped external briefings.[55]

Using this dual-track mode, General Saint was able to maintain USAREUR readiness and training, cope with the increasingly complex and sensitive international scene, acquire approval of his drawdown and restructuring plans, and continue to pursue his vision of a larger, more mobile, two-division capable corps prepared to meet any contingency, at least in Europe.

CFE/Restructuring

Through 1989 and 1990, as international developments continued to shatter former assumptions, plans, and requirements, the CFE cell, which during this period was restructured and enlarged, still under Pflaster, to form the CFE Division of the Office of the Deputy Chief of Staff, Operations, developed plans for reduction to various force structure levels. Based on the criteria established earlier, the division and its small circle of trusted associates in other HQ USAREUR/7A staff offices and the headquarters of USAREUR's major commands came up with prioritized lists of installations that would close and units that would inactivate at various successively lower total strength levels.

This planning allowed General Saint and CFE Division to respond quickly to their first external taskings. As noted above, the first of these had been to identify specific units for inactivation to support President Bush's proposal in May 1989 to limit U.S. troops in Europe to 275,000, which would reduce Army strength by about 20,000. The second such tasker came in January 1990, when President Bush announced in a state of the union message a further reduction in Europe to 225,000 military personnel. The decision meant a reduction of the Army's share of personnel strength in Europe to approximately 158,000. By late spring and early summer of 1990, General Saint and his planners had largely given up on retaining the latter strength and were concentrating on preserving and planning force structure based on an end-state strength of 120,000. Although CFE Division personnel could by this time go to their computers and pull out a list of previously prioritized units whose reduction would bring total U.S. Army unit strength in Europe down to the numbers in the current drawdown option, the ramifications for creating a "capable corps" and the reduction of non-USAREUR Army tenant units became increasingly problematic. Through the summer, the CFE Division prepared lists of units that would stand down each quarter in 1991 and 1992, though it was uncertain whether the final number reduced would be 20,000 or 30,000 annually.[56]

Disposition of Anticipated Treaty-Limited Equipment

USAREUR planners also were preparing to meet equipment restrictions in a CFE treaty. By early 1990 Army leaders believed that a CFE treaty would be signed by late summer or fall 1990. USAREUR had some outdated treaty-limited equipment that would have to be destroyed or disposed of to meet anticipated treaty limitations. Destruction was expensive, complicated, and possibly unnecessary. After USAREUR informed HQDA of excess equipment and the disadvantages of destruction, the Departments of the Army and of Defense found U.S. military organizations interested in acquiring some of the equipment and foreign military sales customers outside Europe interested in purchasing much of the rest. In late April and May 1990 USAREUR shipped at least 2,219 combat vehicles out of Europe. This equipment included 1,202 M113 armored personnel vehicles and 117 M109 howitzers sent to U.S. military organizations and 900 M60A1 tanks, some of which were sent to U.S. military organizations and others to Egypt, Morocco, and Tunisia.[57] This action would not only save money in destruction costs but also gave USAREUR valuable experience in quickly shipping large combat vehicles out of Europe.

POMCUS

Through the 1980s USAREUR had gradually built up pre-positioned equipment and supplies, or POMCUS, for U.S.-based divisions that would quickly reinforce NATO forces, including V and VII Corps, in case of Warsaw Pact attack. These stocks, together with theater reserve stocks covered below, were called war reserve stocks. POMCUS equipment would supply six divisions, plus their support troops.

The changing threat and political situation and the initiatives to restructure USAREUR and reshape the U.S. Army threw into question the continued need for this level of pre-positioned stocks. The expected CFE treaty-limited equipment ceilings applied to this equipment, as well as to USAREUR unit equipment.

In May 1990 the USAREUR Chief of Staff, Maj. Gen. Willard M. Burleson, Jr., directed an organizational review of this program.[58] By summer General Saint received information indicating that the future would see the current ten-division U.S. "essential force" oriented toward the defense of Europe (i.e., four forward-deployed divisions and six reinforcing divisions) reduced to seven U.S. divisions. The seven-division force would consist of two divisions forward deployed, four divisions stationed in the United States with equipment in POMCUS, and one division and its supplies and equipment provided by fast sealift.[59] In the early fall of 1990, General Saint was carefully reviewing plans for POMCUS stocks to determine what would be needed in the future and what could be used to sustain U.S. forces in the Persian Gulf.

Theater Reserve Stocks

Throughout the 1980s USAREUR also built up pre-positioned theater reserve stocks in Europe for use by both forward-deployed USAREUR units and reinforcing divisions in the event of war. Allied Command Europe (ACE) had set minimum objectives for pre-positioning thirty days of supply for all classes of supply except fuels, for which forty-five days was sought. In the 1980s Department of Defense guidance increased the objective for U.S. units to sixty days of supply for all classes of supply except ammunition, for which the goal was seventy-five days of supply.

General Saint reviewed the theater reserve program in February 1989 as part of his broader review of USAREUR force structure, and he established a requirement of thirty days of supply for all classes of supply for the entire ten-division essential force. In June 1989 General Saint directed a complete reassessment of all aspects of the theater reserve program. In December 1989 he further reduced the sustainment pre-positioning goal generally to fifteen days.[60] Through 1990 General Saint continued to reassess these programs, recognizing the likelihood that his command would ultimately need to bring these stockage objectives into line with a two-division forward-deployed force and seven-division essential force.

Drawdown Preparation and Announcement

Although personnel strength limitations eventually were eliminated from the CFE treaty, the growing pressure for personnel cuts stemming from military budget reductions and the apparent growing public expectation of a peace dividend made the prospects for lower USAREUR strength levels ever more likely. For the Army Commanders Conference in August 1990, General Saint asked his planners to outline a possible end-state force with an authorized strength of 70,000, which they labeled a "presence force." Through the late summer of 1990, however, General Saint and his planners continued to develop a preferred force reduction package retaining end-state units with a total personnel strength of 120,000. They regarded a strength reduction to this level necessary to cope with a substantially reduced budget they expected in fiscal year 1992.

Through the late summer and fall of 1990 General Saint and his planners began to concentrate on developing a force structure option based on a personnel strength level of 92,200. This was done on advice from General Galvin. At the 4 September USCINCEUR Component

Commanders Conference and again by message on 14 September, General Galvin tasked General Saint to develop an alternative force structure with an authorized strength of 92,200. As early as May 1990 General Saint was telling his staff that he considered 90,000 the lowest possible troop strength sufficient to maintain a ready combat and contingency force in Europe through a capable corps. Through the late summer and fall General Saint briefed USAREUR's many high-level visitors on his drawdown plans, including Secretary of the Army Michael Stone; Chairman of the Joints Chiefs of Staff General Colin L. Powell; Army Chief of Staff Vuono; and many other top Army leaders. In addition, Generals Saint and Heldstab and Mr. Pflaster briefed, coordinated, and discussed the USAREUR draw-

General Galvin (left) joins soldiers of the 4th Battalion, 159th Aviation, loading rail cars with equipment bound for Saudi Arabia

down concept and the future shape of the Army with Army leaders on their many trips to the Pentagon.[61] By the winter of 1990 Army leaders appeared to agree on a USAREUR force of 92,200, USAREUR's share of total U.S. forces in Europe which would number 120,000, but no final decisions were made.

Mr. Melvin Mitchell of the CFE Division (who later joined a drawdown implementation team) had drafted, briefed, and coordinated a 500-page, draft drawdown implementation plan in twenty-seven days during February 1990. Coordination of the draft with the Pentagon and other services in Europe continued through the spring and summer. The classified plan was published in CINCUSAREUR Operations Order 4352–90, United States Army, Europe, Conventional Forces Europe Reductions, which was dated 1 August 1990, but not distributed until 14 September 1990. The operations order required addressed commanders to prepare supporting plans and submit them to HQ USAREUR/7A by 1 October 1990. The operations order called for notification of each unit scheduled to inactivate 180 days in advance of its inactivation date, thus providing a 30-day warning period and 150 days to complete standdown.[62] The delay in the order's distribution, however, guaranteed that the deadline for notifying the first units, which were scheduled for inactivation on 1 March 1991, could not be met even if HQDA promptly approved USAREUR drawdown plans. Unit inactivation, which often involved base closures and host nation notification, would be a difficult, time-consuming, and expensive process, especially on the scale planned in USAREUR. In the spring of 1990 General Heldstab created a new branch in his Operations Division, the USAREUR Reduction Branch, to implement the drawdown of units beginning as soon as HQDA approved the USAREUR plan and announced specific base closures.

On 2 August 1990, the day Iraq invaded Kuwait, USAREUR's CFE planners, headed by General Heldstab, were participating in a command post exercise called Homeward Bound in the Army Operations Center at the Pentagon. The purpose of the exercise was to determine the maximum, sustained annual rate of withdrawal of personnel from Europe that the Army could accommodate. All major Army commands were represented, as was the Army Staff. The USAREUR team, in addition to General Heldstab, included Col. Roger L. Mumby, Chief, Operations Division, and Mr. Pflaster and Colonel Graham of the CFE Division in the Office of the Deputy Chief of Staff, Operations; Col. Phil G. Phillips, Chief of the Plans, Operations, and Systems Division, and Col. Robert G. Fear, Chief of the Transportation, Energy, and Troop Support Division in the Office of the Deputy Chief of Staff, Logistics; and a lieutenant colonel from the Office of the Deputy Chief of Staff, Personnel. At the conclusion of the exercise, USAREUR and receiving major Army commands in the United States agreed that the maximum drawdown rate in Europe should be set at 30,000 per year.[63]

In late August, four weeks before the Pentagon's official announcement of troop withdrawals from Europe, General Saint found it necessary to take notification of the units projected to inactivate on 1 March 1991 into his own hands. General Saint and his planners and action officers were concerned that the first units and soldiers to stand down, those who would test the procedures and timelines developed for the drawdown, were not being given fair warning. Since it was unclear when the Department of Defense would release the unit announcement, HQ USAREUR/7A went ahead and informed the units that were to inactivate 1 March. These units began to stand down based on the 180-day drawdown timeline.

As summer drew to a close, USAREUR leaders and planners became increasingly anxious to get started with implementation of base closures and unit drawdowns in a measured, orderly manner before further budget decrements made the process more difficult. Final decisions on the substance and timing of the statement were controlled in Washington, however, with Secretary of Defense Richard B. Cheney slated to make the first announcement. Before this occurred, the State Department needed to coordinate announcement of initial base closures with the German government. General Burleson, the HQ USAREUR/7A chief of staff, participated in a working group at the U.S. embassy in Bonn coordinating closures with that government and developing notification and announcement procedures. These rather complex procedures were necessary to maintain good relations with the German federal, state, and local governments. On 18 September 1990, Cheney and Saint simultaneously announced closure of almost 100 USAREUR installations and facilities beginning in 1991.[64]

On 26 September 1990, the Office of the Secretary of Defense and the United States European Command announced the withdrawal of 40,000 U.S. forces from Europe in 1991. The USAREUR share was 30,000 troops to be withdrawn by 30 September 1991. The announcement named thirty-one units, including elements of both corps, that would be withdrawn in 1 March and 1 May 1991 increments.[65] By the time of this announcement, the March units were already well along in the inactivation process, and USAREUR was deeply involved in the support of U.S. forces in Southwest Asia.

Chapter 3

Early Southwest Asia Support

First Reactions

General Saint and his staff had their hands full with drawdown and restructuring, withdrawal of chemical weapons, and normal peacetime USAREUR operations and training in the late summer of 1990. It is hardly surprising that USAREUR leaders, planners, soldiers, and civilians did not suddenly ask for a large slice of the action when President Bush announced on 8 August 1990 that the United States would launch Operation DESERT SHIELD to resist Iraq's 2 August invasion of Kuwait and the threat of further aggression against Saudi Arabian oil fields.

As American troops began to arrive in Saudi Arabia in the first days after the announcement, General Saint made it clear that USAREUR could and should provide important support to U.S. Army units deployed to Saudi Arabia, but neither he nor other USAREUR leaders immediately foresaw major USAREUR involvement. USAREUR had no plans for a substantial out-of-theater deployment or other involvement beyond sustainment support.[1]

Through August and September, General Saint, General Burleson, and the rest of the HQ USAREUR staff devoted more and more time and attention to support of U.S. troops in the Persian Gulf area in response to increasing numbers of requests for equipment and personnel and growing recognition that USAREUR would have to be involved if the United States was to go to war in the desert. As USAREUR's involvement in Southwest Asia support deepened, management processes evolved out of normal staff procedures to ensure that Southwest Asia information was shared throughout the staff and subordinate commands and that quick and effective decision-making forums and procedures were accessible to all staff officers. General Burleson expanded periodic operations and intelligence (O&I) briefings into the primary daily forum for sharing information among all headquarters staff officers and for tasking those staff officers. In this forum, USAREUR's intelligence chief, General Pfister, tried to fill in broad gaps in USAREUR's knowledge of conditions and plans in the USCENTCOM theater. General Heldstab and Colonel Mumby gradually expanded the HQ USAREUR/7A Crisis Action Team, which was located in the HQ USAREUR/7A "war room," while each staff office established and expanded its own staff office crisis action team. The objective, which General Burleson and Colonel Mumby were generally successful in meeting, was to provide 24-hour turnaround on Southwest Asia actions.[2] The expansion of management and capabilities was a gradual process as the role of USAREUR became broader and clearer through August and September, and later it would effectively support the deployment of VII Corps and massive sustainment to Southwest Asia.

Operations and Intelligence Meetings

One of the most important staff management developments of the early period of USAREUR Southwest Asia support was the evolution of the periodic O&I meetings into a headquarters-wide forum for information and decision. Prior to 7 August 1990, the O&I briefings were a meeting between USAREUR's operations chief, General Heldstab, and USAREUR's intelligence chief, General Pfister, and their staffs, held once or twice a week to discuss issues of common concern. General Burleson, seeing a serious need to share Southwest Asia information throughout the headquarters, gradually expanded these sessions to daily, then twice daily, morning and afternoon or evening, meetings for all staff office heads. By mid-September, Generals Saint and Shalikashvili also attended regularly, and the O&I became a forum not only for sharing information, but also for coordinating actions and bringing issues for decision to General Saint. This forum assured all staff officers of early access to the headquarters Command Group and surely reduced the turnaround time on many actions. It also kept the whole headquarters on one track. After adjourning these expanded O&I meetings, Generals Saint, Shalikashvili, Burleson, Heldstab, Laposata, and other appropriate staff officers would meet in smaller groups called "huddles" to discuss and resolve issues that were not of interest to the larger group.[3]

Southwest Asia Intelligence

Although called on to provide significant early support, USAREUR lacked detailed information on the situation in Iraq, Kuwait, and Saudi

Arabia. To help cope with this problem, General Pfister, who prior to coming to USAREUR had served as the intelligence chief of USCENT-COM, arranged to obtain theater, USCENTCOM, and national intelligence information on the situation in the Persian Gulf area. He tailored this information for briefings and distribution to USAREUR forces. General Pfister had only three qualified analysts in August, but he gradually came to devote up to 50 percent of his staff to this analysis and support.[4]

Because information from USCENTCOM and other sources was sparse, the output of General Pfister's staff and help from the Army Intelligence Agency and the Defense Intelligence Agency proved to be indispensable in reaching the force structure and logistic decisions that General Saint and his staff would eventually have to make. But it was not until November that the Army and Defense Intelligence Agencies brought their ten-volume intelligence preparation of the battlefield materials to USAREUR at General Pfister's request to brief division and brigade commanders and their intelligence chiefs.[5]

Crisis Action Team

The administrative functions of the headquarters related to support for Southwest Asia were gradually centralized in Colonel Mumby's HQ USAREUR/7A Crisis Action Team and integrated into the O&I schedule. The HQ USAREUR/7A Crisis Action Team normally dealt with all incoming high-priority messages, sending them to the Command Building and to appropriate staff offices. Before long, Mumby's team was receiving and tracking all incoming and outgoing messages related to operations in Southwest Asia, sending them to the Command Group, the crisis action team of the appropriate staff office, or other responsible action agency. It also collected all O&I and other decisions and periodically sent them out to the USAREUR commanders in consolidated decision messages. To build up the team's staff to cope with the increasingly large workload and to maintain continuous coordination and linkage to all staff offices, each staff office provided at least one officer at all times to Mumby's Crisis Action Team. Together with the staff action control officers in the Office of the Secretary of the General Staff in the Command Building, who were dedicated to tracking the business of each staff office that required action by a member of the Command Group, Mumby's Crisis Action Team provided intensive oversight of each action, while the twice daily O&I sessions guaranteed swift attention, action, and information throughout HQ USAREUR/7A.[6] Each staff office created its own crisis action team or a similar organization that worked twenty-four hours a day, seven days a week, tracking actions internal to the staff office and providing linkage with Mumby's HQ USAREUR/7A Crisis Action Team. This tight organization, which allowed intensive and timely management of early unit deployments and logistic support and later of the deployment of VII Corps, evolved gradually in August and September 1990.

Deployment Requests and Personnel Strength

In the first week after President Bush's announcement of the deployment of U.S. troops to defend Saudi Arabia, HQDA through USEUCOM tasked HQ USAREUR/7A to deploy specialized units and personnel there to become part of USCENTCOM and its Army element, the U.S. Army Central Command (ARCENT). These USAREUR units would provide specialized support that units from the United States lacked or could not adequately supply. Their capabilities included providing intelligence and communication resources, combat aviation assets, including AH–64 Apache attack helicopters, medical evacuation and other medical functions, and chemical reconnaissance, as well as assorted other functions.

While General Saint made it clear that USAREUR was well prepared to support these requirements and requests, he opposed proposals to further reduce overall manning of USAREUR and on 16 August 1990 strongly urged Lt. Gen. William H. Reno, the Army's Deputy Chief of Staff for Personnel, not to create a hollow army in Europe. Saint argued that "to reduce manning from [the] previously agreed 96 percent level will place this command in [a] tenuous readiness posture and significantly detract from its ability to maintain a trained and capable force." He saw no problem with diverting some specialized personnel who were desperately needed both by USAREUR and USCENTCOM, but, Saint continued, "wholesale reduced manning will break our bank. The object is not to reduce your forward deployed force to ineffectiveness."[7]

This was not just more general opposition to thinning forces in lieu of making rational force structure decisions that would maintain the readiness of the essential, deployed USAREUR force. Further undermanning could undermine Saint's ability not only to maintain a ready force in Europe but also to deploy combat-capable units to the Persian Gulf. General Saint foresaw potential problems if USAREUR's already substantially understrength forces were committed piecemeal to Southwest Asia. He wanted to maintain manning levels in the essential force and seek other solutions to problems caused by conventional force reductions, budgetary constraints, and deployment to Southwest Asia rather than thinning and creating a hollow army.

Early Deployments

HQ USAREUR/7A began the deployment of USAREUR personnel and units to Southwest Asia in the first week after the president's deployment announcement. The deployments from Europe in August and September were experiences from which USAREUR was to learn a great deal. An early presumption that deployment through Mediterranean ports would save time as opposed to the more circuitous route via North Sea ports proved wholly false. On the other hand, the early doctrinal assumption that units could deploy themselves proved partially correct. HQ USAREUR/7A relied on higher echelons or the State Department to inform NATO that USAREUR was deploying units committed to NATO out of the NATO area of responsibility, as was the case with the early deployment of the 12th Aviation Brigade.[8] The early experience was particularly valuable because of the varied deadlines for the deployments and the diversity of units deployed, which included a combat aviation brigade, an expanded air ambulance medical evacuation company, a specialized intelligence unit, Fuchs (Fox) chemical reconnaissance platoons, and various signal and other units.

Early Medical Support

The first USAREUR unit to deploy to Southwest Asia was the 45th Medical Company augmented by personnel and equipment provided by the 421st Medical Battalion. The company was requested early because USCENTCOM had no air ambulance capability. On 10 August the company was informed that twelve air ambulance aircraft and supporting medical personnel would deploy to Saudi Arabia to transport patients and provide essential medical staff, as well as critical medical supplies, such as blood.

The first elements of the company, including six UH–60 Black Hawk utility helicopters, deployed on 21 August 1990 and arrived in Dhahran at 0600, 27 August 1990; a second element the same size deployed 27 August. They all self-deployed through U.S. Army Southern European Task Force (USASETAF) facilities in Italy. All 45th Medical Company elements arrived in Dhahran by 2 September, where the company was attached to the 44th Medical Brigade. The unit took eighty-six personnel, seventy-eight of whom were to stay in Saudi Arabia.

The 421st Medical Battalion had to send along essential maintenance personnel because XVIII Airborne Corps maintenance assets scheduled for deployment from the United States were still awaiting transportation at Fort Bragg, North Carolina, with no date established for their arrival in Saudi Arabia. As the first air ambulance medical evacuation unit to arrive in the USCENTCOM area of responsibility, the 45th Medical Company assumed responsibility for providing air ambulance evacuation throughout the ARCENT area of responsibility until other medical evacuation units arrived. Even after the arrival of other units, the 45th retained this mission to some degree, while performing its originally planned ship-to-shore evacuation mission. Five of the company's pilots were carrier qualified before they left; others were to qualify after arrival in Saudi Arabia.[9]

The self-deployment of the company's helicopters provided several significant lessons at the very start of USAREUR deployments. The initial twelve aircraft, which had not been modified for long-range flight, had to use special fuel pods or forward area refueling equipment (FARE) systems for the trip. The 70th Transportation Battalion brought these to Aviano, Italy, from Burtonwood Army Depot in the United Kingdom. The successful use of these systems verified the strengths and weaknesses of these aircraft in long-range self-deployment. The trip was apparently the longest helicopter self-deployment in Army history. The flight extended over 3,500 miles through six countries and took just five days.[10]

The deployment of the medical evacuation unit in the first weeks of Operation DESERT SHIELD was the beginning of massive medical support for the operation from USAREUR and its 7th Medical Command. That command, HQ USAREUR/7A, and HQ USEUCOM began to prepare medical evacuation support plans in mid-August when it became clear that USCENTCOM plans called for evacuating patients from Southwest Asia to hospitals in Europe. In fact this support began on 12 August 1990 when the first evacuee from Saudi Arabia arrived in a USAREUR hospital. Early planning was necessary to ensure that USAREUR could carry out this mission while maintaining basic medical services for the large military community in Europe. On 18 August HQ USEUCOM warned that 25 percent of hospital bed capability in Europe would have to be made available to support patients evacuated from Operation DESERT SHIELD. This concept plan called for USAREUR to make 1,760 hospital beds available.[11] USAREUR's role as a rear medical support base for the evacuation of USCENTCOM patients will be covered in Chapter 6.

HQ USAREUR/7A offered USCENTCOM additional medical units and some of these personnel were deployed early in Operation DESERT SHIELD. On 6 September elements of the 483d Medical Detachment (Veterinary Service) and the 655th Medical Company (Blood Bank) and associated equipment began deploying from Germany to Saudi Arabia. The 763d Medical Detachment provides an excellent example of the sort of medical unit support that USAREUR would offer to USCENTCOM in the early months. The 763d was uniquely qualified to detect and treat chemical casualties, based on its training and experience in connection with Operation STEEL BOX, which had moved chemical weapons out of Germany from June through September 1990. The offer to deploy this unit was typical of USAREUR support of ARCENT and USCENTCOM in at least three ways. First, like many USAREUR units, the 763d had specialized training and experience based on its USAREUR mission. Second, USAREUR offered its services without solicitation. And third, like many other USAREUR units that were of potential value to USCENTCOM, the unit was scheduled for inactivation. In this case, USCENTCOM did not accept the offer, and the 763d Medical Detachment inactivated on 15 February 1991.[12]

By mid-October 133 personnel of the 7th Medical Command had deployed to Southwest Asia, including a liquid oxygen production and distribution team with its equipment. The deployment of the remainder of the 45th Medical Company had been delayed because logistic and administrative support was still not available in Saudi Arabia. USAREUR was also preparing additional medical facilities in Europe in anticipation of the evacuation of USCENTCOM casualties to USAREUR.[13]

Early Intelligence Support

Another of the initial USAREUR units to deploy from Europe to Southwest Asia was a specialized V Corps intelligence unit. Company C, 302d Military Intelligence Battalion, 205th Military Intelligence Brigade, operated the new Tactical Radar Correlator, processing imagery and signal information gathered from TR–1 aircraft and providing it to a tactical force, in this case, USCENTCOM. The TR–1, which flew out of the United Kingdom, was on loan to an element of the British Air Force, which joined the V Corps team to provide airborne imagery and signal information for USCENTCOM. An advance party was deployed on 19 August 1990, and the main body of Company C deployed a few days later by Military Airlift Command aircraft. The company was attached to ARCENT and began operations immediately upon arrival in Saudi

Arabia.[14] The deployment of this unit marked the beginning of substantial support of Operation DESERT SHIELD from intelligence units in Europe, some of which was offered by HQ USAREUR/7A and the units on their own initiative.

Many of the early taskings in this sphere involved individual soldiers, including Arab linguists, who were deployed from Europe to help man fully deployed intelligence organizations from the United States. The Army's personnel staff was looking throughout the Army for Arab linguists and other intelligence specialists. Some of these intelligence specialists were taken from the Intelligence and Security Command's Berlin and Augsburg Field Stations and 66th Military Intelligence (MI) Brigade, which were under the operational control of HQ USAREUR/7A, and military intelligence organizations assigned directly to USAREUR. An example of unsolicited intelligence support was the offer of the intelligence brigade's Imagery Exploitation System stationed at Zweibruecken, Germany. General Pfister found it understandable that USCENTCOM did not call this and other advanced systems forward until late December when it was ready to assimilate new systems and provide the required training. Pfister later noted USCENTCOM eventually accepted all of the intelligence systems offered.[15]

Chemical Reconnaissance Platoons

USAREUR's preparation in the first half of August to deploy four chemical reconnaissance platoons illustrates several of the themes of early USAREUR deployments, including the use of new equipment and the reliance on friendly host nation relationships and support. In anticipation of the possible use of chemical warfare by Iraq, the USCINCEUR, on order of the chairman of the Joint Chiefs of Staff, ordered the commander in chief, USAREUR, to deploy four 26-man platoons to operate thirty German Fox nuclear, biological, and chemical (NBC) reconnaissance and detection vehicles. The German Army, barred from deploying to Southwest Asia by the German government, which cited constitutional prohibitions, loaned the Fox vehicles to USAREUR instead.

The 1st and 3d Armored Divisions and the 3d and 8th Infantry Divisions each would provide one platoon. Each of their twenty-man platoons had to be supplemented with six additional soldiers to meet Fox force structure requirements. Each platoon would consist of a platoon leader, a platoon sergeant, and six four-man crews. The V Corps advised its units to ensure that the best personnel were selected for the new, reinforced NBC reconnaissance platoons. The four USAREUR pla-

German Fuchs (Fox) chemical reconnaissance vehicles at Rhein Main Air Base awaiting shipment to Saudi Arabia

toons were given new equipment training at the German NBC School at Sonthofen, Germany, on a thirteen-hours-a-day, seven-days-a-week schedule for three weeks, beginning on 20 August 1990. While each corps provided two platoons, VII Corps oversaw the preparations and training. A contractor assisted with organizational, direct support, and general support maintenance in USAREUR and in Southwest Asia. After arrival at the aerial port of embarkation at Rhein Main Air Base, the platoons prepared loading plans, palletized their equipment and supplies, conducted predeployment desert training, and made final preparations for overseas movement. By 20 September the two platoons from the 1st Armored Division and the 3d Infantry Division, including ten Fox vehicles, had deployed to Saudi Arabia. The second two platoons from the 3d Armored Division and the 8th Infantry Division were ready to go on 12 October 1990. By the first week of November, three platoons and eighteen of the first thirty vehicles had deployed, while the 8th Infantry Division platoon, the last to deploy, awaited receipt of its vehicles. That platoon left for Saudi Arabia on 16 November 1990.[16]

USAREUR decided to rebuild the deployed teams, expecting to be asked to provide sustainment in this sphere for USCENTCOM, although this did not occur. USAREUR arranged for additional spaces at the German NBC School to train new teams, planning to use additional Fox vehicles and the German Army (*Bundeswehr*) experts who had provided predeployment training to the four deployed platoons. In the meantime, HQDA requested an additional thirty Fox vehicles, planning to send ten of them to the marines and the other twenty to ARCENT. The Army planned to provide on-the-job training to the personnel who would fill the additional teams that ARCENT would require. General Heldstab, USAREUR's operations chief, doubted that on-the-job training would be fully effective with such a sophisticated system and arranged for additional U.S. Army Materiel Command personnel along with at least one British platoon to be trained on the Fox vehicles at Sonthofen.[17] The Fox NBC reconnaissance vehicles and training were the beginning of substantial support that the German and other allied armies offered to USAREUR.

Deployment of the 12th Aviation Brigade

The largest and most instructive of the deployments in August and September was the dispatch of V Corps' 12th Aviation Brigade, popularly called the 12th Combat Aviation Brigade. This deployment included an attack helicopter brigade headquarters; two AH–64 Apache attack helicopter battalions; an OH–58 Kiowa scout helicopter company; a UH–60 Black Hawk utility helicopter company; a CH–47 platoon (five Chinook helicopters); an aviation intermediate maintenance company; the bulk of a chemical company; and an air defense artillery platoon (Stinger). A total of 1,435 aviation personnel would be deployed. The 12th Aviation Brigade was alerted for movement on 14 August 1990, and an advance party left USAREUR for Saudi Arabia within a week. The rest of the unit began moving toward port on 28 August. The planned date for closure in Saudi Arabia was 27 September 1990; the bulk of the brigade actually arrived in Saudi Arabia in mid-September and the last piece of equipment on 2 October 1990. USCENTCOM desperately needed the brigade's thirty-seven AH–64 Apache attack helicopters and support aircraft to reinforce the light combat forces it then commanded in the Persian Gulf region.[18]

This initial large-scale deployment was filled with frustrations and learning experiences as concepts of operations changed and the brigade encountered basic transportation and port problems. Although USAREUR was in the midst of a successful self-deployment of Black Hawk medical evacuation helicopters, Military Airlift Command and

CWOs Paul R. Stein (top) and David M. Conboy of the 12th Aviation Brigade perform a preflight inspection of their Apache helicopter prior to its shipment to Saudi Arabia.

USCENTCOM requested that only the 12th Aviation Brigade's CH–47s self-deploy and that the rest of the brigade be deployed by Military Airlift Command aircraft and, if necessary, by sea. In the end, both the CH–47s, operated by Company B of the brigade's Task Force Warrior, and the UH–60 Black Hawks self-deployed; the brigade headquarters, the two attack helicopter battalions, one OH–58 scout helicopter company, and the rest of the brigade went by train through France to be deployed by sea primarily from Livorno, Italy, and, in cases of last resort, from Rotterdam, the Netherlands.[19] In spite of USAREUR's wealth of REFORGER reception and onward movement experience, many lessons were to be learned in the deployment of this substantial force by sea.

The tasking of HQ USAREUR/7A staff offices and subordinate USAREUR units to assist and support the 12th Aviation Brigade's deployment primarily followed normal USAREUR functional staff and command responsibilities. The commander of the 21st TAACOM, General Flynn, was tasked to help prepare the helicopters for transport and to move their basic load ammunition to departure airfields. General Flynn established an aerial port of embarkation, including a marshaling yard, at Ramstein Air Base on 17 August, and later another at Rhein Main Air Base. USAREUR's 200th Materiel Management Center was tasked to help acquire essential aircraft items and repair parts. HQ V Corps, 12th Aviation Brigade's corps headquarters, submitted airlift requirements to Military Airlift Command through USAREUR's 1st Transportation Movement Control Agency. USAREUR's 7th Medical Command was responsible for establishing immunization requirements, and its 1st Personnel Command assumed responsibility for filling critical shortages in needed military occupational specialties that could not be resolved by reassigning or attaching personnel from other units within V Corps, a process termed cross-leveling personnel. (*Map 1*)

Less conventional approaches were also necessary to prepare the brigade for deployment at full strength and capabilities. The 3d Battalion, 227th Aviation, and an air defense artillery platoon were taken from the 3d Armored Division and attached to the brigade. An augmented aviation intermediate maintenance battalion, the 8th Battalion, 158th Aviation, and a chemical company were attached from the 3d Corps Support Command. The 12th Aviation Brigade was instructed to take along its full unit basic load and to acquire needed supplies or equipment from other units or stocks to ensure this standard was met. This process was called cross-leveling equipment among units. HQ USAREUR tasked VII Corps to assist V Corps and provide equipment and personnel to fill V Corps shortages. This precedent for cross-leveling personnel and equipment across corps lines would be followed in the massive deployments ahead. Obviously the 12th Aviation Brigade had to request relief from current taskings. Other USAREUR instructions tasked the unit to bring along all authorized chemical defense equipment and to follow operations security measures to prevent disclosure of its capabilities and intent.[20]

The first lessons USAREUR had to learn in the deployment of a larger unit to another theater were related to preparing personnel for deployment. HQ USAREUR/7A's initial instructions to V Corps on the brigade's deployment sought to ensure that all soldiers were qualified and pre-

NORTH SEA

Hamburg ✈

●Bremerhaven ⊡
Nordenham ⊡

●Eemshaven ⊡

Berlin ◉

NETHERLANDS

●Rotterdam ⊡

Antwerp ⊡

BELGIUM

●Cologne ✈   GERMANY

Rhein Main
Air Base ●Frankfurt ⊙

CZECHOSLOVAKIA

Ramstein
Air Base   ●Mainz △
LUXEMBOURG

⊙✈Landstuhl   ●Mannheim △

Grafenwoehr ⊙

●Heidelberg ⊛   ●Nuremberg ⊙✈

Hohenfels ⊙

●Stuttgart ⊛✈

▲Berchtesgaden●

⊙ Sonthofen

FRANCE

AUSTRIA

SWITZERLAND

YUGOSLAVIA

⊛ Vicenza●

ADRIATIC
SEA

●Livorno ⊡

ITALY

Rome ◉

GULF WAR FACILITIES IN EUROPE
1990

✈ Airport	⊙ Medical Facilities
△ Barge Terminal	⊡ Port
⊛ Headquarters	▲ Recreation Area
⊙ Training Center	

0 ————————— 200
Miles

MEDITERRANEAN
SEA

MAP 1

pared for overseas movement. This included verifying that all soldiers had in their possession a set of identification (ID) tags, an ID card, and shot records. Soldiers' Government Life Insurance benefits and next of kin notification forms were reviewed and updated. Soldiers were processed through the Office of the Staff Judge Advocate for the preparation of wills and powers of attorney. They were warned not to bring to Southwest Asia illegal drugs, alcoholic beverages, or pornographic materials, to include "such items as 'swim suit issues' of certain sports magazines." Commanders were required to ensure soldiers received Geneva and Hague Convention refresher training and complied with Army Regulation (AR) 608–4, containing war trophy registration requirements. This preparation for overseas movement process obviously was not easy. The first two lessons that V Corps learned, even before deployment was completed, were that soldiers should be prepared for overseas movement regularly if out-of-theater contingency deployments were to continue and that checklists should be developed to ensure that all required procedures were covered.[21]

Medical requirements, which were handled through regional medical centers, also proved difficult to meet in some cases. Soldiers were required to get or have up-to-date immunizations for tetanus-diphtheria, typhoid, and meningococcus, if they had not received the vaccine in the previous five years. Immediately on notification of planned deployment, soldiers also were to start antimalarial medications. Some required vaccines were not stocked in adequate quantities at United States Army Medical Materiel Center, Europe. Soldiers were advised to take a two-month supply of any prescription drug they required and the following protective items: insect repellent, eyedrops, chapstick, sunscreen prep gel, foot powder, and iodine tablets.[22]

By the time V Corps conducted the departure ceremony for the 12th Aviation Brigade at Wiesbaden, Germany, on 28 August 1990, some of the transportation and shipping problems ahead were already beginning to come to the surface. The large standard military containers (MILVANs), which attach to truck chassis, were in short supply, and only three of the twenty rail cars required were available at Wiesbaden. Moreover, V Corps expressed concern about the availability of adequate support to load the brigade on ships at Livorno. The planned 230 personnel who would accompany the rail shipments had neither the skills, equipment, nor manpower to prepare and load the brigade on ships. Then, on the day before the deployment would begin, USAREUR received word that HQDA was asking why USAREUR had not self-deployed the AH–64 battalions. Generals Saint and Heldstab answered that the brigade had wanted to self-deploy, but HQDA instructed

USAREUR initially to move them by air transport and then by ship, and it was too late to change plans.[23]

The 12th Aviation Brigade encountered numerous problems with its rail transportation and with the ships available at Livorno and Rotterdam. After some delays in loading German *Bundesbahn* trains, 14 trains with approximately 380 rail cars moved the equipment, and 96 helicopters self-deployed to Livorno. Italian rail workers refused to work one day, because they had not been given forty-eight hours' notice of work. Trains starting for Livorno were mixed with oversized cars containing combat support and combat service support equipment that would not fit through mountain tunnels. This problem had been created when V Corps, without adequate information on tunnel size, decided to load the trains and ships tactically with this equipment along with the 5th Squadron, 6th Cavalry, and 3d Battalion, 227th Aviation. In France, the trains were stopped and inspected, and the oversized cars were removed. Four trains containing oversized equipment were then sent to Rotterdam for shipment. An elevator broke while loading one ship, and another ship had to be moved to a second dock for loading. Two trains headed for Rotterdam had to be rerouted to Livorno, because the ship available at the Dutch port did not have enough capacity for thirty rail cars of equipment. The brigade's soldiers successfully helped load the ships, and then returned to Germany by bus.[24]

On 10 September General Joulwan, the commander of V Corps, reported that although all aviation brigade equipment had been shipped, he was still troubled about the movement of soldiers by air to meet the equipment in Saudi Arabia. Joulwan expressed growing concern because resources had not been found to move the main body of the 12th Aviation Brigade on 12 September, when advance personnel would begin departing Rhein Main Air Base on flights for Saudi Arabia. For the next week, small groups of fifty departed most nights, and then the main body began to move in larger groups on 17 September 1990. On 19 September, as planned, the brigade was attached to the 101st Airborne Division (Air Assault). On the same day, the last of the 12th's Hellfire missiles were flown to Saudi Arabia. In the end, USAREUR sent the 12th Aviation Brigade to Southwest Asia with one and one-half times its required personnel, and General Saint would be looking for the return of the extra aviators later to support additional USAREUR deployments. By early October all ships had arrived and the brigade was conducting training rotations on desert terrain, developing battle books, and conducting an extensive night training program to prepare for their covering force assignment with the 101st Airborne Division.[25]

As noted above, V Corps compiled a substantial list of lessons learned even before the last ships left Italy. While a lack of experience and shortage of some stocks posed problems, V Corps also found that transportation planning and execution undertaken by HQ USAREUR/7A's Office of the Deputy Chief Staff, Logistics, the 1st Transportation Movement Control Agency, and the 37th Transportation Group lacked centralized organization and had relied on inaccurate rail information. The V Corps recommended that units be required to develop air and sea movement data. Moreover, it reported that aviation units lacked sufficient blocking and bracing materials and shrink wrap for moving helicopters by ship.[26] USAREUR had plenty to learn about and improve before it could make quick deployments with relative ease.

Signal Requirements

Signal requirements were substantial and complex in the early phase of support, and the efforts to respond to them raised issues of tenant unit relationships in USAREUR. The USAREUR Deputy Chief of Staff, Information Management, Brig. Gen. David E. White, was also the commander of the 5th Signal Command. This unit was an element of the U.S. Army Information Systems Command at Fort Huachuca, Arizona, although it was under the operational control of the CINCUSAREUR. The 5th Signal Command was responsible for providing echelon-above-corps signal support to USAREUR. As early as 17 August, the commander, U.S. Army Information Systems Command, tasked General White to provide individuals to fill specific critical vacant positions in units deploying from the United States. He also tasked White to provide two tactical communications centers, one deploying to Riyadh and the other to Dhahran, because existing communication capabilities there were inadequate. The communications centers, including operators, maintenance personnel, equipment, and repair parts, were ready to deploy in August, but the aircraft they were slated to use was diverted and their departure was postponed until 12 September 1990.[27]

Although the initial tasking apparently went directly from the U.S. Army Information Systems Command to the 5th Signal Command on 17 August, General White worked closely with General Saint and the HQ USAREUR/7A staff and Crisis Action Team through the O&I sessions to ensure that every tasking from the information systems command headquarters went through the normal validation process, which included ARCENT, USCENTCOM, HQDA, JCS, and USEUCOM before it was tasked through HQ USAREUR/7A. According to General White, General

Saint would cancel any task that had not gone through this approval process, including HQ USAREUR/7A approval. Although General White continued to get direct taskings from U.S. Army Information Systems Command, he was convinced that many problems and much confusion were saved by sticking to the standard validation process. He and his headquarters unofficially began working on these requests when notified by the information systems command but took no action until they were validated and briefed to General Saint at the O&I.[28]

This decision-making and information process apparently worked smoothly, at least for USAREUR, for the substantial taskings of August through October. By the first week of September, the 5th Signal Command was augmenting communications centers in Southwest Asia, had prepared tactical secure record terminal equipment and personnel for deployment to them, and was prepared to provide Unified Tactical Command and Control System equipment and personnel to link ARCENT main headquarters with its rear and later forward headquarters.

In September and October, HQ USAREUR/7A and its major commands joined the 5th Signal Command in taking a close look at the communications equipment they could afford to give up to support ARCENT and USCENTCOM. The VII Corps, for example, found that it could give up many assets but that the loss of TTC–39 switchboards and FM radio assets would have a crippling impact on operational readiness. The V Corps had a similar reaction. General White submitted a message, which General Saint approved, telling HQ USEUCOM that USAREUR did not have excess quantities of these switches and recommended working through the Joint Staff to have the United States Army Communications-Electronics Command provide the equipment to meet this requirement. This sort of coordinated action enabled USAREUR to provide its own substantial support to USCENTCOM while maintaining the readiness of USAREUR units. By the end of October, USAREUR had deployed approximately 1,900 personnel to Southwest Asia.[29]

Early General Logistics Support

USAREUR began to receive and respond to USCENTCOM requests for logistics support shortly after the president's 8 August announcement. Generals Laposata and Heldstab began, in the next few days, to get calls requesting immediate support. At first the requests and approval process were informal. General Laposata received his first request at home in a phone call from General Pagonis, who had arrived in Saudi Arabia the day before to take over logistic support of the operation and had found appalling conditions for the arriving troops of the 82d Airborne Division. Pagonis explained that they were eating impromptu host nation meals and asked for two C–130s full of meals, ready to eat (MREs).[30] General Laposata dispatched the MREs that day, apparently viewing this request as the sort of support that would be required of USAREUR. General Saint and his staff officers seem to have received many such calls in the days and weeks after the announcement of Operation DESERT SHIELD.

At first General Laposata focused on arranging proper staffing for logistics decisions and on arranging airlift between USAREUR and USCENTCOM. He met with USEUCOM and Military Airlift Command staffs in the first half of August to work out "air bridges" of sustainment support to the troops in Saudi Arabia. Bringing together key logistics personnel from throughout USAREUR, he warned them that support would be centrally managed and carefully controlled from HQ USAREUR, and he reviewed with them the whole process of deploying sustainment support. From the beginning, Laposata sent every request for support to General Saint for approval. He also had his staff office record every supply and logistics action supporting ARCENT and USCENTCOM on five-by-eight-inch cards, which it maintained on every item supplied for Operations DESERT SHIELD, DESERT STORM, and PROVIDE COMFORT and related activities.[31] The admittedly conventional, basic logistic procedures Laposata established in the first days of Operation DESERT SHIELD would allow him to maintain accountability for the massive support and deployment ahead.

A Need for NATO Release?

One early question that was not conventional, because it had not come up for many years, was whether or not USAREUR was allowed to send equipment and personnel out of the theater without providing notification to and receiving the approval of NATO. General Saint decided to leave this issue to higher Department of Defense echelons and the State Department to resolve. Due to the recent reductions in East-West tensions, a complaint on this issue appeared unlikely, particularly as most NATO allies were part of the broad coalition united in opposing Iraq's aggression.[32] But the question remained as USAREUR's commitment grew larger and coalition politics grew more complex.

Use of War Reserves

Although General Saint and his staff officers at first continued to concentrate primarily on internal USAREUR issues, major logistical matters quickly demanded Saint's attention, decision, and guidance. Huge early requests from ARCENT, USCENTCOM, HQDA, Forces Command, and Army Materiel Command for specific items, such as cots and M15 mine fuzes, made it clear that these headquarters viewed USAREUR's war reserve stocks as a general reserve that could be tapped to meet any shortages in USCENTCOM or the units deploying to that command. In addition, HQDA began to divert to USCENTCOM and deploying units equipment, supplies, and ammunition that had been ordered and produced for USAREUR units and war reserve stocks. While the reduction of USAREUR sustainment reserves would damage the command's readiness less fundamentally than thinning its personnel strength, the reductions certainly could cripple USAREUR's capability either to accomplish its European mission or to deploy capable units when needed in Southwest Asia or elsewhere. General Saint had to establish and enforce limits on transfers from unit equipment and withdrawals from war reserves to ensure USAREUR's readiness was not compromised.

While General Saint was eager to support USCENTCOM, he did not want to approve the reduction of USAREUR stocks beyond a certain breaking point. It was his mission to maintain a combat-ready force in Europe for the defense of the NATO nations of that continent or for contingency operations elsewhere, wherever he might be ordered, including the Persian Gulf.[33] Although the Soviet Union was experiencing unaccustomed political turmoil, its forces could still pose a significant threat to NATO. Saint's USAREUR force faced shortages and incomplete modernization, as did units in the United States. Some of the very equipment that USAREUR units lacked was stocked in theater reserve and POMCUS. For many years, HQDA had been reluctant to approve any sort of blanket authority to CINCUSAREUR to withdraw material from theater reserve and POMCUS in order to upgrade his units' readiness.[34]

On 16 August the Army's logistics office announced procedures for the release of overseas theater reserve and operational project stocks to Saudi Arabia–bound units from the United States after balances maintained by the Army Materiel Command and Defense Logistics Agency were exhausted.[35] In response to this announcement, General Laposata advised General Saint that the use of Central European theater reserve stocks for this purpose was not only workable, but would in fact "assist our ability to deal with TR [theater reserve] equipment posturing."[36]

The major question, then, was how much of the theater reserve and POMCUS stocks could be used to meet ARCENT/USCENTCOM and, later, VII Corps needs without crippling USAREUR. As described in the previous chapter, General Saint had already made the basic decisions on which to make this determination. In 1989 and the first half of 1990, he

***War reserve equipment, stored in large humidity-controlled
warehouses, being drawn upon for REFORGER 90 exercises***

had reviewed and reassessed the need for theater reserve and POMCUS
and established new theater reserve stock objectives based on a reassessment of the threat, anticipated reductions in forward-deployed divisions,
and the size of the reinforcing force that would need pre-positioned
stocks. In view of this ongoing reassessment, General Saint and his operations and logistics planners established new minimum theater reserve
storage levels. Much of the existing stock had been justified by plans for
four forward-based divisions and six reinforcing divisions. Since a smaller U.S. force was now likely to be approved, USAREUR appeared to have
substantial excess theater reserve stocks available to support USCENT-
COM. The same applied to POMCUS. And, as General Laposata noted,
these stocks included equipment that would have to be moved out of
Europe in response to an anticipated CFE treaty in any event.

At the end of August, HQDA caught up with General Saint's thinking on reducing theater reserve to fifteen days of supply. The Army's

deputy chief of staff for logistics asked USAREUR to establish lower war reserve levels. USAREUR could then support DESERT SHIELD by drawing upon theater reserve stocks in Central Europe and Southern Europe's Class VII stocks, which included critical items, such as weapons systems and trucks, as these stocks would exceed the lower reserve levels. The Pentagon recommended a level of fifteen days of supply, except for ammunition.

POMCUS also substantially exceeded that required by USAREUR's plans and expectations, but, as late as the end of September, HQDA had not approved these plans. On 20 September 1990, Lt. Gen. Dennis J. Reimer, the Army's deputy chief of staff for operations and plans, briefed Secretary of the Army Stone on sustainment needed in Southwest Asia, including prospective changes in POMCUS, but no alterations in policy were immediately forthcoming.[37]

Early Sustainment Controls and Procedures

Generals Saint and Laposata then established procedures to ensure that USAREUR would give quick and substantial support to USCENTCOM without causing USAREUR to reach its breaking point. Under these rules, General Laposata would give his commander the information necessary for a decision on each request, including information on the type and number of items requested, theater reserve and POMCUS levels before and after the transaction, and a recommendation of approval or disapproval. General Saint would review and approve each request for support, carefully scrutinizing any transaction that would drive reserves below fifteen days of supply.[38]

By early September USAREUR leaders were coming to realize that the modest, emergency type of air-supplied support that had been imagined and supplied in the first weeks of Operation DESERT SHIELD was not what lay ahead for the command. The rather informal process for requesting USAREUR support gradually became a formal validation process carefully enforced by Generals Laposata and Heldstab. The validation process worked as follows: 1) On receipt of a request from Southwest Asia, HQDA or the Department of Defense's National Inventory Control Point would request through USEUCOM that USAREUR issue materiel for DESERT SHIELD. 2) General Laposata and his staff would assess the impact of filling the request and inform General Saint. 3) HQ USEUCOM's Theater Logistics Control Center would request validation of requirements data, including quantity and required delivery date, from USCENTCOM and confirm with HQDA the requests

from the National Inventory Control Point. 4) After this validation by
USCENTCOM or confirmation by HQDA, USEUCOM would task
USAREUR to release the material. 5) At that point General Laposata
would request General Saint's approval of its release.[39] By the end of
September, this complex and formal validation process had become necessary to ensure that adequate communication was maintained with
ARCENT and USCENTCOM, that each action was coordinated among
the various agencies involved, and ultimately that the best decision was
made on where to acquire needed sustainment. Actually USAREUR staff
officers started working on actions as soon as they heard about them
through either formal or informal channels, but final action had to await
formal validation.

USAREUR as a Communications Zone?

On 10 September General Laposata warned Generals Saint and Burleson
that USCENTCOM would be severely overtaxed logistically from the end
of September through October. Based on information gathered in con-
versations and from a review of USCENTCOM situation reports, he predicted severe shortages of Class I supplies and food services, as well as
certain ammunition items. The M624 fuse for the M15 mine, which was
necessary to allow center hits on tanks, provided a good example.
USAREUR had already sent 10,000 of these fuzes to USCENTCOM,
which was short and asking for 26,000 more. There were none of these
fuzes in the United States. USAREUR had 30,000 on hand.

General Laposata was also checking USAREUR's capacity to support
Class VII requests, including heavy equipment tractors, generators, and
line-haul cargo trucks and tractors and its Class IX assets, including
repair parts and maintenance items for M60 and M1 tanks. USAREUR
had begun to get requests for these items but would not send them
unless they were excess to the command's requisitioning objectives.
Laposata also noted that the transfer of repair and maintenance items
from USCENTCOM to USAREUR, or even to Mainz Army Depot which
was operated by the Army Materiel Command, would tax direct support
and general support maintenance in USAREUR. While he continued to
express confidence in USAREUR's capability and the advantages of drawing down some USAREUR stocks through support of Desert Shield,
Laposata expressed concern about the severe demands on 21st TAA-
COM, which would be serving two theaters, USAREUR and USCENT-
COM. Provocatively, Laposata asked if USAREUR was becoming a communications zone for USCENTCOM.[40]

General Saint responded positively to Laposata's thoughts and urged him to determine what ports would be used and how long it would take ships to get from Bremerhaven to Saudi Arabia in comparison with ships traveling from the United States to Saudi Arabia. Saint observed that if USAREUR became the communications zone for USCENTCOM, he wanted the mission, not just directives from higher and lateral head-quarters.[41] Saint knew that no such status would be recognized for USAREUR and wanted simply to remind Laposata that he would con-tinue to give first priority to the European missions that had been for-mally assigned to him.

USEUCOM's Southwest Asia Support Concept

In September USEUCOM, which served as the conduit for requests from USCENTCOM for USAREUR sustainment support, tried to work out a formal support concept with USCENTCOM. Maj. Gen. Herman C. Kammer, Jr., the chief European Command logistics officer, presented support concept briefings to General Schwarzkopf on 20 September 1990 and to General Galvin on 25 September 1990. In the matter of force structure, General Kammer recommended to General Schwarzkopf that USEUCOM provide both augmented units and personnel with crit-ical skills, much as it had been doing. Relative to logistics support, General Kammer offered Schwarzkopf additional intelligence assets and communication equipment. He also offered general maintenance sup-port for tracked and wheeled vehicles to be performed by the 21st TAA-COM; medical care for evacuees (at the level of 5,500 beds in case of hostilities) and additional medical supplies; the use of firing ranges and other training areas and related support; and access to European Command recreational facilities. General Schwarzkopf answered that he did not want to build up heavy echelon-above-corps support in theater, particularly medical support and combat service support, and he did not currently need training areas.[42]

After the briefing General Kammer and Maj. Gen. James D. Starling, his Central Command counterpart, worked out some of the details. They agreed, with General Saint's subsequent approval, that ARCENT could ask USAREUR directly only for emergency requirements or supplies. Other requirements would go through the normal validation system. Since ARCENT reported that it could meet most of its logistical needs through host nation support and contracts, aided by maintenance at Mainz Army Depot, General Kammer concluded that USEUCOM should not honor requests for shipping tanks or other major assemblies provided by the Army Materiel Command or Class VII items sought for time-phased force deployment list units. General Kammer reported to General Galvin that his trip to USCENTCOM would help to minimize USEU-COM involvement in Saudi Arabia. General Galvin was pleased.[43]

Growing Logistics Requests

From August through October the number and size of requests for USAREUR war reserve stocks and for unique equipment available only in Europe grew significantly. *Table 2* lists August shipments, reflecting the diversity and numbers involved even in this early support. *Table 3* summarizes significant shipments in September. Tables in Chapter 6 give cumulative sustainment totals of selected items, including ammunition, through March 1991. The early support included a large quantity of chemical protective suits and equipment, including masks, battle dress overgarments, and footwear. MREs and tents were shipped from depots in Burtonwood, Germersheim, Kaiserslautern, and Pirmasens, completely exhausting the Burtonwood stocks.[44] By 4 September 1990, USAREUR had dispatched $424,000 worth of Class VIII medical supplies. USAREUR also supplied substantial amounts of communications equipment and even provided two C–12 aircraft with crews to ARCENT.[45] By 28 September, 176 supply sorties had been flown from Europe to Saudi Arabia.[46]

A noteworthy ARCENT request of 12 September 1990 shows how diverse and substantial were the requirements which it asked USAREUR to fulfill: seventy rough-terrain fork lifts of varying capacity, ninety 5,000-gallon tankers, sixty 5-ton tankers, twenty 10,000-gallon collapsible tanks, over one hundred radios of various types, seventy-two 250-gallon bags, sixty 5-ton trucks, and two hundred forty 500-gallon collapsible drums. Movement was requested as soon as possible by sea to Dhahran, Saudi Arabia.[47] By this time, even the Army's deputy chief of staff for logistics was asking USAREUR to break the very fifteen days of supply floor that the Department of the Army had recommended that USAREUR establish two weeks earlier. His logistics office requested USAREUR to dip below the fifteen- days-of-supply stockage level in chemical protective gear to provide 350,000 battle dress overgarments.[48]

POMCUS Tanks to USCENTCOM

When making his early, basic, logistical decisions on sustainment of USCENTCOM, General Saint had to balance or juggle at least three basic requirements: USCENTCOM needs, USAREUR readiness, including war reserve requirements, and anticipated CFE and drawdown requirements. Because he had to have a plan to dispose of excess tanks under the anticipated CFE treaty, Saint planned a revision of USAREUR tank-retention policy well in advance of actual Department of the Army requests for excess tanks to support USCENTCOM and, for that matter, Department of the Army reconsideration of POMCUS requirements. In early September 1990, Department of the Army first asked what tanks might be excess and available without specifying what or how many USCENTCOM needed or what revisions in POMCUS requirements were anticipated. General Saint considered the issue in a 12 September decision briefing that also addressed generally what units USAREUR could send to Southwest Asia. General Laposata told General Saint that USAREUR had 600 M1A1s potentially available in Army Readiness Package – South, theater reserve, POMCUS, and drawdown units. Existing requirements of USAREUR units could largely be met from units inactivating in 1991. Confronted with unapproved CFE limitations and drawdown plans, mission uncertainties, and unspecified USCENTCOM requirements, Saint suggested that USAREUR could offer 100 M1A1s immediately or 500 in June 1991 as the drawdown progressed. He viewed this modest proposal as likely to encourage HQDA and USCENTCOM to figure out their real requirement.[49] General Saint was not going to transfer tanks out of POMCUS until HQDA approved. When General Reimer briefed Secretary of the Army Stone on lowering POMCUS levels on 20 September, General Saint wanted senior Army leaders to understand that if he did not move tanks out of the Atlantic-to-the-Urals region, he might have to destroy some to meet CFE treaty provisions.[50]

In early October, General Reimer observed to General Saint that USAREUR had already identified quantities of M1- and M60-series tanks as excess to anticipated treaty limits and USAREUR end-state requirements. Reimer understood that the CFE treaty would be signed 19 November 1990, which meant that the excess tanks needed to be moved out of Europe before that date. He thus proposed that USAREUR move M60A3 tanks to Southwest Asia for sale to Saudi Arabia and send excess M1-series tanks from POMCUS to Saudi Arabia to modernize USCENTCOM's forces and provide theater reserve. According to Reimer, most of the M1A1 tanks from POMCUS would be used to modernize a division and an armored cavalry regiment that might rotate from the United States to Southwest Asia, but some would be left in USCENTCOM theater reserve. At this time, General Reimer believed that one division would rotate from the United States and another from Europe to Southwest Asia to replace forces there and that the current force in

Southwest Asia would not be modernized. He noted that M1A1 production was insufficient to modernize rotating divisions without using USAREUR assets. He therefore proposed that one division in the United States be modernized using newly produced equipment and another be modernized from USAREUR POMCUS assets. He added that transportation and funds for the movement of USAREUR tanks were currently available. General Saint responded positively, asking his staff for a quick response naming the ports to be used, since USAREUR was already prepared to act on this type of clear-cut request.[51]

TABLE 2—MAJOR SHIPMENTS FROM THEATER RESERVE AND POMCUS
STOCKS TO USCENTCOM IN AUGUST

Desert Battle Dress Uniforms (BDUs)	8,507 sets
Meals, Ready to Eat (MREs)	76,428 meals
Chemical Suits	87,000
Chemical Masks	59,000
Fuzes for M15 Mines	10,000
Mobile Laundry Trailers	10

Source: Memo, AEAGS for DCSOPS, 31 Aug 90, sub: Briefing slides for CCC.

TABLE 3—MAJOR SHIPMENTS FROM THEATER RESERVE AND POMCUS
STOCKS TO USCENTCOM IN SEPTEMBER

Meals, Ready to Eat (MREs)	1,655,148 meals
T-rations	2,201,040 meals
NBC Overgarments	244,000 sets
Mobile Laundry Trailers	16
Fuzes for M15 Mines	36,000
TOW 2 Missiles	3,450
Cots	6,663
Tents (GP Med & Lg/Maint)	2,912
Fest Tents	9 pallets
C–12 Aircraft	2
M60 Tanks (for foreign military sales)	220

Source: Briefing slides, DCSOPS, AEAGC-CAT, 28 Sep 90, sub: DESERT SHIELD.

The Joint Chiefs of Staff and Department of the Army confirmed that the Office of the Secretary of Defense had approved the movement of the Ml-series tanks before the anticipated signing of the CFE treaty on 19 November 1990, and the American embassy in Bonn informed the appro-

*New M1A1 Abrams tanks loaded on flatbed rail cars
at Rhine Ordnance Barracks in Kaiserslautern, Germany*

priate offices in Germany of the action. By the end of October all tanks were delivered to port, and they were shipped by the end of the first week of November. HQDA directed the Army Materiel Command to ensure that the tanks met current maintenance standards and to reinforce the front turret for protection against Soviet high-explosive, penetrating tank munitions. USAREUR provided an inspector in Southwest Asia to ensure USAREUR was charged only for repairs necessary to bring tanks to current maintenance standards. The M1A1s were used not as theater reserve, but to replace M1 tanks of 1st Cavalry Division; 24th Infantry Division; 1st Brigade, 2d Armored Division; and 197th Infantry Brigade. In a not unusual postscript to this successful major support story, one of the ships carrying the M1A1s blew a boiler en route to a stop in England before heading to the Persian Gulf and could not be repaired. USAREUR then had to send M1A1 drivers and mechanics to England to unload the ship and transfer the tanks to another ship.[52] By the time the new ship left for Saudi Arabia on 10 November, HQDA had already requested additional M1A1s from POMCUS, from both the authorized stockage list and prescribed load list, to upgrade forces already in Saudi Arabia. By then, however, USAREUR was preparing to deploy VII Corps, and General Saint insisted on filling USAREUR units' needs first.[53]

USAREUR also made available M60A3 tanks and diverse other equipment for foreign military sales to support DESERT SHIELD. By 11 October, 150 of these tanks had been accepted for sale to Saudi Arabia and 47 to Oman, with 109 already in port and the remainder ready for shipment in the next week. USAREUR also made machine guns available for the tanks as well as 105 mm. artillery rounds, 1 1/4-ton trucks, M578 recovery vehicles, M85 and M240 machine guns, and substantial quantities of chemical protection equipment. The U.S. Congress meanwhile was considering approval of the sale of 150 additional excess tanks to Turkey and 27 to Bahrain.[54]

Early Ammunition Support

USCENTCOM requests for ammunition support began approaching safety limits on USAREUR's reserve of multiple-launch rocket system canisters and launchers and its tube-launched, optically tracked, wire-guided (TOW) missiles by the end of August. These requests for ammunition illustrated early the sort of decisions that would have to be made in USAREUR throughout Operations DESERT SHIELD and DESERT STORM. USAREUR was requested to provide large quantities of multiple-launch rocket system canisters and TOW 2 missiles, both of which were fully stocked to the thirty days of supply level. But filling the requests would reduce stockage below thirty days of supply even for the anticipated lower 1990/1991 requirement.[55] In order to issue the materiel, General Saint directed a postponement in the fielding of a new multiple-launch rocket system battery from October 1990 until January 1991 when stock would presumably again be available.[56] An additional problem USAREUR confronted in providing ammunition support in these early months was the unavailability of the best port in Germany for that purpose. Nordenham was totally engaged in the shipment of old U.S. chemical weapons to the Pacific in Operation STEEL BOX.

As soon as Nordenham became available, USAREUR placed the ammunition to fill most early USCENTCOM ammunition requests on ten trains and sent them to Nordenham for shipment on a single ship, the maritime service (MS) *Greenwave*. The ship was loaded with multiple-launch rocket system canisters, 25-mm. rounds for the Bradley fighting vehicle, Ablative B panels, M60 tanks with blades, and 105-mm. tank rounds. The MS *Greenwave* left Nordenham on 3 October for the two-week trip to Saudi Arabia. At the same time, over 800 rounds of 105-mm. tank ammunition, 1,000 cots, 3 fest tents, 5 rough-terrain forklifts, and more were waiting for flights.[57] Again, this description of sustainment provided to USCENTCOM gives only a flavor of the massive support that would continue through March 1991. Later sustainment support, including ammunition sustainment, is described in Chapter 6.

Depot Maintenance Support

Provision of sustainment stocks was only one of the logistical issues involved in early USAREUR support of Southwest Asia. Another was the provision of maintenance support by Mainz Army Depot, an Army Materiel Command facility in Germany. U.S. Army equipment was shipped to and from depots across Europe for maintenance and repair at Mainz Army Depot. As early as 16 August, the commander, Army Depot System Command, activated a 24-hour emergency operations center at Mainz Army Depot, that provided theater-wide, depot-level maintenance and repair to USAREUR. In September the commander, Army Materiel Command, Europe, agreed to coordinate with USAREUR's 200th Theater Army Materiel Management Center (200th TAMMC) the release of equipment at the Mainz Army Depot to support DESERT SHIELD. The Depot System Command also announced that Mainz Army Depot would be used as a wholesale source of repair for depot-level equipment from Southwest Asia. Concerned that these decisions not adversely affect USAREUR, Generals Saint and Laposata worked out an agreement in October with the headquarters of the Army Materiel Command, Europe, that improved management of equipment turned in to the depot and helped it to repair USCENTCOM equipment without degrading support to USAREUR.[58] Again USAREUR's monitoring and close cooperation with Army Materiel Command; Depot System Command; Army Materiel Command, Europe; and Mainz Army Depot ensured that the depot could provide support to Southwest Asia with minimum impact on USAREUR readiness.

Chapter 4

Planning a Major USAREUR Role in Southwest Asia

Changing Perceptions of USAREUR's Role

Through September and October, as the United States and its coalition allies continued to build up their defensive strength in Saudi Arabia, American political and military leaders reevaluated the type of force that would be best suited to counter Iraq's aggression and threats against its Persian Gulf neighbors. By the second week of September 1990, USAREUR leaders understood that their units might be called on to make a substantially larger contribution than heretofore to the counter-Iraqi effort. On 11 September the chairman of the Joint Chiefs of Staff, General Powell, told the Senate Armed Services Committee that his and Secretary Cheney's staffs were considering a rotation policy that might involve deploying units from Europe to Southwest Asia. In mid-October, after administration and Defense Department leaders had rejected an offensive concept relying primarily on the already deployed XVIII Airborne Corps that had been developed by a USCENTCOM planning group, General Schwarzkopf directed his planners to develop a heavier two-corps flanking attack. Such an attack would require the infusion of substantial additional American troops into the theater.[1]

The deficiencies of the defensively oriented force that USCENTCOM assembled in August and September appeared quite evident to USAREUR leaders and planners. From their European perspective, these officers worried that the units deploying from the United States to Saudi Arabia lacked the full-strength divisions, modernized equipment, and support elements required to field the type of mobile, heavy force with massive firepower that they believed would be necessary to conduct a successful offensive operation in the desert against Iraq's combat-tested divisions.

In the view of USAREUR's CFE Division, there was not a single full-strength Army division in the United States, most units in the United States were not modernized, and the XVIII Airborne Corps in particular lacked the armored mobility and firepower needed to deal with Iraq's Republican Guards. Moreover, combat support and combat service support appeared hopelessly deficient in the deployed forces, and almost all such support available in the United States had already been committed to the current defensive operation. The Office of the Army's Deputy Chief of Staff for Operations had substantiated the deploying units' comparative lack of modernization in determining their need for USAREUR equipment discussed above.[2]

In September and October as HQDA first planned a long-term defense of Saudi Arabia and later evaluated offensive options, General Saint and other USAREUR leaders recognized real dangers for USAREUR. An extended rotation of USAREUR units to Southwest Asia could delay its drawdown schedule and disrupt Saint's efforts to reduce his expenses slightly faster than his budget was cut. More important, by mid-October HQDA and USCENTCOM requests for units, soldiers, and equipment threatened to degrade USAREUR's readiness and undermine its ability to field an effective force in Europe, Southwest Asia, or anywhere else. This had already occurred in the case of V Corps in August, as the deployment of its 12th Aviation Brigade had left the corps largely without an offensive helicopter capability.

In August 1990 and before, General Saint and his commanders and staff were certain that USAREUR troops were the best trained and best equipped in the U.S. Army and had foreseen, but had not specifically planned, an out-of-theater contingency role for them in the post–Cold War environment.[3] In September and early October, as General Saint and HQ USAREUR/7A organized to rotate divisions to Southwest Asia, sustain USCENTCOM, and, in some cases, equip units from the United States deploying to Saudi Arabia, they also began to think about possible roles for its larger combat organizations. In discussions with General Vuono in early October about USAREUR's ability to contribute to the force deployed to Saudi Arabia, General Saint offered to send a complete, capable corps there as the heavy offensive force. The Army did not immediately accept this offer. During the night of 4–5 October, Vuono called Saint to ask him to ready one division and possibly a second, an armored cavalry regiment, an artillery brigade, a corps support command, and extra aviation for deployment to Southwest Asia by 20 December. The next day General Saint told General Heldstab, General Laposata, Mr. Pflaster, and Colonel Graham to prepare to deploy the units, which, he noted, looked a lot like a corps. He also asked them to begin studying the impact of sending a corps in January.[4] Because HQDA requests added up practically to a corps anyway, Saint and his planners relied for the possible deployment of a corps in January on the same preparations they undertook to send one or two divisions, a cavalry regiment, and aviation, artillery, and support elements by December.[5]

Early Deployment Options and Plans

Before 1989 it would have been almost impossible for the United States to deploy a large armored force from Europe without dangerously weakening the North Atlantic alliance. But after the collapse of the Communist regimes of the Soviet Union's Warsaw Pact allies in 1989 and 1990 and after the achievement of broad international support for United Nations economic sanctions against Iraq in August 1990, neither General Powell nor General Galvin expected any serious complaints from NATO nations about the commitment of NATO assets to the Persian Gulf. General Galvin told reporters on 19 September that there existed a complete consensus among NATO nations in support of sending to the Persian Gulf U.S. forces that had been dedicated to the defense of Europe. General Saint, although not directly involved in this issue, had already come to similar conclusions and discussed the issue with General Vuono and probably with General Galvin.[6]

The deployment of USAREUR forces to the Gulf, whether as replacement, rotational, or reinforcement units, or as a main offensive force, would entail extremely complicated planning issues. The size and type of force that USAREUR could and should send to Southwest Asia were only two of many complicated considerations. Deployment planning also would have to take into account units that were already drawing down, turning in equipment, and closing facilities. Moreover, in spite of Saint's August protest against undermanning, USAREUR personnel strength would slip below 94 percent of its authorized level by the end of October 1990. USAREUR was already deploying personnel with critical skills and equipment during the first three months of its support for Operation DESERT SHIELD. Deployment would have to leave an adequate force in Europe, as well as a viable community structure to support 200,000 USAREUR family members, including those left behind by deployed sponsors. Deployment would have to allow USAREUR to meet drawdown plans for fiscal years 1991 and 1992, unless changes were made in those plans. The complexities of planning to deploy a USAREUR force, combined with the ambiguity of Defense Department and Army plans and their initial reluctance to use the largest USAREUR combat organiza-

General Vuono

tions, led to many planning excursions, through which the parameters of USAREUR's eventual VII Corps deployment were gradually defined.

On 4 September 1990, General Burleson directed General Heldstab to establish a small planning group to examine the pros and cons of designating units that would be leaving Europe under drawdown plans as potential replacements for units currently deployed from the United States in Saudi Arabia. Such a replacement scheme would have been essentially a personnel operation, because USAREUR units would have simply left their equipment in Europe and obtained new equipment that other units would have left in Saudi Arabia rather than carrying it back to the United States. The concept evidently involved rotating units both into Saudi Arabia and back to Europe, because Burleson suggested that families might stay in Europe if the rotations were for less than six months. Burleson asked Heldstab to consider personnel, logistical, installation, and family issues and determine how USAREUR would handle such an operation.[7]

Early on, the USAREUR Command Group foresaw a possibility that deployment of USAREUR units to Southwest Asia could disrupt drawdown plans, schedules, financing, and rationality. However, members of the Command Group probably also saw deployment as a possible means to cope with potential budgetary shortfalls in implementing drawdown plans, for USAREUR leaders were already concerned that swift reductions in USAREUR's budget, aimed at procuring a "peace dividend" in Europe, could undermine USAREUR's ability to draw down units and close installations efficiently and effectively—a complicated, expensive, and time-consuming process at best. They hoped that a Persian Gulf mission might help them resolve some of these problems.

On receipt of General Burleson's 4 September directive, General Heldstab directed Mr. Pflaster, the chief of his CFE Division, to put together a briefing on deployment issues for General Saint. CFE Division was chosen for this task because it had been studying USAREUR force structure for the previous two years and had, with the help of Generals Saint, Shalikashvili, Burleson, and Heldstab and other staff officers, put together a drawdown concept that named units and installations, provided tentative inactivation and base closure schedules, and included plans for a USAREUR end-state force structure to be reached by 1995. The CFE Division thus had the data and the experience to propose deployment structures and options, and it already held carefully conceived plans for drawdown and restructuring on a close-hold basis. Its first reaction to this tasking was concern that deployment would complicate its drawdown work. The division was still waiting for the Department of Defense to announce 1991 unit inactivations and installation closures before really getting started with the implementation of its drawdown and restructuring plan, even though the first increment of unit inactivations was already under way.[8]

General Heldstab

Pflaster and other CFE Division personnel presented the first of many proposed deployment force structures and scenarios to General Saint on 12 September 1990. In this first planning round, Pflaster proposed using only residual units or units that were not scheduled for inactivation within the timeframe of the rotations to and from Southwest Asia. At this time USAREUR's combat force consisted of 4 three-brigade divisions and 2 separate brigades. All together these included 7 mechanized infantry brigades and 7 armored brigades, containing 21 infantry battalions and 23 armor battalions, plus 2 armored cavalry regiments. Deleting units scheduled for drawdown during the anticipated rotation period, USAREUR had a residual force of 7 armored brigades, containing 9 mechanized infantry battalions and 14 armor battalions, plus the 2 armored cavalry regiments. The CFE Division proposed leaving at least one battalion at each installation in Germany to manage the installation and its family support. On this first cut, they proposed three options for a deploying force: 1) up to three mixed brigades and an armored cavalry regiment; 2) up to two heavy armored brigades and an armored cavalry regiment, and 3) up to two heavy infantry brigades and an armored cavalry regiment. Pflaster's briefers preferred their second option because it met the goal of keeping one battalion at each installation and gave all units twelve months between rotations. They considered option 3 the worst choice, based on the heavy infantry structure of the Iraqi Army.[9]

General Saint did not endorse any of these options. Instead he gave his CFE Division planners additional guidance and sent them back to their drawing boards and computers more than once in the following week before approving three options that would be briefed to HQDA. His key guideline was that USAREUR units would deploy to Southwest Asia for six months and then return to USAREUR for eighteen months before deploying again. He also suggested that USAREUR could send some battalions training at Grafenwoehr and Hohenfels to Southwest Asia prior to their inactivation.[10]

During the next week, General Saint and the CFE planning group refined three options for battalion, brigade, and division rotation packages, and on 18 September General Heldstab faxed the resulting product to General Reimer. The plans basically did not interfere with scheduled fiscal year 1991 inactivations, but they included in the 1991 rotations units scheduled for inactivation in 1992. The three packages each achieved the commander's goals of providing six-month rotations with eighteen months between unit rotations and of leaving one battalion at each home installation, variously used inactivating and residual force units, and left USAREUR with a range of capabilities to sustain the rotations. The options offered were: 1) a brigade package of (1a) heavy armor or (1b) heavy infantry in which battalions had not previously been affiliated with the brigade; 2) a battalion package of mixed armor and heavy infantry battalions, plus a brigade headquarters, made up of either both inactivating and residual force battalions or strictly battalions that were not scheduled for inactivation; and 3) a heavy division set. The proposal recommended option 1a, the heavy armor brigade, although USAREUR could not sustain this option after eighteen months. Option 1b, heavy infantry, and option 3 could be sustained only for twelve months. Moreover, the heavy division, option 3, required the readjustment of fiscal year 1992 inactivation dates.[11]

Mr. Pflaster and Ms. Virginia Jay of the CFE Division also briefed these options to General Reimer on 18 September. Their discussions with the Army's operations chief focused on USAREUR's provision of heavy divisions for rotations, the use of units scheduled for fiscal year 1992 inactivation for the March 1991 rotation, the possible use of POM-

CUS to support USCENTCOM, and the idea of sending equipment from inactivating USAREUR units to Southwest Asia. In line with these discussions, the USAREUR options were partly incorporated in and partly superseded by plans which General Reimer presented to the secretary of the Army on 20 September and which Mr. Pflaster brought back to USAREUR.

Briefing Secretary Stone on sustaining the force in Southwest Asia, General Reimer proposed basically the same goals USAREUR recognized at this time: long-term sustainment of forces in Southwest Asia, maintenance of readiness Army-wide, and a continued reshaping of the Army to new force levels. He considered two scenarios in Southwest Asia: 1) defending the Arabian Peninsula with four divisions, preferably including three heavy divisions, until December 1991, or 2) deterring the Iraqis, without fighting them, with three divisions until September 1992. Reimer discussed the possibility of having USAREUR serve as a rotation base using two heavy divisions, two armored cavalry regiments, and one separate brigade, plus inactivating units, beginning in March 1991. USAREUR units were well down the list of deployment options for the smaller deterrence mission. Reimer called for the deployment of USAREUR forces by 1 March 1991 under the defend option. He admitted that units on USAREUR's fiscal year 1991 inactivation list might have to rotate to Saudi Arabia under this option and that these units would subsequently have to return to Europe for inactivation. His plan called for modernizing the tanks of the 24th Infantry Division and the 1st Cavalry Division in Southwest Asia, implicitly by drawing modernized tanks from POMCUS in Europe. Their replacement divisions would inherit this modernized equipment, while the 24th Infantry Division and the 1st Cavalry Division would return to the United States with their original armor.[12] Reimer's proposals in this sphere apparently led the Army to approve in October guidelines under which M1A1 tanks were drawn from USAREUR theater reserve and POMCUS and shipped to Southwest Asia as described in Chapter 3.[13]

After reviewing Reimer's briefing, General Saint asked his planners to put together a rotation plan by 26 September. He now apparently favored deploying a short-term surge of heavy forces to Saudi Arabia by January 1991, possibly for offensive action. But Saint first had to respond to HQDA plans for long-term rotation of divisions or smaller units, or even parts and pieces of units, which, in the long run, might seriously disrupt his and the Army's plans for drawdown and restructuring, as well as dash his hope to contribute to an offensive deployment without destroying USAREUR's readiness. He gave his planners the following guidance: USAREUR could contribute seven battalions in long-term rotations or more to a surge force. Saint wanted HQDA to understand that he was determined to achieve 100 percent manning of active USAREUR units even if it was necessary to inactivate other units to accomplish this. He would need to retain four divisions in Europe to support six-month rotations with an eighteen-month stay in USAREUR between rotations and to maintain a meaningful level of readiness in Europe.[14] In ten days, Saint and his planners worked out proposals for swapping USAREUR battalions and brigades for comparable units in Southwest Asia; rounding out, with USAREUR brigades, divisions stationed in the United States; deploying a USAREUR division; and sending a USAREUR division together with an echelon above corps combat service support slice.[15]

Division Rotation Plans

On 6 October USAREUR planning suddenly shifted from a relatively low key consideration of various possible deployment arrangements to intensive, close-hold planning to send actual units, specifically a USAREUR division and an armored cavalry regiment, to Saudi Arabia by 20 December 1990. On that October day, General Saint told Generals Heldstab and Laposata, Mr. Pflaster, and Colonel Graham to prepare to send a division and an armored cavalry regiment and to look at sending a corps. Heldstab and Laposata also met with Mr. Pflaster, Colonel Graham, and Ms. Jay of CFE Division and with Colonel Phillips, Laposata's chief of the Plans, Operations, and Systems Division. General Heldstab told the group that General Saint had received a call from HQDA the night before, asking that USAREUR deploy a division plus an armored cavalry regiment to Saudi Arabia by 20 December 1990. The members of the group decided that they first needed to determine whether or not they could simultaneously meet the new requirement, maintain the drawdown, and execute probable CFE requirements. Then they would pick a division.[16]

On 13 October 1990, the planning group reported its conclusions to General Saint. The planners recommended sending modernized units that had recently completed training in a ten-battalion division. They argued that this could be done without using units announced for inactivation in 1991. They also planned to leave a unit in each military community. General Saint responded that as many inactivating units as possible should be deployed. When their time was up, they could leave their equipment in Saudi Arabia and depart.[17]

Although the planners presented two options, mechanized infantry heavy and armor heavy, it was clear that both they and General Saint preferred the armor-heavy option. General Saint was convinced that USCENTCOM had adequate infantry but needed more armor to face Iraq in the desert. Generals Saint and Heldstab and their planners all seem to have agreed that VII Corps' 1st Armored Division was the best choice for the December 1990 deployment. The VII Corps' commander, General Franks, also preferred the armor-heavy option and agreed with the choice of the 1st Armored Division. Nevertheless, throughout the early October discussions, the planners continually considered deployment options involving VII Corps' 1st Armored Division and V Corps' 3d Armored Division. This indicated that they were prepared to send both armored divisions if asked to deploy a corps.[18]

To determine the composition of the 1st Armored Division, General Saint and his planners applied the selection principles they considered most significant: modernization, training, inactivation status, and community coverage. No USAREUR division, including the 1st Armored Division in its existing organization, perfectly met their criteria. Therefore, some mixing and matching of divisional elements was necessary. The plan briefed by the CFE planners on 13 October would have deployed two 1st Armored Division brigades. The headquarters and headquarters companies of both brigades, two of their armor battalions, and one of their infantry battalions were scheduled for inactivation in the second half of 1991. General Heldstab noted that the planners would have to reexamine sending those battalions if the deployment were delayed until March. The third brigade the planners proposed to deploy with the 1st Armored Division was the 3d Brigade, 3d Infantry Division, whose headquarters company and three battalions were scheduled for inactivation in 1992. The planners also selected a number of artillery, aviation, and support units from the 2d Armored Division (Forward), of which the artillery and support units were mostly scheduled for inactivation in 1992. The engineer, air defense, signal, military intelligence, military police (MP), and chemical units were strictly 1st Armored Division elements, and they were also scheduled for inactivation in 1992.[19]

Even with the 1st Armored Division filled with the elements of their choice, the planners had to confront problems caused by low personnel levels in the units selected. The 1st Armored Division stood at 95 percent of authorized strength, short 800 personnel with an additional 300 who were nondeployable. A total of 1,100 personnel would have to be reassigned or cross-leveled from other units for the division to deploy with a full strength of 16,966. In order to begin unloading in Saudi Arabia by 20 December 1990, planners built a time line for its preparation, loading, and transportation, assuming a Department of the Army decision by 20 October 1990.[20] HQDA never decided to deploy just a single USAREUR division. Nevertheless, the planning for this contingency surely helped Generals Saint and Franks and their staffs to identify the preferred ingredients for a major deployment and thus went a long way to shape the corps that would later be called upon to deploy.

At this time General Saint and his planners also made other decisions of eventual importance, including which armored cavalry regiment to send, how to rotate aviation brigades, and how to support other HQDA and USCENTCOM requirements. They applied their standard planning factors and selection principles to the question of which cavalry regiment was best suited to deploy. The planners envisioned a reorganized 2d Armored Cavalry Regiment made up of two current 2d Armored Cavalry Regiment squadrons and one squadron from the 11th Armored Cavalry Regiment. They planned to leave one 2d Armored Cavalry Regiment squadron in Germany, because its subcommunity would be totally unsupported by any tactical military unit if the squadron deployed.

General Saint's planners concluded that the 11th Aviation Brigade would be prepared to deploy in March, but only if they could arrange to bring back to USAREUR the extra aviators they had deployed with the 12th Aviation Brigade. They also put together a corps support contingent requested by HQDA. In this contingent they planned to send the 87th Maintenance Battalion, a military police company, a finance unit, a personnel services company, an aviation intermediate maintenance battalion headquarters, and a company-level headquarters from the 200th Theater Army Material Maintenance Command (TAMMC) for a total of 2,700 personnel. The total number of personnel proposed for deployment with the division, the armored cavalry regiment, and the corps support contingent, together with the previously deployed aviation brigade, was 25,936. General Saint still wondered what other support DA would need.[21] The answer to this question would become apparent in the next two weeks.

In the week immediately following, USAREUR planners engaged in considerable discussion about which unit would replace the 1st Armored Division in the second rotation. This discussion helped resolve issues that would become important when USAREUR was required to deploy a corps. General Saint's planners were convinced that it was best to deploy one division from each corps in turn, and, to make this possible, they proposed completing the modernization of the 8th Infantry Division before the second rotation would begin. General Saint and his planners were still trying to maintain their 30,000-soldier drawdown schedule in 1991 and 1992. Each USAREUR division thus presented problems because some units were in the process of turning in their equipment in preparation for a March 1991 inactivation while others were scheduled for inactivation in May 1991. To send the 3d Armored Division in March 1991, for example, would probably have required its reconfiguration using 8th Infantry Division battalions and other elements that were not scheduled for inactivation either in 1991 or early 1992. USAREUR would then have to use residual force or end-state divisions for later rotations.[22]

During the same week, Colonel Graham of the CFE Division prepared a draft deployment order that would send the 1st Armored Division to Southwest Asia by 20 December 1990. The draft addressed many of the issues that would arise later during the deployment of VII Corps. Under the plan it outlined, the division would be task organized and essentially would deploy itself. The plan relied on U.S. Air Forces in Europe to provide space and facilities for deploying forces on its bases, United States Transportation Command to provide sea and air transportation, and USCENTCOM to perform reception and onward movement missions in Southwest Asia. It identified three seaports of embarkation: Bremerhaven, Rotterdam, and Antwerp. The order named the commander, VII Corps, as the USAREUR executive agent for the operation; he was tasked with overseeing the deployment operations. The order made supporting USAREUR commands responsible for the following assignments: V Corps for providing ground transportation, general maintenance, and emergency medical support; 21st TAACOM for establishing marshaling areas at seaports of embarkation and for providing related maintenance, transportation, and technical loading support; 1st Personnel Command for bringing units to 100 percent strength; and 7th Medical Command and 5th Signal Command for medical and signal communications requirements.[23]

With the help of General Laposata, the planners also addressed in the draft order some of the basic logistical issues that any large-scale USAREUR deployment would entail. Units would deploy with their unit basic load of Class I (food), III (petroleum products), V (ammunition), and VIII (medical) supplies and equipment and their prescribed load list of Class IX (repair parts). Ammunition would be placed on vehicles to maintain unit load identity at the battalion level. For Class II (expendable items) and IV (barrier) supplies, units were required to submit requisitions for two sets of desert battle dress uniforms and one desert battle dress uniform hat and kevlar helmet cover, and to order sunglasses for each deploying individual. Each unit was to take its basic load of barbed wire and sandbags and its current stock of camouflage nets and tents. It was also to take two sets of NBC protective suits, filters, and decontamination kits and one training set per person. For Class VII (major end items), the operational readiness float—a pool of extra vehicles and other major equipment items—would accompany units to replace vehicles that might become unavailable to the unit during maintenance or combat. Cross-leveling within VII Corps was authorized to secure serviceable equipment for the operational readiness float. The transportation section of the draft order specified that each unit would have to submit its movement plans through VII Corps to the 1st Transportation Movement Control Agency within seven days of an alert to move. Military Traffic Management Command, Europe, would provide port facilities and space. M1A1 tanks were to be processed through Bremerhaven and aircraft though Antwerp. The 21st TAACOM was responsible for providing material for blocking, bracing, and tying down equipment that would be sent to port by rail.[24]

The draft order also covered administrative matters and personnel processing. It would have halted the reassignment and most other departures of soldiers from USAREUR, implementing what were called stop-loss provisions. The order proposed the cross-leveling of personnel within corps to fill shortages of critical occupational specialties and the referral to the 1st Personnel Command of any shortages that could not be filled in that way. It would establish an Operation DESERT SHIELD strength report, but have individual personnel records remain at each soldier's USAREUR home station. The order also outlined responsibilities for casualty reporting and mail service.[25]

General Heldstab sent the draft deployment order to General Burleson for review on 17 October 1990. Burleson asked about numerous issues left unresolved in this first draft order. For example, General Saint wanted to paint vehicles desert tan on the way to port, but the draft order made no provision for painting. Where and how ammunition and other sensitive items would be shipped seemed ambiguous or neglected. The chief of staff also wanted to know if ammunition would be shipped through the port of Nordenham, Germany, which had long held authority from the German government to allow ammunition shipments, in addition to the three ports mentioned in the draft order. General Burleson asked General Heldstab to answer these questions and refine the whole plan. Colonel Graham's draft and Burleson's review very much facilitated the drafting of a final deployment order when HQDA ultimately decided to send a USAREUR corps to Southwest Asia.[26]

At this time General Saint and his planners carefully reexamined the functional impact of the drawdown, their early USCENTCOM support, and the planned December deployment to determine what and how much more they could offer USCENTCOM. Using a standard matrix, the planners examined a wide variety of military functions, including aviation, including air evacuation; artillery, including the multiple-launch rocket system; engineer; signal; combat support and combat service support; medical and dental; chemical; military police; and finance and personnel service support. They found, for example, that already very few chemical assets were left in USAREUR; indeed, only two USAREUR chemical decontamination companies remained.[27]

The planners observed again and again that they could offer substantial initial support but only limited support for future rotations. Rotations after March 1991 would have used up nearly all aviation and multiple-launch rocket system assets. Further rotations would have had a serious impact on artillery, engineer, and signal support in USAREUR. After drafting plans to deploy a division, an armored cavalry regiment, and a corps support contingent and after completing a thorough functional analysis, General Saint and his planners could respond more quickly and accurately to USCENTCOM wish lists. The limits and impact of potential future USAREUR deployments were now clearer to USAREUR leaders and planners. General Saint planned to brief General Vuono on these subjects, including their relationship with drawdown planning, in Washington on Wednesday, 23 October 1990.[28]

Meanwhile a small group consisting of General Saint and his planners had continued to consider the possibility of sending a corps. Saint had offered to deploy a USAREUR corps to Southwest Asia in discussions with General Vuono since early October. General Heldstab had also raised the corps option with General Reimer, arguing that USAREUR could put together full-strength, heavy divisions and a complete corps support command, while Forces Command had no fully manned divisions nor any complete corps support commands available.[29] By mid-October, Saint and his planners had decided the VII Corps flag and headquarters would deploy if required. Among the considerations that underlay this decision was the fact that V Corps was about to undergo a change of command.[30] On 9 November, Lt. Gen. David M. Maddox would become commander, V Corps, replacing General Joulwan, who had been appointed commander in chief, U.S. Southern Command, and would receive a promotion.

General Saint went to the Pentagon about 16 October for the Army Commanders Conference and direct discussions with General Vuono and other Army leaders. During this ten-day trip, General Saint surely contributed to the process that led to the decision to send VII Corps to Southwest Asia in January as the main armored formation in an "enhanced" USCENTCOM force with offensive capabilities. Some key USAREUR planners also went to Washington at this time. While General Saint was at the Army Commanders Conference, he received General

Reimer's options for a USAREUR division and armored cavalry regiment to rotate to Southwest Asia, which were based to some extent on concepts that USAREUR had previously developed. Since he had continued to collect Army requests for USAREUR assistance beyond this rotation, the corps support command contingent, and the other support already requested, General Saint asked Ms. Jay to compile a list of these requests. She reported that overall the Department of the Army had asked for 96 units with 42,168 soldiers.[31]

Mr. Pflaster and Ms. Jay returned to Heidelberg with the list, and the CFE Division went to work on planning how to fill the total requirements. The division used its force structure data base to identify units that could meet the new requirements and quickly sought approval from the USAREUR subordinate commands to which those units were assigned. The division's staff found that USAREUR was short combat service support units, including medium truck and other transportation units; petroleum-oriented units; and signal units. These would have to be drawn directly from USAREUR's residual requirements. But the CFE Division found that USAREUR could fulfill most of the requests by providing 74 to 77 units with 39,524 people (see Appendix A). On 24 October Mr. Pflaster faxed these results to General Saint, who was continuing his briefings and discussions at HQDA, along with a note observing that it might be easier to send an understrength corps to simplify command and control and avoid continued uncontrollable piecemeal support.[32]

VII Corps Deployment Plans

On the morning of Saturday, 27 October 1990, Generals Shalikashvili, Burleson, and Laposata; General Heldstab's deputy, Col. William D. Chesarek; Engineer Col. Joe N. Ballard; and Mr. Pflaster, Colonel Graham, Lt. Col. Paul N. Quintal, and Ms. Jay of the CFE Division met with General Saint in his office to discuss Saint's trip and to refine division-plus rotation plans. The USAREUR commander announced that he had received a call in the middle of the night asking if he could deploy a corps with two divisions to Southwest Asia by 15 January 1991. A division stationed in the United States would be added to the corps. He reported that the decision to deploy a second corps had been made in the "Tank," the conference room used by the Joint Chiefs of Staff at the Pentagon, the night before. Although the decision was placed on close hold pending public announcement, USAREUR needed to get key personnel into the planning process immediately. Taking advantage of the planning that his staff had already accomplished, General Saint said he would send the 1st and 3d Armored Divisions with one armored cavalry regiment and a field artillery brigade that was heavy on multiple-launch rocket systems. He told the planners they needed to meet with him again on Sunday afternoon to begin to identify component units, prepare a movement plan, review its impact on the drawdown schedule, and list caveats. Deploying the corps would have first priority in USAREUR; drawdown execution and restructuring would be relegated to second.[33]

VII Corps Force Structure Decisions

General Saint's close-hold announcement that USAREUR would plan to send a corps to Southwest Asia by 15 January 1991 ignited two weeks of intense force structure decision-making and logistical planning. The USAREUR commanders needed to make prompt decisions on which units to deploy. More extensively than he had in the division rotation planning, General Saint now applied, as much as he could, the Army's AirLand Battle and his own capable corps concepts to the force structure decisions. He also maintained the unit selection principles worked out in the previous two months. Thus he and his corps commanders modeled VII Corps' structure around the units previously proposed for deployment in both of the first two six-month rotations of the 1st and 3d Armored Divisions and accompanying corps support units. Many additional decisions were required, however, to build up the combat service support required for a heavy corps that would include at least one division from the United States.

USAREUR was well prepared for a time-sensitive requirement to deploy an enhanced, highly mobile, armored capable corps ready for combat to Southwest Asia. Over the previous two months, General Saint and his staff had established the basic principles they would use in whatever deployment was finally required. First, USAREUR would send primarily armor. Second, deployed units had to be modernized or capable of being modernized before departing Europe. Third, they had to have completed a recent training cycle. Fourth, deployed units would be brought to 100 percent or higher personnel strength through reassignments, cross-leveling, or whatever means necessary. Fifth, USAREUR would retain at least one battalion in each community. Meanwhile, General Saint would maintain a credible force in Europe as best he could, and he would carry out the 1991 and 1992 inactivation plans to the extent possible. In addition, the planners had already addressed such issues as painting of combat vehicles, transportation, and the maintenance of family support facilities.[34] They had also prepared a draft deployment order, which could quickly be revised, coordinated, and released to get the deployment rolling.[35]

Considering the international aspects of carrying out this massive deployment, General Saint reexamined briefly the need to get NATO approval to deploy a corps and its equipment that was dedicated to the defense of America's European allies. As before, he quickly decided this was not a problem for USAREUR: first, all NATO nations and indeed most nations worldwide supported a determined response to Iraqi aggression and, second, higher military echelons and the State Department would coordinate the deployment with the NATO allies.[36]

Basic Plan Adopted in First Planning Meeting

At 1400 on Sunday, 28 October, Generals Saint, Shalikashvili, and Burleson met with General Franks and a small group of staff officers from their two headquarters, plus a representative of Headquarters, V Corps, to begin planning the deployment of VII Corps.[37] In this first planning session, Generals Saint and Franks expressed some well-defined ideas about the force they wanted to deploy and the sequence and schedule of its deployment, both of which they had surely discussed earlier. They agreed that the 1st and 3d Armored Division headquarters and flags would each lead a composite of six armored and four mechanized infantry battalions.[38] Based on their perception of U.S. forces already deployed and USCENTCOM battle plans, Saint and Franks believed this was the best mix of these two combat arms.[39] Using staff reports on unit modernization, new equipment training, and recent rotations at USAREUR training areas, the two commanders discussed and decided, or in a few cases deferred decision on, which combat units to send, generally down to battalion level. General Franks declined an aviation brigade from the United States, preferring to deploy his own 11th Aviation Brigade.[40]

Generals Saint and Franks did not decide all unit deployment issues in this first planning session. They reserved decision on whether to take the 1st Brigade, 1st Armored Division, from Vilseck or the 3d Brigade, 3d Infantry Division, from Aschaffenburg with the 1st Armored Division. They were also undecided whether to deploy V Corps' 1st Brigade, 3d Armored Division, or its 1st Brigade, 8th Infantry Division, with the 3d Armored Division. While the ultimate composition of the 3d Armored Division remained to be determined, General Saint asserted that he wanted to deploy those 3d Armored Division units that were drawing down.[41] The armored cavalry regiment to be deployed was not named at this meeting. The 2d Armored Cavalry Regiment was clearly the choice, but its composition would remain undecided for several days. Plans for the corps support command, engineers, signal, military police, and military intelligence elements were also incomplete as this first session concluded.

AirLand Battle/Capable Corps Issues

General Saint raised numerous force structure issues with an eye to providing the deploying corps with maximum mobility in line with AirLand Battle doctrine, capable corps concepts, and his understanding of USCENTCOM campaign plans. Generals Saint and Franks implemented some of the ideas proposed to enhance corps mobility, but time did not allow them to act on others. For example, General Saint believed that the division cavalry should be reorganized to better support division mobility, but he reluctantly decided that it was not advisable to make such a reorganization while deploying. On the other hand, he insisted that each division artillery brigade be composed of two 155-mm. battalions and one multiple-launch rocket system battalion each but include no 8-inch artillery, which he thought could not keep up with the corps' anticipated fast-moving, long-distance attack. This configuration was lighter than some desired, and General Saint eventually agreed to deploy extra multiple-launch rocket system assets, sending eight of his twelve batteries armed with this system to Southwest Asia. He decided that only one air defense artillery battalion of Patriot and Hawk missiles would accompany the corps, although General Franks and Maj. Gen. Gerald H. Putman, commander of the 32d Army Air Defense Command (AADCOM), wanted to send an air defense artillery brigade. Other capable corps issues, including a restructured engineer force and a robust corps support command, were also raised. Although final decisions were not made on all of these issues at this time, the decisions made in October and November and the concepts and training that had been implemented in the previous year meant that the VII Corps that would deploy and fight in the desert basically met Saint's and Franks' standard of the AirLand Battle capable corps.

Through all his planning, General Saint's foremost concern was the ability of the deploying forces to move long distances quickly and to bring maximum possible firepower to bear promptly and unexpectedly. Therefore he stressed that, to the greatest extent possible, deploying units had to be fully modernized with the latest tanks and vehicles. He authorized deploying units to trade their commercial utility cargo vehicles for Army high-mobility multipurpose wheeled vehicles and their 5,000-gallon fuel trucks for heavy expanded-mobility tactical trucks and to make other equipment upgrades covered in the logistics section of the earlier draft deployment order. Also with an eye to mobility, he would basically limit the equipment units could take to that authorized by their tables of organization and equipment, fearing that extra equipment might burden them.

Early Corps Support Command Planning

While General Saint and his planners on 28 October lacked a complete assessment of what combat service support was available, they were almost certain that USAREUR units could not fully support the non-USAREUR units that would be attached to VII Corps. Although VII Corps' 2d Corps Support Command was short only three companies (one of fuel haulers and two of medium trucks, which would have to be supplied by V Corps) it would need to be supplemented substantially for Southwest Asia. CFE and VII Corps planners returned to their offices on Sunday afternoon to begin to identify units to bolster the 2d Corps Support Command. Using units identified earlier to support division rotations and recent USCENTCOM requests, the planners added some of the extra combat and combat service support elements needed to create the robust corps support command required to make the capable corps essentially self-contained. As then conceived, this unit would have had just 8,700 personnel. It was expanded substantially again before deployment to enable it to provide services not available in USCENTCOM and to try to cover, as much as possible, the attachment to VII Corps of non-USAREUR units. Additional elements would be added to the corps support command in Saudi Arabia to bring it to an operating level of over 25,000 soldiers.[42]

Impact on CFE/Drawdown

USAREUR planners immediately recognized that the deployment of VII Corps would make it impossible for USAREUR to meet its scheduled 1991 objective of inactivating units with 30,000 personnel. Its CFE planners conceded that they were unsure they could inactivate units with more than 7,000 personnel in 1991 and still deploy an enhanced capable corps. There appeared, however, to be a major consolation in giving up this goal. Although 1991 inactivation schedules would not be met, deployed units that would be inactivating could plan to leave their equipment in Saudi Arabia, since it was thought that the United States would build up POMCUS there. The personnel of these units could then return to Europe to stand the units down, pick up their families, and either return to the United States or join another USAREUR unit.[43] This would surely make drawdown cheaper. It would also probably be easier and quicker to withdraw a large number of units from USAREUR after conclusion of their involvement in the Persian Gulf.

Saint's Response to the Pentagon

General Saint returned the late night call he had received from the Pentagon, probably on 28 October, with the response that USAREUR soldiers were trained and ready to go. The VII Corps, the 1st and 3d Armored Divisions, the 2d Armored Cavalry Regiment, and a robust corps support command would deploy. To get them to the Persian Gulf in January, however, he would need ports, ships, money, international support, and an early November announcement.[44] He probably told General Vuono that he would need to use theater reserve and POMCUS stocks and that he would require help rebuilding adequate USAREUR personnel strength, particularly in specific functions, including medical specialists. USAREUR medical personnel strength was inadequate to support the deploying corps, as well as the personnel and families remaining in USAREUR and likely evacuees from Southwest Asia. Saint undoubtedly mentioned that the deployment would jeopardize plans to reduce personnel strength by 30,000 through unit inactivations in 1991. He may have mentioned some of the other noteworthy issues that planners and commanders had identified. For example, it was very unlikely that all vehicles could be painted before departure from Europe. His planners were concerned that part of the peak period for commercial movement to the ports might fall during the winter holiday period in Germany, when larger firms traditionally closed down for two weeks.[45]

USAREUR Planning Documents Sent to HQDA

After the planning sessions of 28 October and another held in General Saint's office the following morning, Mr. Pflaster faxed USAREUR force structure plans for VII Corps to General Heldstab, who had remained in Washington. Heldstab delivered these plans to General Reimer and Brig.

Gen. Robert B. Rosenkranz, Reimer's director of force programs integration. The 1st and 3d Armored Divisions as configured for the corps deployment at these meetings varied little from either the divisions that General Saint, his corps commanders and their staffs, and the CFE planners had worked out in the previous three weeks or from the divisions that would ultimately deploy to Southwest Asia, which are shown in Appendix B. Except for many combat service support units that were added to the corps either in Europe or Saudi Arabia, the corps that was described to HQDA in the 29 October package was essentially that which would deploy from USAREUR to Saudi Arabia.[46]

The planning documents transmitted to HQDA on 29 October also listed some of the problems USAREUR would face in deploying these units. USAREUR personnel strength would be 93 percent of its authorized level in December 1990, when VII Corps personnel began to deploy, and USAREUR clearly foresaw that it would need personnel fillers. Equipment shortages that could not be filled by cross-leveling would have to be filled from theater reserve and POMCUS. USAREUR would need to replace commercial utility vehicles with the high-mobility multipurpose vehicles. Residual missions would have to shift from VII Corps to V Corps. Training schedules might have to change. Some communities would not be served as well as desired, and there would be a medical shortfall throughout USAREUR.[47]

3d Armored Division Versus 3d Infantry Division

After reviewing USAREUR's plans, General Vuono apparently inquired why USAREUR was sending V Corps' 3d Armored Division rather than the 3d Infantry Division, which had been part of VII Corps. General Saint responded that he had decided to deploy USAREUR's two armored divisions because he perceived a fundamental need for armor-heavy divisions in the desert. In his view, the deployment of the 1st and 3d Armored Divisions gave a better tank-over-mechanized mix and maximized the corps' warfighting capability in Southwest Asia. In addition, Saint observed that 3d Armored Division was preferred over the 3d Infantry Division, because the former was farther along in modernization than the 3d Infantry Division, had more modernized tanks, and had converted to mobile subscriber communications equipment.

Although the 3d Infantry Division was not slated for inactivation, it was in the midst of upgrading its attack aviation, and its units would require more cross-leveling to deploy. The 3d Armored Division, on the other hand, ultimately had more elements slated to inactivate and could leave much of its equipment in Southwest Asia. HQ USAREUR/7A argued that sending a division from each corps would allow better residual support in USAREUR and keep both end-state division headquarters in Europe (although the 8th Infantry Division would eventually have to be reflagged as the 1st Armored Division). The converse was also true in that both division headquarters scheduled for inactivation would be deployed to Southwest Asia. Both corps commanders agreed on the switch, and General Saint apparently emphasized these facts to the General Vuono.[48] General Saint also may have argued, as he did on other occasions, that "you cannot be worried about division and corps cohesion when you have been mixing and matching brigades all over."[49]

HQDA Requests 2d Armored Division (Forward) and Other Units

On Tuesday, 30 October, the commanders of USAREUR's major commands—V and VII Corps, 21st TAACOM, United States Army, Berlin, and the Army's Southern European Task Force—were in Heidelberg for the October Commander in Chief's Commanders' Forum, and General Saint worked with them throughout the day. Late in the afternoon, General Saint met separately with General Franks, General Joulwan, and his USAREUR planners. Relying upon a conversation with General Heldstab, who was still at the Pentagon, General Saint told his commanders that General Reimer believed USAREUR deployment of a corps could be a "done deal today." Reimer also made other requests on which Saint and his commanders and staff were apparently already working. Reimer had asked that a separate brigade, the 2d Armored Division (Forward), containing approximately 4,000 additional personnel, be deployed to round out the 1st Infantry Division, which would send its elements stationed in the United States to Southwest Asia to join VII Corps.[50]

USAREUR had already considered the possibility of deploying one of its two detached infantry brigades—the 2d Armored Division (Forward) or the 1st Infantry Division (Forward). It now quickly agreed to the 2d Armored Division (Forward), which would deploy to join the Fort Riley elements of the 1st Infantry Division in Saudi Arabia. The 1st Infantry Division already had a long association with USAREUR and VII Corps through the assignment of its forward brigade to VII Corps and through the division's participation in REFORGER exercises. However, the 1st Infantry Division (Forward) was not in shape to deploy, because its artillery, armor, and infantry battalions had already learned that they

General Franks

would inactivate by May 1991 and had begun standing down.[51] This meant that the M1A1 tanks previously held in POMCUS stocks for use by the 1st Infantry Division in reinforcing European defense could instead be shipped to Saudi Arabia by the January deadline. The soldiers of the 1st Infantry Division (Forward), meanwhile, were able to play a significant role in the deployment as they were called upon to serve as stevedores unloading ships in Saudi Arabia.

General Reimer had evidently also continued to press for release to USCENTCOM of VII Corps' 11th Aviation Brigade. General Saint repeated that he would let General Franks decide whether he would take his own aviation brigade or the aviation brigade from the United States that had been offered earlier. He did not mention the fact that deployment of the 11th would leave USAREUR virtually without attack helicopters. General Saint did tell his commanders on 30 October, however, that he wanted to protect his war reserve stocks in Italy for possible use by a USAREUR contingency force in southern Europe or elsewhere. Saint and the attendees at his Commanders' Forum seem also to have decided that Maj. Gen. Roger K. Bean, commander of the 56th Field Artillery (FA) Command in Schwaebisch Hall, would be responsible for VII Corps communities in southern Germany during General Franks' absence.[52]

Additional Force Structure Decisions

In addition to their intense work on selecting units for deployment, General Saint and his commanders and planners in the last days of October and early November continued to struggle with the question of whether to modify further their deploying units' internal composition in an effort to build the most effective force structure possible. The force alignment proposals under consideration would have matched the corps

*Campbell Barracks, Heidelberg, Germany, home of Headquarters,
United States Army, Europe*

almost completely with Saint's capable corps concepts, as applied to the desert, except for a second armored cavalry regiment, which had been abandoned early in drawdown and capable corps planning for budgetary reasons. These issues presented difficult decisions, because General Saint did not want to reorganize unnecessarily on the move, and there simply was no time for some otherwise desirable adjustments and reorganizations.[53] They also posed difficult choices between greater mobility and better support. In addition, the severe drain on specialists to which some reorganization plans would subject the forces Saint would retain in USAREUR presented him with a choice between sending the best possible force to fight in the desert and maintaining a modicum of readiness and community support in Europe.

The Engineer Restructure Initiative

As USAREUR had begun to draw down and restructure its force as a capable corps in early 1990, General Saint planned to reorganize combat engineers into the E-Force envisioned in the engineer restructure initiative that Maj. Gen. Richard S. Kem had developed earlier at the U.S. Army Engineer School. The engineer restructure initiative provided an engineer brigade for each division and a small, mobile engineer battalion for each maneuver brigade. In order to increase VII Corps' mobility in the desert, General Saint; General Franks; Brig. Gen. Robert C. Lee, USAREUR deputy chief of staff, engineer; and Maj. Gen. Daniel R. Schroeder, who was the current commandant of the Engineer School, agreed that the deploying corps and division engineers would be restructured to establish this reorganization of division engineers as much as possible. While planning and preparing for the deployment, division engineer battalions were restructured according to these concepts and attached to the maneuver brigades. This created smaller, more mobile combat engineer battalions that could assist the brigade commanders better than could the engineer companies attached to the brigades under the old assistant division engineer force structure. Division engineer brigades were not activated, but new colonels were assigned as division engineers and advisers to the division commander.[54]

Air Defense

The issue of how much air defense artillery force structure and weaponry the deploying corps should take erupted repeatedly in these critical planning days and later. On 30 October, the commander of the 32d Army Air Defense Command, General Putman, presented six deployment options that ranged from deploying three Patriot units and two Hawk units, plus support, with 956 personnel, to eight Patriot and eight Hawk firing units plus supporting units with 2,706 personnel.[55] General Shalikashvili met with General Putman on 2 November to discuss these options. While no final decision was apparently made at this meeting, all plans and the final deployment orders would conform to General Saint's consistent advice to send one air defense artillery battalion. The number of Patriots was increased, however, to four firing units, while the battalion retained two Hawk firing units. Saint and Shalikashvili apparently based their decision to limit the corps' air defenses on the need to maintain the mobility of the corps, the availability of the U.S. Air Force in Southwest Asia, and the clear inferiority of the Iraqi Air Force.[56] They may also have anticipated the later critical need for Patriots throughout Southwest Asia, as well as a need to maintain some air defense capability in Europe.

2d Armored Division (Forward)

General Shalikashvili also met on 2 November with Brig. Gen. Jerry R. Rutherford, the commander of the 2d Armored Division (Forward), to discuss some missions that might be given to his brigade and how its deployment would be handled. At General Reimer's request, the 2d Armored Division (Forward) would round out the 1st Infantry Division. While supporting port operations at Bremerhaven with a battalion-size unit, the rest of the brigade could serve as an advance party and the third brigade for the 1st Infantry Division in Saudi Arabia. The limited air defense artillery assets of the 2d Armored Division (Forward) would have to be made up by deploying elements of the 1st Infantry Division. The deputy commander in chief recommended that the brigade get an early start in preparing personnel and equipment for overseas movement.[57]

Supplemental Communications Structure

General Saint ensured that the deploying force was supplemented to provide the command and control capabilities that would enable VII Corps' headquarters to communicate effectively both with the units deploying with it from Europe and with the reinforcing units coming from the United States. He and General White, who was Saint's information systems manager and also the commander of the Army Information Systems Command's 5th Signal Command in Europe, worked together on many signal and information management issues to strengthen the deploying force. General Saint approved the attachment of the 5th Signal Command's 1st Signal Battalion to VII Corps' 93d Signal Brigade to give it the enhanced strength and information management capabilities it would need to communicate effectively with the five divisions and myriad supporting units that would be attached to VII Corps in Southwest Asia. In the end, the 5th Signal Command would dispatch, with General Saint's approval, about three-fourths of its echelon-above-corps capability, including about 2,000 soldiers, to augment the 6th Signal Command in Southwest Asia.[58]

Medical Support Structure

The provision of medical units and related logistical support for the deploying corps highlights the complex challenges USAREUR confronted in supporting USCENTCOM. USAREUR's peacetime medical force structure was simply inadequate to carry out the three medical missions that were assigned it by November 1990. USAREUR and its 7th Medical Command were expected to provide the wartime medical force structure for the deploying corps; to serve as the rear medical evacuation, treatment, and logistical base for USCENTCOM; and to maintain adequate medical services for some two hundred thousand USAREUR personnel and family members who remained in Europe. (Chapter 6 describes subsequent deployments and sustainment support including medical support.) USAREUR had to determine how to apportion its efforts to meet each of these critical missions prior to putting together the medical force structure for the deploying VII Corps.

On 11 November 1990, ARCENT and Forces Command requested the repacking and shipment of twenty-four massive deployable medical systems (DEPMEDS), as the Army termed its mobile hospitals. This request alone illustrates the expectation that USAREUR could perform extraordinarily vast logistical and medical work while deploying VII Corps. USAREUR eventually sent twenty DEPMEDS, containing 7,400 beds, and with them it deployed two specialized teams to give new equipment training.[59]

Medical elements and personnel from the 7th Medical Command, from V Corps units, and from VII Corps units remaining in Europe, such as the 3d Infantry Division, were attached to the deploying VII Corps to make up part of the difference between VII Corps' peacetime medical structure and its wartime medical requirements in Southwest Asia. The 7th Medical Command sent eleven units with VII Corps. These were mainly medical and dental detachments, but they also included a medical supply unit and an air ambulance company. The V Corps sent the 12th Evacuation Hospital. The 7th Medical Command provided 112, V Corps provided 27, and nondeploying VII Corps units provided an additional 22 physicians and physician assistants to deploying VII Corps hospitals and divisional units. Overall, more than 1,200 of the 7th Medical Command's medical personnel deployed to Southwest Asia. USAREUR expected that two of the DEPMEDS hospitals approved for shipment would support VII Corps, and Forces Command apparently planned to supplement VII Corps medical units with six reserve component mobile Army surgical hospitals (MASH) and six evacuation hospitals. As it prepared to deploy a large part of its medical assets, USAREUR requested Department of the Army and Forces Command help in reconstituting its medical structure to enable it to meet its missions as a logistical base for USCENTCOM.[60]

Factors in Unit Deployment Decisions

USAREUR decision makers largely resolved last-minute questions regarding which units to deploy in line with the procedures and criteria General Saint had identified and established in September and early October. A review of the October and November 1990 decisions will show clearly that a unit's level of training and modernization were the two most critical factors in determining whether it would be sent to Southwest Asia. Secondary considerations included preferring to send units scheduled for drawdown, to leave at least one unit in each community, and to maintain as much unit cohesion as possible.

Modernization and Training Versus Unit Purity

The complexity of USAREUR's deployment decisions was evident in one of the larger unit decisions that Generals Saint and Franks discussed and decided in these last days of October—whether or not to send the Vilseck-based 1st Brigade, 1st Armored Division, or the 3d Brigade, 3d Infantry Division, based in Aschaffenburg, with the 1st Armored Division. The CFE planners had earlier, during divisional rotation planning, recommended sending the latter brigade in place of the former.

As was true with most decisions to send one unit over another, the commanders based their decision to send the 3d Brigade, 3d Infantry Division, largely on superior modernization, recent training, and inactivation plans. The 3d Infantry Division brigade was totally modernized, had more recently returned from Grafenwoehr and Hohenfels, and would stand down in 1991 and 1992. Its military community, Aschaffenburg, moreover, could be covered by the nearby Frankfurt community. It could leave its equipment in Saudi Arabia, and its facilities were going to be closed on its return. Although the 1st Brigade, 1st Armored Division, had habitually high readiness ratings and was already part of the 1st Armored Division, it was still accessioning Bradley fighting vehicles, and while its community was also covered, none of its battalions were slated for inactivation and its equipment would have to be returned to Europe.[61]

Modernization and Training Versus Drawdown

Modernization and training status generally took precedence over drawdown status and schedules in determining which units to deploy. Despite the fact that it was not slated to inactivate, the modernized 1st Battalion, 37th Armor, which had been a part of 1st Armored Division's nondeploying 1st Brigade, was transferred to and deployed with the division's 3d Brigade from Bamberg, Germany, to obtain the desired mix of six armor and four infantry battalions in each division. Modernized units with pending inactivation dates were even more favored for inclusion in the deploying force. USAREUR leaders selected the modernized 4th Battalion, 34th Armor, of the 1st Brigade, 8th Infantry Division, a battalion scheduled for inactivation on 1 May 1991, to replace the 2d Battalion, 32d Armor, in the 1st Brigade, 3d Armored Division, a division that they had now tentatively decided to deploy. Similarly, the modernized 6th Battalion, 6th Infantry, which was also scheduled for inactivation on 1 May 1991, although displaced from the 3d Brigade, 1st

Armored Division, by the 1st Battalion, 37th Armor, nevertheless deployed as part of 2d Brigade, 1st Armored Division, instead of that brigade's 2d Battalion, 6th Infantry, which was undergoing transition to Bradleys and had not completed new equipment training. Other units deploying from Europe that had already been announced for 1 March or 1 May 1991 inactivation included the 3d Armored Division's 3d Battalion, 8th Cavalry, and its Company E, 122d Maintenance Battalion, and a detachment of the 1st Infantry Division's 101st Military Intelligence Battalion.[62]

Unit Purity Versus Residual Community Support Issues

The need for units to remain in USAREUR to provide community services was a significant consideration complicating the selection of the armored cavalry regiment and its squadrons. General Saint and his commanders and planners were all intensely conscious that they confronted an unusual situation with this deployment. They were deploying an already forward-deployed force and leaving soldiers' families to face, in a foreign and possibly even threatening environment, the difficulties and uncertainties of having one or even two parents in combat. Through the changing deployment plans of October, personnel in the HQ USAREUR/7A Office of the Deputy Chief of Staff for Personnel and CFE Division calculated the numbers of units and personnel left to cover each community under the various deployment options.[63]

Because sending the entire 2d Armored Cavalry Regiment or the entire 11th Armored Cavalry Regiment would leave certain subcommunities with little or no military support structure, CFE planners considered deploying virtually every possible combination of the squadrons of USAREUR's two armored cavalry regiments. Deploying the entire 11th Armored Cavalry Regiment would leave the Bad Kissingen and Bad Hersfeld subcommunities uncovered, while deploying the entire 2d Armored Cavalry Regiment would leave Bindlach and Amberg without coverage. At the end of October, however, Saint, Franks, and Holder decided to send the entire 2d Armored Cavalry Regiment and make other arrangements for community coverage at Bindlach and Amberg.[64]

Progress by 31 October

By the end of October USAREUR planning for the deployment of VII Corps to Saudi Arabia had worked up a full head of steam among commanders and USAREUR staff offices. Though deployment planning was still close-hold, the circle of personnel and organizations intensely scrutinizing deployment issues had widened substantially. Force structure and other general plans had developed sufficiently for Colonel Graham of CFE Division to expand the scope of his draft division deployment order to a corps and send it to selected staff agencies for review and comment.[65] On 31 October, these staff agencies were seeking to perfect Graham's draft corps deployment order as it related to their specific functional responsibilities. Brig. Gen. Walter J. Bryde, the deputy chief of staff, personnel, USAREUR, and Brig. Gen. Mary C. Willis, the commander of the 1st Personnel Command, meanwhile, were laying the foundations for cross-leveling personnel to fill shortages prior to overseas movement. General Laposata and a few members of his staff and those of the 1st Transportation Movement Control Agency and Military Traffic Management Command, Europe, were refining deployment and transportation plans. Generals Pfister, Lee, and White and other key staff officers worked on the deployment in their functional areas. Maj. Gen. Richard T. Travis, USAREUR's chief surgeon, who was also the commander of the 7th Medical Command, was assessing his medical resources and needs, estimating potential shortfalls, and establishing plans. The deputy chief of staff, host nation activities, was identifying likely concerns of USAREUR's host nations and areas in which they might provide support. Subordinate commands, including the headquarters of both corps and their deploying units, as well as the 21st TAACOM, 32d AADCOM, and other commands, had begun planning. USAREUR seemed to be off to a quick start.

Deployment Planning Stopped, 1 November

Then suddenly on Thursday, 1 November, USAREUR was told to stop planning to send a corps to Saudi Arabia. General Saint was given that instruction rather informally by General Vuono. General Heldstab also was called by the vice chief of staff's office late Thursday afternoon, after which he directed his planners to "cease and desist" all planning.[66] It soon became clear that this halt in planning had been called to ensure that the decision to deploy a USAREUR corps with a powerful offensive capability would not become a last-minute factor in the U.S. congressional elections to be held the following Tuesday, 6 November. General Saint understood simply that the Department of Defense and the White House were not quite ready to announce the decision. In any event, the planning that was already under way continued very quietly both at HQ USAREUR/7A and its corps. Secretary of the Army Stone surely discussed the deployment with his host, when he stopped overnight, 2–3 November, in Heidelberg on his way to Saudi Arabia and had dinner at General Saint's quarters. Stone also met with General Franks during his stopover in Germany.[67]

ARCENT Combat Support/Combat Service Support Add-On

On the day after the election, 7 November, Forces Command faxed USAREUR a 31 October request from ARCENT Rear for an additional combat support and combat service support package. This new "wish list" included several supply and service battalions and various transportation, maintenance, petroleum, and water supply units. Forces Command noted that this package might be modified based on additional USAREUR input.[68] The request list was updated and substantially expanded over the following weeks, presenting USAREUR many decisions on further USCENTCOM support. While USAREUR leaders and planners waited anxiously for word that VII Corps would deploy, they were bound to react to these ARCENT wish lists with less enthusiasm than they had in the past.

Announcement of Corps Deployment

Late on 7 November General Galvin had called General Saint to give him a "heads up" that the deployment would be announced soon.[69] On 8 November General Saint called a meeting of his corps commanders, Generals Franks and Joulwan, and the commanders of the 21st TAA-COM, 32d AADCOM, 2d Armored Division (Forward), and 56th Field Artillery Command, as well as all HQ USAREUR/7A staff principals, to prepare for the announcement and discuss unresolved deployment issues. While most force structure issues had been resolved in the previous two weeks of planning, General Saint, his commanders, and staff confirmed those decisions shortly before the official announcement of the deployment. Up to this point, after all, the work and discussion had involved only contingency plans. Now it was an actual deployment with which the United States, USAREUR, and VII Corps would have to live or die. The group reaffirmed that the 2d Armored Cavalry Regiment would deploy complete with all its squadrons. Although General Franks again requested two battalions of air defense artillery, he agreed to wait until he knew more precisely how his USCENTCOM mission would be defined. It was decided that all deploying V Corps, 21st TAACOM, 7th Medical Command, and other non–VII Corps units would be attached to VII Corps on arrival in Saudi Arabia. While some other force structure decisions also remained tentative, General Saint directed General Franks to proceed as best he could to develop his corps' final task organization.[70]

In the evening hours of 8 November, HQ USAREUR/7A received a top secret execution order. Well into the evening European time, President Bush announced on American television networks that the United States would deploy reinforcing forces to Saudi Arabia, including units currently stationed in Europe. Following the presidential broadcast, Secretary of Defense Cheney and General Powell held a televised news conference in which they announced that units deploying from Europe would include VII Corps with the 1st and 3d Armored Divisions, the 2d

The Stars and Stripes *announces the deployment of VII Corps, 9 November 1990.*

Armored Division (Forward), and the 2d Armored Cavalry Regiment. The announcement and news conference were carried live on American Forces Network in Europe.[71] Many soldiers and even commanders of units deploying with the VII Corps first learned that they would deploy through the presidential broadcast and subsequent news conference.[72]

Response to the Army Staff

On 9 November General Heldstab sent an organization chart to General Reimer and Forces Command showing the VII Corps force that would deploy and a memorandum explaining the rationale for interchanging the elements of existing organizations. Heldstab explained that most changes were made in an effort to put together and deploy the most modern and capable force possible. In this context, he observed for the first time that the 5th Battalion, 3d Air Defense Artillery, an 8th Infantry Division unit, would accompany the 3d Armored Division in lieu of that division's 3d Battalion, 5th Air Defense Artillery, which had already turned in its equipment in preparation for inactivation.

General Heldstab also explained in this memorandum some other extraordinary features of VII Corps' organization. The VII Corps' aviation was short one attack helicopter battalion because the 3d Armored Division's 3d Battalion, 227th Aviation, had already deployed to Saudi Arabia with the 12th Aviation Brigade and had then been attached to XVIII Airborne Corps. It would rejoin the 3d Armored Division in the desert. Generals Saint and Franks had added additional military police units beyond VII Corps' peacetime complement. At the request of the 1st Infantry Division's combat electronic warfare intelligence battalion, they had decided to deploy with VII Corps the detachment of that battalion that was stationed in Germany. General Heldstab explained that General Saint would not send VII Corps' 8-inch artillery, which, beyond creating additional support requirements, simply could not keep up with an extremely mobile, armored attack. In its place, he would send a mix of multiple-launch rocket systems and 155-mm. artillery. Because V Corps Artillery's 155-mm. units were already standing down, he would use some divisional 155-mm. battalions to replace the 8-inch artillery. Relative to the deploying air defense artillery units, General Heldstab stated that they were a "good mix to fight and move simultaneously."

Heldstab stated that the engineers selected for deployment, including the topographic unit, represented USAREUR's best judgment of what would be needed. He explained that petroleum, oils, and lubricants companies and transportation companies had been added to the 2d Corps Support Command because of the shortage of these types of units in USCENTCOM and USAREUR's concern that VII Corps be capable of fulfilling its transportation requirements. On the other hand, he admitted that the support command remained short one evacuation hospital because USAREUR could not spare any more medical units of that type. Finally, General Heldstab noted that the robust 2d Armored Division (Forward) would be sent as it was currently constituted to provide a solid roundout for the 1st Infantry Division. He attached a list of all the units USAREUR proposed to deploy, with the exception of corps support command units. However, this list was subsequently expanded to include information about the units' personnel strength and status of equipment modernization.[73]

A Last-Minute Major Force Structure Decision

By the afternoon of 9 November, except for the reinforcement of the 2d Corps Support Command, the composition of VII Corps had been resolved except for one brigade. The failure to reach a final decision on whether to deploy the 1st Brigade, 8th Infantry Division, or the 1st Brigade, 3d Armored Division, may have been a misunderstanding or oversight among General Saint, his corps commanders, and his planners, or it may have reflected the USAREUR commander's desire to involve General Maddox, the incoming commander of V Corps, in the decision. In any event, late on 9 November, the day which saw the change of command at V Corps, General Saint called General Maddox and told him that his first job as corps commander was to decide, in ten minutes, which brigade to deploy. General Maddox quickly called back to say that the 1st Brigade, 3d Armored Division, would deploy. This deployment was already shown in the force structure planning documents that had been sent to HQDA and Forces Command. The basic combat forces of the deploying VII Corps were now set, although some further modifications would still be made to the support structure.[74] That evening USAREUR sent a message to the commanders of major deploying units together with CINCUSAREUR Deployment Order 21, Deployment of VII Corps to Southwest Asia, to get deployment moving.

CINCUSAREUR Deployment Order 22

The next day, 10 November, HQ USAREUR/7A published CINCUSAREUR Deployment Order 22, which dealt with the same subject in more detail. (See Appendix C.) Both CINCUSAREUR Deployment Orders 21 and 22 derived from the draft deployment order that Colonel Graham had initially written to deploy the rotating divisions. The second order prescribed policy, procedures, and responsibilities for deployment and listed the task organization developed over the previous two weeks. It also implemented logistics decisions that had evolved over the previous two months.

For example, Deployment Order 22 directed that trains and barges would be the primary means of transportation to ports. Road convoys would be held to a minimum. It basically limited deploying units to taking along their unit basic load. In the personnel arena, it immediately put stop-loss into effect for all USAREUR soldiers. The commander in chief, USAREUR, would retain command of all deploying units until they entered the USCENTCOM area of responsibility, when they would be attached to ARCENT. The order designated the commander, 56th Field Artillery Command, as the deputy commanding general, VII Corps, Rear, for community operations in the VII Corps area of USAREUR.[75]

General Burleson pointed out later that the quick publication of the deployment order allowed deploying units to get started preparing their personnel and equipment for overseas movement, while HQ USAREUR/7A and HQ VII Corps struggled to complete the deployment plan. The brief order reflected General Saint's conviction that the way to get something done was simply to issue mission orders giving very specific instructions describing what needed to be done, not how to do it, and to make sure adequate resources were available.[76]

The few force structure modifications made to the deployment order over the next couple of days continued to beef up the corps support command and add other support personnel. These changes were primarily designed to fill out the VII Corps personnel and finance groups. By mid-November VII Corps had grown to 71,500 personnel. With force structure largely decided, the USAREUR deployment story for the next two months would shift to decisions and actions relating to logistics, personnel, and home front planning.

Force Structure Results

The most significant lesson illustrated by this detailed account of USAREUR planning in September and October is that the ambitious effort that General Saint undertook in these months, going well beyond the planning required simply for the piecemeal reinforcements and the divisional rotation initially anticipated by the Pentagon, prepared the way for USAREUR's eventual quick and successful deployment of an enlarged, "capable" corps to Southwest Asia. Saint's offer to General Vuono of USAREUR providing the main heavy offensive force against Iraq may have appeared facile to those unaware of Saint's vision of a capable corps or his broadly conceived planning. In fact, it was based on two years of commitment to restructuring efforts and training initiatives aimed at enhancing unit mobility amid force and budget reductions, two months of planning and providing support to Southwest Asia, and one month of planning for the rotation of USAREUR divisions (and contemplating the deployment of a corps), all overlaid on the rich USAREUR REFORGER experience.

In shaping VII Corps' force structure, General Saint had applied complex planning considerations to achieve, as much as possible, apparently contradictory objectives. His primary objective was to send the most capable, mobile, modernized and well-trained, armor-heavy corps he could to the desert, while not losing sight of his responsibility to defend the NATO nations of Europe and to reduce his forces and budget. Through all his planning, it was clear that a major concern was the ability of the deploying units to penetrate enemy forces deeply and decisively, bringing maximum possible firepower to bear quickly and unexpectedly. His desire to send the most capable units, based on his vision of the modern army and the specific needs of ground warfare in Iraq, underlay the specific decisions he made in building the deploying force. As General Saint later admitted, the development of the force structure proved both difficult and controversial.[77]

General Saint's ability to meet his other objectives also shaped and were shaped by the corps' deployment. USAREUR continued to provide massive logistical support and crew replacements to USCENTCOM. General Saint was able to maintain or quickly restore sufficient basic readiness in the two divisions and other units that remained in Europe to meet, if necessary, another contingency there or elsewhere. He was able to provide a support structure for USAREUR families and military communities in which the families proved very successful in caring for themselves and their neighbors.

General Saint was also able to modify his CFE/drawdown plans to meet treaty, budget, and Army restructuring requirements. He continued to draw down many units already announced for inactivation. Although it was impossible to meet the 1991 objective of inactivating units with 30,000 personnel, it would be possible to increase substantially the pace of inactivations after USAREUR units returned from the Gulf. The VII Corps force of 71,500 selected for deployment included over 30,200 personnel in units scheduled for inactivation. Most deployed units that were scheduled to inactivate in 1991 and 1992 would move their equipment out of the European theater, use it in Southwest Asia, and leave it there or send it back to the United States.[78]

Above all, the planned deployment of over half of USAREUR's combat units would show that USAREUR had successfully transitioned from the Cold War anchor in the allied defense of Central Europe against the Soviet Bloc threat to a flexible force capable of defending a more secure Europe and simultaneously deploying to another continent perhaps the most capable warfighting corps in military history.

Chapter 5

Deployment of VII Corps

First Logistics Considerations

When General Saint was asked in the early morning hours of 27 October whether or not he could get a corps to Saudi Arabia by 15 January, no one in Europe or Washington really knew the answer, including General Saint. He and his commanders and staff officers had confidence in themselves and, above all, in the officers, noncommissioned officers, and soldiers in their units. They and their troops had considerable experience with deployment issues. Virtually all USAREUR generals had REFORGER experience, as did most other USAREUR officers and noncommissioned officers and many USAREUR soldiers; they were also accustomed to loading their units and debarking for training at Hohenfels, Grafenwoehr, or local training areas. Such exercises were at the heart of the modern professional Army.

But the upcoming deployment was unprecedented in many ways. Not since World War II had there been a deployment by U.S. forces in Europe of this size and speed, nor had so many forward-deployed U.S. soldiers been taken directly from one theater to another in that period. Moreover, the deploying units were expected to be ready to go into action shortly after arrival in Saudi Arabia. The deployment was dependent on host nation commercial transportation, on which USAREUR had, to be sure, relied for many years, and on shipping and air transport over which USAREUR had little ultimate influence.

It was impossible to weigh the logistical pros and cons precisely or persuasively. General Saint and General Franks concluded it would be possible to send a heavy corps plus more from Germany to Saudi Arabia by 15 January based mainly on their confidence in themselves and their soldiers and on their unwillingness, under the circumstances, to answer the question in any other way. In the intense, late October planning meetings, General Saint asked not whether timely deployment was possible, but rather what support was needed to make it a reality. Again and again he asked General Laposata how many ships were necessary and how many railroad cars were required, sensing surely the improbability of a precise answer and the likelihood of problems with ships. The planning done in this period by General Heldstab and his Operations, Plans, and CFE Divisions and by General Laposata and his deployment team could not fully assure General Saint that the deployment could be carried off within the time allotted, but it did convince him that at least there were no insoluble problems.

General Laposata set several planners to work calculating the volume of cargo space and the number of ships required, as well as the number of trains and barges. He quickly put together a five-man corps deployment planning team, composed of Colonel Phillips, his Plans, Operations, and Systems Division chief, and two other members of the HQ USAREUR/7A logistics staff; Col. Carl Salyer, Commander, 1st Transportation Movement Control Agency; and Col. Rick Barnaby, Commander, Military Traffic Management Command, Europe. This group identified problems, answered General Saint's early concerns about deployment as best they could, and came up with a general corps movement plan.[1]

General Saint's Answer to HQDA

At the end of October, General Saint told HQDA what support the CIN-CUSAREUR required in order to deploy a corps to Southwest Asia by 15 January. He needed at least three ports, Bremerhaven, Antwerp, and Rotterdam; sufficient ships, probably five at a time, to be available when needed for continuous loading; the notification of NATO and host and allied nations by the Department of Defense and the State Department and the securing of those nations' concurrence and support; and a timely announcement that a USAREUR corps would deploy, so that he could openly begin to follow a timeline that would get the corps to Southwest Asia by 15 January 1991. At this point, in late October, he said he needed an announcement by 2 November. Money should be no object.[2]

At the same time, General Saint sent HQDA a projected timetable that his staff had worked out backwards from the required arrival date in Saudi Arabia. The first proposed deployment timeline envisioned a decision and announcement from Washington by 2 November, the departure of the first trains by 12 November, and the loading of the first ships by 15 November. Under this schedule, the corps would be ready to fight by

15 February 1991. General Laposata's planners also proposed a deployment sequence, starting with the armored cavalry regiment and followed in order by the 1st Armored Division, corps headquarters and corps support units, and the 3d Armored Division.[3] Subsequently the 2d Armored Division (Forward) was added, and on 8 November the deployment was announced. The date for the completion of the deployment to Saudi Arabia remained 15 January 1991.

Deployment Planning

The key decisions involved in the actual deployment were grounded to a large extent on the advice and planning of General Joseph Laposata, USAREUR's Deputy Chief of Staff, Logistics. Laposata had acquired a good idea how to deploy a corps from his study of relevant Army doctrine, his previous exercise experience, the early USAREUR deployments to Southwest Asia, and the close-hold planning for deploying a division or corps that had begun in early October. He had deployment experience at the Pentagon and in three REFORGER exercises, including service a dozen years earlier as chief of logistics of the 5th Infantry Division when elements of the division deployed to Europe during REFORGER 78. In 1989 and 1990 General Laposata had also gained experience moving excess military equipment, including 2,223 vehicles, out of Germany to meet anticipated CFE treaty limitations. To do this, he had used barges on the Rhine River as the preferred mode of transportation because of their lower cost. He found this not only cheaper but also efficient, if he had three to five days to get the equipment rolling. As General Laposata saw the VII Corps deployment, he did not need to find new ideas or procedures, but simply "went by the book" and used time-tested methods. To him, it was just a matter of identifying what needed to be done and doing it.[4]

General Laposata drew heavily on the experience gained in the deployment of the 12th Aviation Brigade and other early unit deployments and through the provision of early sustainment support to USCENTCOM. The 12th Aviation deployment convinced Laposata that a corps could not move itself. Indeed, V Corps had a hard time even identifying what the aviation brigade would take along. This the corps eventually did, but it could not handle the movement. Personnel from the 1st Transportation Movement Control Agency had to be collocated with the corps headquarters to help run the movement operation. This experience reaffirmed Laposata's conviction that a corps could not effectively do movement planning and that deployment would be successful only through strong leadership, strict centralization and control, and disciplined adherence to the established rules.[5] Deployment of the 12th Aviation Brigade also warned him that USAREUR might encounter trouble obtaining usable ships from the Military Sealift Command and that it was not a good idea to rely on the port of Livorno.[6]

General Laposata was one of the very small group of USAREUR leaders who on 6 October had begun planning the rotation of a USAREUR division to Southwest Asia and who were also told to think about deploying a corps. In early October, he had his logistics planners begin to look at deploying a rotating force of about 45,000 personnel. By including Colonel Barnaby of Military Traffic Management Command, Europe, in this small, close-hold logistics group, they accomplished the first coordinated interheadquarters planning in Europe for deployment to Southwest Asia. This group also contributed, of course, to the late October discussions, decisions, and preparations to deploy VII Corps.

On the first weekend in November, General Heldstab's Plans Division decided to test the Joint Operations Planning Execution System (JOPES) in an exercise that would try the planners' patience and find the system wanting. JOPES was the worldwide computer-driven processing system that was supposed to generate the data base and distribute the paperwork necessary to alert and move deploying units. JOPES had been tested repeatedly with units reinforcing USAREUR in annual REFORGER exercises. Now, according to General Burleson, to try to get a head start on implementing the deployment of USAREUR units, Plans Division put the VII Corps structure developed in the last week of October into JOPES as a possible deploying, or "notional," force.[7] The division desperately needed a head start, because USAREUR was substantially changing the corps' force structure and its assigned units. At first, this effort seemed to be paying off. When Forces Command on Wednesday, 7 November, sent the Plans Division a tape of its reinforcing unit Time-Phased Force Deployment Data, the division found that it took account not only of ARCENT guidance but also, apparently, of the "notional" force that USAREUR had fed into JOPES the previous weekend. Before long, however, JOPES failed to keep up with the demands of the deployment. Due both to the changes in the corps force structure and to computer breakdowns and other technical problems, JOPES worked so slowly that it most often produced deployment schedules, orders, and other paperwork after the units had actually deployed.[8] People—USAREUR's leaders, soldiers, and staff—would have to drive, manage, and carry out the deployment.

General Laposata and his planners came up with several estimates of the time it would take to get the corps to Saudi Arabia, a task they initially estimated would take eighty to ninety days. They had, therefore, originally sought a 2 November announcement date, and even then they predicted the deployment might not be completed before 30 January 1991. In a deployment support planning meeting on 30 October, however, General Laposata was much more optimistic, estimating that they could move VII Corps to Saudi Arabia with "56 ships in 56 days," between 15 November and 9 January. Even at that early meeting, Laposata admitted that modifications to USAREUR's early planning would be necessary and expressed concern about potential problems, including what to use as blocking and bracing material, where to get containers, and what ports to use. As the early days of November passed and the deployment was not announced, General Laposata's estimates became less optimistic than they had been at the end of October, predicting that the corps would close in Southwest Asia on 1 February 1991 given "a perfect world and no lost days to holidays."[9] Laposata and his planners then concluded that moving VII Corps' equipment to Saudi Arabia before the end of January would require 62 ships, and they later revised this figure first to 75 and then 90 as they struggled to find a way to get the corps to the desert by 15 January.

At first USAREUR's logisticians preferred to use only trains to move the VII Corps' 4,500 tracked vehicles; 20,000 wheeled vehicles; and 1,000 containers, but they found that the German railway, *Deutsche Bundesbahn*, could not support this requirement within the desired timeframe. They decided, therefore, to move the containers and tracked vehicles by train but to transport at least 60 percent of the wheeled vehicles by barge. Convoys would be used to move these vehicles to barge ports in Mannheim and Mainz on the Rhine River and to carry the 2d Armored Division (Forward) to the North Sea port of Bremerhaven, near where it was stationed in northern Germany.

General Laposata and his planners also worked out the division of deployment responsibilities. Under this scheme, General Franks and his senior staff would, in conjunction with USCENTCOM, determine priorities for his units' movement to ports and their arrival in Saudi Arabia, and VII Corps' operations staff would oversee implementation. Parent units would be responsible for preparing their elements for movement to ports in accordance with VII Corps' priorities. The 1st Transportation Movement Control Agency would determine mode of transportation and arrange transport. The 21st TAACOM would operate rest stops and provide other support. The V Corps would run Departure Airfield Control Groups at designated aerial ports of embarkation. Military Traffic Management Command, Europe, would make port selections, arrange shipping, and manage ship loading.[10]

A Saudi-bound truck hovers in the air as it is loaded on a barge at the Rheinau barge terminal near Mannheim, 13 December 1990.

Supervising all these efforts, Generals Laposata and Heldstab would be jointly responsible for coordinating and tracking the flow of units to ports. These logistics decisions were incorporated into USAREUR Deployment Orders 21 and 22, published on 9 and 10 November.

At the outset Saint and Laposata identified a long list of logistical problems that would have to be addressed. They were concerned about the availability of desert battle dress uniforms or fatigues, of water supply equipment, and of MILVANs and other containers; about the packing and crating of materials; and about methods of blocking, bracing, and tiedown. They were also worried about adequate space and facilities at the ports of Rotterdam, Antwerp, and Bremerhaven. General Saint observed that Nordenham would be used to ship ammunition and decided that tanks would be loaded with fuel and ammunition before shipment.[11]

The actual deployment orders issued on 9 November 1990 superseded some of this movement planning, however, by setting 15 January 1991 as the date the corps would close in Saudi Arabia. Using that closing date, Laposata's and Heldstab's organizers again attempted to plan deployment milestones working backwards. According to their best estimates of ship availability and loading and sailing time, they concluded that all USAREUR equipment needed to be at Antwerp, Bremerhaven, and Rotterdam by 20 December 1990. Concerned with safety in the months of November and December, when temperatures in Belgium, the Netherlands, and Germany normally fluctuate around freezing and roads become icy and dangerous without warning, General Saint desired, at this time, that all movement to port be by rail and barge rather than highway. Therefore, the deployment organizers planned equipment moves from railheads and barge terminals, which, in General Laposata's

units were also given priority service at direct maintenance centers and allowed, at least in some cases, to swap nonrepairable equipment.[20]

The VII and V Corps used all the methods described above to fill shortages including cross-leveling or trading equipment between units within each corps. If, after employing these means, units were still short equipment or supplies, the corps passed the resulting requests to HQ USAREUR/7A along with requests for equipment that exceeded authorizations. Initially, VII Corps asked its subordinate commands to identify the equipment and supplies their units lacked. As time became short, units began to submit their requests directly to HQ USAREUR/7A. The V Corps directed all inactivating units that had been instructed to turn over their equipment to deploying units to transfer the equipment immediately. The equipment of other units drawing down would be used to augment the supplies of similar deploying units. For example, the 8th Infantry Division's 1st Battalion, 68th Armor, an inactivating unit in V Corps, was to use its equipment to fill shortages and meet requirements of the 4th Battalion, 34th Armor, another 8th Infantry Division unit, which was, however, deploying with the 3d Armored Division.[21] The VII Corps did much the same internally and USAREUR theater-wide. These attempts to cross-level and to use equipment from inactivating units were followed by hundreds of requests for equipment and supplies that flowed directly from the corps, divisions, and their units to HQ USAREUR/7A.

Supply and Equipment Management

As shown above, General Saint had established two or three basic policies on what units would take. First, he wanted to deploy units with 100 percent of the most modernized, authorized equipment in top running order. Wishing to ensure that units were not burdened with unnecessary equipment, he directed that they take basically only those items authorized on their tables of organization and equipment, although he would approve the release of some additional equipment if it would not slow down the corps or disrupt USAREUR's operations. While he wanted to send the most lethal and mobile force possible, he recognized that time was too short to field much new equipment.[22]

In pursuit of these objectives, Generals Saint and Laposata tightly centralized and controlled most USAREUR-level equipment requests. This was not a surprise for USAREUR logisticians. At the very outset of the sustainment and unit deployment operations in August and September, General Laposata had called every logistician in USAREUR and reviewed all the logistics actions that would be involved in deploying units and supplying USCENTCOM. He had also warned them that everything that left the theater would be managed centrally at HQ USAREUR/7A.[23]

General Saint implemented this centralization policy vigorously. He had every USAREUR-level request for equipment sent to him for approval and ensured that each request he approved was accurately recorded and accounted for at General Laposata's logistics office. Units also had to get Saint's approval to take any equipment beyond that authorized by their tables of organization and equipment. Through February 1991 Laposata wrote 960 brief notes or memorandums to General Saint for decision on supply and equipment transactions. These notes and decision memorandums listed the number of items requested, the number authorized and on hand, and the number in theater reserve and POMCUS; Laposata included in each a recommendation for approval or disapproval.[24] In each case Laposata obtained the opinion of General Heldstab's operations office and, if appropriate, that of other staff offices. He extended his consultations to the VII Corps staff, bringing VII Corps logisticians to Heidelberg to support or oppose every VII Corps request. General Saint then approved or disapproved the requests in line with his basic principles. Throughout the deployment process, these requests were acted upon within twenty-four hours.

While Generals Saint and Laposata favored units' acquiring needed equipment and supplies from inactivating units or trading items between units within each corps, they were reluctant for two reasons to allow deploying units to take equipment from nondeploying, end-state units that were not part of the same major subordinate command. First, the equipment was usually available in POMCUS or theater reserve, which Saint and Laposata preferred to use in these cases. Second, equipment taken from any units remaining in USAREUR, except those already in the inactivation process, would lower USAREUR readiness after the departure of the VII Corps. Therefore, Saint approved borrowing or trading in these cases only if the deploying unit could prove that a needed item was in short supply everywhere or that the unit required it immediately.[25] In some cases equipment was traded between V and VII Corps units without approval. Stories would be told for some time afterwards about units remaining in USAREUR that had traded a good piece of equipment to a deploying unit in exchange for a nonfunctional item. Saint and Laposata also maintained their strict control over requests for additional equipment to maintain the mobility of the corps, to avoid excess, to maintain USAREUR readiness, and to encourage use of POMCUS when available.

Generals Saint and Laposata were able both to eliminate shortages and to modernize the deploying force while limiting cross-leveling between non-corps units and avoiding a drastic drop in the equipment readiness of units remaining in USAREUR. They could do this because they were generally able to fill requirements from POMCUS or theater reserve stocks. POMCUS stocks were designed as unit sets for formations reinforcing Europe, but in this case the sets were broken up to fill individual unit shortages. The equipment taken from POMCUS included many expensive, late-model items, including tanks (which were provided to units deploying from the United States), Bradleys, armored recovery vehicles, heavy expanded-mobility tactical trucks, HMMWVs, and radios. By the middle of February, USAREUR had withdrawn $2.1 billion worth of equipment from POMCUS, representing just 8 percent of the number of inventory items but over 25 percent of their dollar value, to supply and modernize units deploying from both Europe and the United States and to sustain USCENTCOM. In a broader sense than anticipated, POMCUS thus accomplished the goal for which it had been established. When VII Corps and other USAREUR units left USAREUR, they were highly modernized and ready to fight, having obtained nearly 100 percent of their equipment authorizations. POMCUS and European theater reserve were indispensable in preparing for war in Southwest Asia.[26]

Training

In the brief period before deployment, while units were lining up and preparing their equipment, they also undertook any training they could and filled their personnel requirements. Since 1989 USAREUR units had been training to standards established by General Saint to correspond with his capable corps concepts. Since early 1990, when the armored cavalry regiments ended their border patrols and the corps were relieved of most of their general defense plan missions, USAREUR training had been intensified, sharpening individual and team skills which would prove so valuable in Southwest Asia. HQ USAREUR/7A selected units for deployment partly on the basis of when they had last completed gunnery and tactical training. The 3d Armored Division's combat brigades, for example, had been to Grafenwoehr in early October 1990 and had just left the Hohenfels Combat Maneuver and Training Center when the deployment was announced; the 3d Brigade, 3d Infantry Division, which would deploy as part of the 1st Armored Division, had completed training at Hohenfels in July and gunnery

qualifications at Grafenwoehr in September 1990.[27] When the deployment was announced, other 3d Infantry Division tankers, who were
qualifying in gunnery at Grafenwoehr, loaned their tanks to gunner and
vehicle-commander pairs from deploying units who had not previously
fired together.[28]

The soldiers of the 2d Armored Cavalry Regiment were involved in
exceptionally appropriate training right up to their deployment. The regiment conducted a command post exercise in October 1990 that
required the movement of the regiment over 100 kilometers. Following
General Saint's guidance on capable corps operations, the regiment
moved everything (including the entire headquarters) at least 100 kilometers and tested its communications during the long march. The 2d
Armored Cavalry Regiment was testing and practicing exactly those
mobile functions that Saint had stressed since 1989 and that would be
required in Southwest Asia.[29]

USAREUR also tried to help deploying units organize training aimed
specifically at the potential battlefield in Iraq and Kuwait, using the limited resources made available to it. General Pfister acquired available
intelligence on Iraqi units and probable operations in Southwest Asia,
put together an intelligence briefing, and sent briefing teams to provide
some initial preparation for operations to the units deploying to
Operations DESERT SHIELD and DESERT STORM. (He would later provide
similar briefings to USAREUR soldiers deploying to Operations PROVEN
FORCE in Turkey and PROVIDE COMFORT in the Kurdish provinces of
northern Iraq.)[30] General Lee, USAREUR's chief engineer, distributed
information packets to deploying engineer units and sent mobile training teams to brief them on current engineer issues and the desert battlefield environment. The information packet described the most com-
monly used Iraqi mines and means for crossing pipelines. The briefing
teams discussed many engineer topics, including mine warfare, obstacle
breaching, camouflage, and force protection.[31]

The 7th Medical Command, which did not deploy to Southwest
Asia, worked to prepare its many deploying elements and personnel. On
15 November 1991, General Travis, USAREUR's chief surgeon and the
commander of the 7th Medical Command, instructed each deploying
medical unit to add two elements to its mission-essential task list: preparation for operations in harsh desert conditions and the possibility of
attack by chemical weapons. In addition, Travis asked commanders to
focus immediately on those other tasks that would likely be undertaken
during service in Southwest Asia.[32]

HQ USAREUR/7A assisted VII Corps units in equipping themselves
to continue training once they reached Southwest Asia. With General

Saint's approval, Grafenwoehr Training Area assembled targetry and associated equipment for shipment with the corps, and Seventh Army Training Command trained soldiers in the operation, maintenance, and troubleshooting of this equipment so that they could replace the nondeployable, host nation employees who performed these jobs in USAREUR. The loaned equipment enabled VII Corps units to conduct Tables VIII (intermediate qualification) and XII (advanced platoon qualification) training for tank and Bradley gunnery and for M16 qualification transition and combat pistol qualification in Southwest Asia.[33]

Personnel Planning and Realities

When the deployment of VII Corps was announced, many deploying units were short necessary personnel, including noncommissioned officers and soldiers in critical military occupational specialties, because USAREUR had been manned at no more than 96 percent of its authorized strength for over a year. General Saint established a policy calling for units not only to deploy at 100 percent strength but also to fill all positions, if possible, with the military occupational specialty and grade called for in their tables of organization and equipment.

The staffing of USAREUR units became a significant concern for General Saint and his associates soon after the announcement in early August that U.S. units and personnel would deploy to Saudi Arabia. General Reno, the Army's personnel chief, informed HQ USAREUR/7A on 12 August 1990 that some soldiers would be deleted from movement orders to USAREUR and that others with specialized skills who were already in Europe might be reassigned to Southwest Asia. Maj. Gen. Ronald E. Brooks, at that time USAREUR's deputy chief of staff, personnel, estimated that in consequence by December overall USAREUR strength might drop to 93.6 percent and in some military occupational specialties to as low as 80 percent.[34] As described above, General Saint forcefully answered HQDA that USAREUR would contribute whatever was necessary to the effort in Southwest Asia, but urged the Army not to request that support in a way that would substantially reduce USAREUR personnel strength and thereby create a hollow force in Europe. Saint warned that "wholesale reduced manning will break our bank."[35] In order to understand his concern and the eventual importance to DESERT SHIELD and DESERT STORM of his efforts to protect his units' personnel, it is necessary to backtrack briefly and examine personnel strength issues during the entire period of General Saint's command of USAREUR prior to the announcement of the deployment of VII Corps.

In developing his personnel policies, General Saint was assisted by his deputy chief of staff for personnel and by the commander of the 1st Personnel Command. Brig. Gen. Walter J. Bryde replaced the previous personnel chief, General Brooks, on 15 August 1990, and he was soon deeply involved in deploying the 12th Aviation Brigade, planning for the rotation of divisions, and eventually deploying the VII Corps and needed replacement teams. Generals Brooks and Bryde were successively the staff officers responsible for personnel policy in USAREUR, and they were assisted in developing policy and procedures for deploying units and personnel by Brig. Gen. Mary C. Willis, who commanded the 1st Personnel Command, the military personnel operating agency for USAREUR.

As the commander, 1st Personnel Command, General Willis had been responsible for personnel management and distribution operations in USAREUR during the difficult previous year. USAREUR's overall strength had been nearly 100 percent on 1 October 1989. Fiscal year 1990, which began on that date, would see the implementation of an HQDA decision to reduce USAREUR personnel strength to 96 percent in the midst of serious budget shortfalls and the initiation of drawdown and restructuring actions geared to the budget and the anticipated CFE treaty. The decision to man USAREUR at 96 percent required that General Saint, aided by Generals Brooks and Willis, make difficult choices on where to effect personnel cuts. They excepted some selected units from the 96 percent policy and kept them at 100 percent; they kept armored and infantry divisions within approximately 2 percent of each other; and they worked out a fair-share distribution plan for all nonexcepted units. They also developed special management plans for specific military occupational specialties. When the 1st Personnel Command began in early 1990 to participate in the close-hold planning group for USAREUR drawdown and restructuring, General Willis, together with the CFE planners who had been involved earlier, suggested reducing manning in units planned for inactivation to around 75 percent, while keeping combat units staffed at over 90 percent and maintaining the sparse Army structure of combat service support at 100 percent strength.[36]

General Saint consistently tried to discourage the Pentagon from making strength cuts or budgetary reductions before USAREUR restructuring plans had been approved or announced by HQDA. Therefore, he had been reluctant to implement the proposed DCSPER/1st Personnel Command strength policy proposals before the Department of Defense announced its drawdown and restructuring plans in September 1990; until then, he might need or be called on to provide the services of all

USAREUR units. The 75 percent policy in his view would effectively take these reduced units out of the force. It would also damage morale, because so large a drop in unit strength could hardly go unnoticed by unit personnel or interested neighbors. Saint's reluctance to implement this policy, like his insistence on strictly close-hold planning, proved justified in November 1990 when deployment of a corps in DESERT SHIELD, other USCENTCOM requests for USAREUR personnel and unit support, USAREUR logistical support for USCENTCOM, and the concurrent need to maintain readiness and a large military community in Europe combined to require all the personnel and unit resources he could possibly put together.

By summer, however, increasing budgetary and personnel pressure confronted General Saint with the choice of reducing strength in units he hoped to inactivate in the following year or permitting a serious drop in the readiness and strength of all USAREUR units. At this point he chose to cut off some replacements to units planned for inactivation rather than weaken his units across the board. USAREUR's overall strength figures for September 1990 showed 15,506 officers and warrant officers assigned, 96.2 percent of the 16,126 USAREUR was authorized, and 168,286 enlisted personnel assigned of the 178,121 authorized, or 94.5 percent of authorized enlisted strength.[37] By 25 October USAREUR aggregate strength had dropped to 93.9 percent strength, being short 916 officers, 318 warrant officers, and 10,883 enlisted personnel, a total of 12,117 personnel. By early November, when USAREUR was called on to provide a corps plus additional units to USCENTCOM, units selected to deploy ranged in strength from 83 to over 100 percent (see Appendix B for a listing of the personnel strengths of deploying combat and combat support units on November 8). Units that had been announced in September for inactivation had substantially lower average personnel strength.

To help cope with USAREUR's reduced personnel levels, General Saint had asked General Willis to develop a personnel management tool that would allow USAREUR to reduce its personnel strength (and later deploy almost half of its military personnel) without inadvertently breaking down any specific function in Europe. The management tool Willis developed vividly presented information on USAREUR personnel status by functional area and military occupational specialty. It could provide both theater-wide and subordinate command data, as well as the location of individuals with specific military occupational specialties.[38] The theater-wide career management field data for September 1990 presented in *Table 4* illustrates the challenging problems Generals Saint and Willis and other USAREUR commanders faced in trying to maintain sufficient strength, leadership, and skills in various types of units.[39]

The announcement that the VII Corps and supporting units would deploy to Saudi Arabia found USAREUR units with widely varying levels of personnel strength. Nevertheless the actions deemed necessary to deploy fully manned units and still maintain USAREUR readiness seemed fairly straightforward: stop people from leaving their units through transfers or separations and fill unoccupied positions in deploying units through attachment of personnel from units that were remaining in Europe, and, ideally, were scheduled for drawdown. Stop-loss rules proved fairly simple to implement, and USAREUR had in fact applied them to soldiers in the units that deployed earlier, with the approval of HQDA. But in November, HQDA granted authority to implement stop-loss command wide only to major Army commands designated as DESERT SHIELD "direct support major Army commands," and it did not so designate USAREUR. In fact, HQDA decided not to approve a request that units selected by the CINCUSAREUR be designated as direct support.[40]

TABLE 4—USAREUR STRENGTH BY CAREER MANAGEMENT FIELD
(September 1990)

MOS/Function	Career Management Field	Percentage of Total Authorized	Number Excess (+) or Deficient (-)	
			Total	NCO
Maneuver	11, 18, 19, 93	100	+19	-350
Fire Support	13, 11C	95	-1,044	-202
Air Defense	16	100	+12	+62
Intelligence Ops	96, 98	92	-186	-223
Command & Control	31, 74C	98	-351	-17
Engineer	12, 51, 81	92	-660	-213
Chemical	54	92	-191	-129
Maintenance	23, 27, 29, 33, 63, 67	94	-1,771	-265
Communications	55	90	-253	-75
Logistics Svc	76, 77, 94	91	-1,985	-436
Transportation	88	93	-462	-520
Personnel & Administration	25, 46, 71, 74, 79, 97	93	-631	+104
Law Enforcement	95	93	-465	-83
Medical	91	95	-471	-410

Source: Chart, USAREUR Personnel Status, in tab B to incl 2 to interv, Virginia Jay, CFE Div, ODCSOPS, HQ USAREUR/7A, 20 Nov 90.

Stop-Loss

Nevertheless, on 10 November 1990 General Saint implemented, with limited exceptions, a broad, temporary, command-wide stop-loss policy and permanent-change-of-station freeze to prevent personnel from leaving USAREUR units. The exceptions at first included resignation for the good of the service, pregnancy, extreme hardship, and unsatisfactory performance and also permitted retirement. The first colonel in an individual's chain of command could approve exceptions for extreme personal hardship or for other reasons that made good sense.[41] To make these temporary policies apply in USAREUR for the duration of the Gulf conflict, General Saint repeated USAREUR's earlier requests to be designated a direct support major Army command. Saint also reminded HQDA that it should not lose sight of its commitment to man the residual USAREUR force at 100 percent.[42]

As noted above, USAREUR did not stop all departures from deploying units, allowing a few exceptions to its stop-loss policy. However, these exceptions were generally given only if medical or other reasons made the soldier unsuitable for wartime service. The removal of a field grade officer from a deploying unit required CINCUSAREUR approval.[43] USAREUR commanders, including General Saint, were extremely reluctant to exempt personnel from deploying to a theater where there was a strong possibility of combat operations.

Officers and enlisted personnel scheduled to separate from the Army were for a time prevented by stop-loss from leaving either the Army or their USAREUR units. This policy was initially implemented in USAREUR in September 1990, but it applied only to units deploying to Southwest Asia. After it was decided that VII Corps would deploy to Saudi Arabia, however, USAREUR applied stop-loss to all its military personnel who were scheduled to leave the Army between 10 November 1990 and, as it later turned out, April 1991. Approximately 4,800 USAREUR soldiers were affected, including some who deployed with their units to Southwest Asia and others who remained in USAREUR. The policy thus helped USAREUR not only to deploy its units to Southwest Asia at full strength but also enabled it to maintain personnel readiness and services in Europe.[44]

The involuntary extension of foreign service tours had an even more dramatic effect on personnel strength, the stability of deploying units, and USAREUR readiness. These extensions were given to the many service members who were scheduled to rotate to assignments in the United States. USAREUR had imposed such extensions since September on personnel in units deploying to Southwest Asia. In November it requested that these involuntary extensions be given to all USAREUR personnel. While this step was not approved, HQDA and USAREUR eventually worked out a Date Eligible for Rotation from Overseas (DEROS) readjustment program that would affect approximately 125,000 USAREUR soldiers by the time the program ended in May 1991.[45] These two programs significantly assisted both the deployment of VII Corps and the maintenance of USAREUR readiness, though they may have disappointed some soldiers and would complicate personnel management after the war.

USAREUR also suspended its normal replacement operations on 19 November and, thereafter, assigned incoming personnel to fill high-priority vacant positions. Combined with stop-loss, involuntary extension of foreign service, and cross-leveling of personnel among units, this allowed VII Corps units to deploy from USAREUR with an overall personnel strength of nearly 100 percent.

Cross-Leveling Personnel Among Units

Personnel deficiencies in units deploying to Southwest Asia were filled primarily by cross-leveling soldiers from units remaining in USAREUR to deploying units, a process undertaken until 15 December. The soldiers affected included some 2,000 personnel transferred at theater level and another 3,000 soldiers transferred within V Corps or VII Corps.[46]

At the outset cross-leveling threatened to undermine the tracking of personnel, the reporting and processing of casualties, and even the support of soldiers' families. The corps did not have adequate accountability systems, and their weakness in this sphere was highlighted when HQDA directed that personnel be attached rather than reassigned to units deploying to Southwest Asia. The Pentagon envisioned that USAREUR soldiers would join the deploying units temporarily and return after the operation to their old units in USAREUR. Their records, families, and homes, as well as the basic units to which they were assigned, would remain in USAREUR.[47] In the event, cross-leveling in USAREUR was accomplished by both reassigning and attaching. In general, unaccompanied soldiers who could be reassigned with little or no permanent change of station cost were reassigned. Accompanied soldiers and unaccompanied soldiers whose reassignment would require a full-cost permanent change of station were simply attached.[48]

The 1st Personnel Command froze its USAREUR personnel data base as of 31 October 1990, and HQDA agreed that personnel would be attached on orders, enabling the 1st Personnel Command to track the transferred soldiers on its Standard Installation/Division Personnel System rosters and in its casualty and strength reporting. The soldiers also took their casualty information with them to their new units. These measures meant that 1st Personnel Command could quickly find the basic unit and personnel records of all cross-leveled USAREUR personnel.[49]

General Saint had instructed his personnel administrators to cross-level as much as possible without destroying the readiness of his army in Europe or disrupting the first phase of his drawdown schedule. This first phase would last through March 1991 and reduce USAREUR strength by some 7,000 soldiers, representing nearly one-quarter of the 30,000-soldier drawdown planned for fiscal year 1991. On 12 November HQ USAREUR/7A published guidelines formalizing cross-leveling priorities. Soldiers in units that would be inactivated in fiscal year 1992 and after May in fiscal year 1991 were to be considered for cross-leveling first and second, respectively. Just four days later this guidance was modified to add to the second group soldiers in units scheduled for inactivation in February through May 1991, if enough soldiers would remain to keep preparation for inactivation on track. Saint authorized the reduction of the personnel strength of units that were pending inactivation and remaining in USAREUR to 65 percent, or lower with battalion commander approval, if this would not totally bankrupt the units in some functional capacity or dangerously reduce the strength of any specific military occupational specialty in USAREUR. Soldiers assigned to units not scheduled for inactivation in fiscal years 1991 or 1992 were to be considered for cross-leveling last. General Saint authorized cross-leveling of soldiers from end-state units, however, as long as the overall personnel strength of the end-state force was not reduced below 95 percent. Requirements that could not be filled within V or VII Corps, according to this guidance, were to be sent to the commander, 1st Personnel Command. HQ USAREUR/7A guidance also stated that soldiers should be cross-leveled in a way that would allow their families to stay at their present locations.[50]

General Willis had already developed the management system that gave Generals Saint and Bryde a vivid picture of theater-wide military occupational specialty strength and personnel assignments, both in deploying units and those remaining in Europe. This system allowed the 1st Personnel Command to identify nondeploying units with sufficient personnel in low-strength or critical occupational specialties and grades to permit cross-leveling without seriously depleting USAREUR. General Willis examined the end-state units for available personnel in every occupational specialty needed by the deploying force. Generally it was possible to estimate cross-leveling needs and meet them quickly within

General Saint's guidance, without severely lowering the overall strength of individual units or altering dramatically the balance of each unit's military occupational specialties. In most cases, cross-leveled soldiers joined their deploying units before departing for Saudi Arabia.[51]

On 10 December HQ USAREUR/7A warned VII Corps that its ability to cross-level personnel had been exhausted. Although USAREUR and its subordinate commands had been able to fill most vacancies in deploying units with soldiers in the right occupational specialty and grade while still maintaining needed capabilities in Europe, HQ USAREUR/7A at this point requested that HQDA fill remaining vacancies from outside Europe. These vacancies tended to be in the very combat support and combat service support positions that HQDA was having such a hard time filling, despite the desperate requests of ARCENT and USCENTCOM. These shortages included aviation and vehicle mechanics, petroleum clerks, and supply personnel.[52] Personnel qualified in military intelligence, signal, and medical specialties were also in short supply.

USAREUR could not provide some of these personnel because they were critically needed in USAREUR. Many personnel in these support specialties were assigned to the 21st TAACOM, which performed the echelon-above-corps logistic support functions in USAREUR and would now be providing transportation and port support not only for VII Corps' deployment but for all the sustainment USAREUR was giving to USCENTCOM. The 21st TAACOM was normally organized at a low authorized level, as were combat support and combat service support organizations throughout the Army. Therefore, 21st TAACOM and other USAREUR combat service support organizations were not sufficiently staffed to provide all the personnel needed by VII Corps and other deploying units, while continuing to perform their essential functions in USAREUR. In the end, VII Corps and its units deployed very well staffed, particularly in comparison with most units deployed from the United States. In the time between VII Corps' deployment from USAREUR and the beginning of the ground war in Iraq, HQDA filled the relatively few positions that were unfilled when VII Corps departed USAREUR.[53]

Personnel Preparation for Overseas Movement

The deployment of a forward-deployed corps raised a number of significant family and community issues that will be addressed in detail in Chapter 7. The preparation for overseas movement of individual soldiers must be examined here, however, because it was an integral part of soldier and unit preparation and fundamentally affected VII Corps' deployment. In order to complete their preparation for overseas movement, soldiers were required to get physical and dental clearances, update their personnel records, ensure that their individual clothing and equipment were complete and serviceable, and take care of their personal and family responsibilities. From the soldiers' point of view, these procedures helped organize those administrative and personal chores that were necessary to leave their homes and go to war. From the personnel administration point of view, preparation for overseas movement requirements identified those who were unfit for deployment, helped prepare those who were fit for war, and tried to create as comfortable and supportive an environment as possible for the families left behind.

Soldiers of the 71st Maintenance Battalion at Fuerth, Germany, process through medical, dental, legal, finance, and personnel stations in preparation for deployment to Operation DESERT SHIELD.

Family Care Plans

Providing appropriately for dependent children of single parents or those with two parents deploying to Southwest Asia became a major challenge early in the deployment process. This problem was exacerbated by the fact that these soldiers were already assigned to a forward-deployed army that was far from grandparents and other sources of family support. All of these parents had been required to establish a formal child-care plan to ensure that in the event of combat their children would either be cared for in Europe or returned to family members or other responsible persons in the United States. An actual deployment brought this system under extensive scrutiny for the first time. Many soldiers had developed plans tied to the existing noncombatant evacuation order process, but this did not work in 1990 as no noncombatant evacuation order was issued in Europe for the Gulf War. As a result, over 1,000 soldiers were required to revise their family-care plans to ensure that they could be implemented. In some cases, commanders allowed soldiers to make quick trips to the United States to transport children to the homes of relatives. Under an exception to USAREUR's stop-loss policy, USAREUR officers discharged some forty to fifty soldiers with prime parental responsibility who had not developed or did not implement adequate child care plans.[54]

Nondeployability

Understandably, the issue of nondeployability aroused considerable attention and some emotion in USAREUR. The large-scale VII Corps deployment was a significant test of the viability of the modern all-volunteer Army that Saint and other contemporary Army leaders had been trying to build since the end of the Vietnam War. Pregnancy was sure to contribute to nondeployability in a volunteer Army that had given a larger role to young women as it sought to widen the pool of qualified Americans from whom it could recruit. Some 7.4 percent of VII Corps' women soldiers were pregnant in November 1990, a figure marginally above the pregnancy rate of all women then in the Army. According to General Bryde, pregnancy was not the leading cause of medical nondeployability. Pregnancy accounted for just over 17 percent of those deemed nondeployable. Bryde observed that other medical condictions—undiagnosed injuries, allergies, and asthma—contributed surprisingly high numbers of medical disqualifications. Some people who were supposed to deploy to fight an enemy who had previously used chemical weapons could not wear a protective mask. General Saint questioned why people who were permanently incapable physically of going to war had been assigned to a forward-deployed force.[55]

Other personnel were nondeployable because of pending disciplinary action. General Saint pushed his commanders and their judge advocate advisers to process quickly personnel who could not deploy because of pending administrative discharge or Uniform Code of Military Justice action and to press charges within thirty days against personnel who failed to comply with their movement orders. Some 637 soldiers in deploying units were declared nondeployable because administrative or Uniform Code of Military Justice action was pending against them. By 28 March 1991, 97 percent of the administrative discharges and 87 percent of the actions under the Uniform Code in these cases had been completed. Of the 51 soldiers charged with having missed movement without authorization, 17 were at that time still absent without leave (AWOL) and actions against only 11 had been completed.[56]

Overall the USAREUR nondeployability rate was about 3 percent of the soldiers in the deploying units, a slightly lower rate than that of units from the United States.[57] This rate of nondeployability, however, increased by more than 50 percent the number of vacancies that had to be filled in order to send a fully staffed force. The vacancies were filled as discussed above, and VII Corps deployed at roughly 100 percent, although at a cost of some 2,000 more vacancies in the residual force left in USAREUR. Personnel who were nondeployable when their unit deployed, but who became deployable before the ground war began, went to Southwest Asia along with replacements.[58]

Narrative Account of the Deployment

The announcement of VII Corps' deployment to the Gulf on 8 November 1990 unleashed a burst of activity in the U.S. Army, Europe, that would not abate until late December. As befitted their positions, USAREUR's top generals took the lead. The day after the announcement, General Saint asked his counterparts and other key personnel in allied armies for assistance. They immediately agreed and asked for details. On the following day, a Saturday, General Shalikashvili visited the Belgian and Dutch territorial commands; early the next week he met with German Army leaders. He informed the allied commanders that USAREUR troops would start moving in the next few days and that his command had been given a sixty-day deadline to ship the entire enhanced corps. He also outlined the support that would be necessary.

On Sunday Generals Shalikashvili and Laposata went to Stuttgart to talk to VII Corps leaders and logisticians about deployment requirements. Shalikashvili visited the director of the West German national railroad, the *Bundesbahn*, on Monday to let him know as early as possible what was coming. The two men reached a substantial understanding on the support the German railroad could provide. Based on close, long-term, institutional and personal relationships developed in REFORGER exercises and other allied and bilateral experience, detailed agreement for support was then quickly arranged. General Laposata called other key transportation contacts to begin to acquire containers and make transportation arrangements. Within USAREUR, the temporary stop-loss policy was implemented on 10 November. Deploying units were released from their peacetime responsibilities and turned in their sensitive communications-security and other controlled materials. The VII Corps began attaching some units and requesting the activation of reserve component combat support and combat service support units. General Franks and his commanders headed to Saudi Arabia for a five-day coordination trip, and on 13 November they attended a strategy conference held by General Schwarzkopf. They were told then that their mission would be to attack and destroy the Republican Guard.[59]

As discussed earlier, HQ USAREUR/7A Deployment Order 22, issued on 10 November, required deploying commanders to start planning the deployment of their personnel and equipment. Most commanders had probably been given a head start in late October in thinking through what equipment to take and how to load and transport it, as well as how to prepare personnel for overseas movement. That was certainly true in the 2d Armored Cavalry Regiment, whose commander, Col. Leonard D. Holder, Jr., was then warned by General Franks to calculate what he would need from VII Corps to move his regiment to port and deploy it to Saudi Arabia ready to fight.[60]

HQ USAREUR/7A also geared up its administrative procedures for the uncharted, but undeniably difficult, road ahead. The O&I sessions began to meet twice daily, with General Saint attending often, General Shalikashvili nearly every day, and General Burleson every meeting. Burleson established a requirement to respond to every incoming DESERT SHIELD request within forty-eight hours of receipt of the message, and Colonel Mumby's HQ USAREUR/7A Crisis Action Team established a system to ensure that these suspenses were met. Actually, most issues, whether internal or external, would be considered at the O&I sessions when they arose and decided and acted on no later than the following day. Mumby's Crisis Action Team was enlarged and placed on 24-hour operation, while staff office crisis action teams made parallel adjustments to ensure quick responses to taskings and requirements. The many quick, verbal decisions made in the daily O&I sessions and hastily called decision briefs in General Saint's office reduced paperwork and time compared to the more formal staff action procedures established in USAREUR Memorandum 1–10, but they also made historical reconstruction of these actions more difficult.

On the weekend after the president's announcement, Generals Shalikashvili and Laposata discussed deployment with VII Corps leaders and logisticians at VII Corps headquarters in Stuttgart, Germany. According to General Laposata, he and Shalikashvili described some of the requirements the corps would face and offered their help. Corps planners needed to ascertain their container and blocking and bracing requirements, to determine their rail transportation needs, and to begin working with movement control teams.[61] The VII Corps representatives estimated their requirements and gave Generals Shalikashvili and Laposata ideas about how to meet them, which the USAREUR generals explained in the next few days to key personnel on their own transportation and support staffs. The VII Corps had apparently already asked some deploying commanders for this kind of information. The commander, 2d Armored Cavalry Regiment, for example, was asked to determine his rail transportation requirements in late October. General Shalikashvili could use this information in early November when he talked to the director of the *Bundesbahn*, and General Laposata could discuss it with London container contractors, whom he had contacted within twenty-four hours of the president's announcement.[62]

General Saint acted to get the deployment started by ordering the 2d Armored Cavalry Regiment to begin loading its equipment on rail cars. He made the decision after he found that the combat service support elements of VII Corps' 2d Corps Support Command would not be able to begin deploying immediately. General Burleson later said that General Saint made this decision "because we had to move something . . . and he knew, if he asked a cavalry regiment, he could move a cavalry regiment."[63] The decision to order the 2d Armored Cavalry Regiment to initiate the deployment had probably been made before General Franks left for Saudi Arabia on 11 November. The 2d Armored Cavalry Regiment began loading its equipment on rail cars in Bamberg on 12 November, the fourth day after announcement.

Preparation for the movement of the 2d Armored Cavalry Regiment was already under way on 10 November, when USEUCOM received USCENTCOM's deployment concept and preferred sequence and, that evening, forwarded them to USAREUR. USCENTCOM requested that the movement of supporting elements, specifically engineer, transportation, and base support units, precede combat unit deployment. It gave its preferred sequence for the arrival of combat units as the 2d Armored Cavalry Regiment initially, followed by the 1st Armored Division, the 1st Infantry Division (from the United States), the 2d Armored Division (Forward), the 3d Armored Division, and the combat aviation brigade. The deployment sequence General Franks brought back from USCENTCOM and ARCENT contained no surprises, again requesting combat support and combat service support first.[64]

General Saint eventually approved the VII Corps deployment flow shown below, although he allowed the 2d Armored Cavalry Regiment to lead the movement:[65]

A. VII Corps headquarters advance party
B. Combat support and combat service support units
C. 2d Armored Cavalry Regiment
D. Combat support and combat service support units
E. 7th Engineer Brigade
F. Combat support and combat service support units
G. 1st Armored Division

H. 11th Aviation Brigade
I. HHC VII Corps
J. Corps artillery
K. 2d Armored Division (Forward)
L. 3d Armored Division

The VII Corps quickly filled in the details of its unit deployment sequence based on this approved flow. All USAREUR agencies helping to deploy the corps similarly organized their efforts in accord with that sequence.[66]

The 2d Armored Cavalry Regiment's soldiers launched the deployment when they began loading trains on 12 November. The first trains left on 14 November, and by the 16th eight trains had departed. Then on 16 and 17 November, the advance party of the corps headquarters (Corps HHC[-]) and various 2d Corps Support Command and 7th Engineer Brigade units that USCENTCOM had requested be sent first began to load on trains. On 19 November the 2d Corps Support Command's advance party—VII Corps' lead combat service support element—flew to Saudi Arabia on five C–141 transport planes. At the same time the signal, maintenance, and transportation companies that would help set up USAREUR's and the corps' reception operation in Saudi Arabia began the long deployment to the Gulf, reporting to their respective seaports of embarkation beginning on 20 November. The first twenty of these units were ordered to arrive at port by 22 November, and seventy more were scheduled to reach port by the 24th. In addition, almost 100 units with different responsibilities in Saudi Arabia had ready-to-load dates no later than 23 November.[67] Although trains and barges would transport most VII Corps equipment to port, General Saint found it necessary on 19 November to reverse his earlier guidance to avoid virtually all road convoys. On that date he announced procedures to begin sending VII Corps convoys to ports.[68]

Immediately after VII Corps' deployment was formally announced and the ports of embarkation were selected, the 21st TAACOM and other nondeploying USAREUR units began to perform the varied additional responsibilities required of them to deploy the corps. Complying with Deployment Order 22, the 5th Signal Command installed communications to the seaports and later to the airports of embarkation even before any deploying soldiers or equipment arrived.[69] The 21st TAACOM, aided by the local military communities, quickly established life support areas at the seaports of embarkation for the truck drivers, maintenance and security staffs, and personnel who would help load the ships. The 21st TAACOM already had some experience in a similar sphere, as it had set up a Departure Airfield Control Group at the aerial port of embarkation at Ramstein Air Base in August 1990 to support personnel departures and the shipment of equipment and supplies.[70] The 21st also set up rest areas and refueling stations for convoys to various ports of embarkation. Many other USAREUR units provided the 21st TAACOM with transportation, security, and loading support as it moved deploying units from their German bases to their ports of embarkation. These units included the Combat Equipment Battalions, East, West, North, and Northwest, of the Combat Equipment Group, Europe; the 51st Maintenance Battalion; the 202d Support Battalion (Forward); the 26th Support Group's Support Battalion (Provisional); and the 14th, 27th, and 39th Transportation Battalions. These logistical units were supported by the 4th Battalion (Mechanized), 8th Infantry; the 527th Military Intelligence Battalion; and the 95th and 97th Military Police Battalions of the 42d Military Police Group. The 543d Area Support Group in Bremerhaven and the 80th Area Support Group, also known as the NATO/Supreme Headquarters Allied Powers, Europe (SHAPE), Support Group, in Belgium and the Netherlands provided a wide variety of support near and at the seaports. Other units remaining in USAREUR pitched in to help their neighboring and associated units load their equipment and organize their communities in a manner designed to help families cope as well as possible during the deployment.

The soldiers of the 3d Infantry Division who would remain in Europe supplied the manpower needed by Military Traffic Management Command, Europe, to run the ports. Moving to Bremerhaven and Rotterdam to serve as stevedores, the 3d Infantry Division soldiers immediately began unloading equipment at marshaling yards and loading it onto the ships. Units that participated in this work included the 4th Battalion, 69th Armor; the 5th Battalion, 15th Infantry; the 4th Battalion, 3d Air Defense Artillery; the 10th Engineer Battalion; the 3d and 203d Support Battalions (Forward); the 703d Support Battalion (Main); and the 3d Infantry Division Support Command. Other units remaining in Europe, such as Company B, 1st Battalion, 16th Infantry, 1st Infantry Division (Forward), at Boeblingen, Germany, established and ran railhead operations, helping get the corps loaded and headed for port on time. Host nations in Europe also helped out at the ports by supplying facilities, including showers, latrines, and messes for the life support centers and marshaling areas and by providing guards and other security support. The Bremerhaven and NATO/SHAPE local military communities were also able to provide much useful support.[71]

In mid-November, the deployment appeared to be off to the quick start that was necessary to get the corps to the Gulf by 15 January 1991. Still, the complexities often seemed overwhelming, and while General

Franks and his commanders visited USCENTCOM and ARCENT to learn the campaign plan and the desired deployment sequence, some in Europe began to wonder who would actually lead the deployment. USAREUR leaders had expected that the corps would deploy itself, but it soon became apparent that the very people who should oversee the corps' deployment in Europe, including the commander, VII Corps, were also needed in the ARCENT area of responsibility to plan and oversee the reception, onward movement, and training of the deploying force to ready it for the coming campaign.

General Laposata and the USAREUR Command Group at first professed total confidence in the corps' ability to make the critical decisions involved in its deployment, but they also recognized the essential nature of their assistance. General Laposata, for example, while recognizing General Franks' dilemma, understood that it was a commander's responsibility and prerogative to plan and carry out his organization's deployment. However, reflecting on the deployment of the 12th Aviation Brigade as well as his previous experience, Laposata could only conclude that units were in fact incapable of self-deploying and that the most rigorous centralization and control were necessary to achieve a quick and successful deployment.[72] According to General Burleson, deployment uncertainties, exacerbated by General Frank's five-day absence, reached such a crisis in the second weekend after announcement that the Command Group and staff had to admit they really did not know exactly what they were supposed to be doing, nor could they discern a workable VII Corps plan to move itself to port.[73]

On the following Monday, 19 November, Generals Shalikashvili and Laposata went to VII Corps headquarters in Stuttgart and set up a movements control center. Already in late October, Laposata had expressed concern about VII Corps' ability to handle its transportation requirements while deploying and had suggested to General Saint that he be attached to VII Corps to plan and run the transportation of VII Corps equipment. In November General Laposata moved to Stuttgart, intending to remain there to guide the deployment until the last unit departed; General Shalikashvili meanwhile visited often and helped continually to solve problems. According to General Laposata, the corps commander remained in control of the movement of the corps. Laposata's role was to do whatever General Franks wanted to get VII Corps to Saudi Arabia.[74]

General Laposata brought his logistical experts to the movements control center to serve, as he described it, as "technicians and facilitators." He brought most of the 1st Transportation Movement Control Agency from its headquarters in Oberursel, Germany, leaving behind only those parts necessary to move deploying V Corps units and scattered other USAREUR units. Maj. Richard Cawthorne of the Royal Transport Corps, who was the British liaison officer to the 1st Transportation Movement Control Agency, served as his operations officer at the center. In addition to these movement control agency personnel, Laposata staffed the movements control center with officers and sergeants who were experts in their logistical specialties, bringing in some from his own logistics office at HQ USAREUR/7A. For example, he assigned Maj. William G. Arnold, whom he brought with him from HQ USAREUR/7A, to manage the challenging problem of containers and requested a VII Corps soldier to assist him. In addition to bringing a VII Corps liaison officer into the center, he assigned a member of his HQ USAREUR/7A staff, Maj. Stephen B. Howard, to act as liaison between the movements control center and the VII Corps' deployment action team, which handled transportation arrangements and scheduling for the corps. General Laposata and the staff of his movements control center stayed in Stuttgart until the last piece of equipment reached port on 20 December 1990.

Under General Laposata's direction, the movements control center monitored the implementation of VII Corps' movement plans. It identified problems, brought them to the attention of the appropriate corps officers, and helped solve them. These problems included shortages of containers, blocking and bracing material, and railroad cars; delays at the barge port; and the unpreparedness of some units to move as scheduled. If Laposata could not solve a problem, he would ask General Shalikashvili or General Saint for help. When major problems arose, Laposata might call the president of SeaLand, Shalikashvili might call the *Bundesbahn* director or a high host nation official, and Saint might call the Army staff in the Pentagon. Every few days, General Laposata returned to USAREUR headquarters to check on his own office's operations, attend O&I meetings, and discuss major logistical issues with General Saint.[75]

To keep the rail and barge movements of unit equipment bound for Southwest Asia flowing smoothly, VII Corps, USAREUR's logistical planners, and the movements control center established a staging area at the barge terminal in Mannheim, Germany; several regional railheads; and marshaling areas at the ports. Then the logisticians asked transportation providers to position at these barge and rail heads the number of barges and railroad cars the Army planners estimated would be needed per day to get VII Corps unit equipment to the ports by 20 December. At first they had arranged with the *Deutsche Bundesbahn* for 600 trains, or 15 trains per night, with allowances for adjustments later.[76] They also found that over 100 barges were available in the first two weeks.[77]

The logisticians then scheduled units to load their equipment into the pipeline. M. Sgt. Gerald R. Thompson III, a food service supervisor from Laposata's Heidelberg office, used his computer skills to generate spreadsheets showing daily unit movement schedules and data. The data were transferred to large boards at the offices of the VII Corps' deployment action team and to the movements control center to highlight schedules, movements, and problems. Then the units and VII Corps, aided by the movements control center, had only to ensure that units met their ready-to-load dates and moved their equipment into the pipeline on schedule, after which the center monitored the flow in the rail and barge pipelines to see that each item of unit equipment met its latest arrival date at port.[78]

On 3 December, when the equipment pipeline was flowing effectively, VII Corps conducted its official departure ceremony at its headquarters at Kelley Barracks near Moehringen, Germany, just south of Stuttgart. Generals Galvin, Saint, and Franks participated, as did other concerned American commanders, and important German friends. Saint and Franks addressed those attending in both English and German, stressing the success of VII Corps soldiers in preparing for deployment, the rich traditions of VII Corps, the challenge ahead to deploying soldiers and their families, and the importance of the support given them by Germany and other host nations. Meanwhile, a small group of German demonstrators could be heard in the background. German officials, including General Frank Schild, commander of the Baden-Wuerttemberg military district (*Wehrbereichskommando* 5), and Stuttgart mayor Manfred Rommel, discussed increasing their nation's support to families of deployed soldiers.[79] General Franks and other corps leaders departed for Saudi Arabia in the next few days.

The deployment of VII Corps' equipment was never an easy matter. One of the first issues that HQ USAREUR/7A, VII Corps, and 21st TAACOM faced was whether or not to repaint in a tan, desert-camouflage design USAREUR's green camouflage tanks, Bradleys, and other vehicles. General Saint preferred that USAREUR vehicles be repainted before shipment to enhance their readiness for war when they arrived in Saudi Arabia. Personnel from the 21st TAACOM and Laposata's Heidelberg logistics office briefed General Shalikashvili on 25 October on the costs and methods of repainting wheeled and tracked vehicles. The costs were high and the problems many, but USAREUR decided to proceed nevertheless.[80] Although a serious effort was made, in the end time simply did not allow USAREUR to finish the job. USAREUR painted as many vehicles as it could before deployment, but on 23 November 1990 it diverted to ARCENT the 15,000 gallons of Tan 686 paint it had

A repainted M1A1 tank being loaded on a C–5 aircraft at Rhein Main Air Base for shipment to Saudi Arabia

originally requisitioned for painting in Europe and soon gave up the project.[81]

At the beginning of the second week of deployment, it became clear that reduced barge capacity due to high water on the Rhine and scheduling complexities at ports would make some road convoys necessary to keep the equipment pipeline flowing. Although General Saint had wanted to avoid the dangers and problems of winter driving—which in Central Europe could involve confronting extended rain, ice, fog, wind, and snow—on 19 November he approved road convoys to ports of embarkation when required for efficient movement. Only the 7th Engineer Brigade, the 1st Armored Division, and the 2d Armored Division (Forward) made substantial use of convoys in their deployment. This limited convoying was accomplished successfully with few accidents or fatalities.[82]

Containers were continually a problem. Before the establishment of the movements control center, VII Corps did not have enough container express (CONEX) containers, and it did not receive any before the first units began loading to deploy. So when the trains started moving, some unit equipment had to be left behind to await containers. The container shortages persisted through the deployment, despite General Laposata's vigorous efforts to lease SeaLand containers and to have the movements control center closely manage all containers obtained by USAREUR.[83] Although ARCENT assured General Franks it could deliver individual CONEX and SeaLand containers to the proper units in Saudi ports, the VII Corps commander was concerned as he directed the use of SeaLand containers that would move separately from the units whose equipment they would contain.[84]

It proved to be extremely difficult to predict not only how many containers would be needed, but also the number of rail cars and ships required. By 23 November General Shalikashvili was warning that USAREUR had grossly underestimated the need for rail road cars. Laposata's logistics office at HQ USAREUR/7A now estimated that 25 trains per day were required. The question of "how many ships?" had been discussed repeatedly since the end of October. Laposata's logisticians predicted that 62 to 90 ships would be required depending on the size of the ships obtained. Questions about the size, speed, and reliability of transport ships, which had already challenged USAREUR logisticians in the deployment of the 12th Aviation Brigade, again posed major problems in the deployment of VII Corps.[85]

General Saint expressed repeated concern not only about numbers of ships but also about the capacity to load them. Around 20 November he asked Maj. Gen. Wilson A. Shoffner, the commander of the 3d Infantry Division, to examine the issue of port capacity. General Shoffner reported that Bremerhaven and Antwerp could handle about a division at a time and Rotterdam a brigade. Bremerhaven could load as many as 1,000 vehicles per day, while Antwerp and Rotterdam could load about half that number. Shoffner's overall assessment was that the capacity at these ports was adequate to avoid delays.[86] Nevertheless, on 24 November Colonel Barnaby, the commander of the Military Traffic Management Command, Europe, informed Maj. Gen. John R. Piatak, Commander, Military Traffic Management Command, that he was talking to contractors at Antwerp and Rotterdam about increasing the number of berths at each from three to four and establishing an ammunition port at Eemshaven, the Netherlands, in addition to the two existing berths for ammunition at Nordenham, Germany. This port expansion effort followed USEUCOM's conclusion, reached in the previous day or two, that it would need 3 million additional square feet of shipping for a total of 10 million square feet by the end of December.[87] If Eemshaven were added, USAREUR could use up to five ports, which would be adequate, but the size and dependability of the fleet that the U.S. Transportation Command could put together remained in doubt.

One problem that confronted USAREUR throughout this period was the competition for transportation resources between VII Corps equipment and equipment that USAREUR was providing to modernize or sustain USCENTCOM units deploying from the United States. USAREUR had accepted the mission of getting the corps to Saudi Arabia by 15 January, and it gave the highest priority to this task. General Saint repeatedly admonished his subordinates to focus on the deployment of VII Corps.[88] In general, USAREUR adhered to the following order of equipment movement priorities: 1. Deploying unit equipment, deployable medical system equipment, and heavy equipment tracked transport systems, all with top priority; 2. German ambulances, water trucks and trailers, and 5-ton trucks; 3. Other German-provided equipment; 4. Ammunition, both unit basic load and sustainment; and 5. Force modernization equipment. USCENTCOM had agreed with these priorities early in the deployment process.[89] Questions of movement priority assumed new significance on 19 December when General Piatak advised General Shalikashvili that he would have to reallocate ships to move units faster from the United States to Saudi Arabia. This warning came the day before the final USAREUR shipments arrived at their European ports.[90]

In an attempt to improve communication and coordination with its USCENTCOM partner, HQ USAREUR/7A dispatched a liaison team to HQ ARCENT on 26 November 1990. General Burleson asked CINCUSAREUR's liaison officer to the commander in chief of the French Forces in Germany, Col. James E. Callahan, and his liaison team members to move from Baden Baden, Germany, to Riyadh, Saudi Arabia, and set up a liaison mission to HQ ARCENT. The mission was designed to act as General Saint's representative to General Yeosock and his staff, and it was to deal both with issues related to VII Corps deployment and other USAREUR matters.

Although the team's mission had been planned cooperatively by Colonel Mumby's Crisis Action Team and the ARCENT G3 office, when the team arrived in Riyadh, no one in ARCENT seemed to know about its mission. The team brought its own STU III and tactical satellite radios, but HQ ARCENT provided no work space, transportation, or communications. This early resistance led Colonel Callahan, who was invited to General Yeosock's morning meetings, to focus only on key issues.[91]

The liaison team's tribulations underscored a communications gap between USAREUR and USCENTCOM. Callahan even had difficulty getting ARCENT to respond to USAREUR requests for ARCENT shipping priorities, since HQ USEUCOM had been handling this problem. Communication at the joint level thus sometimes interfered with direct army-to-army contacts.[92] The USAREUR liaison effort was not a success, and General Burleson and Brig. Gen. Robert S. Frix, the chiefs of staff of the two headquarters, agreed to end the attempt.[93] On 18 December the team returned to Heidelberg.

The size and complexity of the deployment made some human error entirely predictable. Some units or parts of units showed up at the wrong port, causing them to miss their port call or latest arrival date.[94] Some units were late, while others arrived at port ahead of schedule. Numerous units scheduled for early departure reached port up to four days late.[95] The complex geography of USAREUR's stationing patterns made these mix-ups hardly surprising.

The division of individual units' equipment among several ships caused many serious problems in getting these units unloaded, out of port, and ready to fight in Saudi Arabia. At the beginning of each large unit deployment, each division and separate brigade had been required to send a liaison officer to each of the European ports that USAREUR was using in an effort to ensure, among other things, that unit integrity was maintained during loading.[96] But for a variety of reasons, unit integrity could not be maintained. Above all, there were simply not enough big, fast, reliable ships. The 105 ships that the Transportation Command used to deploy VII Corps varied substantially in size from a capacity of as little as 9,000 to as much as 185,000 square feet. While the average ship capacity was 72,400 square feet, two-thirds of the ships used were smaller than average. The use of small ships congested ports, slowed loading and unloading operations, dispersed the equipment of both headquarters and combat organizations, and complicated the rapid reconstitution of combat forces in Saudi Arabia.[97]

Army unit commanders' plans created other reasons for dispersing a unit's equipment over several ships. Since units were expected to arrive ready to fight, their commanders often used their task force organization in organizing their shipments. This could directly contradict the goal of maintaining unit integrity and result in a unit's equipment being dispersed over several ships. The Stuttgart movements control center's advice against shipping by task organization was sometimes rejected by commanders who were confident that they had a better understanding of the mission ahead. Another factor was that supply officers could not always get all their equipment to port at the same time. If they were still seeking a piece of equipment to cross-level from another unit, repairing a piece of equipment, or waiting to receive a requisition for equipment, such additional unit equipment might arrive at port, be shipped, and arrive in Saudi Arabia several weeks later than the unit's original shipment.[98] The consequence of the failure to maintain unit integrity in shipping was that units or parts of units would remain at the ports in Saudi

Arabia awaiting the arrival of the last of their equipment; even so, they would have a hard time finding it when it did arrive.

To have troops ready to fight as soon as possible after their arrival in Saudi Arabia, USAREUR sought host nation approval to transport ammunition in the ready racks of tanks and to carry a basic load of small arms ammunition in vehicles transported by barge. The German, Dutch, and Belgian authorities all quickly approved this exception to normal safety procedures. On 15 November HQ USAREUR/7A informed deploying units and the supporting 21st TAACOM that these host nations had authorized the shipment of small arms ammunition up to .50 caliber by rail to Nordenham and Bremerhaven in Germany and by road, rail, and barge to Antwerp and Rotterdam. USAREUR then also established weight limits, blocking and bracing requirements, and labeling and certification requirements for the transport of ammunition.[99] The next day General Saint informed Generals Vuono, Galvin, and Schwarzkopf that Antwerp, Bremerhaven, and Rotterdam would all accept tanks and Bradleys loaded with ammunition.[100] Toward the end of November, HQ USAREUR/7A instructed deploying units that other tracked vehicles, including self-propelled artillery (both 155-mm. and 4.2-inch) and the combat engineer vehicle, could also carry munitions.[101] These host nation authorizations, which were typical of the support given by the European allies in deploying U.S. forces to the Persian Gulf, substantially reduced American shipping requirements. In late November the Military Traffic Management Command began using as well the port of Eemshaven in the Netherlands, a secure and uncluttered harbor which could handle two ammunition trains per day.[102]

A network of personal contacts with host nation and allied government officials, military officers, and private citizens, built up over years of cooperation on REFORGER and other exercises, considerably smoothed the deployment process. These contacts made it possible for Generals Saint and Shalikashvili to obtain pledges of support from military, transport, and local officials within a day or two of their requests. These were not idle promises but specific offers of support, based on previous experience of what was needed gained from the earlier exercises. German transport authorities waived prohibitions on convoy travel on Sundays, and German defense officials provided Fox vehicles, heavy equipment tracked transport systems, ambulances, water transport vehicles, five-ton trucks, and other equipment. Dutch and Belgian military officials found port support facilities. The German, Dutch, Belgian, and Canadian Armies helped U.S. forces meet their transportation requirements, with the Dutch providing, at one point, 151 free rail cars.[103]

Soldiers from the 2d Armored Cavalry Regiment watch a ship bearing their equipment from Germany prepare to dock in Saudi Arabia.

These official actions, however, were a small part of the host nation support that contributed so much to the deployment. Probably the most inspiring and helpful host nation and allied support came from below rather than above. Members of host nation military units worked alongside their U.S. partnership units to load trucks and trains; some even used their own trucks to help their U.S. partners deploy.[104]

To bring VII Corps' equipment deployment to a successful conclusion, USAREUR also had to provide support for off-loading the ships that carried the corps' equipment to Saudi Arabia. This required a difficult decision by General Saint, who was still trying to maintain the drawdown schedule he had proposed before the Iraqi attack. Saint first approved sending the 4th Battalion, 16th Infantry Brigade, 1st Infantry Division (Forward), which was scheduled to inactivate in May 1991, to act as stevedores unloading corps equipment in Saudi ports. On 22 November 1990, Brig. Gen. John R. Landry, VII Corps' chief of staff, formally proposed sending the soldiers of the same brigade's 3d Battalion, 34th Armor, to Saudi ports as well. This battalion was scheduled for inactivation by March 1991, and its deployment would probably delay

that inactivation. General Saint nevertheless approved sending both battalions, thus providing the soldiers needed to off-load five ships simultaneously at each Saudi port. Under the direction of Brig. Gen. William
J. Mullen III, the commander of the 1st Infantry Division (Forward),
Task Forces 4–16 at Ad Dammam and 3–34 at Al Jubayl unloaded 152
ships containing 50,500 pieces of equipment and provided housing,
food, and other basic needs for 107,000 soldiers who were waiting for
or receiving shipments of their equipment. The two task forces of the 1st
Infantry Division (Forward) would complete this mission, which it
called Operation DESERT DUTY, and return to Germany in mid-February
to continue drawing down.[105]

Personnel Movement

During the same Thanksgiving week when General Laposata moved to
Stuttgart to guide the movement of equipment, Generals Saint,
Shalikashvili, and Heldstab made a careful review of the plans and
mechanics of moving personnel to Southwest Asia. One product of this
review was General Saint's decision to send his operations chief, General
Heldstab, to Stuttgart to set up an air movement control center with a
mandate to get it running by Monday, 26 November. There was a pressing need for an operational center to plan, coordinate, and monitor all
movement of personnel by air between Europe and Saudi Arabia. All
available logisticians in USAREUR headquarters were then working on
equipment movement to cover for the corps planners and logisticians,
who were working on preparing for the campaign ahead. Col. Gerald E.
Thompson, the deputy community commander in Heidelberg, had
shortly before proposed to General Shalikashvili, the Heidelberg community commander and deputy commander in chief, the concept of
establishing an air movement control center to coordinate and oversee
the air movement of personnel. The idea was derived in part from
Colonel Thompson's experience as the supply officer (G–4) of the 82d
Airborne Division. Thompson and Shalikashvili had briefed the concept
to Generals Saint and Heldstab, and Saint approved. The weekend after
Thanksgiving, General Heldstab moved to Stuttgart to organize and
oversee the air movement operation, and he asked Colonel Thompson to
head the air movement control center.[106]

Collocated in Stuttgart with HQ VII Corps, the air movement control center grew to number 140 personnel, who manned the center
around the clock. It was organized in six deployment teams and some
additional functional cells, and it included representatives of various air

deployment agencies. Each deployment team consisted of two officers and two noncommissioned officers, split into day and night shifts. Each team was responsible for coordinating the movement of the personnel of a major VII Corps unit. The additional cells were responsible for overall planning and the coordination of specific functions or programs. A Long Range Planning Cell, for example, worked with the Joint Operations Planning Execution System, the Worldwide Military Command and Control System, the corps, and the movements control center to develop personnel deployment plans well in advance. Serving with the air movement control center were representatives of the Military Airlift Command, V Corps, VII Corps, and 21st TAACOM, including a liaison officer from the departure airfield control groups operated by V Corps. However, the only two logisticians on board were the 37th Transportation Group commander and one of his battalion commanders, who helped arrange buses and trucks to get deploying soldiers and their baggage from their European stations to the airfields.[107]

From the first flight on 1 December 1990 to the last on 9 January 1991, the air movement control center scheduled flights to Saudi Arabia for over 71,500 soldiers. During the first two weeks of their operation, its staff members analyzed the steps involved in air deployment from home unit to Saudi Arabia, established procedures to get the soldiers moving, and deployed the first VII Corps soldiers according to the corps' priorities. The U.S. Air Force established four aerial ports of embarkation, its Rhein Main and Ramstein Air Bases and the German commercial airports at Hamburg and Stuttgart, with an alternate for the former at the Cologne/Bonn airport and for the latter at Nuremberg/Ingolstadt airport.[108] As planned, V Corps was tasked with establishing departure airfield control groups at all aerial ports of embarkation that lacked them, and the departure airport control group that 21st TAACOM had established during the earlier deployment was placed under the operational control of V Corps. The departure airfield control groups were run by the 3d Corps Support Command's 8th Maintenance Battalion at Rhein Main, 19th Maintenance Battalion at Hamburg, 85th Maintenance Battalion at Nuremberg, 181st Transportation Battalion at Stuttgart, and by the 21st TAACOM's 29th Area Support Group at Ramstein.

Although some problems arose, personnel movement was a major success. The 21st TAACOM's 37th Transportation Group used approximately 1,700 vehicles, including buses, to move soldiers and trucks to carry their accompanying clothing and personal equipment from their European stations to airports with an on-time record of over 99 percent. Every available type of aircraft was used in the deployment, including commercial 747s, DC–10s, and L1011s; Air Force C–5s; and Navy C–9s.

USAREUR soldiers waiting in a warehouse in Saudi Arabia for their equipment to arrive by ship

Later, when the demand for wide-bodied aircraft to carry troops based in the United States increased, the Air Force drew upon its many C–141s. The wide-bodied aircraft flew on schedule 77 percent of the time and the C–141s about 83 percent of the time.[109] Although the Air Force agreed to give the 37th Transportation Group at least twenty-four hours' notice before arrival of each aircraft to allow soldiers some time with their families after being notified of the time of their departure, this could not always be arranged.[110] However, there were no accidents and no unsolvable problems. Departures peaked during the period 24–26 December, when over 9,000 soldiers left for the war. On 9 January 1991, six days ahead of schedule, the air movement control center saw the last VII Corps soldiers deploy to Saudi Arabia. Its personnel then returned to their normal units of assignment.[111]

While the movement of personnel had run much more smoothly than the shipment of equipment, it had also encountered some problems. At the end of November, as the demand for aircraft escalated everywhere, General Saint found it necessary to appeal for additional airlift.

Simple arithmetic showed that at the current rate USAREUR would not be able to deploy the VII Corps to Southwest Asia by 15 January 1991. Moreover, Saint wished to avoid the need to fill every seat every day, as he preferred to tie departures to the anticipated arrival of ships in Southwest Asia.[112] In planning and scheduling personnel deployment, the air movement control center closely monitored equipment sailings in an effort to match the arrival of soldiers by air with the arrival of their equipment by sea.[113] This effort implemented a USAREUR policy promulgated on 10 November 1990, whereby personnel departure dates were aimed at getting soldiers to Southwest Asia one day before the ship carrying their unit's equipment would arrive. Unfortunately, this was not always possible.[114]

Deployment Success

The deployment was a success overall because USAREUR soldiers and equipment arrived in time and in shape to play a major role in the ground war. The administrative procedures, problem solving, and other assistance provided by HQ USAREUR/7A created only the preconditions for a successful deployment. The credit for the success of so many USAREUR units in moving their equipment from home station to sea and aerial ports and onto ships and planes before 20 December 1990 and all deploying soldiers to Saudi Arabia before 10 January 1991 should go primarily to the commanders and soldiers of the deploying units and of the units that immediately supported them.

Through the combined efforts of USAREUR units at all levels and soldiers from private to general, VII Corps moved its equipment to the ports by 20 December 1990, just forty-two days after its deployment was announced. The 21st TAACOM then closed its rest and life support areas and reduced the manning of its tactical operations centers to the minimum necessary to respond quickly to sensitive sustainment missions.[115] Many elements of USAREUR supporting the deployment could go home for the holidays, knowing they had accomplished their mission. Others, like the soldiers of the 3d Infantry Division acting as stevedores at the port of Bremerhaven, were released to their home stations in early January.[116] The soldiers of the 1st Infantry Division (Forward) serving at the ports in Saudi Arabia would return to Germany in February.[117] The VII Corps soldiers moved into position for the combat ahead.

The deployment showed that a forward-based, enhanced, corps-size force could move quickly to meet contingencies even in another theater. Over 70,000 USAREUR personnel deployed by air to Saudi Arabia in

*A soldier directs the first of the 2d Armored Cavalry Regiment's
M1A1 tanks off a ship in Saudi Arabia.*

November and December 1990. Aerial ports of embarkation at Rhein
Main, Nuremberg, Stuttgart, Hamburg, and Ramstein (in order of use)
handled 437 flights.[118] *Table 5* shows the number of personnel in each
major USAREUR unit that deployed to Southwest Asia and the number
retained in Europe as of 31 December 1990. Subsequent deployment of
echelon-above-corps units, Patriot missile batteries, and squad, crew, and
team replacements would bring the total number of USAREUR troops
that deployed to Southwest Asia by the beginning of the ground war to
over 78,000—the equivalent of seventy-eight battalions.

This deployment involved the transport of over 30,000 pieces of
equipment, including 19,800 wheeled vehicles; 5,200 tracked vehicles;
almost 3,000 containers; and over 23,000 tons of unit ammunition. This
massive cargo movement used the varied transportation modes available
in Central Europe. USAREUR moved 45 percent by train, 35 percent by
barge, 19 percent by convoy, and 1 percent by air. Long, hard, and competent work by USAREUR soldiers; intensive management of the over-
land deployment process; and valuable host nation support combined to
get the corps to port on time. The shipment of VII Corps equipment

from Europe to Saudi Arabia required 6.94 million square feet of cargo space on 105 ships. Of these, 36 ships sailed from Rotterdam, 29 each from Antwerp and Bremerhaven, 10 from Nordenham, and 1 from Eemshaven. Ship transit time ranged from 11 to 45 days and averaged about 17 days for large ships and over 22 days for small ships. The last ship carrying VII Corps equipment arrived in Saudi Arabia on 7 February 1991, ninety days after the presidential announcement of its deployment.[119]

In General Saint's opinion, the deployment operation was successful precisely because HQ USAREUR/7A did not tell commanders and their soldiers how to deploy; it simply gave them the mission. Nevertheless, USAREUR analysts also concluded that HQ USAREUR/7A should be responsible for future strategic deployments of the full corps, while corps headquarters should be responsible for deployments of division strength and below, whether in support of unilateral or NATO missions. In corps deployments, HQ USAREUR/7A responsibility would ensure that the corps could concentrate on reception, onward movement, and the mission assigned in the employment area.[120]

TABLE 5—USAREUR ASSIGNED TROOPS STRENGTH, 31 DECEMBER 1990

Unit	Remaining in USAREUR		Deployed to CENTCOM	
	Authorized	Assigned	Authorized	Assigned
32d AADCOM	9,338	8,863	2,462	2,780
3d Bn (Air Traffic Control), 58th Avn	605	412	0	161
AFCENT Reserve Corps	90	97		
2d AD (Fwd)	99	422	4,010	4,441
U.S. Army, Berlin	3,836	3,406		
V Corps (non div)	27,894	23,558	5,931	6,160
11th ACR	4,666	4,598		
3d AD	224	1,023	17,222	16,558
8th ID	15,704	13,738	909	967
VII Corps (non div)	2,217	2,812	17,089	16,497
2d ACR	0	159	4,745	4,609
1st AD	515	747	13,748	13,726
1st ID (Fwd)	4,406	2,361	98	1,151
3d ID	17,323	16,477	4,137	3,918
18th Engr Bde	2,529	2,081	830	828
Finance & Acctg Ctr	142	142		
56th Fld Arty Cmd	3,526	2,546		
7th Med Cmd	7,151	6,991	428	617

TABLE 5—USAREUR ASSIGNED TROOPS STRENGTH, 31 DECEMBER 1990 (CONT.)

Unit	Remaining in USAREUR		Deployed to CENTCOM	
	Authorized	Assigned	Authorized	Assigned
200th TAMMC	215	197		
42d MP Gp	624	653		
1st Personnel Cmd	643	714		
Postal Group	413	467	39	73
59th Ord Bde	6,321	6,009		
21st Repl Bn	0	8		
Seventh Army Tng Cmd	1,570	1,888		
26th Support Gp	778	872		
Special Forces Spt Units	500	492		
21st TAACOM	8,741	8,364	930	861
Misc Transport Units	458	420		
USASETAF	3,288	3,300		
USMLM to Soviet Forces	40	0		
HQ USAREUR/7A	1,094	1,260		
Other	0	115		
USAREUR Totals	124,950	115,077		
Non-USAREUR Totals	15,535	15,820		
Theater Totals	140,485	130,897		
USAREUR DESERT SHIELD Totals			72,578	73,347
Non-USAREUR DESERT SHIELD Totals			2,449	2,088
Theater DESERT SHIELD Totals			75,027	75,435
USAREUR Grand Total			197,528	188,424
Non-USAREUR Total			17,984	17,908
Theater Grand Total			215,512	206,332

Source: USAREUR Authorized/Assigned report, troop strength by command code, 31 Dec 90, 1st Personnel Command, RPT ID No. 403210–01/RCS CSGPA–1140; *HQ USAREUR/7A Historical Review, 1990–1991*, Table 14, p. 159.

Chapter 6

Additional Deployments and Sustainment Support

Follow-On or Add-On Force Packages

Even while focusing on the massive task of deploying the VII Corps, USAREUR attempted with considerable success to meet ARCENT requirements for additional forces. General Saint's attitude was that USAREUR would provide additional support to ARCENT, if possible, but he wanted verification that Forces Command did not have the needed units available before he would provide units or personnel that might reduce below minimum standards the readiness or capabilities of the units remaining in Europe. During November and December 1990 USAREUR continued to schedule the deployment of echelon-above-corps units and personnel in addition to deploying VII Corps. After 20 December, when the last corps equipment reached port, and especially after 9 January, when the last corps personnel left for Saudi Arabia, USAREUR concentrated again on providing support in the specific areas where ARCENT's unmet needs were greatest. The last of the follow-on units left Europe on 28 January 1991.

USAREUR's most substantial follow-on contribution came in the form of two engineer combat battalions, one of which was drawn from USAREUR's 8th Infantry Division. The two signal battalions in the follow-on package brought with them significant communications capabilities. The 63d Signal Battalion was trained and equipped to install, maintain, and operate the multifaceted communications facilities required by a theater headquarters, including telephone switching centers and teletypewriting, facsimile transmission, and radio communications. USAREUR also provided in the follow-on package a signals intelligence company trained to intercept enemy communications, a Chinook heli-

copter company, and two additional heavy truck companies. The units
that comprised USAREUR's follow-on force package are listed in *Table 6*
with the exception of special task forces, replacement crews, and additional air defense, which will be discussed separately.[1]

TABLE 6—FOLLOW-ON FORCE PACKAGE

Unit	Personnel
Company B, 6th Battalion, 158th Aviation (CH–47)	67
12th Engineer Battalion (Heavy Division)	767
54th Engineer Battalion (Combat) (Mechanized) (Corps)	714
Company A, 204th Military Intelligence Battalion (Signals Intelligence)	169
44th Signal Battalion (Area) (Corps)	460
63d Signal Battalion (Theater) (Command Operations)	438
2d Transportation Company (Heavy Truck)	143
377th Transportation Company (Heavy Truck)	138
326th Transportation Detachment (Trailer Transfer Point)	16
Total	2,912

Source: Briefing slide, Ops Div, ODCSOPS, HQ USAREUR/7A, 21 May 91, sub: United States
Army, Europe, Contributions to the Victory in the Gulf.

Joint Task Force Proven Force

The deployment of very substantial U.S. and allied forces to Saudi Arabia
in the fall and winter of 1990 and 1991 was accompanied and followed
by smaller, related operations, to some of which USAREUR also made
significant contributions. In early January 1991, for example, the North
Atlantic alliance's Defense Planning Council decided to deploy to Turkey
the more than forty German, Belgian, and Italian fighter jets that comprised the air component of the Allied Command, Europe (ACE), Mobile
Force. This would be the first deployment ever of the ACE Mobile Force
(Air), and it raised the possibility that ACE Mobile Force (Land) might
be deployed, which would entail substantial USAREUR responsibilities.[2]

Meanwhile, in the late fall of 1990, the U.S. Air Forces in Europe had
helped develop a plan to establish a multinational force in Turkey to
deter hostilities against that nation and, in the event of war, to reinforce
Turkish defense and conduct multinational operations in northern Iraq.
For these purposes, on 23 December 1990, General Galvin, who was
both the United States Commander in Chief, Europe, and NATO's
Supreme Allied Commander, Europe, established Joint Task Force (JTF)
Proven Force. Commanded by USAFE's Deputy Chief of Staff for

Operations, Maj. Gen. James L. Jamerson, the task force comprised primarily USAFE tactical air forces in Turkey; it also included a joint special operations task force and Army and Navy elements stationed in or sent to Turkey. Under JTF PROVEN FORCE's charter, USAREUR assumed responsibility for providing medical support and psychological operations staff to the joint task force and for coordinating the handling, processing, and repatriation of its detainees.[3]

Through the rest of December and early January, USAREUR made plans to provide additional logistical and technical support to the special operations portion of PROVEN FORCE and in particular to the American combat search and rescue teams, known under the operational name of ELUSIVE CONCEPT, that were created to carry out personnel recovery operations in northern Iraq. CINCUSAREUR exercised command, less operational control, of deployed Army special operations forces through the commander, 21st TAACOM. Under the commander, JTF PROVEN FORCE, the commander, Joint Special Operations Task Force–Europe (JSOTFE), exercised operational control of these forces. USAREUR would deploy the 1st Battalion, 10th Special Forces, to assist in these special operations efforts. Under the provisions of the USCINCEUR operation plan for PROVEN FORCE, General Saint tasked the commander, 21st TAACOM, to support JSOTFE headquarters and its elements at forward staging bases in Turkey. To do the work, the 21st TAACOM reorganized the 66th Maintenance Battalion into a forward support battalion and placed it under the operational control of 21st TAACOM's 7th Special Operations Support Command. The battalion would provide supply, transportation, and direct support maintenance to the special operations effort. USAREUR also deployed the 324th Signal Company to provide communications support.[4]

After these deployments were officially approved by the Turkish government, ACE Mobile Force (Air) deployed to Turkey on 13 January, and components of JTF PROVEN FORCE deployed from 14 to 25 January. Meanwhile, on 13 January 1991, USAREUR received an order from the secretary of defense, sent through USEUCOM, to deploy as soon as possible two Patriot missile firing units to Incirlik, Turkey, to support JTF PROVEN FORCE. The leaders of the 32d AADCOM and USAREUR decided to deploy the battalion headquarters and two firing batteries of 4th Battalion, 7th Air Defense Artillery. The battalion's advance party left for Incirlik on 14 January, and the firing batteries followed soon after.[5] The beginning of the air war on 17 January and the more pressing need to provide emergency Patriot support to Israel, which was attacked by Iraqi Scud missiles, delayed completion of the Patriot fielding in Turkey, however, until 25 January.[6]

Task Force PATRIOT DEFENDER

Within thirty hours of the start of the air offensive portion of Operation DESERT STORM at 0001, 17 January, Greenwich Mean Time, Iraq retaliated with Scud missile attacks against targets in Israel and Saudi Arabia. Iraq's missile attack on Israel, a noncombatant in the Persian Gulf War, was apparently calculated to bring that nation into the war and thereby undermine Arab support for the international alliance against Iraq. Whatever the likelihood that this Iraqi plan would split the coalition opposing it, the immediate reinforcement of Israel's air defenses with the best available air defense weaponry appeared vital both to defend Israel and to deter it from entering the war. The demonstration by USAREUR, its 32d AADCOM, and supporting commands of the ability to establish a Patriot firing capacity in Israel within twenty-six hours had a significant impact. While it did not create an invincible barrier against missile attack, USAREUR's Patriot deployment undoubtedly helped retain Israel's cooperation and thus protected the alliance against Iraq. It is necessary to recount some of the background to understand this noteworthy deployment success.

By mid-January 1991, USAREUR had substantial experience in deploying Patriot missile battalions by sea. USAREUR had deployed the four Patriot batteries of the 8th Battalion, 43d Air Defense Artillery, with VII Corps. In early January, USAREUR sent the four batteries of the 2d Battalion, 43d Air Defense Artillery, to defend the Hafar al Batin and King Khalid Military City in Saudi Arabia. The 59th Ordnance Brigade had loaded both battalions on rail cars for shipment to port. Although the 2d Battalion, 43d Air Defense Artillery, was an echelon-above-corps air defense asset, it had suffered the same shipping problems as VII Corps units had experienced earlier. Its equipment was loaded on seven different ships.[7]

The USAREUR air defense artillery battalions that were sent to Southwest Asia there joined two Patriot battalions that had deployed from the United States—the 2d Battalion, 7th Air Defense Artillery, and the 3d Battalion, 43d Air Defense Artillery—in providing land-based air defense in the region under the direction of the 11th Air Defense Artillery Brigade. Only a single Patriot training battalion remained in the United States during the Gulf War.[8] Although General Saint would not allow the staff of the 11th Air Defense Artillery Brigade to inquire directly of his 32d Army Air Defense Command staff about the readiness of USAREUR Patriot battalions, he directed that the HQ USAREUR/7A Crisis Action Team quickly provide the air defense artillery parts requested by ARCENT.[9]

Soldiers of the 6th Battalion, 43d Air Defense Artillery, prepare a Patriot launching station during training in Ansbach, Germany, 28 January 1991.

Although the huge, complicated, and high-tech components of the Patriot air defense missile system, including launchers, generators, and communications equipment, had not been designed for air deployment, USAREUR planning for such an eventuality, beginning in late December, helped the 32d AADCOM get a quick start on deployment to Israel the following month. On 2 January 1991, General Saint decided to alert for deployment at least one additional Patriot battalion, the 4th Battalion, 43d Air Defense Artillery.[10] On the same day General Shalikashvili received two different estimates of the airlift requirements for deploying such a battalion and asked the 32d AADCOM to reconcile them.[11]

According to General Shalikashvili, General Saint sensed that Patriot missile battalions would be required shortly as the talk of Scud attacks increased.[12] In the days before the air war began, General Saint asked General Putman to keep some Patriot battalions in a high state of readiness so that they could move out very quickly.[13] Putman ordered some of his Patriot batteries to be ready to deploy at air departure sites on twelve hours' notice. According to Saint, "We tried to do it so that a) we got ready, but b) we didn't harass the troops by keeping them lying around the barracks. So I had different lengths of string." Saint concluded that Putman did an extremely good job on both counts.[14]

Just hours after the Iraqis fired their first Scud missiles at Israel on the night of 17–18 January, the American Joint Chiefs of Staff issued a deployment order to U.S. Army Forces Command to send Patriot maintenance and support personnel to Israel. The order did not mention the deployment of firing batteries.[15] Only in the very late afternoon of 18 January, Central European Time, did the Joint Staff first order USAREUR to deploy Patriot missiles and crews to Israel.[16] About 1800 that day General Shalikashvili instructed General Putman to deploy two Patriot batteries to Israel; the units were formally alerted at 1900. Deployment started immediately. Within five hours of their notification, two batteries of the 4th Battalion, 43d Air Defense Artillery, were on their way to the airfield. At 0635 on 19 January the first aircraft with USAREUR Patriot personnel and equipment took off for Israel. The first of the battalion's Patriot firing units was ready to defend the skies over Tel Aviv at 2045 that evening, within twenty-six hours of its unit's deployment alert.[17]

USAREUR Patriot crews in Israel remained under the control of the United States European Command. The 32d AADCOM's 10th Air Defense Artillery Brigade headquarters at Darmstadt, Germany, remained responsible for the command, task assignment, training, logistics, and personnel requirements of the deployed elements of the 4th Battalion. The 10th Air Defense Artillery Brigade handled all contacts for the battalion with the Israeli Defense Forces. General Galvin and his United States European Command staff were responsible for providing mission direction, assuring operational status, and processing situation and engagement reports. The American Patriot missile crews not only operated their own firing units but also helped or trained Israeli personnel to operate their Patriot systems.[18]

Members of the 1st Battalion, 7th Air Defense Artillery, at Rhein Main Air Base preparing to deploy to Israel with their equipment aboard a C–5 transport plane

USAREUR and 32d AADCOM monitored the performance and problems of Patriot missiles throughout the Gulf War, provided whatever support was needed by USAREUR air defense artillery units and other elements of the 11th Air Defense Artillery Brigade, and deployed additional Patriot batteries when required. *Table 7* lists the USAREUR Patriot units that deployed to Southwest Asia and Turkey. USAREUR deployed two firing batteries of a second Patriot battalion, the 1st Battalion, 7th Air Defense Artillery, to Haifa, Israel. This was accomplished within twenty-four hours on 25 and 26 January; at the same time USAREUR was completing the deployment of the 4th Battalion, 7th Air Defense Artillery, to Turkey. Overall, USAREUR deployed 648 personnel manning 32 launchers to Israel and 471 personnel manning 16 launchers (as well as providing maintenance and support) to Turkey, in addition to the 9 batteries sent to Saudi Arabia. USAREUR sent most of its limited supply of advanced Patriot missiles (PAC II) to Israel and Saudi Arabia where they were sorely needed. Units in Turkey had only a few PAC II missiles, but USAREUR was prepared to move more of the advanced missiles there from other units in Southwest Asia if required. From 2 through 7 February, another USAREUR Patriot battery from the 1st Battalion, 7th Air Defense Artillery, was deployed to Saudi Arabia. By the start of the ground war, USAREUR had deployed 15 Patriot batteries and 4 of its 7 battalion headquarters; 9 batteries remained in USAREUR, some without battalion headquarters, some already in the advanced stages of drawing down, and some committed to the defense of air bases. USAREUR retained less than a seven-day supply of Patriot missiles.[19]

TABLE 7—DEPLOYMENT OF USAREUR PATRIOT BATTALIONS AND BATTERIES

| Battalions | | Deployment Dates | | |
(Batteries)	Destination	Start	Completed	Personnel
Task Force 8–43 ADA (HHC, 4 btry)	Saudi Arabia VII Corps	1 Dec 90	18 Dec 90	942
2–43 ADA (HHC, 4 btry)	Saudi Arabia EAC package	24 Dec 90	5 Feb 91	702
4–7 ADA (HHB, 2 btry)	Turkey PROVEN FORCE	15 Jan 91	29 Jan 91	471
4–43 ADA (HHB, 2 btry)	Israel PATRIOT DEFENDER	19 Jan 91	22 Jan 91	514
1–7 ADA (A and B btry)	Israel PATRIOT DEFENDER	25 Jan 91	26 Jan 91	134
(D btry)	Saudi Arabia EAC Package	2 Feb 91	7 Feb 91	88
			Total	2,851

Sources: Task Force 8–43 ADA: CFE Div, ODCSOPS, HQ USAREUR/7A, computer data and *32d Army Air Defense Command Annual Historical Review, 1990*; other units: Chart, Doctrine, Concepts, and Analysis Div, ODCS74OPS, HQ USAREUR/7A, USAREUR DESERT STORM and DESERT SHIELD Theater-Level Observations, Feb 92.

Crew and Individual Replacements

USAREUR provided individual replacements for VII Corps soldiers who were medically evacuated as well as individual and crew replacements throughout the USCENTCOM theater. It made the decision to provide individual replacements to VII Corps even before all VII Corps soldiers had departed for Southwest Asia, although this responsibility had not been self-evident initially. On 5 January General Burleson asked General Heldstab what replacement system existed for the seventy-two VII Corps soldiers who had already been evacuated from Southwest Asia.

At the O&I meeting the following day General Saint announced that USAREUR would provide replacements for heavy forces in Southwest Asia, and he asked his staff to find out what training individual ready reservists were receiving in the United States both as replacement crews and individuals before being sent to USAREUR.[20] He wanted to evaluate whether to use these reservists as replacements for evacuated VII Corps soldiers.

On 11 January 1991, HQ USAREUR/7A published an operation order for providing individual and crew replacements to ARCENT. The commander's goal in approving this order was to meet ARCENT requirements for weapons crew replacements by making available currently trained platoons prepared for immediate overseas movement.[21] Under this order USAREUR would send active Regular Army crews first and later prepare, train, and deploy to Southwest Asia Army Reserve personnel to form a ready reserve of platoon, squad, crew, and individual replacements. General Saint directed V Corps to send the initial replacement squads and crews to Southwest Asia by 30 January. For this purpose, the V Corps commander was authorized to reduce his residual end-state units to 80 percent of authorized manning and non–end-state units to 65 percent without CINCUSAREUR approval. The V Corps commander was tasked to brief CINCUSAREUR on how his command would meet requirements to provide replacement crews for Bradley fighting vehicles, which were expected to reduce manning in V Corps Bradley units to nearly 50 percent of authorized manning. Saint expected that individual reservists would arrive at V Corps from Training and Doctrine Command schools to receive two weeks of training and then leave for Southwest Asia in two equal installments about 24 February and 26 March.

On 14 January 1991, General Maddox, the commander of V Corps, protested in a memorandum to General Saint that this replacement mission would prevent him from restoring the readiness of his units for further deployment to Southwest Asia or elsewhere and would undermine his broader training mission. He explained that providing the replacements would require drawing down critical units below the "floors" that General Saint had specified and would also conflict with Saint's goal of keeping at least a battalion-size force in each V Corps community. Maddox recommended that instead of executing the individual ready reservist training mission, entire combat-ready V Corps battalions be deployed to provide the required crew capabilities.[22] General Saint did not approve the suggestion.

At the end of January, as USAREUR prepared to send crew replacements to Southwest Asia from 31 January through 11 February, in line with an ARCENT reception and training plan, General Saint warned Generals Vuono and Galvin that the deployment was "tearing the heart out of the command." Saint told his superiors that drawing crews equivalent to four tank battalions and four Bradley battalions from well-trained and cohesive USAREUR units would leave each unit a "shadow of itself, even after personnel are replaced."[23] Nevertheless, USAREUR deployed 1,900 Regular Army personnel to ARCENT in the form of replacement crews. Although individual reservists were given the planned two weeks of training as crews in USAREUR and prepared for deployment to ARCENT, the reserve crews did not deploy.[24] The weapons systems personnel replacement operations worked successfully in Southwest Asia, but this outcome may be ascribed in part to the fact that additional crews were not needed due to the short duration of the ground war.

The USAREUR crews that deployed also experienced some serious problems. Over 75 percent of USAREUR replacement crew members interviewed said they were not accepted in their new units in Southwest Asia. Artillery crews were split up and assigned forward as individuals to full or overstrength units. Armor and infantry crews fared better and were assigned as crews to infantry or armor battalions.[25] Overall, V Corps provided ARCENT 390 replacement crews, comprising 1,900 soldiers, of the types shown in *Table 8* below:

TABLE 8—SUMMARY OF CREW REPLACEMENTS FOR ARCENT

Crew Type	Number of Crews Provided
M1	116
M2	108
M3	24
155-mm	24
203-mm	8
OH–58	10

Source: Briefing slide, Ops Div, ODCSOPS, HQ USAREUR/7A, 21 May 91, and ODCSOPS, USAREUR, Theater Level Observations, p. 8.

Ammunition Sustainment

USAREUR also made a vital contribution to the war effort by shipping to USCENTCOM a large portion of USAREUR's massive ammunition war reserves. The requested shipments were so large that they are difficult to describe in a meaningful way. In late October, when the deployment of

VII Corps was secretly being planned by a small group of USAREUR leaders, USAREUR received a USCENTCOM request for approximately 55,560 tons of ammunition. General Saint approved the request. The ammunition shipments were scheduled to take place in November and December, while USAREUR also deployed the corps. USAREUR would take the ammunition from war reserves maintained in Central and Southern Europe. The shipments would cause shortages in European war reserves of some projectiles, fuzes, and primers.

By 8 November USAREUR had moved 4,200 tons of the ammunition to port at Nordenham, Germany, using 240 rail cars dedicated to the mission by the German railway. In the middle of November the 21st TAACOM and 60th Ordnance Group struggled to deploy VII Corps equipment and USCENTCOM sustainment ammunition at the same time. The *Cape Farewell* loaded sustainment ammunition at Nordenham from 13 through 22 November. From its departure until 15 December, USAREUR shipped VII Corps equipment from the berth the *Cape Farewell* had occupied, but it continued ammunition sustainment shipments at another Nordenham berth and began to plan to dispatch more ammunition from Eemshaven, the Netherlands.[26]

It was not long before HQDA, the Army Materiel Command, and ARCENT increased their ammunition requests to the point where USAREUR recognized it lacked the capacity to ship these vast quantities of ammunition at the same time as it was attempting to move VII Corps units to Southwest Asia. It authorized ARCENT to requisition the difference between on-hand stocks and three normal loads for each unit, one to be loaded on its weapons systems, one in unit trains, and one in reserve stocks. The Army Materiel Command was to fill the requisitions from production or stocks on hand in the United States, to the extent they were available, and to pass to USAREUR or the Eighth United States Army in Korea the requisitions it could not fill. HQDA recognized that the transfer of some USAREUR items might "adversely impact" on USAREUR's mission and thus sought USAREUR comments. Nevertheless, on 21 November HQDA requested that USAREUR provide large additional ammunition quantities by 15 January 1991, the same day on which VII Corps deployment was to be completed.[27]

During the deployment of VII Corps, USAREUR gave sustainment ammunition a slightly lower priority for shipment. Only at the end of December could USAREUR logistics leaders turn their primary attention from VII Corps to meeting ARCENT's ammunition sustainment requirements. General Shalikashvili began to meet weekly with the key personnel involved, Generals Burleson, Laposata, and Tipton and Colonels Salyer and Andrew. Brig. Gen. Carl W. Tipton was the commander of the

*Members of the 184th Ordnance Company use a 10,000-pound-
capacity forklift to load 155-mm. howitzer ammunition at a
railhead in Muenster, Germany, for shipment to Saudi Arabia.*

200th TAMMC, and Col. Gary Andrew was his ammunition division
chief. Together these officers managed the movement of ammunition to
port, solving many serious problems along the way. They devised a complicated inland transportation plan, including convoys when necessary.
They worked with host nation authorities to expand port capabilities, to
arrange the complicated timing of the huge number of rail cars needed,
to secure additional loading and transportation support, and even to
acquire more ammunition from Germany. This group also helped establish an air bridge to Saudi Arabia for critical, high-priority ammunition,
including training ammunition for VII Corps.

The total ammunition requested for Southwest Asia sustainment
grew to 146,000 tons by the end of January, and the required delivery
date was adjusted to 15 March 1991. The delivery of the last VII Corps
equipment to port, on 20 December 1990, cleared the way to ship large
amounts of sustainment ammunition. Eleven trains of ammunition were
loaded and sent to ports between 21 December 1990 and 4 January
1991; the equivalent of six trainloads of ammunition sailed on 5 January
aboard the *American Shanti*. USAREUR's January ammunition shipments
peaked in the second and third weeks of the month. In the fourth week
of January, the shipment of Army ammunition dropped when USCENT-
COM changed its priorities to focus on replenishing its depleted Air
Force ammunition stocks. As the air war progressed it gave priority to
requests for the U.S. Air Forces in Europe to send a total of approxi-

mately 41,000 tons of sustainment ammunition. By 1 February, the Military Traffic Management Command, Europe, reported that it had dispatched 87,236 tons of sustainment ammunition for both Army and Air Force units from Ridham and Newport in the United Kingdom and Tombolo Dock in Italy, as well as from the four ports in Belgium, the Netherlands, and Germany.[28]

By the beginning of February General Shalikashvili and his sustainment ammunition management team had to admit they were behind schedule and needed to find new resources to complete the move of ammunition to Southwest Asia by 15 March. Additional ammunition had been added to the USCENTCOM request, and shipping priorities had changed, accounting in part for their being about a week behind. They were moving ammunition from forty-three ammunition supply points in USAREUR and needed to move an additional 500 tons per day beyond the 3,000 tons per day originally planned. The armed forces of Belgium, Canada, Germany, and the Netherlands were contributing substantially to moving the ammunition. The Dutch armed forces, for example, were loading and transporting 600 tons per day by truck.[29] By 19 February, the commander, 200th TAMMC, reported that USAREUR was back on schedule to make USCENTCOM's 15 March required delivery date.[30]

Using over 400 trains to carry to port average loads of nearly 550 tons each, USAREUR had, by the end of combat operations in the desert, shipped to ARCENT by boat a total of 207,872 tons of ammunition, including the types and total amounts shown in *Table 9*. In addition, USAREUR had shipped by air 2,168 tons of critically needed ammunition, as is also detailed below.[31]

TABLE 9—USAREUR AMMUNITION SHIPPED TO SOUTHWEST ASIA

By Ship	
Type	Amount in Rounds
Small Arms	40,000,000
Tank Ammunition	236,000
Mortar	69,000
Artillery	1,685,000
Mines	117,000
Pyrotechnics	175,000
Small Missiles	40,000
Multiple-Launch Rocket Systems	10,338
Demolitions	2,360,000
Patriots	322

TABLE 9—USAREUR AMMUNITION SHIPPED TO SOUTHWEST ASIA (CONTINUED)

By Air	
Type	Amount in Rounds
25-mm.	422,000
MICLIC	227
TOW Missiles	5,482
Copperhead Missiles.	840
Chaparral Missiles	572
120-mm.	2,160
40-mm.	223,000
165-mm.	1,500
2.75-inch	10,750
Patriot Missiles.	194
Hellfire Missiles	357

Source: HQ USAREUR/7A Historical Review, 1 Jan 90-31 Dec 91, pp. 269–70.

General Sustainment

The diversity of sustainment supplies and equipment USAREUR provided to Southwest Asia from November 1990 through March 1991 defies succinct description. *Table 10*, which lists the quantities of some of the most significant items provided, gives an indication of the size of that support. USAREUR sent, in addition, a wide variety of medical equipment; intelligence and communications equipment, including thousands of combat net radios; and even office furniture. It also sent floodlights, generators, tires, cots, maps, and steam cleaners.[32]

TABLE 10—SELECTIVE LIST OF SUSTAINMENT ITEMS PROVIDED BY USAREUR

Item	Quantity
Chemical Defense Kits and Related Items	1,063,000
Protective Masks.	2,000
M1A1 Tanks.	880
M60 Tanks With Dozer Blades	20
M2/M3 Bradley Fighting Vehicles	122
M113 Armored Personnel Carriers	37
HMMWVs	3,130
5-ton Cargo Trucks.	10
Heavy Equipment Transporters	24

Table 10—Selective List of Sustainment Items Provided by USAREUR (Cont.)

Item	Quantity
M880 Vehicles	73
Rough Terrain Forklifts	80
400-gallon Water Trailers	68
Laundry Trailers	16
M16 Rifles	38,000
Pistols	2,500
Fest Tents	103
Meals, Ready-To-Eat, cases	411,000
T-Ration Meals	2,404,980
Deployable Medical Systems	19

Source: Briefing slide, Ops Div, ODCSOPS, HQ USAREUR/7A, 21 May 91.

In addition to supplies and equipment provided from its own stocks, USAREUR was willing to pursue almost any avenue to fill critical USCENTCOM requirements. For example, General Shalikashvili, who oversaw contracting in USAREUR, approved use of a letter contract to speed the purchase and delivery of forty Czechoslovak heavy equipment transporters.[33] USAREUR regional contracting offices processed requirements for over 50,000 cots, most of which were delivered to ARCENT.[34] When operational maps became critically short, VII Corps probably had an advantage in that USAREUR had already decided to attach to the corps a direct support, topographical engineer unit that could produce maps. USAREUR also helped arrange the shipment of some equipment loaned by Germany in addition to the Fox equipment mentioned earlier; much of this equipment would help USCENTCOM meet its ground transportation requirements, as illustrated by the examples shown in *Table 11*:

Table 11—Examples of Loaned German Equipment

Equipment	Number	Equipment	Number
Trailer, 8-ton	120	Truck, repair	14
Tank hauler	59	Reefer	10
Water hauler	26	Truck, water	5
Fork lift	14	Battery charger	6
Trailer, reefer	66		

Source: Briefing summary, Maj. P. Phillips, SACO, OSGS, HQ USAREUR, 1 Apr 91, sub: O&I.

Soldiers of the 649th Engineer Battalion (Topographic) retrieving maps from the USAREUR map depot in Schwetzingen, Germany

Throughout the preparations for war, Generals Burleson and Frix, the USAREUR and ARCENT chiefs of staff, helped keep the massive sustainment support on track by discussing the supply situation over the phone almost every day. The efficiency of this support was also significantly increased by the establishment of a daily "Desert Express" air bridge between Rhein Main Air Base in Frankfurt, Germany, and Dhahran, Saudi Arabia, for very high priority cargo.[35]

Medical Support

In supporting Operation Desert Shield, USAREUR's 7th Medical Command confronted the need to perform four separate missions simultaneously. First, the 7th Medical Command would be responsible for providing medical care for evacuees from the Gulf during Desert Shield and for U.S. casualties during armed conflict there. Plans for this mission quickly transformed into fact when the first Desert Shield evacuee arrived in a USAREUR hospital on 12 August 1990. Later, the mission would include providing mortuary services, a function performed by USAREUR's U.S. Army Memorial Affairs Activity, Europe, and casualty reporting provided by the 1st Personnel Command. Second, the 7th Medical Command was quickly involved in August 1990 in deploying medical units and individual personnel to USCENTCOM. These personnel requirements would grow substantially during the following months as USAREUR worked to support an enhanced force for war. The 7th Medical Command deployed with VII Corps a reinforced 30th Medical Group, which included three hospitals, three ambulance companies, the 428th Medical Unit (Supply, Optical, and Maintenance), and a plethora of medical and dental detachments. A third sphere of activity for the 7th Medical Command was to provide medical supplies and equipment for Operation Desert Shield. By 31

December 1990, the medical command had shipped 2,722,865 pounds of Class VIII medical supplies valued at $19,348,408. Fourth, whatever happened in Southwest Asia, 7th Medical Command remained responsible for providing normal health care services to USAREUR personnel and family members in Europe. The plans that the 7th Medical Command developed in late October and November addressed all of these medical responsibilities and called for a threefold expansion of the command's normal peacetime medical care system.[36]

General Travis, the USAREUR chief surgeon and commander of the 7th Medical Command, submitted his initial medical plan to General Saint on 24 August 1990. USAREUR's initial share of USEUCOM's requirement to provide beds for evacuees from Southwest Asia was 1,760 beds. General Travis planned to devote

Sgt. Stephen Marquez, 128th Combat Support Hospital, readies an operating room tactical shelter drawn from USAREUR's theater reserves prior to its shipment to Saudi Arabia.

three existing medical facilities at Frankfurt, Landstuhl, and Nuremberg to care for these evacuees. He had already decided to cross-level personnel from peacetime medical assignments to support casualty operations that would ensue if there was a ground war. This would require the suspension of some medical services, such as surgery and pediatrics, for civilian employees and all family members, who would have to seek these services from host nation sources. Other services, such as emergency and outpatient treatment, could probably continue.[37]

The medical facilities that General Travis prepared to meet evacuation needs were all located near major airports. These were the 2d General Hospital at Landstuhl near Ramstein Air Base; the 97th General Hospital in Frankfurt near Rhein Main Airbase; and the 98th General Hospital in Nuremberg near Nuremberg Airport. Rhein Main and Ramstein Air Bases were already designated casualty evacuation aerial ports of embarkation, and USAREUR requested that USEUCOM give a similar designation to Nuremberg Airport in the event of hostilities in Southwest Asia.[38] The USAREUR chief surgeon's initial plans also specified the need for substantial augmentation of USAREUR medical units from the United States.

In early November 1990, as the 7th Medical Command's planners prepared to deploy medical units and personnel with VII Corps, its personnel outlook was bleak. According to the planners' calculations, at the end of October 1990 the units that should deploy with VII Corps were short 184 doctors, 56 dentists, 237 nurses, 94 medical service personnel, and 1,417 other personnel for a total personnel shortage of 1,988. These personnel would have to be obtained by 15 November 1990 in order to deploy to Southwest Asia on schedule. The planners also calculated that 7th Medical Command required an additional 1,591 health care providers by the start of ground operations to accomplish the medical support mission in Europe. To 7th Medical Command planners, the bottom line at this time was that VII Corps might deploy without full medical support, USAREUR might have inadequate personnel to meet the anticipated needs of casualty evacuees from a ground war, and the peacetime USAREUR health care system might fail.[39]

The 7th Medical Command, VII Corps, and USAREUR filled the shortfalls of medical personnel in the deploying units by cross-leveling medical and medical services personnel within USAREUR from nondeploying to deploying units. Except for one field hospital, VII Corps deployed to Southwest Asia medical units that were essentially full. This left the 7th Medical Command seriously short of personnel to perform its three missions of providing medical support to evacuees, sustainment for USCENTCOM, and normal peacetime medical care in Europe. To provide essential services in these areas, it was necessary to reduce some peacetime services at least temporarily, while filling vacancies as quickly and fully as possible.

USAREUR and the 7th Medical Command were well prepared to request and employ individual and unit replacements. The 7th Medical Command began to identify requirements and make requests for additional personnel in September, based on its need to treat evacuees from Southwest Asia as early as August, the early deployment of 45th Medical Company (Air Ambulance), and early planning to deploy a substantial number of USAREUR combat units. The USAREUR and 7th Medical Command staffs identified additional replacement requirements as they formulated plans to deploy VII Corps in late October. On 11 November 1990, USAREUR requested 1,374 personnel to restore peacetime health care in USAREUR and 1,645 personnel to expand its capacity to ensure 1,760 hospital beds would be available to treat evacuees from Southwest

Asia, including any casualties. Forces Command was able to identify ten U.S. Army Reserve and five National Guard medical units by 22 November, and their personnel, mobilized to report for duty at the end of the first week of December, began arriving in Europe as early as mid-December.[40] Appendix D lists the U.S. Army Reserve and National Guard units that served in USAREUR during the Gulf crisis.

The mobilized reserve and guard units included general and station hospitals; a mobile army station hospital; an air ambulance company; medical clearing companies; medical (blood) detachments; dental detachments; a veterinary detachment (food inspection); and a medical supply, operations, and maintenance unit. The personnel included physicians, including surgeons and various specialists, dentists, nurses, medics, technicians, and other support people.[41]

By the time these units began to arrive in Europe, the new USAREUR Chief Surgeon and Commander, 7th Medical Command, Maj. Gen. Michael J. Scotti, Jr., M.D., had worked out a plan to distribute the units and individuals throughout USAREUR to fill vacancies created by the deployed medical personnel and to build up the medical organization needed to treat and care for evacuees from Southwest Asia. Some of the incoming units were sent fully or in halves to replace deployed units or build up support for evacuees. Other units were split up even more finely to send individuals with specific specialties or skills to replace personnel with similar qualifications who had deployed to Saudi Arabia. To help ensure that all requirements were met, the Army Surgeon General's Office and Health Services Command provided USAREUR with an additional eighty-seven active duty physicians and fifteen active duty registered nurses from various Army medical facilities. The units and individuals filled medical needs in military facilities and communities throughout western Germany as well as in England, Belgium, Italy, and Turkey. The arrival of these units and individuals restored predeployment medical strength in USAREUR by early January 1991.[42]

The prompt arrival of Army Reserve and National Guard medical units meant that the curtailment of medical treatment and services for Army civilian personnel and family members, the initial and less satisfactory method of coping with reduced personnel and additional missions in the medical sphere, did not have to be employed extensively. General Scotti later reported that some communities apparently received curtailed services for a few weeks. Emergency care was managed individually, apparently by 7th Medical Command personnel, using either available American medical personnel or German medical personnel and facilities financed by the Civilian Health and Medical Program of the Uniformed Services (CHAMPUS).[43] Army Community Service and fami-

Army reservists assigned to the 7th Medical Command assembled in Heidelberg on 14 March 1991

ly assistance centers also helped family members use German medical services and facilities with CHAMPUS, when necessary.

By the end of the first week of January 1991, USAREUR had received 3,447 newly assigned medical personnel, and its leaders had begun to consider whether to ask for more. Except for several internists and twenty-seven pharmacy specialists, which USAREUR continued to request, these personnel provided the staff needed to restore USAREUR predeployment medical personnel strength and to make available 1,760 beds for evacuees. On 11 January 1991, as USAREUR was busily preparing to receive battle evacuees, USEUCOM reported that USCENTCOM had changed the USEUCOM evacuee mission to one of short-term care or "flow-through" care en route to hospitals in the United States. General Saint, however, rejected the change in mission, at least in the case of evacuated USAREUR soldiers, noting on the USEUCOM message, which he forwarded to Generals Shalikashvili, Burleson, and Scotti: "We determine who should be evacuated." USAREUR had already begun to develop plans to provide convalescent care to wounded USAREUR soldiers near their units and families and to expand services for nondeploying USAREUR patients at medical facilities not far from the hospitals that would be dedicated to the evacuees from Southwest Asia needing more intensive medical attention.[44]

The plan to keep USAREUR casualties who could be cared for in USAREUR hospitals as near their units and families as possible was one element of the campaign to convince military families to stay in Europe when their military members deployed to Southwest Asia. The overwhelming majority of the families of USAREUR soldiers who deployed to Southwest Asia in fact stayed in Europe. USAREUR planned to use the 2d General Hospital, Bremerhaven; 5th General Hospital, Bad Cannstatt; 34th General Hospital, Augsburg; 67th Evacuation Hospital, Wuerzburg; and 130th Station Hospital, Heidelberg, to provide convalescent care for returning USAREUR soldiers who were wounded in action or medically evacuated for other reasons, as well as to care for the general USAREUR population.

USAREUR and the 7th Medical Command recognized that casualties in the conflict with Iraq might require more than 1,760 beds, but, due to the uncertainty of what lay ahead, they made no further request to expand their medical facilities. At the end of January USAREUR again requested the internists and pharmacy specialists it needed and warned that additional requirements might be forthcoming, depending on the USCENTCOM battle plan and the number of casualties it expected.[45] Fortunately, additional medical staff proved unnecessary. The timely receipt and competent assignment of reserve component medical personnel not only limited the curtailment of services offered to USAREUR personnel and their families, but also meant that USAREUR and the 7th Medical Command were well equipped to fulfill their mission of providing medical care for the medical evacuees and later casualties from Southwest Asia.

Casualty Evacuation and Medical Treatment Operations

As a result of early planning and the work of medical replacements, reserves, and regular medical staff, USAREUR and the 7th Medical Command successfully provided the medical care needed by U.S. Army casualties and other Army medical evacuees from the USCENTCOM theater and the Persian Gulf War. Some 7,256 evacuees from Southwest Asia were treated in the three USAREUR hospitals dedicated to their care between 12 August 1990 and 4 August 1991 as shown in *Table 12*. Six of these evacuees died in USAREUR hospitals; none had been wounded in action. Of the 338 evacuees who had been wounded in action, 14 were women soldiers and 1 was a civilian employee. Of the 7,228 personnel evacuated from Southwest Asia to USAREUR hospitals by 1 August 1991, 4,446 (62 percent) were further evacuated medically to the

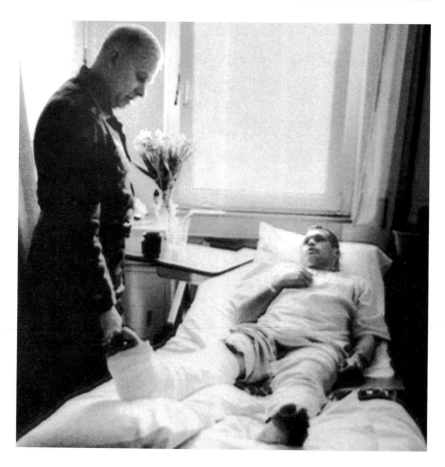

General Saint visits Specialist Jon Price, a VII Corps soldier wounded in Operation DESERT STORM, at the Landstuhl Army Regional Medical Center.

United States, 2,747 (38 percent) were returned to duty, 3 were absent without leave (AWOL), and about 30 remained in USAREUR hospitals.

USAREUR cared for its own personnel in hospitals near their assigned communities, if their families had remained in USAREUR and if those hospitals could provide the required medical care. Among the soldiers evacuated to U.S. Army hospitals in Europe, 1,411 were USAREUR soldiers, including 127 who had been wounded in action. Of the USAREUR soldiers evacuated, 1,086 (77 percent) were returned to duty in Europe and 308 (21 percent) were further medically evacuated to the United States. The USAREUR soldiers who were further evacuat-

ed were primarily unmarried soldiers or those with medically disabling illnesses or injuries. Families of soldiers in the latter category were authorized to move permanently to the United States, or, if the injuries were life threatening and the attending physician recommended it, to travel at government expense on emergency travel orders to the Army hospital in the United States.[46]

TABLE 12—EVACUEES TO USAREUR PRIMARY CARE HOSPITALS
12 Aug 90–4 Aug 91

	Nonbattle Injuries	Battle Casualties	Sex M / F	Deaths
Frankfurt	2,928	69	2,622 / 375	1
Landstuhl	3,091	208	2,986 / 313	5
Nuremberg	899	61	872 / 88	0
Total	6,918	338	6,480 / 776	6
Grand Total		7,256		

Source: Chart, Barbara Slifer, Public Affairs Ofc, 7th Medical Command, n.d.

Casualty Reporting Plan

USAREUR's role of caring for evacuees from Southwest Asia carried with it a requirement to provide reports to family members and to Washington in this highly sensitive area. Elements of the Department of the Army informed USAREUR's 1st Personnel Command in August 1990 that it should report to the appropriate medical facility in Europe the extent of injuries, wounds, or illness, together with other pertinent information on each individual evacuated from Southwest Asia. USAREUR was also asked to identify the remains of U.S. and allied personnel processed through the USAREUR mortuary system and to report the circumstances of soldiers' deaths and other pertinent data. This mission included providing full medical, casualty, and mortuary notification support. The 1st Personnel Command alerted General Burleson, the 7th Medical Command, and appropriate USAFE organizations of these taskings.[47]

General Saint asked General Willis to design a new casualty reporting system for USAREUR because, as with many other USAREUR functions, few of the peacetime procedures—or even those planned for wartime—currently applied. USAREUR's existing casualty reporting plans were based on the scenario of a European war before which families would have been evacuated to the United States. The casualty area commands established by those plans were based on areas of general courts-martial jurisdiction in USAREUR, and these had to be reshuffled due to the departure to Southwest Asia of many general officers responsible for overseeing courts-martial.

General Bean, who had taken command of the VII Corps rear area covering all of southern Germany, created instead casualty area commands headed by the four brigadier generals subordinate to him. Under the plan he and General Willis worked out, the 3d Personnel Command in ARCENT would make the initial notification to HQDA and 1st Personnel Command of soldiers killed in action, missing in action, or wounded in action. The 1st Personnel Command would confirm the arrival of evacuees or remains in Europe. It would also notify HQDA, the 3d Personnel Command, and the XVIII Airborne Corps, if appropriate, of any unreported evacuees. In all USAREUR cases, 1st Personnel Command would notify the appropriate casualty area command, which would inform the soldier's community and, through it, the soldier's unit.[48]

USAREUR needed to be able to track all patients, whether or not they had been serving in Europe, quickly and without error. The establishment of an adequately efficient and error-free reporting system posed substantial challenges whose resolution was vital to the command. USAREUR soldiers were far removed from the families in which they had been raised. Unofficial news traveled quickly, however, due to the availability of private means of communication and the sometimes rapid involvement of news media. Members of soldiers' families in the United States who might privately learn of casualties could quickly fly to Europe to visit them.

USAREUR undertook several initiatives to cope with this situation. It made the commanders of casualty area commands responsible for ensuring that communities in their areas notified and assisted next of kin. Communities established casualty working groups, which included representatives of all key family support activities. The 1st Personnel Command trained notifying officials and casualty assistance officers. The Office of the USAREUR Deputy Chief of Staff, Personnel, developed and distributed a community casualty assistance planning book and kit, which included handouts for family members that explained exactly how the casualty notification system would work.[49]

In order to carry out these USAREUR responsibilities, the 1st Personnel Command implemented a casualty reporting system that gave unaccustomed functions and capabilities to some USAREUR soldiers. Under this system enlisted personnel of the grade of sergeant, first class, and above were authorized to handle family notifications for any evacuee, whether an officer, enlisted soldier, or civilian employee. (Normally notifications were made by an official of the same rank or higher.) The 1st Personnel Command brought in ninety-five personnel to augment its own staff in tracking patients. It installed computers, facsimile machines, and telephones and provided staffing in eight Army and Air Force hospitals in Germany, the United Kingdom, Italy, and Spain to ensure that it obtained complete information on patients within four hours of their arrival in the hospital. It also staffed international airports in Germany with command personnel to help parents and other family members arriving from the United States to visit patients in USAREUR hospitals. If the family members could provide the patient's social security number, date and place of birth, or other specified personal identifying information, command representatives in the airports would tell them where they could find the patient. Along the same lines, USAREUR communities established family reception centers. USAREUR also planned for the worst case scenario. General Heldstab, the USAREUR deputy chief of staff, operations, was tasked to prepare a mass casualty/fatality operations plan for USAREUR to cope with large war casualties or a plane crash in which there were more than ten casualties in one USAREUR community.[50] Chapter 7 provides more details on community and family support for evacuees and their families.

General Saint cautiously supported the views of General Robert C. Oaks, Commander in Chief, United States Air Forces in Europe, that relatives of evacuees should be discouraged from traveling to Europe to visit them in USAREUR hospitals. Saint understood that many evacuees would be kept in European hospitals such a short time that visits would prove impractical. He expressed concern, however, that relatives might view such discouragement as deriving from reluctance to provide full information about sick or wounded relatives. Thus he recommended that the Department of Defense establish an "800" telephone line in the United States that would give relatives a realistic assessment of visit prospects, if they wanted to visit.[51]

USAREUR published its public affairs plan relating to DESERT STORM patients at the end of January 1991. The plan apparently had been delayed by disagreements with HQDA and USEUCOM over proposed language, which USAREUR leaders saw as usurping USAREUR prerogatives concerning the release of personal information about individual USAREUR casualties and related issues. Public affairs activities were to be handled through the normal chain of command, beginning with the doctor and hospital commander, and normal public affairs channels. Under the USAREUR plan, the public affairs staffs of the 7th Medical

Command and the three primary evacuee care hospitals were each provided with one additional public affairs officer and one or two additional public affairs noncommissioned officers. The rules and procedures contained in the plan were designed to allow media news coverage while carefully protecting the patients' welfare and privacy, as well as that of their next of kin. General Saint and his public affairs officer, Col. Paul W. Childress, decided that USAREUR would not release the names of USAREUR soldiers who were killed, wounded, or missing in action. They viewed this as a family matter and wanted to avoid making it a media spectacle.[52]

USAREUR and the 100-Hour Ground War

By the middle of February USAREUR had completed almost all preparations to support the ground war. USAREUR had provided an expanded, modernized, highly trained armored corps that General Schwarzkopf had selected to serve as his main armored attack force to drive north through Iraq, parallel to Kuwait's western border, and then turn east to attack the positions of the Iraqi Republican Guard. USAREUR had included in this corps the 1st and 3d Armored Divisions, the 2d Armored Cavalry Regiment, a Corps Support Command, and other corps-level combat support proportioned to support a robust four- or five-division force that could move rapidly hundreds of miles over the desert to fight and destroy a heavily armored enemy. USAREUR also contributed aviation brigades to both the VII and XVIII Airborne Corps. The latter corps would drive straight north through the desert, covering VII Corps' left flank. In addition USAREUR helped deploy with VII Corps the 2d Armored Division (Forward), which rounded out the U.S.-based elements of the 1st Infantry Division (Mechanized) to give it essentially the structure of an armored division. USAREUR also delivered vast quantities of supplies, equipment, and ammunition. In Europe, HQ USAREUR/7A organized medical care personnel and facilities to support both the air war and the ground war. HQ USAREUR/7A and the 1st Personnel Command also devised and put into place a casualty reporting system to provide information on hospitalized personnel to their family members.

Although USAREUR leaders and planners had prepared for and worried about a devastating and prolonged war with high U.S. casualties, rapid victory and departure from the Persian Gulf area were not entirely unexpected in USAREUR. On 15 February 1991, General Burleson told the O&I meeting at HQ USAREUR/7A that General Saint sensed that the

Army would be able to leave Southwest Asia very quickly and that the drawdown might well resume very quickly as well. General Burleson observed in this connection that 70,000 soldiers could be leaving USAREUR in fiscal years 1991 and 1992. At the same time, Saint, Shalikashvili, Burleson, and the entire USAREUR military community would await the ground attack certain of their soldiers' and units' success, but fearful of the possible casualties, particularly in view of the substantial danger that Iraq would use chemical weapons.[53]

On 17 January 1991, the United States and its allies initiated Operation DESERT STORM with an air war that aimed at quickly destroying Iraq's Air Force and its air defenses, disrupting communications and the command and control of Iraqi ground units, and inflicting as much damage as possible to those ground forces before the opening of a coalition ground offensive. The 38-day air war was basically successful in attaining all three objectives, although a significant part of the Iraqi Air Force escaped physical destruction by taking refuge in Iran and the extent of damage to ground forces was debatable. The VII Corps' artillery contributed to the initial offensive by firing Army tactical missiles at Iraqi air defense sites.[54] On 18 January, the Iraqis retaliated against the air offensive with Scud missile attacks on Saudi Arabia and Israel. The objective of the latter attacks was to bring Israel into the war and thereby undermine Arab support for the coalition. USAREUR successfully helped calm Israel and other threatened coalition allies by quickly deploying Patriot air defense batteries to nations throughout the Gulf region, including Israel, Saudi Arabia, and Turkey.

As the air war progressed, the VII and XVIII Airborne Corps moved into position on the Iraqi border for the planned ground offensive, leaving the U.S. Marine Central Command and two coalition forces commands to their right, assigned to breach the border between Saudi Arabia and Kuwait. The VII Corps would grow to comprise one British and four American heavy divisions, four self-propelled artillery brigades, an armored cavalry regiment, a combat aviation brigade, and expanded numbers of combat service and combat service support units under an enlarged support command.[55]

The ground war was launched on 24 February. The two ARCENT corps, the U.S. Marine Central Command forces, and the eastern coalition command each breached the opposing Iraqi border defenses the first day. The XVIII Airborne Corps elements penetrated farthest against the scattered enemy forces they encountered in the Iraqi desert around As Salman, located more than one hundred miles west of the Kuwait border. While the American 1st and 3d Armored Divisions and 1st Infantry Division, leading the VII Corps attack, also encountered little opposition,

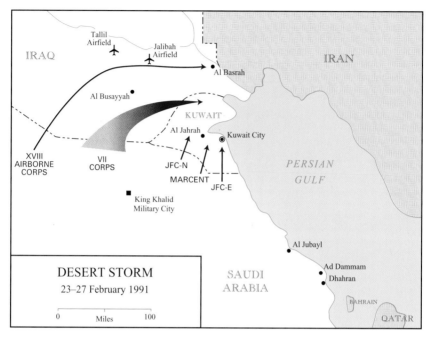

MAP 2

General Franks halted them on the evening of 24 February some twenty miles into Iraq. On 25 and 26 February the XVIII Airborne Corps continued north and northeast to Highway 8 in the Euphrates River valley and to the edge of Iraq's large Tallil and Jalibah Airfields.[56] (*Map 2*)

The VII Corps moved into position for its assault on the heavy Iraqi divisions in its zone somewhat more deliberately. On 26 February the 1st Armored Division advanced to and captured the town of Al Busayyah, Iraq, on VII Corps' left flank. Commanding over 1,500 tanks, 1,500 Bradley fighting vehicles and armored personnel carriers, and 600 artillery pieces, General Franks then swung his VII Corps east toward Kuwait, attacking Iraq's elite Republican Guard divisions that had turned to face this heaviest formation in the coalition drive. Engaging the enemy on the right of the VII Corps line, the 2d Armored Cavalry Regiment spent much of that afternoon fighting determined elements of Iraq's Tawakalna and 12th Armored Divisions in the four-hour "Battle of 73 Easting." Although outnumbered and outgunned, the 2d Armored Cavalry took merciless advantage of its superior thermal-imaging and laser range-finding systems to destroy at least twenty-nine tanks and twenty-four armored personnel carriers in this engagement. The regiment also took 1,300 prisoners. Farther north the 1st Armored Division's Task Force 1–37 Armor attacked the 9th Brigade of the Tawakalna Division. Although four tanks of the American task force were hit, the advancing American M1A1 tanks managed to kill seventy-six modern Soviet-built T–72 tanks, destroying in the process a force later judged to have been "the best equipped and most competent force in the Iraqi army."[57]

As the armor-laden VII Corps drove into Iraq's best equipped and most determined elements, the 2d Armored Division's 1st (Tiger) Brigade joined the 2d Marine Division on 26 February in pushing north across southern Kuwait to Al Jahrah, a western suburb overlooking Kuwait City and the open desert to the north. There, from Mutla Ridge, it could observe many enemy vehicles desperately attempting to flee to Iraq. The next day, the Marine command gave the Kuwaitis, Saudis, and Egyptians the honor of occupying the city.[58]

Meanwhile VII Corps, with four divisions now advancing abreast, continued to destroy the heaviest Iraqi formations as it entered northern Kuwait. Engaging five battalions in the assault, the American 1st Armored Division at dawn on 27 February pounded Iraq's T–72-equipped Medina Division in the largest tank battle of the war. By mid-afternoon, every weapon in the Medina Division's defensive positions, including more than 300 armored vehicles, had been destroyed or set ablaze. The Iraqis now ordered a full-fledged retreat toward Al Basrah on the Euphrates. Since the XVIII Airborne Corps, after capturing Jalibah and Tallil Airfields and advancing to the Rumaylah oil field, had not yet closed the escape route that ran north of Kuwait toward that Iraqi city, a number of Iraqi Army units that had avoided destruction managed to reach safety as the cease-fire declared by President Bush took effect on the morning of 28 February, timed to produce a "100-hour war."[59]

In terms both of its goals at the start of the fighting and American objectives in the war, VII Corps' attack into the main Iraqi forces defending the occupation of Kuwait was overwhelmingly successful. Franks' armored and mechanized divisions either destroyed or dispersed Iraqi defensive forces and their operational and tactical reserves. Although the campaign did not fully meet either Saint's vision of fluid mobile armored warfare nor Schwarzkopf's vision of a left hook, end run, and encirclement, the American forces did effectively rely on mobility, complicated and disciplined large unit maneuvers, and effective use of sophisticated technology. Typically, Franks' Abrams tanks destroyed Iraqi tanks before the American armored forces even appeared in the sights of the Iraqi tankers or entered the range of their guns. As the Defense Department later reported to Congress, the VII Corps estimated that in

A Soviet-built Iraqi tank destroyed during Operation Desert Storm

ninety hours of engagement it had destroyed 1,300 Iraqi tanks, 1,200 fighting vehicles and armored personnel carriers, and 285 artillery pieces. It had also captured nearly 22,000 enemy troops.[60] The emphasis in USAREUR training over the previous two years on long marches accompanied by full logistical support, disciplined and flexible maneuvers, and concentrated, devastating firepower surely contributed substantially to the success of VII Corps' desert operations.

During the ground war, a total of 148 U.S. soldiers were killed in action, and less than half of those losses were suffered on the armored battlefield. Despite these remarkably low U.S. casualties, USAREUR personnel paid a significant percentage of this most fundamental price of war because of the central combat roles their units played. As of 13 June 1991, twenty-three USAREUR soldiers had died in consequence of combat action; another twenty-six USAREUR soldiers had lost their lives through nonbattle causes in Southwest Asia. All of the twenty-three USAREUR soldiers killed in action had served in the enlisted ranks; four officers and twenty-two enlisted soldiers died of nonbattle causes. The nonbattle deaths included five resulting from ground vehicle accidents and four from land-mine detonations. Another four died from gunshot wounds, three from collapse of bunkers, three in unloading accidents, two in helicopter crashes, two with heart attacks, and one from viral infection; one soldier drowned while pursuing an intruder.[61]

The fact that VII Corps had not suffered heavier casualties either from fratricide or enemy fire in its long, broad sweep into Kuwait derived in part from General Franks' insistence on maintaining the integrity of his advancing line within his assigned area of responsibility. That insistence, however, left Franks vulnerable to charges by some military analysts that he had been slow off the mark in his breaching operations and swing east into the Republican Guard and thus had allowed some Iraqi units to retreat without being engaged. A number of analysts, however, focused their criticism on Schwarzkopf's overall strategic plan, observing that, despite the XVIII Airborne Corps' rapid drive north and east on VII Corps' left flank, it had been unable to advance fast enough to close the escape route north to Al Basrah by the time VII Corps had routed the Republican Guard forces anchoring Iraq's defenses on the western border of Kuwait. This, combined with the decisions to keep both corps south of the Euphrates River and to halt the attack after one hundred hours, left the envelopment incomplete and permitted the escape of significant numbers of Iraqi troops and equipment. Franks' corps had, nevertheless, clearly destroyed the strongest Iraqi forces that attempted to hold Kuwait and had achieved the critical objectives the United States' senior leaders and commanders sought from it far more rapidly than any of them had initially anticipated.[62]

During the ground war, USAREUR leaders and troops all craved accurate and detailed accounts of the progress of the fighting. As had also occurred earlier in Operations DESERT SHIELD and DESERT STORM, this craving seems to have been more often satisfied by the international television coverage of Cable News Network (CNN) than by official status reports. General Saint, who traveled to Washington during the ground war, undoubtedly provided USAREUR with some additional news, both on the fighting and on the decisions that surrounded it.

On 1 March 1991, General Saint returned from Washington. He joined the O&I on his arrival in Heidelberg to deliver a congratulatory victory speech to his staff. Saint reported that USAREUR's performance had won accolades in every department. He mentioned in particular compliments he received for the strength of training and squad leaders. He said it was clear that USAREUR had sent the right units.

General Saint directed General Burleson to appoint a major general to assemble an after-action report, which would include lessons learned. He underscored the command's responsibility to take care of the families of those killed or wounded in action. He also expressed concern about the availability of armed forces recreation centers for the use of returning soldiers and their families. Saint observed that history books teach that the Army usually loses control at the end of combat, and he addressed the issue of how to draw down in some detail. He concluded that the drawdown, combined with redeployment and ending the special measures required by war, was going to be confusing and warned his staff to "stay cool."[63]

Chapter 7

The Home Front

General Saint and his commanders faced a difficult and pressing task in reconstituting USAREUR at the same time that they helped deploy VII Corps and sent massive sustainment to USCENTCOM in Saudi Arabia. The task could not be delayed because USAREUR had important, continuing missions in Europe. Nondeploying, or residual, USAREUR units, soldiers, and civilian employees, while deploying and sustaining VII Corps and providing general support to USCENTCOM, also needed to restore USAREUR readiness and to maintain basic services and community life for U.S. military personnel in Europe. The last of these tasks had probably never been more difficult, for the American community now included over 32,000 families whose military sponsor or head of household was deploying to Southwest Asia. This task was complicated by the fact that many family members of deploying soldiers lived in military communities from which the largest and primary military units were deploying to Saudi Arabia. The families whose sponsors were deploying included almost 75,000 individuals remaining behind in Europe.[1]

Post-Deployment Community Demographics

Many of the families with absent military sponsors were concentrated in specific communities in southern Germany. *Table 13* provides deployment figures for the communities in Germany where the number of soldiers remaining dropped to 50 percent or less of predeployment totals. It also shows the number of individual installations within these communities at which less than 25 percent of the assigned soldiers remained. Nine installations in other communities in Germany—three in the Seventh Army Training Command, three in Frankfurt, and three in Hanau—were reduced below 25 percent.

Each of USAREUR's forty communities included a number of installations, many of them relatively small, scattered across an area of tens or hundreds of square miles. USAREUR aimed to maintain at least one battalion in every community to provide guard duty and other community support functions. This proved possible in all communities, although some subcommunities, such as Bindlach and Amberg, Germany, home to elements of the 2d Armored Cavalry, had to seek support from neighboring subcommunities. If 1991 drawdown plans for residual units had been fully carried out, most communities in the table below would have been reduced in personnel strength an additional 5 to 20 percent, the Mainz and Goeppingen communities would have fallen under 50 percent strength, and the number of installations with less than 25 percent of the currently assigned force would have risen from 34 to 46 installations.[2] In late October and early November, USAREUR planners had studied the impact on communities of deploying various units to Southwest Asia and had identified the communities and installations that would require extra attention and help during and after the departure of the units selected to deploy. (*Map 3*)

TABLE 13—COMMUNITIES REDUCED TO 50 PERCENT STRENGTH OR LESS BY DEPLOYMENT TO SOUTHWEST ASIA AND DRAWDOWN

Community	TOE+ Soldiers to SW Asia	TOE+ Soldiers Remaining	Percentage Remaining After Deployment & Inactivations	Number of Installations Under 25%
Ansbach	5,750	1,520	15	5
Aschaffenburg	3,750	450	25	2
Bamberg	5,460	1,550	25	2
Giessen	*	*	50	2
Heilbronn	2,330	1,290	25	2
Norddeutschland	*	*	45	1
Nuremberg	9,600	3,450	20	4
Stuttgart	7,180	3,040	50	7
			Total	25

*Figures not available.

+These figures include only soldiers assigned to numbered or lettered units organized under a table of organization and equipment.

Source: Tab B to encl 4 to interv, author with Jay, 20 Nov 90.

Family Members in USAREUR

General Saint encouraged families of soldiers deploying to Southwest Asia to stay in Europe, assuring them in a message issued on 14

USAREUR LOCATIONS
IN GERMANY
1990

0   Miles   100

BALTIC SEA

NORTH SEA

NETHERLANDS

POLAND

Berlin

Garlstedt

Friedberg
Frankfurt   Gelnhausen
Wiesbaden   Hanau
Aschaffenburg   Bindlach
Bad Kreuznach   Bamberg
Darmstadt   Wuerzburg   Grafenwoehr   CZECHOSLOVAKIA
LUXEMBOURG   Giebelstadt   Erlangen   Vilseck
Kaiserslautern   Heidelberg   Illesheim   Nuremberg   Amberg
Ansbach   Katterbach
Pirmasens   Heilbronn   Hohenfels
Karlsruhe

Stuttgart

Augsburg

FRANCE

AUSTRIA

SWITZERLAND

MAP 3

November 1990 that they were "vital to the lifeblood of our communities. They are the community." In the same message, General Saint argued that "Now, perhaps more than ever, is the time for you to remain in the home you have built for yourselves, and to take advantage of the familiar surroundings for yourself and children as well as the mutual support you can gain and give to others in similar situations." USAREUR leaders believed that they could provide families more comfortable conditions and better care than they would receive elsewhere. Relocating, particularly without the help of the family's sponsor, would impose severe additional pressure at an already tense and difficult time. USAREUR leaders also believed that family stability would be greater and readjustment easier if the families remained in Europe, in part because soldiers deploying to Southwest Asia would initially return there. At first, the leaders believed that personal communications with Southwest Asia would be faster from Europe than from the United States, although this did not always turn out to be the case. They were right, however, that family members would be better informed if they remained part of the support group of their sponsor's military unit and close to their friends and neighbors than they would be if they returned to their families in the United States.[3]

USAREUR also needed the family members. About 60 percent of civilian positions in USAREUR that were designated for American citizens were filled by military family members, as were about 40 percent of Department of Defense schoolteachers' positions. Family members were simply a vital element of the American military community in Europe.[4] They were part of their neighborhoods in military housing areas, members of church groups and other community organizations, and, in many cases, employees of USAREUR agencies. To each of these, military family members made a vital contribution and from each they received emotional and physical support. Finally, USAREUR lacked sufficient funds to return families with an absent military sponsor to the United States.

General Saint and his staff confronted the issues of family return during the first deployments from USAREUR in August 1990. Saint decided then that the families of soldiers deploying to Southwest Asia could return early to the United States at government expense only for normally accepted reasons. There was some provision for advance return of family members under the existing Joint Travel Regulations. Although deployment to Southwest Asia did not in itself justify the advance return of family members at government expense, the 1st Personnel Command would consider compelling personal reasons associated with the deployment. Family members could, of course, always move back to the United States at their own expense.[5]

Announcement of the deployment of VII Corps on 8 November led to a quick modification of USAREUR procedures in an effort to facilitate the review of families' requests for early return for compelling personal reasons. The new procedures left the requirements for qualifying unchanged but shifted the approval authority from 1st Personnel Command to the sponsor's community commander or his or her deputy. Soldiers were reminded that after completing their service in Southwest Asia, they would generally serve out their tour in Europe until their originally scheduled return to the United States. If family members moved to the United States at government expense, the government would not pay for them to come back to Europe after their sponsor returned there from Southwest Asia. On 29 November USAREUR further delegated approval authority for the advance return of family members for compelling personal reasons associated with the sponsor's deployment to the sponsor's first commander in the grade of lieutenant colonel or higher or to designated representatives in the community.[6]

On 10 November USAREUR authorized funded travel to single parents or to one member of military couples who were both deploying for the purpose of escorting children under the age of twelve to a designated location, to the extent predeployment schedules would allow. In this case, both the unit commander and either the community commander or deputy community commander had to approve the travel and absence. By 19 January 1991, 784 single USAREUR parents had deployed to Southwest Asia.[7] All, of course, had completed family care plans.

In his 14 November message encouraging families of USAREUR soldiers deploying to Southwest Asia to stay in their military communities in Europe, General Saint promised that the community and family support structure, including schools, child development centers, Army Community Service, doctors, chaplains, and recreational services would remain firmly in place. He argued that during the challenging time ahead, families of deployed USAREUR soldiers had the most both to give to and to gain from their military community. No one was better prepared to recognize the needs or solve the problems of USAREUR families than were other members of the same USAREUR community. It was, he said, a time to come together for mutual support in a way that would reassure those deployed that their families were settled and supported while they did their duty in Southwest Asia. General Saint promised that additional community and family services would be added before the soldiers deployed.[8]

Although the length and outcome of the deployment to Southwest Asia was uncertain and even the future of USAREUR was unclear, the overwhelming majority of families remained in Europe and contributed to the common welfare of their military communities. Some 3,416 families, slightly over 10 percent of the USAREUR families with a deploying military sponsor, returned to the United States between the end of November 1990 and the end of February 1991. These figures include some 600 children under twelve whose return to the United States was escorted. Most families and almost all escorted children returned in November and December 1990.[9]

The high percentage of families remaining in USAREUR testified not so much to the appeal of General Saint's message to families as to its simple truth. For most families, their home was in their USAREUR military community. This basic fact made it critical for General Saint and his subordinates to ensure that the communities would provide the assistance, stability, and comfort needed and expected by USAREUR families.

In early January 1991 USAREUR was asked to provide input to congressional testimony being prepared by General Galvin on why family members should or should not return to the United States when their sponsors were deployed to Southwest Asia. General Bryde responded following the same approach as had Saint's November message to USAREUR families, and Bryde added an outline of the community and family programs USAREUR had available, including those it had just established. Reviewing General Bryde's response, General Saint observed that most families would have nowhere to live in the United States until their soldier members were reassigned there. In mid-January the Army's deputy chief of staff for personnel announced that the assistant secretary of defense for force management and personnel had formulated a position on the early return of families of soldiers deployed to Southwest Asia that corresponded closely to that of General Saint. "The bottomline [sic] was early return was an avenue of last resort to improve a problem situation overseas." Under this decision, the early return of dependents was to be evaluated as an extra permanent change of station that had to be fully justified according to the Joint Travel Regulations.[10]

The VII Corps Base and Community Organization

The first issue that needed to be addressed in attempting to maintain and upgrade USAREUR's military community and family support services was how best to ensure continuity of an effective unit and community command structure. As noted above, General Franks and other key commanders who were responsible for overseeing military community administration in southern Germany would deploy with VII Corps. To maintain continuity in military community administration in southern Germany and to oversee the execution of the remaining rear or base functions of deployed VII Corps units, General Franks created a VII Corps Base organization. He and General Saint agreed to name General Bean, who led the 56th Field Artillery Command, to command the VII Corps Base and, in that capacity, to oversee the military communities in the VII Corps area. In addition, General Burleson approved the temporary exemption of VII Corps from the scheduled reduction in community area support positions that was to be part of the ongoing transition to a new community structure. USAREUR saw these positions as necessary to help support the families of soldiers deployed to Southwest Asia living throughout the VII Corps area.[11]

Rear Detachment Commanders

The practice of appointing a rear detachment commander, mandated in Department of the Army directives for deploying company- and battalion-size units, was followed throughout the deploying unit structure. The rear detachment commander was responsible for taking care of rear unit business and for providing needed community and family support to the families of deployed members of the unit. In early December, General Saint sent his commanders a message emphasizing the importance of making sure the right individual was chosen for the critical job of rear detachment commander. He envisioned that this commander would be the key to the community/family support system. The rear detachment system, however, did not always function very smoothly.

An HQDA general officers' steering committee report in July 1991 would find that the effectiveness of rear detachment commanders during Southwest Asia deployments had been uneven and recommended that formal policy be developed and plans formulated relative to rear detachments. It also urged that rear detachment personnel be trained before units were alerted for deployment. The Office of the USAREUR Inspector General (IG), meanwhile, in its Special Inspection of Key Post-Deployment Operations, found that while USAREUR rear detachment commanders were generally capable, they were unprepared in some cases for a much more complex mission than expected. Fortunately, General Saint did not rely exclusively on rear detachment commanders for the provision of community services during the deployment. Following his principle that redundant systems were sometimes necessary to ensure vital functions were performed effectively, General Saint advised community commanders to organize at least three community and family support systems in each community with a large number of deployed service members.[12]

Community and Family Support Plans

General Saint focused considerable attention on community support planning from the early days of VII Corps deployment. On 14 November he invited his commanders with regional community responsibilities in areas with many deploying soldiers, namely the commanders of V and VII Corps, the 21st TAACOM, the 56th Field Artillery Command, and the Seventh Army Training Command, to meet with him in Heidelberg on 26 November to discuss the community programs they were developing for those communities from which a significant number of soldiers would deploy. He asked each commander to address community organization; security plans at different threat conditions; schools; child development services; youth activities; Army Community Service programs; morale, welfare, and recreation programs; and medical and legal support. He also asked them to discuss their plans for reinforcing their "chain of concern" support networks, ensuring mail distribution, providing space and support to designated community "mayors," protecting private vehicles and other personal property of deployed soldiers, preserving laundry contracts, operating dining facilities, and transmitting information to and from families of deployed soldiers, as well as any other issues they wished to raise.[13] The HQ USAREUR/7A staff was also invited to attend the meeting.

General Saint provided basic guidelines for community organizations' support efforts during the Southwest Asia deployment to these commanders on 17 November 1990. He called for the creation or reinforcement of three overlapping support structures: unit family support groups, community family assistance centers, and community mayors. Although he recognized that the efforts of these support structures would overlap one another, which might not please efficiency experts, he believed that the duplication was justified to make doubly sure that, when families needed help, they could find it.[14] With the exception of area mayors, Saint's recommended community organization essentially adhered to the guidance contained in Department of the Army Pamphlet 608–47, *A Guide to Establishing Family Support Groups*, 6 January 1988, and to the section on "Family Assistance During Deployment or Mobilization and Emergencies" in the recently revised Army Regulation 608–1, *Army Community Service Program*, 30 October 1990.

Saint's 17 November message also proposed a variety of basic ideas for providing assistance to families of deployed soldiers. It suggested that the substantial deployment of soldiers from some communities might make it possible to designate some nontactical vehicles, some recreational facilities, and a community building to support DESERT SHIELD families. It recommended that the community commander convene periodic information update meetings for family support groups and for spouses who were not part of any such group. It suggested that training be provided for teachers and child care workers to sensitize them to the special needs of children of deployed soldiers, and it urged commanders to extend, when possible, the hours of programs and facilities for children. It also proposed the establishment in each community of a family assistance team of community leaders to help coordinate services, disseminate accurate information, and dispel rumors.[15]

After the 26 November meeting with his area community commanders, General Saint issued new guidance on community organization and programs derived from ideas exchanged there. Saint now required all communities to establish family support groups immediately, using DA Pamphlet 608–47 as a guide. While the family support group's organizational structure had to be created immediately, its level of activity would be determined by the extent of deployment of the soldiers in the community. Each family support group was to brief all of its family members whose sponsors had deployed to Southwest Asia about the special support available to them.

The message Saint issued on 3 December also initiated some of the small, but important, additional programs that USAREUR would offer. It required all communities to establish a "Helpful 1" telephone line using the standard community telephone number 111. This line was designed to make available at all times a knowledgeable and responsive person who could answer questions or refer callers to someone else who could help. The message also established procedures for bundling mail by battalion for direct shipment to the unit in Southwest Asia. It suggested storing unused privately owned vehicles in motor pools. It recommended hiring military family members to fill vacant mail clerk positions and hiring any additional needed employees part-time to give more people jobs. It solicited ideas on how German communities could help, as some German cities and towns were already offering to do. The message asked communities to survey their dining facilities and determine how many cooks they needed. And it required that each community commander have a town hall meeting of the entire community within two weeks after deployment.[16]

In the 3 December message, General Saint provided USAREUR units with guidance about the regulatory status of family support groups, and he outlined the types of support that could be provided to them and to area mayors. Family support groups, he explained, were officially recognized volunteer organizations and a component of Army Community Service outreach programs authorized by Army regulations. As such, family support groups were entitled to office and administrative support, government franking privileges, and transportation in support of their missions. Other forms of support would have to be approved by the local Army judge advocate. Mayors, who had been instructed to assist directly families whose military members had deployed to Southwest Asia, were similarly authorized government support in the performance of their duties.[17]

With this series of messages and meetings, USAREUR had, within a month of the announcement of VII Corps' deployment, established a system designed to meet the needs of U.S. military family members who would live in Central Europe while their sponsors deployed to Southwest Asia. To provide ongoing support to this effort, General Bryde established a Family Support Task Force, which met weekly. It brought together HQ USAREUR/7A staff members involved with various community- and family-related functions and programs to answer questions and to consider and publicize good ideas. Col. Ron Joe, the chief of General Bryde's Human Resources Division, oversaw the operation of USAREUR's family support programs.[18] General Saint remained interested in this work, and on 24 January 1991, he again met his area community commanders to review their community programs.

Community and Unit Family Support Organizations

Family Support Groups

The primary organizations through which USAREUR units provided support to the families of deployed soldiers were the company and battalion family support groups. Family support groups were established at this level for virtually every deployed unit, although some were still in the process of organizing as late as February. The groups were composed of unit soldiers and family members, and leadership roles in the groups often paralleled the unit's chain of command. Some communities from which only a small number of soldiers had deployed organized community-wide family support groups rather than unit groups.

In each family support group, volunteers provided information, assistance, and social and emotional support to family members of deployed soldiers. Some communities' education centers offered training courses for family support group volunteers as part of their Advanced Skills Education Program. The family support group would identify and help families that needed special support. Through this organization, families could come together to provide mutual reassurance and share experiences. Each unit group, moreover, served as a liaison between the rear detachment commander and the unit's community and families. The basic objective of each group was to "ease the strain and alleviate possible traumatic stress associated with military separation for both family members and the soldier."[19]

USAREUR's family support groups appear to have been reasonably successful in meeting their objectives. The 1991 USAREUR Personnel Opinion Survey showed that 51 percent of the spouses of deployed soldiers participated frequently and an additional 24 percent sometimes participated in their unit's family support group. Most spouses reported that family support groups performed at least adequately, although 25 percent felt there could be improvement in all areas, except for emergency assistance. A review of key post-deployment operations in USAREUR made by the command's inspector general in late January and early February found that family support groups were effective. The inspector general observed, however, that working with these groups placed a heavy burden on a few individuals and that the leadership and participation in some groups closely paralleled the chain of command. The Army's deputy chief of staff for personnel, General Reno, who visited some USAREUR communities and talked to family support groups observed some signs of burn-out and resentment among them, which testified to their hard work, if not necessarily to their effectiveness. All measures of the work of family support groups noted greater involvement by, and therefore presumably help to, the spouses of officers and senior noncommissioned officers. Families of junior enlisted soldiers proved hardest to reach.[20]

Family support groups gave military spouses a collective voice in their community and an effective two-way channel of information exchange with their community and rear detachment commanders. This collective family voice repeatedly reached General Bean, the VII Corps Base commander, and he passed family concerns on to General Saint. The USAREUR commander then addressed major issues of family concern and confronted persistent rumors on American Forces Network (AFN) television in Germany and in other media. General Bean found that two of the major concerns expressed in family support groups were the duration of the deployment, about which no reassurance could be given, and the uncertain future of USAREUR. Responding to rumors that a continuing drawdown of USAREUR could close installations and communities where families of deployed soldiers lived, General Saint went on AFN TV to assure families that although force reductions would continue, no community would close while its soldiers were deployed to Southwest Asia.[21]

Family Assistance Centers

Community commanders also established community family assistance centers, a second organization to assist families of deployed personnel. These centers were designed to provide information about and access or referral to many basic services and military agencies in one central location. The agencies and services represented included Army Community Service and the Red Cross, and employment, financial, housing, medical, mental health, religious, and transportation services.

Family assistance centers were established in most USAREUR communities, including all of those from which over 50 percent of the soldiers had deployed to Southwest Asia. They operated twenty-four hours a day, seven days a week, in communities that had deployed large numbers of soldiers and somewhat expanded work hours in other communities. Most centers operated 24-hour "hotlines" to answer questions related to community services and military agencies. A majority of respondents to the USAREUR Personnel Opinion Survey found their family assistance centers to be equally valuable to them as their family support groups and rear detachment commanders. The USAREUR inspector general reported that the family assistance centers had been tailored to meet community needs and were well received. They provided basic multilingual services to family members when required and, in the inspector general's view, relied on the work of a good blend of Army Community Service and Community Counseling Center professionals and volunteers.[22]

Area Mayoral Program

In addition to the aforementioned programs, which were specifically authorized by the Department of the Army, General Saint suggested that community commanders appoint area mayors, each of whom could present the concerns of an installation, a subcommunity, or a whole community to the community command. After wrestling unsuccessfully with the question of how to make the mayoralty a full-time, paid job, General Saint decided that the position would have to be voluntary and that its incumbent would have to rely upon community support in the performance of official duties. Area and community mayors could lead town meetings and speak with commanders on behalf of the members of their jurisdiction.[23]

Mayors were appointed in many communities and areas within communities in USAREUR, particularly in those from which large numbers of soldiers had deployed. The Aschaffenburg community, for example, had five mayors serving five distinct areas within the community. The fact that mayors were not initially appointed in some USAREUR communities, including those of the 21st TAACOM, may account for the relatively low approval ratings received by the mayoralty program in the 1991 USAREUR Personnel Opinion Survey. In that survey 48 percent of spouses of deployed soldiers said they were unaware of the mayoral program, and only 10 percent said they found the mayoralty program supportive. The inspector general found a well-established mayoral program operating in the V Corps area, but concluded that even there uncertainty persisted about the mayor's role and his or her relationship to other support organizations.[24] The mayoralty program was thus one initiative that seems not to have fully matured during the deployment of USAREUR soldiers to Southwest Asia.

Community Response

The 1991 USAREUR Personnel Opinion Survey indicates that both officially sponsored organizations and private interpersonal relationships assisted the families of the command's deployed soldiers. According to the survey, those families obtained support from the following groups, agencies, or people:

83 percent	Another unit spouse
65 percent	Army Community Service
62 percent	People in their housing area
57 percent	Family support group
57 percent	Family support center
56 percent	Rear detachment commander
56 percent	Supervisors at work
49 percent	A church group
45 percent	Army chaplains

Surely the multiplicity of support groups, systems, and programs contributed to the well-being of the Army families of deployed Army personnel and, by extension, of everyone in USAREUR, during this tense and difficult time.

Focusing on these support groups and programs, however, may exaggerate the needs of many spouses and families. The personnel opinion survey also showed that 80 to 90 percent of spouses of deployed soldiers reported no problems with landlords, banks or creditors, or even with using powers of attorney. Fully 93 percent of the spouses of deployed soldiers reported no difficulty managing the household budget, a proportion even larger than the 89 percent of those married to soldiers who remained in Europe who made that claim.[25] Apparently most families were quite well equipped to take care of themselves in the military community. The command's support groups and programs, meanwhile, were ready to provide support whenever the stresses and difficulties of having their sponsors away at war might challenge their ability to cope.

Family Support Programs

Helpful 1

At General Saint's instruction all USAREUR communities established Helpful 1 telephone services. With the inauguration of this service, individuals and families, particularly the families of deployed soldiers, could obtain assistance, counseling, and information twenty-four hours a day by dialing 111. The service was designed to provide an additional or final place to turn for help when other channels had failed to resolve a problem or provide support. While this service was meant to connect the family member with another concerned and knowledgeable member of the deployed unit, it was sometimes combined with family assistance center hotlines, which typically provided more "official" information, services, and referrals to community agencies and organizations. The inspector general found that the Helpful 1 system was working effectively; that the people answering it were well trained, concerned, and competent; and that the phones were answered "live." The personnel opinion survey found that 27 percent of spouses of deployed personnel found Helpful 1 supportive as opposed to only 4 percent who found it unsupportive. However, 23 percent had not heard about it, and 46 percent had no opinion.[26]

Counseling Services

USAREUR leaders, including the USAREUR Family Support Task Force, community commanders, and other USAREUR personnel working in the family support arena, recognized that family separations and the likely ground war ahead were creating an extremely stressful emotional environment for the command's DESERT SHIELD families. These personnel tried to make counselors, crisis intervention teams, chaplains, and family support groups as available as possible to affected families. Some Helpful 1 lines and hotlines automatically referred calls to counselors' personal telephones when "live" telephone respondents were not available in the office. At the suggestion of the USAREUR Family Support Task Force, General Saint recommended that community commanders employ counselors in the drug and alcohol abuse prevention program whose workload was reduced by deployment to provide comprehensive counseling services to families of deployed personnel.[27] It appears that counselors were available when needed, but that friends, neighbors, family support group members, and chaplains also frequently helped out.

Postal Services

One of the most prominent concerns of the families of deployed soldiers was the issue of mail delivery. This was also an important issue to the deployed soldiers themselves, and it received much command attention throughout the deployment. Because the postal infrastructure in Southwest Asia was apparently inadequate and because USAREUR soldiers were in the unique situation of deploying from military communities in a foreign country, General Saint tasked General Willis to devise a separate system for the delivery of mail directly from family members in USAREUR military communities to soldiers in Southwest Asia. Under the system General Willis established, personal mail for each deployed unit was bundled separately at USAREUR Army post offices each day. The bundles were consolidated as VII Corps mail at Rhein Main Air Base and moved quickly to Southwest Asia. Within two to four days, the mail would arrive at a personnel services company that was supporting VII Corps in Saudi Arabia. There, apparently due to inadequate force structure, mail-handling equipment, and transportation, mail was often delayed. Mail between USAREUR and Southwest Asia often took about three weeks to reach its destination.[28] The postal situation became even more frustrating for families of deployed soldiers at the start of the air war in January, when security restrictions led to a temporary prohibition on sending packages weighing over sixteen ounces to Southwest Asia.[29]

E-Mail, Desert Fax, and Telephones

USAREUR leaders recognized from the beginning of the deployment that mail would never be fast enough and that communication would be a major concern for deploying soldiers and their families. They thus searched for alternative means of communication, focusing on telephone-transmitted facsimile communications and on electronic-mail (e-mail) communications to and from personal computers in Europe. General White and his 5th Signal Command worked to set up an e-mail system that would allow spouses to send short messages of fifty words or less; this proved a slow and difficult task because the communications/signal infrastructure in Saudi Arabia was primitive and because satellite time was at a premium. The system gradually worked more effectively.

General White also helped establish a system to enable military family members in Europe to send facsimile messages (Fax) free of charge to soldiers in Southwest Asia. American Telephone and Telegraph (AT&T) volunteered to set up a one-way "Desert Fax" system in Europe similar to that available to families of DESERT SHIELD soldiers in the United States. Desert Fax calls would go via the military European Telephone System to England and from there via AT&T to Saudi Arabia. General White's information management office at HQ USAREUR/7A and his 5th Signal Command initially placed Desert Fax terminals in family assistance centers in the twelve communities that had deployed the most soldiers to Southwest Asia. In mid-February, an additional ten Desert Fax terminals were installed at other key USAREUR locations. Unfortunately, the Desert Fax system relied on the mail in Saudi Arabia right at the point where the mail was stalled, and therefore it proved hardly any quicker than the mail. The Army's Automatic Voice Network telephone lines to Saudi Arabia were also clogged, so that even commanders in Southwest Asia had a hard time reaching their rear detachment commanders by telephone.[30] It was also possible for soldiers to make commercial calls from Saudi Arabia to Germany.

Child Care

Although HQ USAREUR/7A did not give blanket approval to suggestions that priorities at child development centers be rearranged to move the children of deployed soldiers to the top of the centers' waiting lists, General Saint did inform community commanders that they could request from his staff exceptions to the normal order of priorities. He also encouraged and assisted communities and family support groups to create additional child care programs. Hoping to make drop-in care and regularly scheduled care available to spouses during medical appointments or routine errands, Saint urged community commanders to establish immediately whatever temporary child care facility was necessary and then request approval from HQ USAREUR/7A after the fact.[31]

Special Transportation Provisions

USAREUR's senior staff and community leaders were concerned about the problems that a lack of adequate local transportation might cause the families of soldiers who had deployed to Southwest Asia. Although the Army had created shuttle transportation systems between some installations and facilities, the dispersed nature of USAREUR communities and installations made USAREUR military personnel and their families almost as dependent on their cars as typical Americans in the United States. In USAREUR a person's house or apartment, work place, child care center, commissary and post exchange (PX), bank, medical facilities, recreational facilities, and friends' houses might well be located in different areas several miles apart. The personnel opinion survey would confirm that this was a problem, although it appeared to be no greater for spouses of soldiers who were deployed than for those whose spouses remained in Europe.

General Saint and his staff encouraged community commanders to provide local transportation to the families of deployed soldiers and asked mayors of German communities near U.S. installations to grant free public transportation to USAREUR soldiers and their families during the deployment. On 23 November 1990, HQ USAREUR/7A suggested that nontactical vehicles be employed to expand shuttle systems or to develop new transportation routes between facilities. It also recommended use of nontactical vehicles to transport volunteers supporting family and community programs. On 7 December the USAREUR Community and Family Support Agency informed communities that they could purchase and operate shuttle buses in support of morale, recreation, and welfare programs using nonappropriated funds.[32]

General Saint wrote to the mayors of German cities with large USAREUR populations and, while asking them to support the USAREUR community in general, specifically requested free municipal transportation for all USAREUR families. The response he received was very positive. Numerous mayors provided free public transportation or free tickets. These included the mayors of Aalen, Bamberg, Baumholder, Darmstadt, Frankfurt, Heilbronn, Karlsruhe, Pirmasens, Schwaebisch Gmuend, and Wuerzburg. In addition, the German commercial firm Daimler-Benz loaned USAREUR thirty-five mini-vans to support family transportation needs in the communities most affected by deployment. Working through the Overseas Military Sales Corporation, Chrysler and General Motors donated six nine-passenger vans to USAREUR family assistance centers.[33]

Special Housing Provisions and Exceptions

Housing and the uncertain future of some USAREUR installations were among the major concerns facing the spouses of deployed soldiers. Those concerns were heightened by the fact that the first announcement of installations that would be returned to German use had just been made in mid-September 1990. In order to reassure family members and solve special problems resulting from the deployment, HQ USAREUR/7A announced the following housing policies:

— Families were assured that they could remain in current housing for the duration of the deployment and in government housing facilities as long as they remained in USAREUR.

— Families could retain their quarters despite temporary absences of any duration to visit the United States or to stay with relatives in Germany.

— If sole or dual-deployed parents had their children leave their quarters for the duration·of the deployment in line with a family care plan, they would nevertheless retain their family housing.

— Deployed soldiers who had been living in private German rental housing were allowed either to terminate their leases or to retain them for the duration of the deployment, as they preferred.

— Military family members who had come to Europe without qualifying for command support, and who were thus termed non–command sponsored, could be assigned excess family housing as an exception to policy in cases of extreme hardship or for compassionate reasons, such as if a family was living in a German community with no transportation or if a soldier's wife was pregnant.[34]

Space-Available Travel to the United States

While General Saint encouraged military families to continue to reside in Europe, he helped arrange for many of them to visit the United States on "environmental morale leave." In early December, the USAREUR commander in chief announced that he had asked the Department of the Army to allow family members of soldiers deployed to Southwest Asia to fly to the United States and back aboard military aircraft on a space-available basis. On 13 December HQDA announced that command-sponsored family members of soldiers expected to be deployed to Southwest Asia in excess of ninety days could make one round-trip, space-available flight to the continental United States during the sponsor's deployment. Category C, or space-available, travel was normally authorized for unaccompanied family member travel to and from the duty station on a one-time basis during their sponsors' overseas assignments. Now, an additional round trip was authorized for command-sponsored family members during their sponsor's deployment, and non–command-sponsored family members of soldiers deployed to Southwest Asia from an overseas station were authorized one-time, one-way, space-available travel from the soldier's overseas station to the continental United States.

The space-available travel program had its limitations. The authorizing messages warned that space-available flights might be plentiful from Europe to the United States, but unavailable for the return to Europe. In that case, family members would either have to pay for commercial airline tickets or remain in the United States. Moreover, family members would point out later that it was not very practical for a sole parent with several small children to attempt to fly on a space-available basis to whatever air base on the east coast of the United States was receiving flights, given the likelihood of delays and the challenges of arranging domestic transportation. HQ USAREUR/7A tried, without success, to allow spouses to get on passenger lists by facsimile message rather than in person at air terminals and to upgrade their travel to category B.[35]

Additional Employment Opportunities

By opening additional employment opportunities to military family members, HQ USAREUR/7A hoped both to provide better services to deploying soldiers and their families and to accomplish critical duties previously performed by individuals and units that would deploy. General Bryde requested a blanket exception to an existing Army-wide civilian hiring freeze in order to implement this program. While the Army secretariat disapproved the blanket exemption, it authorized USAREUR to create over 2,200 direct support positions, almost 900 of which involved processing or replacing deployed soldiers or providing family support.[36] The Army also provided additional funding for many of these positions. Thus on 17 January 1991, the Assistant Secretary of the Army for Manpower and Reserve Affairs, G. Kim Wincup, authorized USAREUR to make 100 temporary hires for indirect support of DESERT SHIELD. Added to the 450 hires he had earlier approved to support deployed soldiers' families, this action brought to 550 the number of temporary positions in Europe that the Army had decided to finance with DESERT SHIELD, rather than USAREUR, funds.[37]

Additional Educational Opportunities

The staff of HQ USAREUR/7A worked with local community education centers and with the tuition assistance and scholarship programs of private and state educational institutions to make classes more accessible to military spouses who might have time available during the deployment to continue their education. Beginning in November 1990, the command encouraged spouses to enroll in German classes in an effort to increase their independence during the deployment of their sponsors. It also encouraged communities to inform family members that most universities and colleges offering classes at USAREUR installations provided students a tuition assistance or scholarship program. General Heldstab's Army Continuing Education System (ACES) Division reduced minimum class size to three military students for Headstart and Gateway German classes and allowed local community commanders to determine the minimum number of military students required for classes in their Basic Skills Education Program, Advanced Skills Education Program, and High School Completion Program. Spouses of military personnel were allowed to enroll in these classes whenever space was available.

The Army Continuing Education Division published a survey of the educational interests of USAREUR military family members in the 19 and 20 December issues of the European *Stars and Stripes*. The survey was completed by 742 respondents, over half of whom were spouses of deployed soldiers. The classes most desired by these spouses were college courses (60 percent), German classes (19 percent), high school classes (5 percent), and graduate courses (4 percent). The HQ USAREUR/7A staff concluded from the survey that its efforts were aimed in the right directions. By 1 March 1991, USAREUR's Continuing Education Division could report that over 800 spouses were enrolled in college courses using spouse scholarship programs and about 300 spouses were enrolled in no-cost classes, such as the Headstart German classes, the Basic Skills Education Program, and the High School Completion Program.[38]

Department of Defense Dependents Schools Support

The leaders of the Department of Defense Dependents Schools system in Germany quickly recognized that their administrators, teachers, and specialists, including above all their counselors and psychologists, would have important roles to play in community and family support during the deployment and in community crisis intervention in the event of casualties or other emergencies. On 24 August at the very beginning of the school year, the director of the DOD Dependents Schools, Germany Region, Dr. J. H. Blackstead, informed his personnel that military families facing possible separation would need their special support. Shortly after the announcement of the VII Corps' deployment, Blackstead established a regional task force to advise principals, teachers, and school counselors on how they could best ease the burdens on families of deploying soldiers. Based on this advice, each school's staff was expected to prepare the school to meet the needs of individual students and to develop an action plan for the staff's participation in community crisis intervention teams.[39]

Handbooks, Newsletters, and Videos

USAREUR headquarters and subordinate organizations issued materials designed to support families in a number of formats and media. At the end of November, the headquarters published a wide-ranging Family Assistance Handbook. Some deploying units and military communities, such as the 2d Armored Division (Forward) and the Frankfurt and Seventh Army Training Command communities, published their own deployment handbooks. The VII Corps published a rear detachment commander's assistance handbook. Headquarters, 21st TAACOM, issued

In his role as commander of the Heidelberg military community,
General Shalikashvili discusses General Dwight Eisenhower with
Heidelberg elementary school children.

a weekly information packet to aid its communities' efforts to support
families. USAREUR headquarters, meanwhile, periodically published a
compilation of its own initiatives in the DESERT SHIELD Family Support
Task Force Issue Book. Family support groups, family assistance centers,
and the Army Community Service published local newsletters and bul-
letins that supplemented the information provided by community newspapers on the services and programs available to assist families of
deployed soldiers. In February, during the air war with Iraq, HQ
USAREUR/7A distributed to its communities a video entitled "Coping
With a Crisis" for the use of local family support groups.

Other HQ USAREUR/7A, Major Command, and Local Programs

This study cannot fully document all of the varied local programs
made available to families of deployed soldiers. A description of a sam-
pling of them, however, can provide an indication of the range of programs offered to families by USAREUR communities. At Coleman
Kaserne, Gelnhausen, Germany, for example, the Army Community
Service offered workshops on dealing with the deployment, two video

cameras and tapes for families to make video messages for their spouses, special support to new mothers, emergency food lockers, and a television with continuous CNN coverage of DESERT STORM, along with more time-tested programs.[40]

Many of the ideas developed in outlying installations and communities were communicated to the USAREUR Family Support Task Force, which disseminated them in "Good Idea" messages to area community commanders. These good ideas often focused on expanding counseling, educational, and recreational opportunities for young children and teenagers, including suggestions on how to replace deployed coaches of youth sports teams. Other suggestions came in the area of automobile care, including having auto craft shops or rear detachments provide free classes in auto maintenance or assistance in buying and selling cars.

Although most of the programs were aimed at the deployed soldiers' families who remained in Europe, USAREUR leaders also considered the special needs of deploying single soldiers. Some of the ideas recommended for these soldiers included ways to store household goods and private automobiles, encouragement for rear detachments to send newsletters to the parents of single soldiers, and checklists and time off duty to help the soldiers take care of personal business before deployment.

USAREUR's Good Ideas Message Number 5, for example, addressed the issues of pets and paying bills. Differences between American and German attitudes toward pets was one of the many reminders to Americans in Germany that they were living in a foreign environment. Thus HQ USAREUR/7A warned that the abandonment of pets was inhumane, potentially dangerous, illegal, and subject to huge fines in Germany. The message recommended that a visit to the command's veterinarian facilities be a required stop for pet owners departing the command. Message Number 5 also provided many ideas to facilitate paying bills, including the suggestion that married couples establish joint checking accounts. The participation of almost all USAREUR personnel in Sure-Pay, an existing system by which a soldier's pay was automatically deposited in the bank, eliminated many potential cash-flow problems. Community banks also gave helpful talks to family support groups and others, attempting to resolve problems with banking issues and other financial concerns.[41]

Post-Deployment Family Weekend Holidays in the Bavarian Alps

With the support of Secretary of the Army Stone and Generals Vuono and Sullivan, Generals Saint and Bryde developed a plan to establish a USAREUR Soldiers Recreation Center at Berchtesgaden, Germany, in facilities that the Army had been planning to vacate. Furnished with approximately 600 beds, the recreation center was designed to provide all returning USAREUR soldiers and their families a three-day holiday in the Bavarian Alps as a respite from Operations DESERT SHIELD and DESERT STORM and from the demanding assignments that lay ahead of them in Europe. It was decided that USAREUR would assume responsibility for operation and maintenance of the Berchtesgaden facilities and oversee recreation center personnel and functions for this purpose. USAREUR would subsidize room charges with USAREUR morale, welfare, and recreation funds and offer affordable meals and beverages. Both federal and local German officials fully supported the USAREUR recreation center at

Berchtesgaden, Germany, site of a USAREUR Soldiers Recreation Center

Berchtesgaden. Soldiers' participation in the program was administered by unit chains of command. The recreation center would remain open from late April until all eligible units and soldiers had a chance to participate. A variety of sports and recreational programs were offered, as well as entertainment. Participants responded enthusiastically.[42]

Host Nation Support

USAREUR obtained host nation support at every stage of its efforts to assist U.S. forces in Southwest Asia. As has been noted above, the most effective European support of the deployment of USAREUR troops was the spontaneous effort of German military units to help their partnership U.S. units prepare, load, and transport their equipment to port. Similarly the grassroots expressions of support for the USAREUR families and communities left behind may have been just as important as all the official host nation support they received. There was a good deal of both.

At the end of November 1990 the federal German government undertook a campaign called "Project Friendship" to encourage *Bundeswehr* units to support American, British, Canadian, and French soldiers deploying to Southwest Asia, and it asked German citizens and communities to aid the NATO military families remaining in their communities. The campaign was headed by the *Bundeswehr* Inspector General, Admiral Dieter Wellershoff. Encouraged by the American embassy in Bonn, the German government put together a multinational working group that would identify requirements for support and provide procedures for drawing on German sources or assistance to satisfy these requirements. The German Federal Ministry of Defense meanwhile established an organization called Action Friendship, which anyone desiring to make a contribution to the project could join by paying a membership fee of at least thirty *Deutsche Mark* (DM). Each German military district and subdistrict command named a point of contact to receive requests for German support, expanded its contacts with U.S. and other NATO installations, and activated partnership relationships with NATO units stationed in its area.

The campaign encouraged German officials at all levels to adopt a supportive approach and thereby contributed to the success of local free transportation initiatives. It "sanctioned" the spontaneous support provided by *Bundeswehr* units to their allied partnership units. Above all, their government's campaign encouraged German citizens to express and donate a wide variety of support. Noteworthy were the many invitations given to American families to visit German families during the Christmas holiday season and the "adopt a family" programs that developed in some communities.[43]

German politicians at every political level, particularly those from the states and communities that had worked most with American military forces over the years, expressed and sometimes contributed support. For example, the Minister-President of Rhineland-Palatinate, Dr. Carl-Ludwig Wagner, wrote to mayors of key cities in his state encouraging them to offer all possible support to the families of deployed American soldiers in their communities. In addition to offering U.S. military families free public transportation, German cities gave tickets to municipal swimming pools and other recreational facilities to American service-related families and organized events for these families over the Christmas and New Years holidays.[44]

Private donations were sufficiently widespread, varied, and substantial to require the development of official legal guidance on their acceptance and use. For example, the German Military District Administration III and the German-American Steuben-Schurz Society in Duesseldorf

Bundeswehr *soldiers show their appreciation for the U.S. Army mission in Southwest Asia by handing out roses to drivers departing a U.S. Army installation in Heidelberg, 10 January 1991.*

had by 1 April 1991 together donated over DM 10,500 to assist American military families. The Swiss Tourist Association, Grindelwald, offered American families free vacations. Individuals also offered assistance in their own ways. Col. Michael F. Kush, USAREUR's Deputy Chief of Staff for Host Nation Activities, recounted the story of a soldier who was standing guard at Patch Barracks in Stuttgart, Germany, when a motorist drove up to him, handed him an envelope containing two DM 500 bills, and told him to make sure it got where it was needed.

The U.S. federal continuing resolution of 1 October 1990 authorized the secretary of defense to accept conditional contributions from foreign governments and individuals in support of defense operations. On 4 January 1991, General Saint asked General Sullivan for help in convincing Secretary Cheney to delegate to General Saint the authority to approve such gifts and donations given in support of Operation DESERT SHIELD up to a value of $25,000. General Saint noted in his appeal that commanders had been offered video cameras for use by soldiers in Southwest Asia, vehicles for the use of family support groups, and coloring books, specifically for the children of deployed soldiers.[45]

HQ USAREUR/7A tried to help community commanders in making decisions on the acceptance and use of private donations. While the local commanders ultimately made those decisions, HQ USAREUR/7A recommended that donated money be used for morale, welfare, and recreation programs for all USAREUR soldiers and family members, including but not limited to DESERT SHIELD families. Community Morale, Welfare, and Recreation Funds could accept donations and gifts up to $25,000 from any source. Private organizations, such as family support groups, because they were not instrumentalities of the United States government, could receive private donations and gifts of any size. HQ USAREUR/7A pointed out the advantages of each. Most substantial donations were surely channeled into the Community Morale, Welfare, and Recreation Fund for the good of all members of the community.[46]

Local Demonstrations and Other German Political Opposition

In spite of this broad German public support for U.S. and other coalition soldiers in Southwest Asia and their families, opponents of the coalition's intervention against Iraq managed to mount significant demonstrations against it in Germany in the fall and winter of 1990–91. The demonstrations were organized and led by a number of political and church groups that included pacifists and individuals who wished to see an end to the U.S. presence in Germany. Some of these demonstrations took on a distinctly anti-American tone. Aiming at maximum visibility to U.S. personnel and their families, the demonstrations were focused on key American headquarters and locations, such as Heidelberg, Nuremberg, Stuttgart, and Bremerhaven. Demonstrators left printed material opposing the war or even advocating refusal to deploy on doorsteps and under windshield wipers of USAREUR soldiers and family members. Some of this literature contended that family members would not be supported and even spread rumors that their housing was to be taken away and returned to the German government. Some German television stations and newspapers gave time and space to these views.[47]

By early 1991 the antiwar demonstrators produced what Colonel Kush described as a "backlash from the German people, the so-called 'silent majority.'"[48] This response was evidenced in Project Friendship, a number of counterdemonstrations by German supporters of the U.S. policy, and the countless donations and other individual expressions of support described above. But the demonstrations and other very visible expressions of opposition to the intervention surely left Americans in

German demonstrators spell out their support of Americans in the Persian Gulf at the gate to Campbell Barracks, 7 February 1991.

Germany, especially families of soldiers deployed to the Gulf, occasionally feeling isolated and vulnerable.

Security Measures and Their Impact

These stresses and tensions were heightened by the danger of terrorist acts or acts of sabotage directed against the U.S. military in Europe, a threat which led to the imposition of strict security measures throughout USEUCOM and a massive requirement for guards throughout already shorthanded USAREUR. The threat to USAREUR had two facets, each of which required separate security or force protection measures. One goal of the American security effort was protecting the deployment of DESERT SHIELD personnel and equipment to the Gulf. A second, equally important, objective was protecting USAREUR military communities and installations and other places where Americans lived and gathered, particularly in the communities and installations that sent large percentages of troops to Southwest Asia and gathering places in large cities housing significant American populations and activities.

There were two ingredients in decisions to impose security measures. First, information on a potential threat had to be collected and
analyzed. Intelligence personnel assigned to USEUCOM, USAREUR, and
other USEUCOM components were responsible for this function.
Second, affected commanders had to assess the perceived threat and
decide what measures to impose to protect against it. Commanders at
various levels had divergent views of the necessity and feasibility of
imposing different security measures in their sphere. Ultimately, General
Galvin decided that a sufficient threat existed across Europe to justify the
imposition of the second strictest level of protective measures, THREAT
CONDITION C (THREATCON CHARLIE), for the entire European
Command. General Saint strongly dissented from the decision to impose
a uniform level of protective measures throughout the theater; Saint
wanted to give more flexibility on these matters to senior commanders.[49]

Security Plans and Experience

HQ USAREUR/7A had confidence in its ability to deal with security threats, because it had just revised its security plans and successfully implemented them in the movement of chemical weapons to port in
Operation STEEL BOX, which ended in September 1990. CIN-
CUSAREUR Operations Order 90–1, Force Protection, had been
revised and republished on 1 April 1990. This order provided for four
levels of security and force protection, from THREATCON A, the least
restricting, to THREATCON D, which carried the strictest force protection measures. The movement of chemical weapons from
Rhineland-Palatinate to port in northern Germany, which required
faultless security and protection, had demanded close cooperation
with the Germans both in intelligence collection and security implementation. The USAREUR deputy chief of staff, intelligence, General
Pfister, worked with the German government to establish an information and security net that not only tested USAREUR plans, but succeeded in protecting this extremely sensitive operation. Subsequently,
USAREUR could use the same security net to assess the threat to
USAREUR equipment, installations, and communities during VII
Corps' deployment. It could then apply the measures delineated in
Operations Order 90–1 to protect U.S. personnel and property. The
problem, of course, was finding the personnel to implement these
security measures during and after the deployment of over 75,000
USAREUR soldiers, including 1,200 military police, to Southwest Asia,
from some of the very communities and installations that might be the
most likely targets of terrorists and saboteurs or, at least, places where
the U.S. population would feel most vulnerable.[50]

General Saint first made sure that USAREUR was prepared to carry out whatever security measures were necessary. In October and again in November soon after VII Corps deployment plans were announced, HQ USAREUR/7A asked communities to review their force protection plans and to identify the soldiers and units they needed, whether available or not, to implement force protection measures of each THREATCON level. In order to offset developing shortfalls in military police and guard personnel, six Army Reserve and four National Guard military police companies and an Army Reserve infantry battalion deployed to USAREUR. Additionally, selected USAREUR units were slated to reinforce existing security forces, if necessary. General Chidichimo, the USAREUR provost marshal, asked for authority and funding to hire local national and U.S. family member guards to make up in part for deployed soldiers. In December and January General Saint tasked his major commands to identify their requirements for civilian guards to replace deployed soldiers. Generals Saint and Shalikashvili worked with German civil and military authorities to ensure adequate local support, and an additional $11.5 million was authorized to contract civilian guards. In mid-January General Saint directed the creation of primary reaction forces, each composed of four military police platoons in the Nuremberg, Karlsruhe, Kaiserslautern, and Frankfurt areas.[51]

In December and January USAREUR again reviewed its force protection plans and ensured the command was prepared to deal with a substantially increased terrorist threat. General Saint asked each community to test, during the period from 10 through 20 January 1991, its force protection plans to THREATCON DELTA, to execute specific additional measures, and to prepare to implement THREATCON CHARLIE on order for a period to be decided by the community commander. The additional measures Saint requested included checking two forms of identification at all access points to U.S. installations, identifying off-post establishments frequented by U.S. personnel to help focus host nation security efforts there, and more generally coordinating plans with host nation officials. General Saint asked that public information released about the community THREATCON exercises mention that the exercises were geared toward "normal events."[52]

Threat Assessment in December and January

Threat assessments in December and January indicated that U.S. installations and personnel throughout Europe, particularly in large cities, were at a high risk of attack. In the fall of 1990 most intelligence sources agreed that Iraq had mobilized its intelligence-collecting sources in preparation for a violent global campaign against U.S. and coalition targets in the event of war. In December, General Saint instructed USAREUR community commanders to ask their soldiers, civilians, and family members to watch for and report suspicious persons and packages. In December and January HQDA warned that the U.S. intelligence community had concluded that terrorist attacks against U.S. and allied personnel and interests, particularly in the Persian Gulf region and in Europe, were almost a certainty in the event of hostilities. German authorities anticipated attacks against persons and facilities of the nations involved, if war broke out in the Gulf. USAREUR leaders thought the most likely mode of attack would be indiscriminate bombings in accessible places frequented by Americans, including unprotected military installations. USAREUR and German intelligence agencies were particularly concerned about the vulnerability of schools and school buses. In the Heidelberg community, for example, experts saw the danger of attack by two- or three-man teams from several possible terrorist organizations. The most likely perceived threats were from explosive devices, an attack using small arms or automatic weapons, the assassination of a military leader, a kidnapping, or a suicide car-bomb attack.[53] Although there was general agreement that the threat was high and although there had been numerous reports of possible surveillance of U.S. facilities in Europe, little specific information existed to help USAREUR leaders, community commanders, or military police officials to focus protection.

THREATCON CHARLIE Implemented

As the air war with Iraq began on the night of 16–17 January 1991, Headquarters USEUCOM released Operation Order FLEXIBLE DEFENDER and at 0045 local time perceived the terrorist threat to be high and declared THREATCON CHARLIE throughout the European Command. At 0230 on 17 January 1991, General Saint ordered the commanders of his major command support areas to implement THREATCON CHARLIE at all USAREUR military communities and installations until further notice. The stringent security measures were challenging for USAREUR to institute and maintain. In addition to the military and host nation police and contract guards prepared for this contingency, USAREUR had the tactical units remaining in Europe contribute to guarding the command's installations and persons. A total of approximately 23,000 personnel were required to perform security duties daily to implement THREATCON CHARLIE throughout USAREUR. Community commanders adopted whatever additional local measures they deemed necessary. In some communities, schools were closed until adequate protection could be provided to their buildings and buses or until the threat subsided. In Heidelberg, for example, barriers were erected around schools

Soldiers of the 26th Support Group search vehicles entering a U.S. installation in Heidelberg under Threat Condition Charlie, 28 February 1991.

where they adjoined public roads or property. Guards rode school buses. Parking restrictions reduced access to installations for almost everyone. Long lines of cars waiting to be inspected at the entrances to USAREUR installations and housing areas must have made anyone contemplating an attack aware of the U.S. security measures.[54]

Host nation police and army forces made important contributions to the security of USAREUR personnel and installations. German police at both state and local levels cooperated closely with U.S. military authorities. The formal assistance of the *Bundeswehr* was more difficult to arrange. German commanders were willing to help protect Americans off-post, but some of them felt that they did not have the authority to help guard U.S. installations. In the absence of serious terrorist attacks and in view of the spontaneous assistance of German soldiers and units at the local level, USAREUR found it unnecessary to formally request *Bundeswehr* assistance in protecting U.S. installations.[55]

Although USAREUR security elements received many reports of possible surveillance of U.S. facilities by suspicious persons, no significant terrorist acts actually occurred during the war. USAREUR commanders, who were stretching their resources in implementing THREATCON CHARLIE, soon looked for ways to reduce the THREATCON level in communities that were considered less likely targets. However, it was not until 4 March, shortly after the ground war ended, that the Seventh Army Training Command was authorized to reduce protective measures in its communities to THREATCON BRAVO. Only on 15 March 1991 were most other communities in USAREUR given that option, and THREATCON CHARLIE remained in effect in Frankfurt and Stuttgart until 19 March.[56]

USAREUR succeeded in performing a widely expanded force protection mission at the very time that many of its military police personnel and potential guards had deployed to Southwest Asia. The intense security measures were difficult for the command and for its members, but they reduced the danger of serious terrorist activity in Europe during the war.

Reconstituting Units and Restoring Readiness

The deployment of many of USAREUR's units and the dispatch of replacement crews and massive sustainment support to Southwest Asia, together with the implementation of THREATCON CHARLIE force protection measures in Europe, undoubtedly brought USAREUR's readiness to fight a war in Europe to a low point in December 1990 and January 1991. USAREUR had deployed over 40 percent of its personnel and over half of its combat units, plus key crews, much of its combat support structure, and a substantial percentage of its most modern equipment and ammunition. Moreover the forces remaining in Europe were buffeted more extensively than these statistics indicate. For example, approximately 7,000 personnel and much essential equipment were cross-leveled from units remaining in USAREUR to units deploying to Southwest Asia. Cross-leveling brought VII Corps strength to over 98 percent, but the overall personnel strength of USAREUR units remaining in Europe dropped to about 92 percent in December when VII Corps deployed. The deployment of crews, squads, and individual replacements further degraded USAREUR's readiness.

The personnel shortages and readiness problems were not, however, uniformly distributed among the units USAREUR retained. The personnel status of combat units, whose predeployment strength had typically been kept high, was not seriously affected, although their readiness was lowered by the departure of trained crews. On the other hand, some remaining combat service and combat service support units that had endured low personnel strength and equipment readiness levels even before the deployment may have become completely ineffective after cross-leveling. Retained units that were preparing for inactivation were also probably of little use to a combat force. POMCUS and theater reserve stocks, meanwhile, had been pillaged to modernize U.S.-based units deploying to Southwest Asia and to sustain all USCENTCOM forces. According to General Heldstab, it took awhile to gauge the readiness of the force remaining in USAREUR with any degree of accuracy.[57]

General Saint believed the reduction in USAREUR readiness was worth the risk, because the threat of war in Europe was low and the stakes in Southwest Asia were high. Moreover he believed he could quickly restore his command's readiness and field a respectable V Corps of two divisions or even deploy an additional division to Southwest Asia, if necessary. Indeed, by the end of October 1990 General Saint and his planners had developed CINCUSAREUR Concept Plan 4285–90 to deploy residual forces to other possible contingencies virtually anywhere in the world or to reenforce USCENTCOM further.[58]

General Saint and his planners carefully evaluated the force structure remaining in USAREUR after deployment of VII Corps, factoring in the impact of drawdown plans. Saint personally had reviewed every decision to send units or equipment, supplies, and ammunition to Southwest Asia that would lower USAREUR reserves below stated minimum requirements. He had taken two major steps toward maintaining and restoring readiness by instituting stop-loss and a permanent change of station freeze, as described in Chapter 5. These policies substantially reduced departures from USAREUR, while the arrival of reserve replacements gradually bolstered the command's strength. Nevertheless, personnel with certain desperately needed skills or grades failed to arrive in sufficient numbers. Saint therefore solicited specific types of Army Reserve and National Guard units, particularly medical and military police elements, and he requested individual reservists with specific skills to fill critical positions and to replace deploying crews. He revised his 1991 drawdown plans and, as soon as VII Corps departed, he realigned command and control of the remaining tactical force structure as described in the paragraphs below.

Command and Control Realignment

Implementing plans developed concurrently with the decisions on which units to deploy with VII Corps, General Saint attached to V Corps the most important VII Corps units that would remain in USAREUR after the departure of the commander, VII Corps. He did so after briefing General Vuono on the subject on 17 November 1990. HQ USAREUR/7A attached to V Corps the 1st and 2d Brigades, 3d Infantry Division; the 1st Brigade, 1st Armored Division, and remaining 1st Armored Division combat units; the 17th and 72d Field Artillery Brigades; the 7th Engineer Brigade and the three engineer battalions and four separate companies that remained assigned to it; and various personnel and finance units. General Bean, as commander, VII Corps Base, controlled the remaining VII Corps headquarters elements and a number of VII Corps units that were not attached to V Corps.[59] The attachment of VII Corps units at least gave the commander, V Corps, most of the structural building blocks he would need to put an effective corps back together and to accomplish his mission. The VII Corps' European tactical responsibilities had been transferred to V Corps units soon after the deployment of the VII Corps was announced.

Delay of Drawdown and Restructuring

Suspending or delaying the drawdown of those units that were not yet so advanced in the standdown process as to be beyond renewal helped maintain USAREUR readiness and contributed to its ability to provide support to USCENTCOM. During the early planning of Southwest Asia support, General Saint and his staff had tried as much as possible to adhere to existing drawdown plans and schedules. This left units with about 7,000 personnel so far into the drawdown process by November 1990 that their readiness could not be restored even if Saint had so desired. Units with a total of approximately 30,000 personnel had been planned for drawdown during fiscal year 1991. Saint and his staff realized in September as they began to plan division rotations that the drawdown of a number of these units would have to be delayed as they were needed to fill requirements in the deploying force or to help support deployment. This delay of the drawdown indirectly helped maintain USAREUR readiness by keeping additional units in the force structure during VII Corps' deployment. Even when units that had been slated for drawdown deployed, they contributed to USAREUR readiness by meeting requirements that might otherwise have been given to end-state units that could now remain in USAREUR. Admittedly, the drawdown delay also postponed the transfer of some modernized equipment from inactivating units to end-state units. On 3 December, roughly a month after USAREUR had determined VII Corps' force structure, which included many inactivating units, HQDA informed USAREUR that 1991 drawdown inactivations should go ahead as much as possible, although units previously scheduled for drawdown should be deployed to Southwest

Asia when necessary.[60] Further USAREUR action on force reduction and unit inactivation would await the return of VII Corps from Southwest Asia.

Army Reserve and National Guard Reinforcements

HQ USAREUR/7A, V Corps, the 21st TAACOM, the 7th Medical Command, and other USAREUR commands quickly identified critical personnel requirements resulting from VII Corps' deployment and subsequently modified their requests to cope with higher THREATCON levels or to cover developing shortfalls. As described in the previous chapter, the 7th Medical Command identified its personnel requirements early, and it began to receive critically needed United States Army Reserve and Army National Guard units in December. By that time, essential military police, combat support, and combat service support units were also on their way to USAREUR. General Saint reviewed requests from USAREUR commands for additional reserve component units and individuals during the 7 December O&I briefing and continued to receive them and pass them on to HQDA right up until the ground war.

In January and February an additional ten Army Reserve units totaling almost 5,000 personnel arrived in USAREUR, including more medical and military police units, an infantry battalion, ordnance units, a military intelligence detachment, and other combat support and combat service support units, all designed to replace deployed USAREUR units. National Guard units also replaced USAREUR medical, ordnance, engineer, and other units. Appendix D contains a list of Army Reserve and National Guard units that served in USAREUR during DESERT SHIELD. In some cases, the Reserve and National Guard units had earlier received overseas deployment training in USAREUR. The reserve component units made a significant contribution to restoring and expanding USAREUR's combat support and community medical services, in implementing THREATCON CHARLIE throughout the command, and in maintaining critical combat service support responsibilities of the 21st TAACOM and the 3d Corps Support Command.[61]

USAREUR generally processed and supported reserve component unit personnel in the same way as it did the Regular Army replacements it received, except that the Army Reserve and National Guard personnel were considered to be in temporary duty status and thus were not entitled to be accompanied by their families. USAREUR units gave the reservists organizational clothing, individual equipment, and other logis-

The Impact of Crew Replacement Requirements

The crew replacement mission discussed in Chapter 6 above significantly vitiated USAREUR's efforts to reconstitute its divisions and restore its combat readiness. Crew replacement undoubtedly violated General Saint's frequently expressed principle of avoiding hollow forces. General Maddox said that he would prefer to send complete, combat-ready battalions, if he could thereby retain some other combat-ready battalions in USAREUR. General Saint informed the Army Staff that he agreed, but to no avail.[67] As a result, V Corps relied on individual ready reservists to fill the gaps left by deploying crews and provided those reservists with as much relevant training as could be arranged.

USAREUR Personnel Readiness Status

General Saint reported to the chief of staff of the Army and the supreme allied commander, Europe, on 11 January 1991 that the overall personnel outlook in USAREUR was not so bleak. He then tallied the overall personnel strength of residual USAREUR units at 92 percent, with the 3d Infantry Division at 95 percent and the 8th Infantry Division at 89 percent of authorized levels. He pointed out that some units had much more substantial personnel deficiencies. For example, the 1st Battalion, 6th Infantry, was staffed at 78 percent and the 2d Battalion, 32d Armor, at 84 percent. The overall totals also did not reflect the severe shortages the command was enduring in certain combat service support military occupational specialties. But Saint could report real success in restoring medical personnel strength to predeployment levels and in enhancing military police strength, thanks in large measure to the arrival of reserve component manpower. By early February General Heldstab could be even more encouraging about the strength levels in the 3d Infantry Division. He reported to General Saint that, since 15 December, that division had received over 1,900 replacements, although he admitted that shortages persisted in some military occupational specialties. Nevertheless he judged that the division's personnel picture had improved substantially.[68]

USAREUR's Equipment Readiness

USAREUR's assessment of the level of its equipment readiness during the early months of 1991 produced less sanguine results. The command had

been somewhat shy of its authorized equipment levels even before the
deployment of VII Corps, and the need to meet the requirements of
deploying units promptly reduced USAREUR stocks further. Not only
were equipment and repair parts formally cross-leveled between remaining units and deploying units, but deploying units sometimes made last-
minute trades of inoperable equipment and parts for the functioning
equipment of residual units, leaving the latter with repair chores. The
delay in the 1991 drawdown schedule also meant that the units known
to have the most outdated equipment remained in the force structure.
The best equipment of these units had been earmarked to modernize
end-state units or to replenish POMCUS stocks, but it now could not be
used for those purposes. While some modernization plans were thus
delayed, General Saint was nevertheless able to push ahead with others.
Until the cease-fire on 28 February 1991, moreover, USAREUR did not
know how much additional sustainment equipment, repair parts, supplies, and ammunition USCENTCOM might request and need. In sum,
USAREUR's achievements in providing support in Southwest Asia, both
in deploying forces and sustaining them, had left a logistics mess in
Europe.

General Tipton's Operation CLEAN-UP

At the end of December 1990, just one week after the equipment side of
the deployment of VII Corps was completed, General Tipton, the commander of the 200th TAMMC and USAREUR's assistant deputy chief of
staff, logistics, had developed a broad plan "for getting theater logistics
back in order" called Operation CLEAN-UP. Tipton proposed six initiatives in this drive. First, he sought to identify shortages in residual units
and replenish them using theater reserve. His plan was to fill the shortages of combat units first, then those of combat support units, and finally those of combat service support units. He had special plans to focus
on equipment needed for aviation and electronic warfare intelligence
systems. Second, Tipton planned to recompute theater reserve shortages
and start to restore them. Third, he would focus on equipment maintenance, identifying and repairing inoperable equipment held by residual
units or simply left behind by deploying units. Fourth, he proposed to
inventory stocks in all storage areas and ensure that reporting systems
which provided asset visibility and accountability for residual units were
accurate and effective. Fifth, he planned to restructure the "fuel community" and to further reduce the number of fuel supply points. Sixth, and
by no means least, he planned to inventory residual ammunition and

move it to where it was needed, as well as to recommend the closure of unneeded storage sites. General Saint approved each of Tipton's proposals, sped up his suggested timetable for several actions so that they would be undertaken by 1 February, directed that every other initiative be completed by early March, and asserted that Operation CLEAN-UP was as important as the deployment.[69]

Reconstitution Priorities

Since it was impossible to restore equipment levels for all units as quickly and fully as General Saint desired, he had General Heldstab send a memorandum to General Laposata on 29 January 1991, establishing an order of priority of equipment fill for residual units and ongoing USAREUR projects depleted by their support of units deploying to Southwest Asia. Heading the list were the requirements of the 11th Armored Cavalry Regiment, the United States Army Southern European Task Force, the 3d Infantry Division, and the 8th Infantry Division in descending order. Then followed commander-in-chief initiatives, including Combat Maneuver Training Center upgrades, mobile subscriber equipment fielding, and division cavalry modernization. These initiatives were followed by the requirements of the 32d AADCOM, 7th Medical Command, 59th Ordnance Battalion, Seventh Army Training Command, and other units. Retaining previously set standards regarding minimum days of supply, equipment would be taken from available sources in the following order: theater reserve stocks in the central European area, excess stocks of deployed units, equipment from USAREUR operational projects, and POMCUS stocks. These priorities would govern only until current deficiencies had been restored, and they could be overridden by corps or subordinate unit commanders if necessary to meet unit readiness requirements.[70]

Role of War Reserves

Through 1990 and 1991 General Saint was continually able to win approval for reductions in total war reserve requirements, and the reserve stocks thus freed gradually helped provide the equipment needed by USAREUR's residual units. Although the Soviet Union had not yet disintegrated and Soviet troops remained stationed as far west as eastern Germany, the likelihood that the politically embattled Soviets or any of the new East European governments would launch a substantial attack on a NATO nation was very low by early 1991. The improbability of any requirement to rapidly reinforce U.S. troops in Europe reduced the immediate need for POMCUS, except perhaps for the brigade-size contingency force stationed in the less secure Mediterranean region, which General Saint carefully monitored. POMCUS requirements had thus been reduced. Moreover Saint had finally obtained the agreement of General Vuono and the secretary of the Army to a plan to reduce USAREUR to one corps. This reduced his theater reserve stockage requirements to those needed to sustain this one corps and allowed Saint to focus his equipment assets toward restoring residual units in USAREUR. Although USAREUR had reduced its POMCUS and theater reserve stocks substantially to equip and supply its deploying units and to support USCENTCOM, the reduced war reserve requirements made additional POMCUS and theater reserve stocks available to fill critical needs of USAREUR units. General Saint could thus proceed to restore the readiness of the two residual divisions.[71]

Assessment and Conclusion

The record shows that General Saint, commanders of units remaining in USAREUR, and their staffs seriously prepared the residual force to perform any mission it might be given, from deterring or fighting a limited or regional war in Europe to deployment to Southwest Asia or elsewhere. It is likely that General Saint could and would have supplied another division and armored cavalry regiment to Southwest Asia or another contingency elsewhere, if he had been required to do so in the first six months of 1991. It is possible that he could have fielded a corps in Europe of two understrength divisions with two brigades in each and an armored cavalry regiment at almost any time except during December or January. This would not have been Saint's capable corps or even the normal force stipulated by contemporary doctrine. It would have been riddled with shortfalls and holes and would not have been able to fight for many days. Such a mobilization would have denied USAREUR the ability to guard its installations against an Iraqi or pro-Iraqi sabotage attack or to provide a number of basic services like medical care to forces deployed to Southwest Asia. But the quick focus on reconstituting residual forces and their retention in Europe meant that, with allied support, USAREUR was able to fulfill its varied missions there during the absence of VII Corps and probably could have defended the nations of Western Europe and American interests in the region against any hostile force that might have threatened them.

Some of the problems experienced by Saint's depleted force would be continuing realities for the much smaller American army that would remain in Europe after 1991. The ability of the commander to put together and deploy impromptu forces and a willingness to take greater risks will undoubtedly be enduring requirements of the CINCUSAREUR in the post–Cold War world.

Chapter 8

Redeployment

Both USAREUR and VII Corps performed effectively in the first post–Cold War deployment to a combat or contingency mission of a major overseas-stationed U.S. Army force. The deployed USAREUR soldiers were greeted at home as victors and heroes. Their futures as soldiers, however, and the destiny of the units they had served so well were subject to the Army's plans for USAREUR's future. Many of USAREUR's soldiers who had fought in the Gulf War had to adapt themselves quickly from the satisfaction of victory to the emotional trauma of inactivating their units, relocating themselves and their families, and enduring less job security and opportunity for promotion than they had previously enjoyed.

The USAREUR Redeployment Order

USAREUR's establishment of personnel redeployment and reception procedures proved relatively easy, particularly compared to issues involving the disposition of equipment and the drawdown of units. HQ USAREUR/7A approached the redeployment process, which it called DESERT FAREWELL, by attempting as best it could simply to reverse or mirror successful deployment plans and operations. According to the USAREUR redeployment order, units would, as much as possible, prepare and ship their own equipment. This entailed repainting the equipment and returning it to highest operating standards prior to shipment. Property accountability would, of course, be maintained from beginning to end. The redeployment order specified that the three northern ports of Antwerp, Rotterdam, and Bremerhaven would be used again, except that equipment destined for theater reserve in Southern Europe, a stockpile now called Army Readiness Package South, would be shipped directly to Italy. Efforts would again be made to maximize barge and rail transportation for the movement of equipment in Europe in order to minimize convoy traffic. Soldiers would arrive in Europe from Saudi Arabia through the same five airports used before. The order also called for a USAREUR liaison team to travel to ARCENT headquarters to coordinate the redeployment of USAREUR personnel, reflecting a USAREUR approach that had been far from effective in the deployment.[1]

Organizationally, General Saint directed that General Laposata, General Flynn, and the commander of the 1st Transportation Movement Control Agency jointly arrange, schedule, and supervise movement operations. The V Corps would again oversee the airfield control groups that would manage and support the arrival of returning personnel. The 21st TAACOM, with the aid of the 37th Transportation Group, also would provide or arrange bus and truck transportation for arriving troops and convoy support at European ports. The soldiers of the 3d Infantry Division would again serve as stevedores there. Each unit would pick up its own equipment from a nearby barge- or railhead and bring it to its home station or final destination. Saint's order also assigned responsibilities for planning and conducting appropriate ceremonies for returning units.[2]

Redeployment and Drawdown Planning

As seen by USAREUR's leaders, the most challenging aspects of the redeployment appeared to be bringing key units and individuals back to Germany quickly to help resume the drawdown while ensuring that the deployed units shipped back only equipment that would be needed to outfit end-state units and replenish and modernize the heavily depleted pre-positioned stocks. The key initial problem in this planning was that USAREUR leaders did not know the shape or the personnel strength of the end-state U.S. Army in Europe. The ultimate size and structure of that force would also determine the level of theater reserves and POMCUS that would be required. Prior to the Iraqi invasion of Kuwait, HQ USAREUR/7A had proposed the inactivation of sufficient units to reduce its strength to 120,000. It had also privately developed drawdown plans that would produce force structures based on even lower personnel strength levels. In September 1990 Secretary of Defense Cheney approved a schedule of inactivations to reach the 120,000 troop level without agreeing to any ultimate end-state strength for the command. The Pentagon had then instructed USAREUR and other major commands to push ahead with planned 1991 inactivations as far as possible despite the Kuwait crisis. To the extent that inactivations needed to be delayed because of deployment to the Gulf, commands were directed either to reschedule them in 1992 or to seek HQDA approval to inactivate residual units in lieu of units that had deployed.

In January 1991, while making decisions related to the Fiscal Year 1992 budget that President Bush would submit to Congress in early February 1991, Generals Saint, Galvin, Reno, Vuono, and Powell agreed with Secretary of Defense Cheney to tentatively set USAREUR end-state strength at 92,200. Due to the tentative nature of the agreement, HQ USAREUR/7A and HQDA continued to study lower options, particularly those between 65,000 and 70,000. Whatever the outcome of those studies, however, the January agreement required the identification of a substantial number of additional drawdown units. Just as Saint's mobile, capable corps concept was about to be validated in the desert, the new drawdown plan threatened to undermine the implementation of his vision of a completely self-sustaining capable corps in Europe. Under the new drawdown plan, USAREUR would trade one of its two armored divisions for a mechanized infantry division. The corps would lose aviation, artillery, engineer, and other assets that were important parts of the capable corps. General Saint and his planners accepted these changes because they understood that budget reductions would necessitate such cuts in any event and because they recognized that the need in Central Europe for an enhanced capable corps as originally conceived was becoming less and less clear, despite lingering questions about the ultimate political destiny of the Soviet Union. General Saint and his planners now stressed a leaner capable corps that could provide fully deployable, independent, contingency-oriented warfighting organizations of a smaller size, probably up to an enhanced division, or that could form the basis for an enhanced capable corps when reinforced from the United States. They also recognized that USAREUR's post–Cold War assignments would likely include diverse contingency missions other than warfighting. The agreement setting USAREUR strength at 92,200 retained the underlying concept of a capable contingency force under a corps headquarters in Europe. More immediately, it enabled HQ USAREUR/7A to develop "final" unit drawdown and base closure schedules, subject only to the duration of the crisis in Southwest Asia.[3]

General Saint and his staff were well advanced in their planning, because they had considered an end-state of 92,200 a likely alternative for several months. They had identified additional units, at least half of which deployed to Southwest Asia, that would have to draw down if USAREUR's end-state was reduced to 92,200. Their interest in this number was based in considerable part on General Galvin's estimate that the highest end-state number the Army in Europe could expect was 92,000. Under the previous plan for a USAREUR end-state force structure of

120,000, VII Corps units with an authorized strength of at least 30,000 would inactivate upon their return to Europe from Southwest Asia. Under the new 92,000-option plan that CFE Division planners developed in late November, USAREUR would inactivate units with as many as 52,000 personnel that had deployed to Southwest Asia after they returned to Europe.[4]

In the past General Saint had insisted, in line with the conclusions of HQDA's August 1990 HOMEWARD BOUND exercise, that 30,000 personnel were the most that could be drawn down from USAREUR in a reasonably organized way in any one year. HQ USAREUR/7A had already proposed inactivation schedules under which units with approximately 30,000 personnel would draw down in fiscal year 1991, and it planned an equal force reduction in fiscal year 1992. The secretary of defense had announced the 1991 inactivations on 26 September 1990. Even after the decision was made to deploy VII Corps to Southwest Asia, HQDA had directed USAREUR on 3 December to go ahead with these inactivations as much as possible, although it instructed that, when necessary, units previously scheduled for drawdown should be deployed to Southwest Asia.

As we have seen, General Saint and his planners found that there were good reasons to deploy units scheduled for inactivation or to use them in USAREUR to support the deployment. Although it was generally too late to stop the inactivations planned for March 1991, the inactivation of most units scheduled for drawdown later in 1991 was delayed. Over 30,000 personnel in units scheduled for drawdown in 1991 and 1992 were deployed to Southwest Asia. In the end, USAREUR inactivated units with an authorized strength of only about 14,500 soldiers in fiscal year 1991.[5]

General Saint, General Heldstab, and their planners recognized that the drawdown delays, however essential for USAREUR's support to operations in Southwest Asia, might well lead to calls for an accelerated inactivation schedule after the war. They were willing to accelerate the drawdown process in 1992 because they concluded that deployment would offer them an opportunity to reduce the cost and time involved in standing units down. Costs and time could be saved in processing equipment for drawdown, they believed, by leaving it in Saudi Arabia or by returning it directly to the United States from Southwest Asia. To maximize these savings, in December and January they contemplated reprogramming units remaining in USAREUR that were scheduled to draw down into end-state units, in order to enable them to change end-state units in Southwest Asia into drawdown units. They anticipated that these new drawdown units in Southwest Asia would not bring their equipment back to Europe, making their inactivation quicker, easier, and cheaper. They thought this might get USAREUR force reduction plans back on schedule in 1992.

General Saint supported his view that an accelerated 1992 drawdown pace was possible by citing the historical example of Operation GYROSCOPE, which in 1955–58 had quickly swapped the personnel, including families, of USAREUR divisions with those of divisions stationed in the United States. If personnel did not have to turn in their equipment, General Saint thought it would be feasible to inactivate in 1992 units containing up to 70,000 soldiers. In mid-December General Heldstab sent a note to Maj. Gen. Harold T. Fields, Jr., the Army's Assistant Deputy Chief of Staff for Operations and Plans, proposing that USAREUR receive back from Southwest Asia fully equipped units, which would remain in Europe, with an authorized strength of only 7,500 personnel. Heldstab proposed that units with an authorized strength of 62,500 personnel return without equipment as "fastmover" units. Their personnel would close down casernes, quickly pick up their families and household goods, and depart to the United States or to other units in USAREUR. The Army rejected the proposal on the grounds that installations in the United States could not assimilate more than 50,000 soldiers returning from Europe in 1992.[6]

The Army approved, instead, a revised 1992 drawdown total of 52,000 that HQ USAREUR/7A subsequently proposed, which would inactivate both deployed and retained units. General Saint and his planners ultimately decided to stick basically to the end-state units they had previously identified because there had been good military and geopolitical reasons for their original choices. Under the revised plan, the details of which were developed by General Heldstab's CFE Division in December 1990 and January 1991, a total of 36,000 soldiers would return from the desert to Europe without equipment for the quick inactivation of their fastmover units. These soldiers would then be individually reassigned during the summer and fall of 1991 to other units stationed either in the United States or in Europe.[7]

In January and February HQ USAREUR/7A hurriedly completed its basic plans for the return of its elements from Southwest Asia in line with its new drawdown plans and schedules. The redeployment plan was complicated. It grouped deployed units into several categories: end-state units, units that would inactivate in 1992, and units that would inactivate after 1992. The planners grouped units in this way to determine their redeployment priority and the disposition of their equipment. Generally, units scheduled to inactivate within a year of their return would redeploy without equipment. Some end-state units and units drawing down after 1992 would bring back all of their equipment and others just the modernized part of it. A third category of end-state units would bring back no equipment from Southwest Asia but would instead receive the equipment of a unit inactivating in Europe. Approximately 70 percent of the soldiers whose units would leave their equipment in Southwest Asia to speed inactivation in USAREUR would return to the United States while about 30 percent of those soldiers would remain in USAREUR.[8]

VII Corps Redeployment Plans

During the 100-hour war, Col. Thomas J. McGuire, the deputy chief of General Heldstab's CFE Division, had been sent to the Pentagon to talk to the Army Staff about USAREUR's new drawdown plan and schedule for reducing its strength to 92,200. General Heldstab, who was also at the Pentagon, informed McGuire that his next assignment was to brief General Franks and his VII Corps staff and commanders on the same drawdown plan and inactivation schedule and to ask ARCENT to consider USAREUR's goals as it developed its redeployment plans. On Thursday, 28 February 1991, the day the cease-fire with Iraq began, Colonel McGuire flew from Washington, D.C., to Saudi Arabia. There he would have to tell General Franks that, in spite of their role in winning the war, his corps headquarters and many of his subordinate units would draw down and inactivate soon after their return to Europe. Also on 28 February, HQ ARCENT tasked its major subordinate commands, including VII Corps, to submit their desired internal order of redeployment, to be used to establish an ARCENT-wide redeployment schedule.[9]

Colonel McGuire met General Franks at VII Corps' main headquarters on the Iraqi-Saudi border on the evening of Monday, 4 March. Over dinner in the officers' mess, he listened to General Franks tell how the 2d Armored Cavalry Regiment had ripped a seam in the Republican Guard's Tawakalna Division and how the 1st Infantry Division had then slipped through to finish off what the cavalry regiment had started. Franks also described the 1st Armored Division's attack on the Republican Guard's Medina Division. Then McGuire told Franks about the new drawdown plan and inactivation schedule. General Franks quickly understood the concept. He asked McGuire to relay three requests to General Saint. First, Franks wanted to know if the campaigns in Iraq would be considered in determining which unit flags would be retained in Europe. Second, he wanted to ensure that the redeployment would follow his principle of first-in, first-out, as he had apparently already promised his soldiers. Third, he wanted to make sure that USAREUR had a reception plan for returning soldiers and their equipment. He was hoping that equipment reception could be handled with as efficient timing as the 1st Infantry Division (Forward) had achieved in Dhahran and Ad Dammam during deployment, so that his soldiers would not be tied up unnecessarily at ports. Franks was anxious that his troops, including members of units attached to VII Corps only during the deployment, have some time off with their families after they returned to Europe.[10]

While he was in Saudi Arabia, Colonel McGuire also met with ARCENT leaders, including General Yeosock, the ARCENT commander; Brig. Gen. Steven L. Arnold, the ARCENT operations chief; and General Pagonis, the commander of the 22d Support Command, to discuss redeployment plans. The ARCENT leaders planned to have most troops redeployed within six months, assuming adequate support at staging areas and ports, but they expressed concern that a quick redeployment would reduce military stocks in Saudi Arabia below acceptable levels. They believed that a significant quantity of military equipment needed to be pre-positioned in the Saudi kingdom to protect it from further external dangers. Colonel McGuire was able to inform these leaders that substantial elements of the 1st and 3d Armored Divisions as they were configured in Southwest Asia would be inactivated soon after their return to Germany and that these inactivating units could leave as POMCUS in Saudi Arabia much equipment that was not needed to modernize end-state USAREUR units. The ARCENT leaders, particularly General Arnold, were apparently delighted by this information and by Colonel McGuire's attitude.[11] Relations between ARCENT and USAREUR would continue to be much more friendly after the war than they had been before.

USAREUR Redeployment Plans

While Colonel McGuire was briefing General Franks, General Saint was working on drawdown and redeployment plans with Generals Burleson and Heldstab and with Mr. Pflaster and his CFE Division planners. They were preparing to brief the vice chief of staff, General Sullivan, on these plans on Friday, 8 March, and the chief of staff, General Vuono, the following week. Saint and Burleson were also working on a message to Franks that explained why they could not fully support the first-in, first-out rule. The draft message said that USAREUR's priorities could not be achieved under a strict application of the first-in, first-out rule, which they clearly understood General Franks favored, because USAREUR planning was driven by the need both to redeploy and to draw down in a cohesive manner. Thus command and control elements of redeploying units needed to return more quickly than other elements. For example, an advance party of VII Corps headquarters would have to come back early to oversee the return and drawdown of some VII Corps units. USAREUR's draft message observed that the returning VII Corps headquarters should not expect to resume its former role as an operational command. HQ USAREUR/7A would reassign to VII Corps only units that would inactivate before VII Corps headquarters was slated to draw down. Some units needed to return early so that they could inactivate quickly and, in the process, close some installations, as necessitated by budget reductions. For example, although the 1st Armored Division had deployed first, HQ USAREUR/7A wanted some 3d Armored Division units to return in advance so that those units' casernes could be closed. Moreover, HQ USAREUR/7A wanted individual fillers and replacement crews, some of which had not been fully integrated into VII Corps units, returned to Germany first of all to restore USAREUR combat readiness.[12]

Actually there were only a few critical differences between the priorities for redeployment favored by headquarters of USAREUR and VII Corps. HQ USAREUR/7A in general also supported the first-in, first-out principle. Thus, the 12th Aviation Brigade and the 2d Armored Cavalry Regiment were both slated for early redeployment under both plans based on their early deployment. In the first week of March, General Shalikashvili discussed with Generals Yeosock and Arnold USAREUR redeployment needs and the possibility of USAREUR's sending a brigade-size element to round up USAREUR equipment and act as stevedores at Saudi ports. Yeosock and Arnold were agreeable in principle. On 7 March Colonel McGuire brought General Franks' requests to General Saint, who ensured that they were included, along with USAREUR's plans, in the briefings presented to General Sullivan the following day.[13] By mid-March, in fact, the only major differences concerned when to redeploy the 11th Aviation Brigade and the order in which to return some 1st and 3d Armored Division elements.[14]

In March and April General Saint, working with Generals Shalikashvili, Burleson, and Heldstab and with Mr. Pflaster and his planners, again juggled USAREUR's redeployment and inactivation schedules. As the return of the bulk of USAREUR's deployed soldiers was about to begin in earnest in early April, Mr. Pflaster's planners made a final survey of what equipment needed to be returned to Europe and of the ability of USAREUR communities and retained units to support redeployment and drawdown. Based on this analysis, General Saint with his advisers made final revisions to their redeployment plans. Now settled, USAREUR's redeployment priorities needed only the support of ARCENT and VII Corps.[15]

USAREUR Redeployment Liaison Team to ARCENT

In early March General Sullivan instructed USAREUR and Forces Command to send redeployment liaison teams to ARCENT. General Saint sent Colonel McGuire back to Southwest Asia as the head of a USAREUR liaison team, asking him to coordinate redeployment planning with ARCENT and to look after USAREUR interests in the process. It was a sensitive assignment, for McGuire was to promote USAREUR's perspective in the evolution of another theater's plans and actions. Saint explained to team members that USAREUR's earlier deployment liaison team had not done anything wrong; it had failed, he asserted, only because USCENTCOM was, at that point, preoccupied. While Saint said that neither then nor now did USAREUR claim any authority over ARCENT or over USAREUR units that had deployed to Southwest Asia, the USAREUR commander instructed his team to ensure that USAREUR interests were considered in VII Corps' redeployment. The liaison team should represent General Saint in explaining USAREUR's vital interests in the timely return of USAREUR units, personnel, and equipment. Among other sensitive missions, McGuire needed to resolve differences between the redeployment priorities of USAREUR and VII Corps.[16]

McGuire brought with him a ten-member team containing experts on personnel, logistics, force modernization, drawdown plans, and medical issues. The team included representatives of Heldstab's CFE and Force Modernization Divisions and Laposata's logistics office, all of whom attempted to ensure that end-state units would return to Europe with modernized equipment; that equipment needed in Europe to support nondeploying end-state units, theater reserve, and POMCUS would be shipped to Europe; and that equipment that was not needed in Europe would not be returned there. These team members were responsible for protecting USAREUR's general force modernization interests and ensuring that returning units were modernized with the equipment of inactivating USAREUR units whenever possible. They tracked the unit sets and other modernized equipment that USAREUR had worked so strenuously to send with VII Corps, striving to ensure that USAREUR would receive back in Europe all the equipment it still needed. For example, the team tried to arrange to have the command's Sluggers, the geographical positioning devices that had proven so important to the mobile corps, returned to USAREUR. It also attempted to track the foreign equipment that had been loaned to USAREUR and help return it to Europe.

USAREUR wanted to place liaison team members at the headquarters of ARCENT, VII Corps, and the 22d Support Command and at staging areas, airports of embarkation, and seaports. ARCENT allowed the team to spread out across the theater to track down USAREUR organizations, personnel, and equipment assigned throughout USCENTCOM, not just to VII Corps, and to inform the units about the redeployment, the disposition of unit equipment, and their futures in Europe. According to Colonel McGuire, the team's personnel specialists probably had the biggest workload, because soldiers from USAREUR serving in USCENTCOM were starved for personnel information. The team's personnel specialists explained stop-loss, attachment, and other current personnel policies to USAREUR soldiers and examined VII Corps plans for the return of USAREUR personnel. Colonel McGuire worked with VII Corps staff and division commanders in an effort to resolve differences between USAREUR and VII Corps redeployment plans, coordinating closely on these issues with ARCENT and the 22d Support Command. Colonel McGuire and most other liaison team members, once they had completed their part of the mission, returned to Germany at the end of April.[17]

This time the liaison mission was generally a success. It enjoyed excellent relations with ARCENT, although it was not always able to influence ARCENT's and VII Corps' redeployment plans. General Franks ensured that VII Corps' medical units were moved to the front of the redeployment line, as General Saint requested, but he was unable to influence ARCENT's decision to retain longer some other USAREUR medical units in the USCENTCOM theater. The VII Corps also advanced the redeployment of the 11th Aviation Brigade as USAREUR requested, but it returned the 1st Armored Division to Europe before some 3d Armored Division elements needed to start closing 3d Armored Division installations in Germany.[18]

General Saint and his staff assumed that it would be necessary to provide ongoing redeployment support to VII Corps and other USAREUR units in Southwest Asia in addition to the liaison team under Colonel McGuire that it sent in March and a small team from the 200th TAMMC that followed in April and May. USAREUR would thus dispatch teams of equipment experts, customs police, communications personnel, and intelligence specialists for this effort. In addition, approximately 200 soldiers who had deployed in December and January remained in Saudi Arabia as late as August to help load the ships.

General Saint and his staff also recognized that USAREUR would be called on to provide much of the residual force in the USCENTCOM theater. They were not surprised when ARCENT announced in mid-May that it expected USAREUR to replace USAREUR units that were already helping it meet its residual force requirements. In response, USAREUR quickly prepared to replace the 3d Brigade, 3d Armored Division, which was guarding the borders of Kuwait, with the 11th Armored Cavalry Regiment. USAREUR leaders were not, however, immediately prepared to replace USAREUR medical units still serving in Southwest Asia, including the 45th Medical Company (Air Ambulance) and the 483d Medical Detachment (Veterinary Service), two of the first USAREUR units to deploy to Southwest Asia. General Saint asked his staff to inform ARCENT that USAREUR would replace only units or modules, not individuals, to ensure an adequate chain of command.[19]

VII Corps Redeployment Organizations

General Franks tasked VII Corps Artillery to set up a VII Corps Redeployment Command. It included the corps artillery's deputy commander, chief of staff, command sergeant major, other headquarters staff officers, and a port support activity commander and totaled approximately ninety personnel. The redeployment command's mission was to provide command and control at the ports and to ensure the efficient processing for redeployment of VII Corps soldiers and equipment. On 15 May the 2d Corps Support Command took over this responsibility from VII Corps Artillery, which prepared to complete its own redeployment. The VII Corps also required each of its major subordinate commands to establish a port support team at the appropriate port to oversee, under the command and control of the Redeployment Command, its passage through the port. The 1st Infantry Division (Mechanized), 1st Armored Division, 3d Armored Division, and Corps Troops established port support teams at Ad Dammam. Corps Troops covered VII Corps headquarters and most other nondivisional corps units. At Al Jubayl, the 2d Armored Division (Forward); 1st Brigade, 3d Armored Division; 2d Armored Cavalry Regiment; Corps Artillery; and Task Force 8–43 established port support teams. HQ VII Corps also established a Redeployment Action Team at King Khalid Military City to monitor the movement of units to ports and the departure of soldiers from the King Khalid Military City airport. This team was made up of representatives of the corps headquarters staff and liaison teams from the redeploying units. The VII Corps Redeployment Command completed its mission on 11 August 1991.[20]

Redeployment of USAREUR Personnel

Whatever USAREUR's plans or General Franks' redeployment priorities, ARCENT and USCENTCOM controlled the redeployment of the Army units in Southwest Asia, and they preferred to redeploy forces basically on a first-in, first-out basis. This meant that the XVIII Airborne Corps and other units that had come directly from the United States would redeploy before VII Corps and most other USAREUR units, except for the 12th Aviation Brigade, which had deployed early. USAREUR benefited, however, from General Schwarzkopf's decision to make an initial token or symbolic redeployment from each unit. Thus, VII Corps received 850 spaces, including 200 each for the 1st and 3d Armored Divisions; 100 each for the 2d Armored Cavalry Regiment, the 2d Armored Division (Forward), and corps headquarters; 70 for the 2d Corps Support Command; 55 for VII Corps Artillery; 19 for 11th Aviation Brigade; and 5 for the 8th Battalion, 43d Air Defense Artillery. This enabled VII Corps to bring back promptly the corps, division, and brigade headquarters personnel most needed to work in Europe on USAREUR redeployment and drawdown initiatives. This initial redeployment was completed between 8 and 10 March 1991. General Bean met returning flights in Nuremberg and Stuttgart, and local German media and American Forces Network–Europe television covered the arrival both there and at some soldiers' home stations.[21]

The subsequent redeployment of the bulk of USAREUR personnel in Southwest Asia also moved relatively quickly, although most soldiers did not return until May. HQ USAREUR/7A established a liaison cell with HQ ARCENT to monitor the redeployment and notify appropriate USAREUR agencies of the dates, times, and airports at which USAREUR personnel were scheduled to return to Europe. The 12th Aviation Brigade began its return to Europe on 27 March, and by the end of the month 1,103 of its soldiers had returned. The remaining 803 followed in early April. Most USAREUR crews also returned early, thanks in part to Colonel Mumby, chief of General Heldstab's Operations Division, who had kept track of the many individual USAREUR soldiers and crews who were now spread all over the USCENTCOM theater. By the end of March, 1,415 of the 1,927 USAREUR soldiers deployed as crews had returned. On 5 April most of the soldiers in the elements of two air defense artillery battalions deployed to Israel in Task Force Patriot Defender returned to USAREUR. By 27 April, a total of 17,282 USAREUR soldiers had returned, including all of the 2d Armored Cavalry Regiment, half of the deployed personnel of the 7th Engineer Brigade, over one-third of VII Corps Artillery and the 207th Military

Left, soldiers from the 3d Armored Division return to Europe after the Gulf War; right, the Crist family welcomes its soldier husband and father home from duty in the Gulf War in April 1991 at Garlstedt, Germany.

Intelligence Brigade, almost 25 percent of the 2d Corps Support Command, and a few hundred from each armored division.

The redeployment of USAREUR soldiers accelerated in early May. By 15 May, 51,455 or 68 percent of the 75,500 USAREUR soldiers deployed to Southwest Asia had returned to Europe. Those totals rose to 65,440 by 1 June and 73,967 by 1 July. Thus by mid-1991, 98 percent of the USAREUR soldiers who had deployed to Southwest Asia had returned. By 30 August 75,171 or 99.6 percent of those deployed had returned to Europe on a total of 369 flights. Except for personnel newly deployed to follow-on task forces, which will be examined in the last section of this chapter, only seventy-two USAREUR personnel, most of whom were from the 7th Medical Command, remained deployed in Saudi Arabia and Kuwait as of mid-October.[22]

USAREUR soldiers were welcomed home with countless small ceremonies at airfields and other appropriate sites, major welcoming events at home stations upon the return of the unit flag, a giant VII Corps celebration with representatives from its Gulf War units on 27 June, and a big USAREUR-wide celebration over a Fourth of July weekend that was extended by training holidays. USAREUR DESERT STORM units also sent representative contingents to participate in parades and other events in the United States. Upon their return, commanders of redeploying units gave their soldiers time off to spend with their families and to get their affairs in order after their long absence. In addition, large numbers of USAREUR soldiers enjoyed a weekend retreat with their families or friends in the Bavarian mountains at Berchtesgaden over the next year. Before that, however, USAREUR soldiers quickly got back to work. There was much to be done to complete redeployment, support postwar contingency operations, restore readiness, continue the drawdown, and restructure USAREUR.

Redeployment of USAREUR Equipment

The disposition of the equipment of USAREUR units that had deployed to Southwest Asia was the truly complicated part of USAREUR's redeployment plans. It offered opportunities to simplify the drawdown by not returning unneeded equipment to Europe and to modernize and refurbish end-state units with supplies and equipment that were excess after the war. The limits of these opportunities were difficult to discern in some cases. For example, General Laposata proposed to General Saint a one-time cancellation of all back orders for supplies and repair parts for all USAREUR units returning from the Gulf as a way to save much needed money. Saint demurred, contending that supply and the restoration of an adequate stock of repair parts in Europe was more important than the money involved.[23]

The discussion above of USAREUR's plans for redeployment and restructuring should make clear the complexity of the issues involved in equipment redeployment. First, USAREUR had to determine what equipment, ammunition, and other supplies were necessary to equip and supply its post-1992 force and to provide it adequate POMCUS and other war reserve stocks. Second, USAREUR had to locate and inventory USAREUR equipment in Southwest Asia and determine what needed to be returned to Europe to meet the equipment requirements it had identified. Third, some advanced equipment that had been used in Southwest Asia to modernize units from the United States needed, if possible, to be returned to Europe for the same purposes, and the responsibilities and procedures for the return of this equipment had to be determined. Fourth, USAREUR needed to identify which ammunition stocks and other supplies and equipment in USCENTCOM reserves could and should be recovered and returned to USAREUR. Fifth, it was necessary to ascertain the condition of USAREUR equipment and sup-plies, and when and how they could be restored to fully operational capability. Sixth, schedules would be required to address when and how USAREUR equipment and stocks would be returned to Europe.

In May, a team from the 200th TAMMC went to Southwest Asia to try to ensure that USAREUR would receive the assets for which it had identified a need, to establish tighter accountability for USAREUR equipment, and to determine to what extent USAREUR war reserve requirements could be met with equipment from Southwest Asia. Using a list of USAREUR's top twenty-five equipment requirements prepared by Laposata's logisticians in Heidelberg, the 200th TAMMC team, in coordination with ARCENT and DA logistics teams, tried to fill the iden-tified requirements from assets in Southwest Asia.

The USAREUR logistics team also struggled with the remaining issues described above, and in this effort it was assisted by the USAREUR redeployment order and by the work of the 21st TAACOM. The logistics annex of the USAREUR redeployment order instructed units in Southwest Asia that would return without equipment to cross-level Class II, IV, and IX stocks (expendable items, barrier supplies, and repair parts) with units returning to Europe with equipment. All units were to turn in any equipment and supplies that were excess to their require-ments and cross-leveling needs. The 21st TAACOM operated turn-in sites to receive POMCUS and theater reserve equipment as well as excess equipment. Some of the excess equipment would be returned to the United States and some would be sold through the foreign military sales program. With the assistance of HQ USAREUR/7A, the 200th TAMMC team also helped to return or otherwise appropriately dispose of equip-ment that USAREUR had loaned to or borrowed from foreign govern-ments, other services, and ARCENT or other reserve stocks.[24]

Most of the equipment of the 12th Aviation Brigade was returned to Europe in April. The return of other USAREUR units' equipment was fully under way by mid-June. By the beginning of August, 43 of 68 ships allocated to return USAREUR unit equipment had been unloaded in Europe, 4 were unloading, and 16 were en route. An additional 31 ships were then projected to be required to redeploy equipment for Army Readiness Package South, POMCUS, and theater reserve. Personnel from the Military Traffic Management Command, Europe, and the 21st Theater Army Area Command, supplemented by reserve component personnel, operated the port support activities and operations at Rotterdam and Bremerhaven. The reservists deployed in five increments of twenty-two days each as part of their overseas deployment training. In each increment, about fifty reservists went to Rotterdam and thirty went to Bremerhaven.

USAREUR learned from the redeployment of the 12th Aviation Brigade that returned equipment might be in very poor condition, damaged, or even inoperable. In October the commander, V Corps, reported to General Saint that damage to returned USAREUR equipment was serious and ranged as high as 95 percent of certain types of equipment received. USAREUR was still expecting shipments from Southwest Asia in late December 1991.[25] The redeployment of equipment turned out to be less timely and useful in the restoration of USAREUR readiness than USAREUR leaders had expected.

The Fate of 1st Armored Division

The 1st Armored Division provides an excellent example of the diverse missions demanded by the war in the Gulf and its aftermath. After the cessation of their combat mission on 28 February, the 1st Armored Division's soldiers received the new mission of defending and clearing a 2,700-square-kilometer sector of Iraq north-northwest of Kuwait. Over the next three weeks, the division destroyed tons of captured enemy materiel, including 90 tanks, 165 armored personnel carriers, 58 artillery pieces, 90 air defense artillery systems, almost 900 trucks, and great quantities of munitions. On 21 March the division received new orders to move approximately 130 kilometers north along the Military Demarcation Line to take over VII Corps' Checkpoint Bravo and to provide humanitarian assistance to refugees in its new area of responsibility. The division issued almost 5,000 cases of ready-to-eat meals and over 10,000 gallons of bottled water to displaced civilians, while its checkpoints processed over 110,000 refugees and 4,707 enemy prisoners of war.[26]

On 12 April the 1st Armored Division began moving 375 kilometers south into Saudi Arabia to set up Redeployment Assembly Area Kasserine and begin its own redeployment. Most of the combat arms units that served with the 1st Armored Division in Southwest Asia were scheduled to inactivate by 15 January 1992. At Camp Kasserine, these units cleaned their vehicles and other equipment and turned them in for storage in Saudi Arabia. The soldiers in the inactivating units then returned to Europe without their equipment, departing from the airfield at King Khalid Military City.

The elements of the division's aviation brigade and four of the ten maneuver battalions that had served with the division in Southwest Asia were not slated to inactivate in 1991 or 1992. These elements, which would be assigned to the end-state 3d Infantry Division, prepared their equipment for return to Germany. Before returning, the 2d and 4th Battalions, 70th Armor, drew new M1A1 Abrams tanks with heavy armor and used M3A2 Bradley cavalry vehicles. The 1st Battalion, 7th Infantry, and the 1st Battalion, 37th Armor, returned to Germany with the equipment they had used in the war. All of the units returning to Europe with equipment conducted road marches to the departure port and then flew back to Germany from nearby airfields. A detachment of 500 soldier-volunteers remained in the ports to load the 1st Armored Division equipment on to ships. The soldiers of the 1st Armored Division completed their redeployment about 10 May. As the equipment of the end-state units arrived at Amsterdam, Antwerp, and Bremerhaven, those units sent soldiers to the ports to help unload it and return it to their home stations. The VII Corps had authorized its soldiers to take extended leave between 15 May and 15 June, and many 1st Armored Division soldiers took advantage and traveled to the United States.[27]

On 15 June 1991, the 1st Armored Division relinquished command of the armor, aviation, and infantry units that would not stand down in 1991 or 1992, although the soldiers in the reassigned units did not sew on their 3d Infantry Division patches until after the victory celebrations in July. The headquarters of the 1st Armored Division and its inactivating elements remained under VII Corps, while most of its end-state units were reassigned to the V Corps and the 3d Infantry Division. The 1st Armored Division held a victory celebration on 3 July, and its formations were reviewed by Generals Saint and Franks.

The division then began implementing Operation HOMEWARD BOUND, during which most of the soldiers who had served with the division in the Gulf War would inactivate their units and return to the United States. This operation was facilitated by the turn-in of equipment in Saudi Arabia. Much of the equipment that these units had left behind in Germany had similarly been turned in by rear detachments and military communities in Europe. As part of HOMEWARD BOUND, a total of 1,434 1st Armored Division soldiers who had served in Southwest Asia were reassigned within USAREUR and another 6,514 such soldiers were reassigned in the United States. The division was so effective in reassigning personnel, turning in remaining equipment, and readying its facilities for closure that the date of the division's departure from Bavaria was moved up to 16 January 1992. On that day, the CINCUSAREUR, the USAREUR corps and division commanders, and German and other allied representatives attended a noncommissioned officers honors ceremony at Hindenburg Barracks marking the end of the 1st Armored Division service in Ansbach. The next day, 17 January 1992, the

Headquarters and Headquarters Company, 8th Infantry Division, was inactivated and its headquarters at Bad Kreuznach in the German state of Rhineland-Palatinate was reflagged as the 1st Armored Division.[28]

Returning Reserve Component Units to the United States

After the ground war ended in Southwest Asia, HQDA and USAREUR quickly made plans to return from Europe Army Reserve and National Guard personnel serving there. USAREUR published instructions to return home by 20 March 1991 at a rate of 500 to 700 per day the individual ready reserve personnel it had received, a group that numbered over 5,000. On 13 March USAREUR released DESERT SHIELD/DESERT STORM temporary tour of active duty volunteers. Eight Army Reserve and National Guard medical units were redeployed to the United States between 12 and 16 March. The return of some reserve component units and individuals was determined by the date they completed their mission. Other units and individuals did not depart until the unit or individual they were replacing returned from Southwest Asia. This delayed the release of some medical units and personnel, because USCENTCOM retained a number of USAREUR medical units until they could conduct a series of medical examinations in Southwest Asia. By late June, however, most units were scheduled for departure.[29]

Ending Special Personnel Policies

HQ USAREUR/7A and the 1st Personnel Command moved quickly to readjust and terminate personnel policies that had been implemented to build up VII Corps before its deployment and to maintain USAREUR capabilities during the deployment. Based on HQDA instructions ending stop-loss provisions throughout the Army, HQ USAREUR/7A took action in March and early April to end stop-loss procedures effective 13 April 1991 and to establish release dates for those whose terms of service had been extended due to the crisis. Personnel who had remained in Europe would be released by 12 April. Deployed personnel whose service had been extended beyond the normal expiration date would be separated from the Army by 7 July 1991. On 20 March HQ USAREUR/7A issued guidance on handling soldiers who had been cross-leveled to other units. A soldier who had been merely attached to another unit would return to his or her original unit within seventy-two hours after return from Southwest Asia, unless that unit had been announced for inactivation. In the latter case, the 1st Personnel Command would issue new assignment instructions. A soldier who had been formally assigned to the new unit for deployment would remain with it. Not until 19 April, however, did HQ USAREUR/7A act to end extensions of involuntary foreign service tours. It then announced a schedule for readjusting the dates at which individuals would become eligible for return from overseas, moving gradually toward the normal return schedule. After 1 October 1991, soldiers desiring to extend their service in Europe would have to request that in line with normal policies and procedures.[30]

Enhancing U.S.-Based Contingency Capability

Soon after the end of the ground war, the Army developed a program, called Enhancing CONUS (continental United States) Contingency Capability or EC3, to improve its readiness to participate in new operations in Southwest Asia or elsewhere. The EC3 initiative derived from one of the first lessons the U.S. Army learned from its deployment to Southwest Asia. It became painfully evident early in Operation DESERT SHIELD that the Army could not quickly assemble the required combat support and combat service support force structure, including ordnance companies, truck companies, transportation headquarters, and medical units, as quickly and successfully as it could obtain other types of units. The active Army unit structure was clearly inadequate, and the reserve component units expected to meet the support shortfall needed more time than was available to prepare and deploy.

The Department of the Army responded to this deficiency by developing plans in March and April 1991 to add significant combat support and combat service support elements to its contingency force in the United States. General Heldstab and HQ USAREUR/7A planners began meeting with Pentagon planners on this initiative in late March. General Reimer's operations office in the Pentagon selected from USAREUR's list of units planned for inactivation through 1993 a group of units that would redress the support deficiencies. Secretary Stone approved the EC3 initiative on 22 May 1991, and two weeks later, after coordinating plans with Pflaster's CFE Division, HQDA sent USAREUR a list of units that, rather than inactivating in Europe, would return to the United States to become part of this contingency capability. HQDA also provided at this time a redeployment schedule and a list of the units' new stations in the United States.[31]

To assist this initiative, HQ USAREUR/7A decided that the first twenty-two USAREUR EC3 units scheduled to join the CONUS contingency force, all of which were deployed to Southwest Asia, should redeploy from there to Europe without equipment. Although doing this would temporarily lower USAREUR's combat service support readiness, their equipment was sent directly to the United States. The contingency force units included field artillery and air defense artillery elements, combat support hospitals, and chemical, engineer, maintenance, military police, supply, and transportation companies or headquarters detachments. The total USAREUR contribution to EC3 would be fifty-seven units with about 12,000 soldiers. The units began to redeploy from Europe to the United States in October 1991.[32]

The most serious problem this caused, however, was that in order to do this USAREUR would have to delay the inactivation, scheduled for early or mid-1992, of other units that were also redeploying from Southwest Asia without equipment. This seemed to mean that either the soldiers without equipment would remain in USAREUR unable to train, or USAREUR could bring back their equipment even though the unit would inactivate in just over a year and the equipment would not be needed otherwise. In either case, USAREUR would have to keep installations open longer than needed to inactivate a unit, an expensive course of action. HQ USAREUR/7A planners made their best judgments between these two unsatisfactory options. In the end no unit without equipment had to stay in USAREUR longer than a year, and this interval was reduced further for most of these units, when HQDA approved an accelerated 1992 drawdown schedule.[33]

Redeployment of USAREUR Task Forces

USAREUR was able to redeploy its units and personnel that had participated in the special task forces related to the war with Iraq more quickly than it could arrange the return of units and personnel serving in and around Kuwait.

The USAREUR units that participated in the task forces operating from Turkey returned to Europe within two months of the successful conclusion of the ground war. By mid-March, all of these units had redeployed except for the deployed elements of the 4th Battalion, 7th Air Defense Artillery, and the 324th Signal Company. Those units redeployed in April. However, a caretaker force of forty-two 32d AADCOM soldiers remained to retain control of the air defense artillery battalion's equipment. The equipment and the caretaker force would stay in Turkey through the fall of 1991.[34] The redeployment from Israel of USAREUR units that had participated in Joint Task Force PATRIOT DEFENDER started at the beginning of April and was quickly completed.[35]

USAREUR Participation in Postwar Contingency Operations

USAREUR was called on to provide leadership for or to participate in several postwar operations in Southwest Asia. These operations illustrated that USAREUR's mission in the post–Cold War period was to serve as the U.S. Army contingency force forward deployed in Europe. The full story of these highly significant operations must be told elsewhere, but they are summarized below to underscore the continuity of these new missions for the USAREUR that had deployed VII Corps to Southwest Asia, its first major post–Cold War out-of-theater mission.

Operation PROVIDE COMFORT

Beginning in mid-April, USAREUR made a major contribution to Combined Task Force PROVIDE COMFORT, which was designed by the U.S. Defense Department, in coordination with allied governments, to provide humanitarian relief to the separatist Kurds of northern Iraq. At the conclusion of the Gulf War, Iraq's minority Kurdish population fled from persecution by Iraqi military and civilian authorities to inhospitable mountain terrain along Iraq's frontiers with Turkey and Iran and into those two nations. The Joint Chiefs of Staff selected General Shalikashvili, who had played an important role in organizing USAREUR's support for Operations DESERT SHIELD and DESERT STORM, to lead Combined Task Force PROVIDE COMFORT. Shalikashvili departed for Turkey on 18 April, accompanied by Maj. Gen. Jay M. Garner, the deputy commander of V Corps, who became the commander of Joint Task Force BRAVO. Garner's division-size task force, made up of components of eight nations' armies, was responsible for ground security in northern Iraq and, in effect, for showing the Kurds that it was safe to return to their homeland. Shalikashvili's air forces, meanwhile, prevented Iraqi planes from flying over the area.

USAREUR support of Operation PROVIDE COMFORT was diverse and substantial. On 29 May there were 5,315 USAREUR soldiers, including several aviation units and many combat service support units, deployed to Turkey and northern Iraq to support the operation. USAREUR also contributed huge quantities of relief supplies. The operation began to be scaled back in June as many Kurdish refugees gained enough confidence to return home. USAREUR personnel deployed in support of PROVIDE COMFORT thus declined by the end of June to 3,701; by the end of July to 2,005; and by the end of September to 1,649. Most of the remaining USAREUR soldiers would return in the fall of 1991, though a small USAREUR contingent remained.[36]

Task Force POSITIVE FORCE and Task Forces VICTORY I and II

USAREUR continued to help protect Kuwait through the end of the year. In May General Franks informed General Saint that the 3d Armored Division was protecting refugees along Kuwait's border with Iraq and that he believed that it might be necessary to leave a residual force in Kuwait. Although a 1,440-member United Nations (UN) peacekeeping force commanded by Austrian Maj. Gen. Gunther Greindl took control of the Iraq-Kuwait border in late April and early May, the 1st Brigade, 3d Armored Division, called Task Force POSITIVE FORCE, remained in Kuwait to continue its defense until 15 June 1991. It was reconfigured for this purpose to include the 3d Battalion, 5th Cavalry; 2d and 4th Battalions, 67th Armor; 2d Battalion, 3d Field Artillery; 54th Support Battalion; and the entire 23d Engineer Battalion. The brigade established a base camp called Camp Thunder Rock at an industrial complex that the Iraqis had looted in Doha, a suburb of Kuwait City. The delay in the return of the 1st Brigade soldiers prompted about sixty military spouses to write a letter in late May to the American ambassador in Bonn seeking assurances that the unit would return to Germany soon. General Saint, after informing them of the importance of the mission, reassured them that their spouses would be home in June. On 15 June 1991, the brigade was replaced by the bulk of the 11th Armored Cavalry Regiment, a smaller portion of which had deployed to PROVIDE COMFORT. That regiment was a V Corps unit that deployed to Southwest Asia from Europe after the Gulf War cease-fire. The brigade returned to Germany to become the 1st Brigade, 1st Armored Division, although it was placed under the control of the 8th Infantry Division until the latter was reflagged as the 1st Armored Division on 17 January 1992. Many members of the brigade took leave in July. They subsequently picked up their equipment, which had been shipped from the Gulf in August.[37]

The elements of the 11th Armored Cavalry Regiment in Kuwait, which were called Task Force VICTORY I, continued the U.S. combat presence there at the request of the restored Kuwaiti government after almost all of the U.S. troops that served in Southwest Asia during the Gulf War had redeployed. The 11th Armored Cavalry Regiment used some of the equipment of the 1st Brigade, 3d Armored Division, and supplemented it from the stocks of the Combat Equipment Group, Southwest Asia. The 11th constructed a firing range for tanks and Bradley fighting vehicles and a small arms range and then conducted training to maintain its readiness. The cavalrymen were supported by a small number of military police and communications personnel from other USAREUR units. On 7 September, the 11th Armored Cavalry Regiment was itself replaced by a battalion-size force from USAREUR called Task Force VICTORY II, consisting of two companies of the 3d Battalion, 77th Armor, and two companies of the 4th Battalion, 8th Infantry, both 8th Infantry Division units, augmented by a fifteen-member staff from the headquarters of the 8th Infantry Division and V Corps. At the end of November, the Department of Defense and USEUCOM announced that Task Force VICTORY II would redeploy in mid-December 1991.[38]

Operation DETERMINED RESOLVE

USAREUR acquired another new mission, Operation DETERMINED RESOLVE, in September 1991, reconstituting Patriot air defense artillery coverage in Riyadh and providing continued coverage in Dhahran and King Khalid Military City in Saudi Arabia. For this operation, USAREUR and the 32d AADCOM deployed the 94th Air Defense Artillery Brigade headquarters; the 1st and 5th Battalions, 7th Air Defense Artillery; and two support companies with over 1,300 soldiers.[39]

Restructuring USAREUR for Additional Post–Cold War Missions

Through the demanding year of 1991, despite the redeployment from Southwest Asia and the additional contingency missions there, USAREUR pressed ahead quickly in its efforts to draw down its forces and to restructure its elements to form the contingency force under V Corps that would enable it to meet its post–Cold War mission efficiently. On 10 May General Saint issued instructions for a new command realignment that would be effective 15 June. This realignment ensured that units returning with equipment from Southwest Asia would be supported and integrated with USAREUR's end-state forces under V Corps. It meant that, shortly after their return from Southwest Asia, many units would join a new division and a new corps and would begin preparing for new post–Cold War missions.[40] Restructuring and drawdown would continue through 1991 and 1992 at a hectic pace.

Gradually HQDA and USAREUR made some revisions to the command's drawdown plans as it moved swiftly toward its 92,200 strength objective. Secretary of Defense Cheney, the Joint Chiefs of Staff, and HQDA in June 1991 approved a USAREUR plan to draw down its strength by 52,000 in fiscal year 1992. Under the plan, many units once scheduled for drawdown in fiscal year 1991 actually inactivated in the months of October to December in the first quarter of fiscal year 1992. In October 1991 HQDA accelerated the drawdown, and additional units

Maj. Gen. Jerry R. Rutherford, left, commander of the 3d Armored Division, and General Maddox case the division's colors in January 1992 as it marks the end of its service in Europe.

with an aggregate strength of 20,000 soldiers were added to 1992 inactivation lists. This brought the total for the year to 70,000, a figure Saint had suggested ten months earlier. Many of the units added to the 1992 drawdown list had fought in the Gulf War, including the 2d Armored Division (Forward) and the squadrons of the 2d Armored Cavalry Regiment. The headquarters of that regiment, however, continued to serve in the United States, and its squadrons were activated again there in 1993.[41] Retiring the colors of other units whose combat in Southwest Asia had merely capped long traditions of service in the defense of American freedom and liberty, USAREUR adopted a leaner and more flexible profile to face the post–Cold War world that the command had helped bring about and was now prepared to help defend.

Conclusion

The deployment by the U.S. Army, Europe, of VII Corps, other command elements, and massive sustainment support to Southwest Asia and

Operation DESERT STORM was the first, and to date the largest, operational mission of this restructured, forward-deployed command in the post–Cold War world. USAREUR was able to respond quickly and effectively to the Kuwait crisis and to furnish the central battle force for the war in the Gulf, because of the improved political and military situation in Europe and USAREUR's aggressive effort to make the transition to a post–Cold War structure.

Well before the Gulf crisis, General Saint had taken advantage of the significantly reduced danger to begin reshaping his army in Europe into a new mobile force with a flexible structure that could adapt to the more varied contingencies that might arise in the post–Cold War world. By mid-1989 Saint and his planners had determined the need for an enhanced, mobile, heavy force—the capable corps. By the end of 1989 Saint had begun training this force, while preparing, under budgetary constraints, to reduce and restructure it. USAREUR's contribution to the Gulf War was thus shaped by the earlier, unrelated initiatives to restructure and retrain USAREUR. The uncertainty that the USAREUR commander faced in predicting where his forces might be engaged will surely continue to confront future American commanders. Saint's successors will probably know much more about how to produce an effective military organization than where and under what circumstances it may be needed.

In preparing the force that would eventually be called upon to fight in Southwest Asia, General Saint aggressively pursued traditional doctrinal principles. First, he stressed maintaining full-strength, well-equipped, combat-ready units, even at the cost of reducing force structure. Second, he gave top priority to developing modern, automated training facilities focusing particularly on realistic small unit and gunnery training. Third, he modernized his force as quickly and effectively as possible, again even at the cost of smaller forces. What, more than anything else, was "new" in Saint's pursuit of these fundamental principles was the single-mindedness with which he defended them in a time of reduced budgets, changing missions, arms control restrictions, drawdown, deployment, and war.

General Saint strictly applied these principles as he developed his force restructuring, drawdown, and capable corps employment plans and initiatives. By the beginning of 1990, Saint had begun to train his forces under a modified AirLand Battle doctrine designed to enable a heavy, fully mobile, self-contained corps to fight effectively on a nonlinear battlefield. This training underlay the effectiveness of VII Corps the following February in its critical combat role in the desert.

One important element in USAREUR's ability to make available quickly and efficiently the forces required by USCENTCOM at the end of 1990 was the detailed data analysis capability that Saint's command had developed. The USAREUR commander had decided in 1988 to begin force restructure planning at the bottom rather than the top. That decision, combined with the intricacies of arms control negotiations and the prospect of severe budget reductions, led Saint's planners, aided by the staffs of USAREUR headquarters and its major commands, to collect, maintain, and interpret a detailed, wide-ranging, and continually updated body of force management data. When General Saint and his major commanders used this enhanced data management capacity for mixing and matching units and cross-leveling personnel and equipment, they were able to put together a VII Corps battle force that maximized the potential of their trained and modernized battalions.

The initial deployment of a forward-stationed capable corps tested USAREUR's ability to perform a variety of tasks. USAREUR's soldiers responded successfully, largely because they were willing and able to do whatever was necessary to get the job done and performed many duties normally accomplished at higher or lower levels or by other personnel. USAREUR units and individuals showed themselves capable of effective performance even when suddenly attached to new brigades, divisions, and corps. The transportation net in Europe and air links to Southwest Asia were found to be adequate for the task of rapidly deploying a heavy corps there. Sealift capacity, however, proved inadequate, as did communications capabilities between USAREUR and Southwest Asia. The Army community in Europe demonstrated that it was resourceful and capable enough both to care for itself and to provide force protection, although its success in these areas was based on a larger force structure than USAREUR would be able to retain. Army directives on family support seemed sound. USAREUR received support and cooperation from its host nations and allies that reflected both similar views on the current crisis and years of living, working, and training together in pursuit of common goals. USAREUR leaders' long-established personal and official relationships with European decision-makers encouraged the latter to make policy decisions that contributed to the deployment's success.

Although the management principles and methodologies that worked for General Saint and other USAREUR leaders at this time could be effective in other contingencies as well, USAREUR itself will not likely have the capacity to field a similar force or to provide equally massive sustainment in the future. By 1996, USAREUR's total strength was less than that of VII Corps when it deployed to the desert. In 1990, Saint enjoyed the brief luxury of mixing and matching the best prepared units of two corps to build the VII Corps he deployed without having to fear a significant threat to the defense of Western Europe. The massive sustainment provided to ARCENT and USCENTCOM was substantially drawn from American war reserves that have, since then, largely been withdrawn from Europe in the aftermath of the collapse of the Soviet Union and the Warsaw Pact. The supporting force structure and military communities have also been significantly reduced.

The experience of the U.S. Army, Europe, with Operations DESERT SHIELD and DESERT STORM tested the mettle of many of America's best professional soldiers not only in war but also in peacetime planning and organizing. USAREUR leaders and soldiers were required to juggle many overlapping missions and requirements, in addition to risking lives in a war in the desert. During the deployment this meant simultaneously maintaining the security of Europe, fulfilling the Army's community responsibilities, planning for drawdown and restructuring, and, for many soldiers, being attached to new units, serving in a new theater of operations, and participating in war. After the war it meant rapid transition from the alien world of combat, which for a time dominated the lives of those deployed and their families, back to a post–Cold War command obliged to conduct an aggressive restructuring, during which many of the units that had fought victoriously in that war were inactivated. Both in Southwest Asia and in Europe, USAREUR's soldiers proved that they were capable of carrying out these varied, challenging, and sometimes threatening tasks and missions with skill, professionalism, and wholehearted responsiveness to America's democratic institutions.

Appendixes

Appendix A

HQDA Requests by October 1990 for USAREUR Units in January and March 1991 Rotations

JANUARY 1991 ROTATION

Type of Unit	Available in USAREUR	Number of Soldiers
1 Heavy Armored Div[1]	Yes	16,996
Artillery		
2 Fld Arty Bde HQ	Yes	108
2 MLRS Bn	Yes	918
2 155-mm. Bn	Yes	1,162
2 8-inch Bn	Yes	1,188
Engineer		
1 Combat Bn	Yes	809
1 CSE Co	Yes	198
1 Bde HQ	Yes	121
2 Combat Hvy Bn	Yes	1,388
2 Combat Mech Bn	Yes	1,618
Aviation		
1 UH–60 Co	Yes	132
1 CH–47 Co	Yes	183
Combat Service Support		
4 Mdm Truck Co	2 only	338
1 Truck Co (POL)	Yes	164
1 Truck Co (HET)	Yes	143

[1] See the Glossary for the meaning of abbreviations and acronyms used in the appendixes.

Type of Unit	Available in USAREUR	Number of Soldiers
1 Trans Bn HQ	Yes	48
2 Ammo Co (DS)	1 only	216
1 Aerial Exploitation Bn	Yes	390
1 Dental Det	Yes	56
1 Ambulance Co	Yes	98
1 Personnel Svc Co	Yes	144
1 Finance Spt Unit	Yes	122
1 Decontamination Co	Yes	123
1 S & S Bn	Yes	55
1 Sup Co (DS)	No	
1 Field Svc Co	Yes	206
1 Repair Parts Co	No	
5 Maintenance Co (DS)	No	
2 ATE Det	Yes	26
1 LEMCO	Yes	204
3 Maint HHD	No	62
1 MP CID Team	Yes	11
2 Area Signal Bn	Yes	1,464

March 1991 Rotation

Type of Unit	Available in USAREUR	Number of Soldiers
1 Armored Cav Regiment	Yes	4,700
Aviation		
2 AH–64 Bn	Yes	522
4 UH–60 Co	Yes	528
4 CH–47 Co	2 Only	366
1 OH–58 Platoon	Yes	56
Signal		
TRITAC Bn	Yes	627
Comp Bde	No	
Combat Service Support		
1 CSE Co (EN)	Yes	198
1 EOD Det	Yes	23
1 Ord Maint Co	No	

Type of Unit	Available in USAREUR	Number of Soldiers
1 Area Spt Gp Log HQ...............	No	
1 ATE Det	Yes	13
1 Sup Co (DS).....................	No	
1 Sup Co (GS).....................	Yes	174
1 Heavy Material Co	Yes	217
2 Maint Co (DS)	Yes	903
1 Decon Co.......................	Yes	123
2 NBC Teams......................	Yes	20
1 MP Bde HQ	Yes	67
2 MP Bn HQ......................	Yes	166
6 MP Co	Yes	936

March Rotation (Continued)

Air Defense Artillery

1 Patriot Bn.......................	Yes	770
2 Patriot Maint Co..................	1 Only	112

Medical

2 Dispensaries	Yes	19
1 Dental Det	Yes	90
1 Air Ambulance Co	Yes	105
1 Ground Ambulance Co	Yes	98

Total Requested: 95 units with 42,168 soldiers

Total Available: 75 units with 39,524 soldiers

Total Possible 1991 Reduction of USAREUR Strength: 30,000

USAREUR Units Deployed with VII Corps

Section I—Combat and Combat Support Units

Unit	Parent Unit	Unit Location	Equip	Nov 1990 Strength Auth	Asgn	Percentage	Scheduled Drawdown*
1st Armored Division		Ansbach					1992
3d Brigade	3d IN Div	Aschaffenburg		2248	1982	88.2	1992
1–7 Infantry	3d IN Div	Aschaffenburg	M2A2	842	734	87.2	1992
4–7 Infantry	3d IN Div	Aschaffenburg	M2A2	842	749	89.0	1992
4–66 Armor	3d IN Div	Aschaffenburg	M1A1	564	499	88.5	1992
2d Brigade	1st AR Div	Erlangen	M2A2	2488	2228	89.6	
6–6 Infantry	1st AR Div	Bamberg	M2A2	819	740	90.4	1991
1–35 Armor	1st AR Div	Erlangen	M1A1	558	489	87.6	1991
2–70 Armor	1st AR Div	Erlangen	M1A1	555	496	89.4	
4–70 Armor	1st AR Div	Erlangen	M1A1	556	503	90.5	
3d Brigade	1st AR Div	Bamberg	M2A2	1967	1807	91.9	1991
7–6 Infantry	1st AR Div	Bamberg	M2A2	841	767	91.2	1991
3–35 Armor	1st AR Div	Bamberg	M1A1	562	474	84.3	1991
1–37 Armor	1st AR Div	Vilseck	M1A1	564	566	100.4	

SECTION I—COMBAT AND COMBAT SUPPORT UNITS (CONTINUED)

Unit	Parent Unit	Unit Location	Equip	Nov 1990 Strength Auth	Asgn	Percentage	Scheduled Drawdown*
1–1 Cavalry	1st AR Div	Katterbach		545	518	95.0	1992
Aviation Brigade	1st AR Div	Katterbach		802	773	96.4	
2–1 Aviation	1st AR Div	Katterbach	AH–64	265	268	101.1	
3–1 Aviation	1st AR Div	Katterbach	AH–64	266	254	95.5	
G–1 Aviation	1st AR Div	Katterbach		138	134	97.1	
H–1 Aviation	1st AR Div	Katterbach		133	117	88.0	
Division Artillery	1st AR Div	Zirndorf		2323	2147	92.4	1992
2–1 FA	1st AR Div	Zirndorf	155SP	695	604	86.9	
3–1 FA	1st AR Div	Bamberg	155SP	701	651	92.9	1992
2–41 FA	3d IN Div	Bad Kissingen	155SP	704	652	92.6	
B/25 FA	1st AR Div	Grafenwoehr	TAB	91	86	94.5	
A/94 FA	1st AR Div	Erlangen	MLRS	132	154	116.7	
DISCOM	1st AR Div	Fuerth		2560	2485	97.1	1992
26th FSB	3d IN Div	Aschaffenburg		419	384	91.6	1992
47th FSB	1st AR Div	Erlangen		478	469	98.1	
123d MSB	1st AR Div	Fuerth		1009	1000	99.1	1992
125th FSB	1st AR Div	Bamberg		428	390	91.1	1992
1–1 AV (Maint)	1st AR Div	Katterbach		226	242	107.1	1992

SECTION I—COMBAT AND COMBAT SUPPORT UNITS (CONTINUED)

Unit	Parent Unit	Unit Location	Equip	Nov 1990 Strength Auth	Nov 1990 Strength Asgn	Nov 1990 Strength Percentage	Scheduled Drawdown*
Division Troops							
6–3 ADA	1st AR Div	Schwabach		794	756	95.2	1991
69th Chemical Co	1st AR Div	Fuerth		160	134	83.8	1992
16th Engineer Bn	1st AR Div	Fuerth		909	851	93.6	
501st MI Bn	1st AR Div	Katterbach		469	410	87.4	1992
501st MP Co	1st AR Div	Katterbach		153	130	85.0	1992
141st Signal Bn	1st AR Div	Ansbach		681	630	92.5	1992
1st AR Div Band	1st AR Div	Ansbach		41	43	104.9	1992
1st AR Div HHC	1st AR Div	Ansbach		277	442	159.6	1992
Det 5, 7th Wea Sqdn	(Air Force)						
Subtotal						93.4	
3d Armored Division		Frankfurt					1992
1st Brigade	3d AR Div	Kirchgoens		2800	2547	91.0	
3–5 Cavalry	3d AR Div	Kirchgoens	M2A1	839	750	89.4	
5–5 Cavalry	3d AR Div	Kirchgoens	M2A1	839	749	89.3	1991
4–32 Armor	3d AR Div	Kirchgoens	M1A1	561	524	93.4	1992
4–34 Armor	8th IN Div	Mainz	M1A1	561	524	93.4	1991
2d Brigade	3d AR Div	Gelnhausen		1988	1772	89.1	1991
4–18 Infantry	3d AR Div	Gelnhausen	M2A1	866	764	88.2	1991
3–8 Cavalry	3d AR Div	Gelnhausen	M1A1HA	561	504	89.8	1991
4–8 Cavalry	3d AR Div	Gelnhausen	M1A1HA	561	504	89.8	1991

SECTION I—COMBAT AND COMBAT SUPPORT UNITS (CONTINUED)

Unit	Parent Unit	Unit Location	Equip	Nov 1990 Strength Auth	Asgn	Percentage	Scheduled Drawdown*
3d Brigade	3d AR Div	Friedberg		1961	1786	91.1	1992
5–18 Infantry	3d AR Div	Friedberg	M2A1	839	757	90.2	1991
2–67 Armor	3d AR Div	Friedberg	M1A1	561	506	90.2	
4–67 Armor	3d AR Div	Friedberg	M1A1HA	561	523	93.2	
4–7 Cavalry	3d IN Div	Buedingen	M3	547	506	92.5	1992
Aviation Brigade (-)	3d AR Div	Hanau		519	529	101.9	
2–227 Aviation	3d AR Div	Hanau	AH–64	261	267	102.3	
G–227 Aviation	3d AR Div	Hanau		125	141	112.8	
H–227 Aviation	3d AR Div	Hanau		133	121	91.0	1992
Division Artillery	3d AR Div	Hanau		2299	2076	90.3	
2–3 FA	3d AR Div	Kirchgoens	155SP	720	638	88.6	
2–82 FA	3d AR Div	Friedberg	155SP	675	608	90.1	1991
4–82 FA	3d AR Div	Hanau	155SP	675	613	90.8	
A/40 FA	3d AR Div	Hanau	MRLS	131	133	101.5	
F/333 FA	3d AR Div	Hanau		98	84	85.7	
DISCOM	3d AR Div	Frankfurt		2553	2356	92.3	1992
45th FSB	3d AR Div	Gelnhausen		427	390	91.3	1992
54th FSB	3d AR Div	Friedberg		435	385	88.5	
122d MSB	3d AR Div	Hanau		1009	900	89.2	1992
503d FSB	3d AR Div	Kirchgoens		456	403	88.4	1992
1–227 AV (Maint)	3d AR Div	Hanau		226	278	123.0	

SECTION I—COMBAT AND COMBAT SUPPORT UNITS (CONTINUED)

Unit	Parent Unit	Unit Location	Equip	Nov 1990 Strength			Scheduled Drawdown*
				Auth	Asgn	Percentage	
Division Troops							
5–3 ADA	8th IN Div	Wachenheim		NA			
22d Chemical Co	3d AR Div	Frankfurt		160	133	83.1	1992
23d Engineer Bn	3d AR Div	Hanau		909	831	91.4	
533d MI Bn	3d AR Div	Frankfurt		430	433	100.7	1992
503d MP Co	3d AR Div	Frankfurt		153	144	94.1	1992
143d Signal Bn	3d AR Div	Frankfurt		463	535	115.6	1992
3d AR Div Band	3d AR Div	Frankfurt		40	46	115.0	1992
3d AR Div HHC	3d AR Div	Frankfurt		265	288	108.7	1992
Det 2, 7th Wea Sqdn	(Air Force)						
Subtotal						92.7†	
2d Armored Cavalry Regiment		Nuremberg		4951	4906	99.1	
1st Squadron	2d ACR	Bindlach	M1/M3	888	846	95.3	
2d Squadron	2d ACR	Bamberg	M1/M3	896	870	97.1	
3d Squadron	2d ACR	Amberg	M1/M3	896	832	92.9	
4th Squadron (Avn)	2d ACR	Feucht		502	493	98.2	
CS Sqdn	2d ACR	Bindlach		816	806	98.8	
87th Chemical Co	2d ACR	Nuremberg		72	117	162.5	
84th Engineer Co	2d ACR	Bayreuth		200	216	108.0	
502d MI Co	2d ACR	Nuremberg		681	726	106.6	
Det 1, 7th Wea Sqdn	(Air Force)						

SECTION 1—COMBAT AND COMBAT SUPPORT UNITS (CONTINUED)

Unit	Parent Unit	Unit Location	Equip	Auth	Asgn	Percentage	Scheduled Drawdown*
					Nov 1990 Strength		
11th Aviation Brigade		Illesheim		1614†	1563†	96.8†	
2–6 Cavalry	11th Avn Bde	Illesheim	AH–64	266	253	95.1	1992
4–159 Aviation	11th Avn Bde	Stuttgart		325	292	89.8	1991
4–229 Aviation	11th Avn Bde	Illesheim	AH–64	NA			
A/5–159 AV (Mdm Lift)	11th Avn Bde	Schwaebisch Hall		183	181	98.9	
C/6–159 Aviation	11th Avn Bde	Schwaebisch Hall		133	122	91.7	
7–159 AV (AVIM)	11th Avn Bde	Nellingen		631	610	96.7	
HHC	11th Avn Bde	Illesheim		76	105	138.2	
Det 13, 7th Wea Sqdrn	(Air Force)						
VII Corps Artillery	VII Corps	Augsburg		2742†	2568†	93.7†	
42d FA Brigade	V Corps Arty	Giessen		1719	1528	88.9	
3–20 FA	V Corps Arty	Hanau	155SP	589	492	83.5	
1–27 FA	V Corps Arty	Babenhausen	MLRS	455	422	92.7	
2–29 FA	8th IN Div	Baumholder	155SP	675	614	91.0	
210th FA Brigade	VII Corps Arty	Herzogenaurach		1023†	1040†	101.7†	1992
3–17 FA	VII Corps Arty	Ansbach	155SP	568	547	96.3	
4–27 FA	VII Corps Arty	Wertheim	MLRS	455	493	108.4	
6–41 FA	3d IN Div	Kitzingen	155SP	NA			
ADA Task Force							
TF 8–43	32d AADCOM	Giebelstadt	Patriot	960	942	98.1	
A/8–43 ADA	32d AADCOM	Giebelstadt		95	87	91.6	

SECTION I—COMBAT AND COMBAT SUPPORT UNITS (CONTINUED)

Unit	Parent Unit	Unit Location	Equip	Nov 1990 Strength			Scheduled Drawdown*
				Auth	Asgn	Percentage	
ADA Task Force (Continued)							
B/8–43 ADA	32d AADCOM	Giebelstadt	Patriot	95	95	100.0	
C/8–43 ADA	32d AADCOM	Giebelstadt	Patriot	98	90	91.8	
A/6–52 ADA	32d AADCOM	Wuerzburg	Hawk	129	126	97.7	
C/6–52 ADA	32d AADCOM	Giebelstadt	Hawk	129	125	96.9	
57th Maint Co (Patriot)	32d AADCOM	Giebelstadt		98	103	105.1	
569th Ordnance Co (Hawk Maint)	32d AADCOM	Wuerzburg		129	144	111.6	1992
HHB 8–43 ADA	32d AADCOM	Giebelstadt		187	172	92.0	
7th Engineer Brigade	VII Corps	Kornwestheim		3073†	2769†	90.1†	
9th Engineer Bn	7th EN Bde	Aschaffenburg		730	626	85.8	1991
82d Engineer Bn	7th EN Bde	Bamberg		728	669	91.9	
249th Engineer Bn	18th EN Bde	Knielingen		694	600	86.5	1993
317th Engineer Bn	130th EN Bde	Eschborn		814	769	94.5	
A/649th Engineer Bn	8th EN Bde	Schwetzingen		NA			
38th Engineer Co	7th EN Bde	Kornwestheim		107	105	98.1	
207th Military Intelligence Brigade							
207th MI Bde	VII Corps	Ludwigsburg		1249†	1156†	92.6†	1992
2d MI Bn	207th MI Bde	Echterdingen		365	365	100.0	
307th MI Bn	207th MI Bde	Ludwigsburg		436	352	80.7	1992
511th MI Bn	207th MI Bde	Ludwigsburg		448	439	98.0	
HHD	207th MI Bde	Ludwigsburg		NA			

SECTION I—COMBAT AND COMBAT SUPPORT UNITS (CONTINUED)

Unit	Parent Unit	Unit Location	Equip	Nov 1990 Strength Auth	Asgn	Percentage	Scheduled Drawdown*
14th Military Police Brigade							
14th MP Bde	VII Corps	Kornwestheim		859†	839†	97.7†	1992
HHC	14th MP Bde	Kornwestheim		71	84	118.3	1992
HHD, 93d MP Bn	18th MP Bde (V Corps)	Frankfurt		NA			
59th MP Co	21st TAACOM	Pirmasens		158	154	97.5	
92d MP Co	18th MP Bde	Baumholder		157	150	95.5	
109th MP Co	18th MP Bde	Frankfurt		157	154	98.1	
HHD, 793d MP Bn	14th MP Bde	Fuerth		NA			
66th MP Co	21st TAACOM	Karlsruhe		158	146	92.2	
212th MP Co	14th MP Bde	Stuttgart		NA			
218th MP Co	14th MP Bde	Augsburg		158	151	95.6	
93d Signal Brigade							
93d Signal Brigade	VII Corps	Heilbronn		1974†	1866†	94.5†	1992
HHC	93d Sig Bde	Heilbronn		162	177	109.3	1992
1st Signal Bn	5th Sig Cmd	Kaiserslautern		NA			
26th Signal Bn	93d Sig Bde	Heilbronn		649	596	91.8	1992
34th Signal Bn	93d Sig Bde	Heilbronn		613	552	90.0	1992
51st Signal Bn	93d Sig Bde	Ludwigsburg		550	541	98.4	
Co C, 17th Signal Bn	22d Sig Bde (V Corps)	Kitzingen		NA			

SECTION I—COMBAT AND COMBAT SUPPORT UNITS (CONTINUED)

Unit	Parent Unit	Unit Location	Equip	Nov 1990 Strength Auth	Asgn	Percentage	Scheduled Drawdown*
2d Armored Division Forward							
3d Brigade	2d AR Div	Garlstedt		3605†	3485†	96.7†	1992
1–41 Infantry	2d AD Fwd	Garlstedt	M2	839	851	101.4	
2–66 Armor	2d AD Fwd	Garlstedt	M1A1	561	538	95.9	
3–66 Armor	2d AD Fwd	Garlstedt	M1A1	581	560	96.4	
4–3 FA	2d AD Fwd	Garlstedt	155SP	675	635	94.1	
498th Support Bn (FSB)	2d AD Fwd	Garlstedt		777	735	94.6	
D/17 Engineer Bn	2d AD Fwd	Garlstedt		172	166	96.5	
Det, 101st MI Bn	1st ID Fwd	Goeppingen		NA			1991
HHC, 3d Brigade	2d AD Fwd	Garlstedt		NA			1992
Total						94.1†	

*Dates shown only for units scheduled for inactivation in 1991 and 1992
†Incomplete figure

SECTION II—COMBAT SERVICE SUPPORT UNITS

Parent Unit	USAREUR Major Command	Location
7th Finance Group	VII Corps	
HHD	VII Corps	Stuttgart
17th Finance Support Unit	VII Corps	Ansbach
59th Finance Support Unit	21st TAACOM	Bremerhaven
106th Finance Support Unit	VII Corps	Ludwigsburg
201st Finance Support Unit	V Corps	Frankfurt
501st Finance Support Unit	VII Corps	Fuerth
7th Personnel Group	VII Corps	
HHD	VII Corps	Nellingen
115th Adjutant General Co (Postal)	1st PERSCOM	Kaiserslautern
178th Personnel Service Co	VII Corps	Aschaffenburg
259th Personnel Service Co	VII Corps	Bamberg
261st Personnel Service Co	VII Corps	Heilbronn
369th Personnel Service Co	V Corps	Giessen
400th Personnel Service Co	VII Corps	Ansbach
9th Replacement Detachment	VII Corps	Nellingen
VII Corps Special Troops		
HHC, VII Corps	VII Corps	Stuttgart
84th Army Band	VII Corps	Stuttgart
242d Chemical Det (NBC)	2d COSCOM	Nellingen
Det 9, 7th Weather Squadron	(Air Force)	
2d Corps Support Command	VII Corps	Nellingen
30th Medical Group	2d COSCOM	Ludwigsburg
12th Evacuation Hospital	3d COSCOM (V Corps)	Wiesbaden
31st Combat Support Hospital	2d COSCOM	Nellingen
128th Combat Support Hospital	2d COSCOM	Nellingen
42d Medical Co (Air Ambulance)	2d COSCOM	Ludwigsburg
236th Medical Co (Air Ambulance)	7th MEDCOM	Landstuhl
651st Medical Co (Air Ambulance)	2d COSCOM	Ludwigsburg
428th Medical Unit (MEDSOM)	7th MEDCOM	Pirmasens
2d Medical Detachment (Dental)	7th MEDCOM	Heidelberg
17th Medical Detachment	7th MEDCOM	Gelnhausen
71st Medical Detachment	7th MEDCOM	Grafenwoehr
87th Medical Detachment (Dental)	7th MEDCOM	Bindlach
120th Medical Detachment	7th MEDCOM	Erlangen

Parent Unit	USAREUR Major Command	Location
122d Medical Detachment (Dental)	7th MEDCOM	Babenhausen
123d Medical Detachment (Dental)	7th MEDCOM	Bad Kissingen
566th Medical Detachment	7th MEDCOM	Landstuhl
914th Medical Detachment	7th MEDCOM	Augsburg
928th Medical Detachment	7th MEDCOM	Heidelberg
7th Support Group	2d COSCOM	Crailsheim
1st Maintenance Battalion	2d COSCOM	Boeblingen
22d Maintenance Company	2d COSCOM	Heilbronn
263d Maintenance Company	2d COSCOM	Boeblingen
586th Maintenance Company	2d COSCOM	Kornwestheim
71st Maintenance Battalion	2d COSCOM	Fuerth
45th Ordnance Co (Missile Maint)	2d COSCOM	Nuremberg
156th Maintenance Company	2d COSCOM	Zirndorf
317th Maintenance Company	2d COSCOM	Fuerth
87th Maintenance Battalion	2d COSCOM	Wertheim
85th Maintenance Co (Lt Equip)	2d COSCOM	Kitzingen
147th Maintenance Company	2d COSCOM	Schweinfurt
504th Maintenance Company	2d COSCOM	Bamberg
557th Maintenance Company	2d COSCOM	Aschaffenburg
16th Support Group (-)	3d COSCOM (V Corps)	Hanau
4th Transportation Battalion	2d COSCOM	Ludwigsburg
11th Transportation Co (HET)	2d COSCOM	Stuttgart
15th Transportation Co (Mdm Truck)	2d COSCOM	Nellingen
32d Transportation Co (Mdm Truck)	2d COSCOM	Ludwigsburg
109th Transportation Co (POL)	21st TAACOM	Mannheim
369th Transportation Co (Mdm Truck)	2d COSCOM	Ludwigsburg
501st Transportation Company	21st TAACOM	Kaiserslautern
515th Transportation Co (POL)	2d COSCOM	Ludwigsburg
590th Transportation Company	3d COSCOM (V Corps)	Mannheim
13th Supply and Service Battalion	2d COSCOM	Ludwigsburg
11th Supply Co (Hvy Maint)	2d COSCOM	Boeblingen
75th Supply Company	2d COSCOM	Schwaebisch Hall
226th Supply and Service Co (DS)	2d COSCOM	Augsburg
229th Supply and Service Company	2d COSCOM	Kornwestheim

SECTION II—COMBAT SERVICE SUPPORT UNITS (CONTINUED)

Parent Unit	USAREUR Major Command	Location
240th Supply and Service Co (DS)	2d COSCOM	Fuerth
493d Supply and Service Co (DS)	2d COSCOM	Wuerzburg
496th Supply Company	2d COSCOM	Stuttgart
101st Ordnance Bn (Ammo)	2d COSCOM	Heilbronn
144th Ordnance Co (Ammo)	3d COSCOM (V Corps)	Wildflecken
501st Ordnance Co (Ammo)	2d COSCOM	Crailsheim
529th Ordnance Co (Ammo)	2d COSCOM	Erlangen
663d Ordnance Co (Ammo)	2d COSCOM	Schweinfurt
7–159 Aviation (AVIM)	2d COSCOM	Illesheim
2d Corps Support Command Special Troops		
11th Chemical Company	2d COSCOM	Nellingen
51st Chemical Company	2d COSCOM	Nellingen
16th Data Processing Unit	2d COSCOM	Nellingen
179th Maintenance Det (ATE Repair)	2d COSCOM	Fuerth
229th Transportation Center (Mvmt Ctl)	2d COSCOM	Nellingen
800th Materiel Management Center	2d COSCOM	Nellingen
856th Ordnance Detachment (EOD)	60th Ord Gp	Stuttgart

Appendix C

CINCUSAREUR Deployment Order 22

HEADQUARTERS
UNITED STATES ARMY, EUROPE
and SEVENTH ARMY
APO NEW YORK 09403
10 November 1990

CINCUSAREUR DEPLOYMENT ORDER 22

DEPLOYMENT OF VII CORPS TO SWA

TASK ORGANIZATION: See Annex A (Deploying Forces).

1. SITUATION.

    a. Enemy. See USAREUR Counterintelligence Daily Summary (CIDS), the quarterly Counterintelligence Summary, and the current INTSUM.

    b. Friendly.

        (1) USEUCOM assists in the coordination with USTRANSCOM, USCENTCOM, and host nations.

        (2) USTRANSCOM provides sea and air transportation assets to move designated USAREUR units from sea ports of embarkation (SPOEs) and air ports of embarkation (APOEs) to designated ports of debarkation in Southwest Asia (SWA).

        (3) USCENTCOM designates ports of debarkation and performs reception mission in SWA.

        (4) USAF provides space or facilities on its bases used as APOEs for the establishment of reception areas for deploying units.

c. Assumptions.

(1) Host nations will not hinder the movement of USAREUR units through or out of their territories.

(2) Deploying units will use three SPOEs: Bremerhaven, Rotterdam, and Antwerp. A minimum of 5 ships will load at a time.

(3) M1A1 MBTs will be shipped through all three SPOEs.

(4) APOEs will be established at Rhein Main, Ramstein, Stuttgart, Nuremberg, and Munich (if necessary).

2. MISSION. USAREUR task organizes and deploys VII Corps composed of 2 heavy divisions, an ACR, and selected units, as well as 2AD(F) and tanks for 1st Infantry Division (MECH), to support U.S. forces in Southwest Asia.

3. EXECUTION.

a. Commander's Intent. Rapidly and accurately develop Type Unit Characteristic data and input into WWMCCS system. This initial step must be fast and accurate as it is one of the two keys to smooth flow of forces. Then move units quickly and safely to APOEs or SPOEs. Movement sequence will be determined by Commander, ARCENT ICW CINCUSAREUR and VII Corps. Fill marshalling areas at SPOEs to ensure maximum utilization of available sea assets early. This is critical if we are to meet our closure date. Ensure community support structure remains ready to provide family care and support.

b. Concept of Operations.

(1) General. USAREUR deploys VII Corps, with two heavy divisions, corps troops, and 2AD(F) to SWA (see Annex A for task organization) in five phases (Preparation, Movement to SPOEs, Loading at the SPOEs, Movement to the APOEs, and Loading at the APOEs).

(2) Phasing.

(a) Phase 1, Preparation. The first step in this phase is the development of the type unit characteristic data for each UIC deploying. Generic data for each type UIC is extracted from WWMCCS and revised data for the specific unit will be entered after the unit has refined it. Other actions include preparing equipment, loading CONEXs, etc. For USAREUR this phase ends when the last deploying unit completes its loading at home station.

(b) Phase 2, Movement to SPOEs. This phase encompasses the in-country movement of all equipment and supplies to the designated SPOEs. Primary means of movement of all vehicles to SPOEs will be by rail or barge.

Helicopters will self-deploy to the designated SPOE. 21st TAACOM will establish, and run marshalling areas at each SPOE. Phase ends when last elements of a unit arrive at the marshalling area.

(c) Phase 3, Loading at the SPOEs. During this phase the departing units will assist loading all equipment and supplies onto ships as required. For each deploying unit this phase ends when the last ship or aircraft has been loaded. For USAREUR the phase ends when the last unit has completed loading.

(d) Phase 4, Movement to APOEs. This phase consists of in-country movement of all personnel to the APOEs. Personnel will move to APOE by motor transport. Units move to designated APOE at the call of the DACG through the chain of command. Phase ends when unit closes at APOE.

(e) Phase 5, Loading at APOEs. At direction of DACG unit will assist in loading of aircraft as required. V Corps is responsible for DACG operations with reinforcement from 21st TAACOM. Phase ends when last aircraft for each unit leaves. Phase ends for USAREUR when last unit has departed.

(3) Timeline for deployment is as follows (C-Day was 7 AUG 90):

EVENT	C-Day	DATE
Decision/Deployment Order 21	C+94	9 Nov 90
Plan/order trains/convoy clearances		TBD
Containerize/move ammo		TBD
1st trains load		TBD
Begin loading ships		TBD

c. Subunit Tasks.

(a) Headquarters USAREUR Staff Directorates.

(1) Deputy Chief of Staff, Personnel. Provide and coordinate personnel support to forces tasked under this plan during all phases of execution.

(2) Deputy Chief of Staff, Intelligence. Provide theater and national intelligence support, support to technical databases, and counterintelligence support enroute.

(3) Deputy Chief of Staff, Operations.

(i) ICW DCSLOG and deploying units, prepare and maintain Time-Phased Force Deployment Data (TPFDD).

(ii) Coordinate with USEUCOM and ARCENT for the establishment of reception areas in SWA.

(iii) Be prepared to provide staff liaison party to ARCENT/USCENT-COM.

(iv) Track unit movements from home station to Saudi Arabia.

(v) Render all required reports to USEUCOM, USTRANSCOM, HQDA, and other agencies as needed.

(vi) Make subordinate unit operations as easy as possible.

(4) Deputy Chief of Staff, Logistics.

(i) Assist in development of TPFDD.

(ii) Coordinate in-theater transportation assets to move equipment and supplies to SPOEs.

(iii) Provide overmatch of movement to the POEs.

(iv) Fill equipment shortages identified by deploying units.

(v) Provide liaison and/or troubleshooting teams as needed.

(vi) Coordinate with Department of the Army and Army Materiel Command for priority fill of theater shortages such as desert clothing and equipment.

(vii) Monitor readiness of deploying units and expedite delivery of required CL IX.

(5) Office of the Provost Marshal. Develop plan to ensure adequate law enforcement coverage in communities affected by the deployment.

(2) V Corps.

(a) Prepare units for movement and deploy as scheduled.

(b) On order establish Departure Airfield Control Groups at all APOEs. 21st DACG at Ramstein AFB will be placed OPCON to V Corps.

(c) Assist in development of TPFDD.

(3) VII Corps.

(a) Prepare units for movement and deploy as scheduled.

(b) All fixed wing aircraft will self-deploy to SWA.

(c) Deploy advance CP to ARCENT early on.

(4) 21st TAACOM.

(a) Prepare units for movement and deploy as scheduled.

(b) Command and control the draw, movement, and loading of tanks for 1st ID(M).

(c) Be prepared to establish refuel/rest stops for any convoys to SPOEs as appropriate.

(d) Establish and run port support areas in the vicinity of the SPOEs which provide life support to deploying units.

(e) Be prepared to provide transportation support to move equipment, supplies, or personnel to the POEs.

(f) Continue to provide Departure Airfield Control Group at Ramstein AB. Place DACG OPCON V Corps.

(5) 32d AADCOM. Task organize 8–43 ADA Bn. Prepare unit for movement and deploy as scheduled.

(6) 56th FACOM. Commander, 56th FACOM is designated DCG, VII Corps Rear, for purpose of community operation in VII Corps area of USAREUR.

(7) 2AD (FWD). Prepare units for movement and deploy as scheduled.

(9) 18th Engineer Bde. Prepare units for movement and deploy as scheduled.

(10) 7th MEDCOM.

(a) Prepare units for movement and deploy as scheduled.

(b) Ensure sufficient vaccines are on hand to inoculate all deploying soldiers.

(c) Be prepared to assist 21st TAACOM in establishing medical treatment facilities at the SPOEs.

(11) 5th Signal Command. Establish a secure communications link, voice and data, from the SPOEs to 21st TAACOM, and Headquarters USAREUR.

(12) 1st PERSCOM.

(a) Prepare units for movement and deploy as scheduled.

(b) ICW the UMCs initiate action to bring deploying units to 100% ALO authorized strength.

(c) ICW ARCENT and DA PERSCOM develop procedures for any replacement operations for deployed units.

(d) Postal unit will deploy with required USPS postal equipment to accompany troops.

(13) 1st TMCA. Coordinate the movement from home station to SPOE/APOEs of all deploying units. Monitor MCC operations and unit flow.

(14) 66th MI Bde. Prepare UIES [UICs] for movement and deploy as scheduled.

(15) 3–58 ATC Bn. Prepare B/3-58 ATC Bn for movement and deploy as scheduled.

d. Coordinating Instructions.

(1) Units not organic to VII Corps are attached to VII Corps as they arrive in Saudi Arabia.

(2) No NATO classified documents will be taken to SWA.

(3) Classified documents will be consolidated at either the installation or parent unit headquarters and maintained by units not deploying.

(4) Conduct the following training prior to deployment: SWA orientation, chemical refresher training, refresher training in the Geneva and Hague Conventions.

(5) Ensure all soldiers have qualified on their assigned weapon within the last 6 months.

(7) Reporting requirements. See Annex B.

(6) Commander, 56th FACOM, and elements remaining in Europe. Review means of accomplishing security measures at all MILCOMs during increased THREATCON.

(7) Units deploying equipment by sea. Be prepared to provide security detachment to ensure positive U.S. control of sensitive items aboard ships.

(8) UMC elements listed in Annex A. Develop implementing plan and provide copy to this headquarters within 7 days of receipt of this order.

(9) Deploying units. Bring all required life support assets (i.e. tents, water trailers, etc.). No source exists for these type items in SWA.

(10) Personal property of single soldiers will be inventoried, boxed, banded, and left in barracks rooms.

(11) Public Affairs Guidance. Information on unit strengths or movement specifics will not be released. No information that is operationally significant to hostile forces will be released. Further guidance is contained in USAREUR MSG "Public Affairs Guidance: Releasable/Non-releasable Information" (DTG 281625Z AUG 90) and USAREUR MSG "AFN and Stars and Stripes Deployment to Desert Shield Operations" (DTG 301200Z AUG 90).

(12) Visitors from outside of USAREUR to deploying units must be approved by CINCUSAREUR (Office of the SGS).

4. ADMINISTRATION and LOGISTICS

   a. Concept of Support: During Phase 1 (Preparation), units will plan movement of equipment to SPOEs; develop and submit type unit characteristic data; provide data input to TC ACCIS; determine container requirements for ammunition and general cargo and upload ammunition and cargo in containers; identify equipment shortfalls; and load vehicles for movement. During Phase 2 (Movement to SPOEs), units will move to the SPOEs at the direction of the corps MCCs and 1st TMCA. Phase 3 (Loading at SPOEs) is the loading of ships. Deploying units will provide loading teams as required at the SPOEs to assist in the loading of its equipment. 21st TAACOM will provide life support at the SPOEs and 7th MEDCOM will provide medical support. During Phase 4 (Movement to APOEs), units will move to the APOEs at the direction of DACGs in coordination with the ATMCT. V Corps ICW USAFE will provide reception/holding areas at all APOEs. Phase 5 (Loading at APOEs) is the loading of aircraft.

   b. Material and Services.

   (1) Supply.

   (a) Class I: Units deploy with up to five days UBL.

   (b) Class II & IV.

   (i) Submit requisitions for 2 sets desert BDUs, 1 desert BDU hat and kevlar helmet cover, and one night type desert BDU consisting of a parka w/trouser and sleep shirt and order 1 pair sunglasses for each deploying individual. Currently the theater has 8,000 sets of desert BDUs available in tariff sizes. Estimates from the CONUS production base are that the desert BDUs will become available in the late November and December timeframe, but production will not be sufficient to outfit all deploying soldiers. First issues will be to forward deployed units. The remaining requirement will be issued after troops arrive in SWA.

(ii) Deploy with existing camouflage nets, cots, tents, and tarpaulins. If tent liners are on hand, take them for tent insulation. Carpentry kits and tools are required.

(iii) Units deploy with basic load of barbed wire and sandbags. DSUs deploy with 100% authorized ASL.

(iv) Units deploy with 2 sets of Battle Dress Overgarments (BDOs). If sufficient BDOs are not available, 2 sets (unopened) of Chemical Protective Overgarments (CPOs) may be issued in lieu of filters and decontamination kits and one training set per individual. All deploying units will change and inspect mask filters and/or canisters prior to departure and on arrival in AOR. All canisters and filters should be checked against SB 3–30–2 to ensure they are serviceable. Each soldier must deploy with a second set of filters or canisters. Masks will be inspected for serviceability once filters have been changed. Recommend all filter elements be marked with the installation date on the inside of the filter connector with a permanent marker. Canisters would be similarly marked on the outside.

(v) Organizational Clothing and Individual Equipment (OCIE). Deploy with items authorized by column AA-M of CTA 50–900, 1 Aug 90 for climatic zones I, II and III.

(vi) Take 15 days SSSC items.

(vii) Do not take installation property. Request exceptions to LOG CAT at HQ USAREUR.

(c) Class III.

(i) CL III (P): Units deploy with authorized UBL and DSUs with 100% authorized ASL.

(ii) CL III (Bulk): 5,000 gal tankers, HEMTT tankers, TPUs and fuel hauling trailers will not be loaded with fuel for deployment. Ample fuel is available in theater.

(iii) Do not take water in water containers or trailers. Do not purchase bottled water. Water is available in AOR and will be provided as required.

(d) Class V: Units will containerize UBL and load for shipment by rail to port of Nordenham.

(e) Class VII:

(i) Operational Readiness Floats (ORF) will accompany units. Crossleveling within Corps is authorized in order to insure serviceable ORF assets are taken to SWA.

(ii) Water purification units deploy with Erdulators. ROWPUs will be issued from available stocks and NET training will occur upon arrival in SWA.

(f) Class VIII: Units deploy with authorized UBL. DSUs deploy with 100% authorized ASL.

(g) Class IX: Units deploy with 100% authorized PLL and DSUs with 100% authorized shop stocks and ASL.

(2) Transportation:

(a) Movement plans will be as directed by Corps MCCs and 1st TMCA through chain of command.

(b) Equipment movements to SPOEs will use the following modes of transportation:

1. Tracked vehicles will move by rail to the SPOEs.

2. Containers will move by rail to the SPOEs.

3. Wheeled Vehicles:

a. Rail will be used to the maximum.

b. Convoys to Mannheim and Mainz for barge movement will be the primary method of moving vehicles to SPOEs, if not by train.

c. Convoys to the port of Bremerhaven will be held to a minimum with the exception of the 2AD(F).

d. Outsize equipment will move by rail.

4. Helicopters will self-deploy to the designated port.

5. Fixed wing aircraft will self-deploy to Saudi Arabia.

(c) Deploying units will provide loading teams at the SPOE.

(d) Personnel will move to the APOEs by motor transport at the direction of the DACG in coordination with the ATMCT through the chain of command.

(e) HQ USAREUR will coordinate with USTRANSCOM for ships and aircraft for the deployment and coordinate with USCENTCOM for the establishment of a reception capability in SWA.

(f) V and VII Corps will coordinate the transportation of assigned personnel and equipment to APOE/SPOEs. 1st TMCA will coordinate transportation for deploying EAC units.

(g) V Corps forms Departure Airfield Control Groups (DACG) at designated APOEs. 21st TAACOM DACG at Ramstein AB will be OPCON V Corps.

(h) MTMC-EUR provide space and facilities to support port operations at Bremerhaven, Antwerp, Rotterdam, Nordenham, Zeebrugge, and other ports as directed.

(i) 21st TAACOM be prepared to provide blocking, bracing, and tie-down equipment (BB&T) to deploying units to support rail movement of vehicles on an emergency basis.

(j) Wheeled vehicles will be shipped with the windows in the standard up configuration.

(k) Deploying equipment must be documented using LOGMARS bar code labels with two labels on each piece. These labels are a TC ACCIS product. Additionally, all equipment must be separately marked with the unit identification code (UIC). Hazardous cargo must be segregated and properly labeled.

(l) Unit identification markings will be placed on five sides of a container prior to movement. Containers will be loaded for movement with doors facing each other for security.

(3) Services: 21st TAACOM provides life support at SPOEs and establishes port support areas in the vicinity of SPOEs. V Corps ICW USAFE establishes reception/holding areas for personnel at APOEs.

(4) Maintenance.

(a) Priority of maintenance support during all phases of the operation to departing units.

(b) Do not take non–mission capable equipment requiring GS and above repair.

c. Medical.

(1) UMCs with assistance from 7th MEDCOM provide all necessary inoculations to deploying soldiers.

(2) 7th MEDCOM:

(a) Be prepared to establish medical treatment facilities at the SPOEs and be prepared to provide filler medical personnel to deploying units.

(b) Be prepared on a priority basis to provide prescription sunglasses to individuals deploying to SWA.

d. Personnel.

(1) Predeployment Processing.

(a) Deployability Criteria. Deployment criteria for Desert Shield are contained in the following:

(i) AR 614–30, Table 3–1, as corrected by HQDA MSG, DAPE-MPE-DR, DTG 171330Z Oct 90, SUBJ: Corrections to AR 614–30, Table 3–1.

(ii) AR 600–8–101, Chapters 4 and 5.

(iii) CINCUSAREUR MSG, AEAGC-O, DTG 160830Z Aug 90, SUBJ: Personnel Deployment Policies and Procedures for Desert Shield.

(iv) CINCUSAREUR MSG, AEAGA-M, DTG 302205Z Aug 90, SUBJ: Personnel Deployment Policies and Procedures for Desert Shield, Update 1.

(v) HQDA MSG, SGPS-CP, DTG 221400Z Aug 90, SUBJ: Insulin Dependent Diabetic Soldiers.

(vi) Single or Dual M-Service Parents. Family Care Plans (FCP) will be implemented for those individuals alerted for deployment.

(vii) Ensure duplicate panographs are on file at the Central Panograph Storage Facility and are not taken with deploying units/soldiers.

(b) Reporting Procedures. Once a unit/individual soldier has been alerted for deployment, they will be POR IAW AR 600–8–101, AR 612–2 and USAREUR Regulation 612–1. The results of the POR will be forwarded from the units to the USAREUR Major Command (UMC)/Separate Major Command (SMC) who will consolidate the results and forward them to 1st PERSCOM by the most expeditious means available. The report will include as a minimum the total POR'd (separating military from civilian), the number qualified and the reasons associated with any unqualified soldiers/civilians. Additional reports will only be required when additional soldiers POR, etc.

(2) Stop Loss. Effective immediately, implement STOP LOSS provisions for all USAREUR soldiers IAW CINCUSAREUR MSG, AEAGA M, 101430Z NOV 90, SUBJ: STOP LOSS in USAREUR.

(3) Civilian Personnel. DAC Personnel will be processed for deployment using predeployment processing outlined in DA PERSCOM MSG, TAPC-MOB, DTG 111800Z Oct 90, SUBJ: Desert Shield Guidelines for Deploying DA Civilian Employees to SWA. Visas are required for DAC and Civilian Contractors deploying to SWA.

(4) Maintenance of Unit Strength.

(a) Critical MOS/Specialty shortages, less AMEDD officers/warrant officers, that can not be cross-leveled from within Corps assets must be identified immediately to 1ST PERSCOM, ATTN: AEUPE-EPMD-RDAD. Units will deploy at 100% ALO authorized strength. Shortages of AMEDD officers/warrant officers that can not be cross-leveled from within Corps assets will be identified immediately to 7th MEDCOM, ATTN: AEMPE-O. Do not consider 7th MEDCOM mobilization augmentees as assigned or available when determining shortages.

(b) Strength Reporting.

(i) Upon arrival in SWA, deploying units are attached to ARCENT.

(ii) Personnel strength accounting will be accomplished IAW USAREUR Pam 680–3 (Wartime Personnel Requirements System) as supplemented under separate message. Daily reports are required to include negative reports once the unit/individuals have been alerted for deployment.

(iii) All reports will be as of 1800Z each day. Reports will be classified SECRET when identifying deployed units, locations, or unit strength in the message. Reporting requirements may be adjusted as needed by the USAREUR ODCSPER to meet mission requirements. Changes will be identified to the field under separate message.

(c) Replacements. UMC/SMCs will provide individual replacements for deployed units, as required, for soldiers not returned to duty in SWA, or for soldiers on Emergency Leave not returning to SWA.

(d) Return to Duty (RTD). RTD policy and procedures are in CINCUSAREUR MSG, AEAGA-M, 261235Z Sep 90, SUBJ: Desert Shield Return to Duty Policy.

(e) Casualty Reporting.

(i) Once deployed, units will submit casualty reports IAW AR 600–8–1 through command channels to 3rd PERSCOM (ARCENT). Corps Gl will provide info copy of reports to Commander, 1st PERSCOM.

(ii) 1st PERSCOM, as CAC for USAREUR, will pass casualty information to deployed unit's rear detachments for notification/processing as required by Army Regulations.

(5) Personnel Management.

(a) Use of Personnel with Critical Skills and Specialties.

(i) Use of Female Personnel. Female personnel will be employed IAW the Direct Combat Probability Coding (DCPC) policy.

(ii) Linguists. The requirement for linguists may necessitate the assignment of personnel with foreign language skills outside their normal MOS/specialty. Linguist requirements will be submitted to Commander, 1st PERSCOM, by either immediate classified message traffic or STU-III.

(iii) Critical MOS. The requirement for specialists and personnel with critical skills for specific missions will be submitted to Commander, 1st PERSCOM, by either immediate classified message traffic or STU-III.

(b) Promotions. Exceptional promotion guidance for deployed enlisted soldiers is contained in the following MILPER MSG:

(i) MILPER MSG 90–229, DTG 161500Z Aug 90, SUBJ: Promotion and Training Exceptions to Policy in support of Operation Desert Shield.

(ii) MILPER MSG 90–242, DTG 280900Z Aug 90, SUBJ: SGT/SSG Promotion Board Procedural Guidance for Soldiers Deployed in Support of Operation Desert Shield.

(iii) MILPER MSG 90–275, DTG 281600Z Sep 90, SUBJ: Promotion Procedures for Attached Enlisted Personnel.

(c) OER/NCOER Processing. Following policy guidance regarding submission of OER/NCOER will be complied with:

(i) MILPER MSG 90–231, DTG 171100Z Aug 90, SUBJ: Submission of OER/NCOER on Desert Shield Soldiers.

(ii) MILPER MSG 90–260, DTG 131645Z Sep 90, SUBJ: OER/NCOER Processing During Operation Desert Shield.

(d) Personnel Records. MPRJ will remain at the deployed units' home station. MILPER MSG 90–272, DTG 241647Z Sep 90, SUBJ: Disposition of Field Personnel Records for Desert Shield, provides additional guidance regarding personnel records to be deployed with soldiers.

(e) Strength Accounting. SIDPERS data base will be updated to reflect those soldiers deployed IAW CDR, 1st PERSCOM MSG, DTG 191400Z Sep 90, SUBJ: Identification of Soldiers Deployed in Support of Operation Desert Shield. Additional guidance on data base management and procedures will be provided by Commander, 1st PERSCOM, as needed.

(6) Development and Maintenance of Morale.

(a) Chaplain Support. The USAREUR Chaplain will provide coverage tailored to the mission requirement. Unit chaplains will deploy with their assigned units. Senior staff chaplains of the tasked command will ensure that faith group coverage is adequate.

(b) Mail.

(i) MPSA, ICW USAPGE, will issue APO for deploying units. Following are formats for addressing mail:

PERSONAL MAIL
RANK/FULL NAME/SSN
OPERATION DESERT SHIELD
UNIT OF ASSIGNMENT/ATTACHMENT
    (FOR DEPLOYMENT)
APO NEW YORK 09XXX

OFFICIAL MAIL
UNIT DESIGNATION
OPERATION DESERT SHIELD
APO NEW YORK 09XXX

(ii) Family members will continue to receive mail which is addressed to them by name at their current location. Deploying soldiers will make arrangements (i.e., delivery at their current location or forwarding mail to deployment APO address) for any mail which is addressed by name to both the sponsor and a family member (e.g., SGT & Mrs Jones).

(c) Unit MWR Kits. Units will deploy with appropriate MWR materials (e.g., playing cards, sports equipment, board games, etc.).

(d) Radios. AFRTS has begun broadcasting an FM radio service in Saudi Arabia. Soldiers are encouraged to bring their personal portable FM radios when deploying.

(e) Emergency Leaves. Policy and entitlements for Emergency Leave for deployed soldiers are outlined in CINCUSAREUR MSG, AEAGA-M, DTG 271723Z Sep 90, SUBJ: Individual Movements in Support of Desert Shield.

Annex A (Task Organization) to CINCUSAREUR Deployment Order 22

VII CORPS

   1st ARMORED DIV (–)
     3d BDE/3d INFANTRY DIV
       1–7 INFANTRY
       4–7 INFANTRY
       4–66 ARMOR

     2d BDE/1st ARMORED DIV (–)
       6–6 INFANTRY/3d BDE 1st AD
       1–35 ARMOR
       2–70 ARMOR
       4–70 ARMOR

     3d BDE/1st ARMORED DIV
       7–6 INFANTRY
       3–35 ARMOR
       1–37th ARMOR/1st BDE 1st AD

     1–1 CAV SQDN

     4th BDE/1st ARMORED DIV
       2–1 AV BN AH–64
       3–1 AV BN AH–64
       *G/1 CMD AV CO
       *H/1 ASLT HELO CO

   DIVARTY
     2–1 FA BN (155)
     3–1 FA BN (155)
     6–1 FA BN (155)
     *A/94 FA BTRY (MLRS)
     *B/25 FA BTRY TARGET ACQ

   6–3 ADA BN (V/S)

 *69th CHEMICAL CO

   16th ENGINEER BN

   501st MI BN CEWI

 *501st MP CO

   141st SIGNAL BN

   1st ARMORED DIV BAND

 *HHC 1st ARMORED DIV

DISCOM (–)
   123d MAIN SPT BN
   26th FWD SPT BN/3d INF DIV
   47th FWD SPT BN
   125th FWD SPT BN
   *I/1 AVIM CO

3d ARMORED DIV
   1st BDE/3d ARMORED DIV
     3–5 INFANTRY †
     5–5 INFANTRY †
     4–32 ARMOR
     4–34 ARMOR/1st BDE 8th ID

   2d BDE/3d ARMORED DIV (–)
     4–18 INFANTRY
     3–8 ARMOR ‡
     4–8 ARMOR ‡

   3d BDE/3d ARMORED DIV
     5–18 INFANTRY
     2–67 ARMOR
     4–67 ARMOR

   4–7 CAV SQDN

   4th BDE/3d ARMORED DIV (–)
     2–227 AV BN AH–64
     *G/227 CMD AV CO
     *H/227 ASLT AV CO

   DIVARTY
     2–3 FA BN (155)
     2–82 FA BN (155)
     4–82 FA BN (155)
     *A/40 FA BTRY (MLRS)
     *F/333 FA BTRY TARGET ACQ

   5–3 ADA BN (V/S) /8th ID

 *22d CHEMICAL CO

   23d ENGINEER BN

   533d MI BN CEWI

 *503d MP CO

143d SIGNAL BN

3d ARMORED DIV BAND

*HHC 3d ARMORED DIV

DISCOM (−)
122d MAIN SPT BN
45th FWD SPT BN
54th FWD SPT BN
503d FWD SPT BN
*I/227th AV MAINT CO

2d ACR

11th AV BDE (−)
2–6 AV BN AH–64
4–229 AV BN AH–64
4–159 CMD AV BN
*A/5–159 MDM HELO CO
*C/6–159 ASLT HELO CO

7th CORPS FA (−)
210th FA BDE (−)
3–17 FA BN (155)
4–27 FA BN (MLRS)
2–41 FA BN (155)/3d ID
42d FA BDE (−)/V CORPS
3–20 FA BN (155)/V CORPS
1–27 FA BN (MLRS)/V CORPS
2–29 FA BN (155)/8ID

TF 8–43/32d AADCOM
8–43 ADA BN (PATRIOT)
A/6–52 ADA BTRY (HAWK)
C/6–52 ADA BTRY (HAWK)
57th MSL MAINT CO (PATRIOT)
569th MSL MAINT CO (−)
(HAWK)

7th ENGINEER BDE (−)
9th ENGINEER BN
82d CMBT ENGINEER BN
317th CMBT ENGINEER BN/
V CORPS
249th CMBT HEAVY BN/18th EN
[BDE]
*A/649th ENGINEER BN TOPO

*38th EN CO MDM GDR/VII
CORPS

207th MI BDE (+)
101st MI DET/1st ID (FWD)

14th MP BDE (−)
793d MP BN
*218th MP CO
*204th MP CO
*66th MP CO/21st TAACOM
93d MP BN/V CORPS
*92d MP CO
*109th MP CO
*59th MP CO/21st TAACOM

*HHC VII CORPS

93d SIGNAL BDE (+)
*C/17th SIGNAL BN/V CORPS

84th AG DET CORPS BAND

VII CORPS PERSONNEL GROUP

VII CORPS FINANCE GROUP (−)
HHD VII CORPS FIN GP
105th FIN SPT UNIT TYPE A (−)
13th FIN SPT UNIT TYPE B (−)
14th FIN SPT UNIT TYPE B (−)
17th FIN SPT UNIT TYPE B (−)
78th FIN SPT UNIT TYPE B (−)
3d FIN SPT UNIT TYPE C (−)
501st FIN SPT UNIT TYPE D (−)
106th FIN SPT UNIT TYPE E (−)
503d FIN UNIT TYPE C(−)/
V CORPS
201st FIN UNIT TYPE D(−)/
V CORPS
39TH FIN UNIT TYPE E (−)/
V CORPS

2d COSCOM (−)
16th SPT GP (−)/3d COSCOM
4th TRANS BN
*11th HET CO
*15th MDM TRUCK CO
*32d MDM TRUCK CO
*396th MDM TRUCK CO

*109th MDM TRUCK CO/
  21st
*501st TRANS CO/21st
*515th MDM TRUCK POL
  CO
*590th MDM TRUCK CO/
  V CORPS
13th S&S BN
*11th HVY MAINT SUPPLY
  CO
*75th S&S CO
*229th DS SUPPLY CO
*226th DS SUPPLY CO
*240th DS SUPPLY CO
*493d DS SUPPLY CO
*496th REPAIR PARTS CO
101st ORD BN
*144th ORD CO AMMO/
  V CORPS
*501st ORD CO AMMO
*529th ORD CO AMMO
*663d ORD CO AMMO

7th SUPPORT GP
1st MAINT BN
*22d MAINT CO
*263d MAINT CO
*586th MAINT CO
71st MAINT BN
*45th ORD CO MSL MAINT
*156th MAINT CO
*317th MAINT CO
87th MAINT BN
*85th LT EQP MAINT CO
*147th MAINT CO
*504th MAINT CO
*557th MAINT CO
7–159th AVIM BN

30th MED GP
12th EVAC HOSPITAL/V CORPS
31st COMBAT SPT HOSPITAL
128th COMBAT SPT HOSPITAL
*42d AMBULANCE CO

*651st AMBULANCE CO
428th MEDSOM/7th MEDCOM
17th MED DET/7th MEDCOM
120th MED DET/7th MEDCOM
566th MED DET/7th MEDCOM
914th MED DET/7th MEDCOM
928th MED DET/7th MEDCOM
2d DENTAL DET/7th MEDCOM
87th DENTAL DET/7th
  MEDCOM
122d DENTAL DET/7th
  MEDCOM
123d DENTAL DET/7th
  MEDCOM
*236th MED AIR AMB CO/7th
  MEDCOM

SPECIAL TROOPS BN
*HHC 2d COSCOM
*11th CHEMICAL CO DECON/
  SMOKE
16th DATA PROCESSING DET
*51st CHEMICAL CO DECON/
  SMOKE
179th ATE REPAIR DET
229th MCC
242d CHEMICAL DET NBC
800th MMC

2d ARMORED DIV (FWD) (–)
1–41 INFANTRY BN
2–66 ARMOR
3–66 ARMOR
4–3 FA BN (155)
*C/26 FA BTRY RADAR
*D/17th ENGINEER CO
498th CS BN FWD SPT
*HHC

*B/I&A BN 66th MI BDE (–)

*115th POSTAL CO/lst PERSCOM

*B/3–58th [AV] AIR TRAFFIC CTL (+)

*A company-size unit whose movement status must be reported to Headquarters, USAREUR, as specified in Annex B.

†The 1st Brigade, 3d Armored Division, included the 3d and 5th Battalions, 5th Cavalry, both of which were organized as infantry battalions. The 3d and 5th Battalions, 5th Infantry, did not serve with the 3d Armored Division in 1990–91.

‡ The 2d Brigade, 3d Armored Division, included the 3d and 4th Battalions, 8th Cavalry, both of which were organized as armor battalions. There were no units in the U.S. Army designated as the 3d and 4th Battalions, 8th Armor, in 1990–91.

Annex B to CINCUSAREUR Deployment Order 22

Reporting Requirements

1. MSC submit a DAILY SITREP as of 1800Z due to Headquarters USAREUR NLT 2100Z, beginning on order. Incorporate the report matrix at page B–2 [not reproduced] into paragraph 2, Operations, of the USAREUR SITREP format below.

2. Unit movement status will be reported to and tracked by USAREUR at UIC level of detail down to battalion and separate company level. Companies identified with an * in Annex A (Task Organization).

3. Planned/actual date time groups will be used in each column.

4. Commander's Assessment, paragraph 9 of SITREP, will include a short assessment of execution covering actions on any issues in the following areas: personnel, logistics, or community operations.

5. USAREUR SITREP Format

PARAGRAPH	SECTION
1	Situation Overview
2	Operations
3	Intelligence
4	Logistics
5	Engineer
6	Communications
7	Personnel
8	Medical
9	Commanders Assessment

Appendix D

Reserve Component Units Serving in USAREUR

	MEDICAL UNITS	
U.S. Army Reserve	U.S. Location	Basic USAREUR Location
44th General Hospital	Wisconsin	Landstuhl
45th Station Hospital	Washington	Frankfurt
56th Station Hospital	Virginia	Nuremberg
94th General Hospital	Texas	Frankfurt
300th Medical Detachment (Dental)	New York	Nuremberg, Augsburg
306th Medical Company (Clearing)	Tennessee	Darmstadt
308th Medical Detachment (Dental)	Illinois	Landstuhl
324th Medical Unit (MEDSOM)	Pennsylvania	Pirmasens
325th Medical Detachment (Blood Collection)	Texas	Landstuhl
328th General Hospital	Utah	Frankfurt
548th Medical Detachment (Blood Processing)	Wisconsin	Landstuhl
719th Medical Detachment (Veterinarian)	Illinois	Frankfurt, Berlin, Augsburg
919th Medical Detachment (Dental)	Colorado	Frankfurt, Mannheim
Army National Guard		
112th Medical Company (Air Ambulance)	Maine	Schwaebisch Hall

MEDICAL UNITS (CONTINUED)		
Army National Guard	U.S. Location	Basic USAREUR Location
204th Medical Detachment (Dental)	Arizona	Wuerzburg, Berlin
245th Medical Company (Clearing)	Oklahoma	Wiesbaden
300th Surgical Hospital (Mobile Army)	Tennessee	Bad Cannstatt
1467th Medical Detachment (Blood Distribution)	Puerto Rico	Landstuhl

MILITARY POLICE UNITS		
U.S. Army Reserve		
307th Military Police (MP) Company (Combat Support)	Pennsylvania	Kitzingen
HHD, 336th MP Battalion	Pennsylvania	Ludwigsburg
340th MP Company (Combat Support)	New York	Hanau
352d MP Company (Combat Support)	Pennsylvania	Schwaebisch Gmuend
433d MP Company (Physical Security)	Louisiana	Ramstein
447th MP Company (Physical Security)	Ohio	Pirmasens
Army National Guard		
323d MP Company (Combat Support)	Ohio	Frankfurt
870th MP Company (Combat Support)	California	Karlsruhe
933d MP Company (Hvy Security)	Illinois	Nuremberg
3175th MP Company (Hvy Security)	Missouri	Mannheim

OTHER		
U.S. Army Reserve		
3d Battalion, 87th IN	Colorado	Friedberg

OTHER (CONTINUED)		
U.S. Army Reserve	U.S. Location	Basic USAREUR Location
189th Ordnance Company	Missouri	Darmstadt
295th Ordnance Company	Nebraska	Babenhausen
962d Ordnance Company	New York	Miesau
283d Military Intelligence Detachment	Missouri	Stuttgart
Army National Guard		
224th Engineer Battalion (Mechanized)	Iowa	Vilseck
1457th Engineer Battalion (Combat)	Utah	Grafenwoehr
623d Service Company	Missouri	Kitzingen
1072d Maintenance Company	Michigan	Nuremberg
3678th Ordnance Company	Puerto Rico	Bamberg
144th Transportation Company (Light Truck)	Florida	Kaiserslautern

Source: Printout, Col M. McCracken, Senior ARNG Adviser, HQ USAREUR/7A, 1 Mar 91, and *Reserve Components Troop Basis of the Army,* Annex 1, 30 Sep 90.

Notes

Chapter 1

1. The VII Corps story was first told from the Army point of view by Lt. Col. Peter S. Kindsvatter, VII Corps historian during the crisis and war, in "VII Corps in the Gulf War: Deployment and Preparation for *Desert Storm*," *Military Review* 72, no. 1 (January 1992): 2–16, "VII Corps in the Gulf War: Ground Offensive," *Military Review* 72, no. 2 (February 1992): 16–37, and "VII Corps in the Gulf War: Post–Cease-Fire Operations," *Military Review* 72, no. 6 (June 1992): 2–19. Since then additional U.S. Army studies have been published, including Brig. Gen. Robert H. Scales, Jr., *Certain Victory: The U.S. Army in the Gulf War* (Washington, D.C.: Office of the Chief of Staff, United States Army, 1993); Richard M. Swain, *"Lucky War": Third Army in Desert Storm* (Fort Leavenworth, Kans.: U.S. Army Command and General Staff College Press, 1994); and Frank N. Schubert and Theresa L. Kraus, gen. eds., *The Whirlwind War: The United States Army in Operations DESERT SHIELD and DESERT STORM* (Washington, D.C.: U.S. Army Center of Military History, Government Printing Office, 1995). Two commercially published works also merit mention: H. Norman Schwarzkopf, *General H. Norman Schwarzkopf: The Autobiography: It Doesn't Take A Hero* (New York: Linda Grey Bantam Books, 1992), and Tom Clancy with Fred Franks, Jr., *Into the Storm: A Study in Command* (New York: G. P. Putnam's Sons, 1997).

2. Swain, *Lucky War*, pp. 17–60; Schubert and Kraus, *The Whirlwind War*, pp. 69–82.

3. Schubert and Kraus, *The Whirlwind War*, pp. 98–99.

4. Swain, *Lucky War*, pp. 71–85. Quote from Schwarzkopf, *It Doesn't Take a Hero*, p. 362. See also Chapter 4 below.

5. See General Crosbie E. Saint, "CINC's View of Operational Art," *Military Review* 70 (September 1990): 65–78; Lt. Gen. Crosbie E. Saint, "Foreword," *III Corps Maneuver Booklet*, comp. Lt. Col. Leonard Donald Holder (May 87), pp. 1–3, copy in Military History Office (MHO), Office of the Secretary of the General Staff (OSGS), Headquarters, United States Army, Europe, and Seventh Army (HQ USAREUR/7A) files, Heidelberg, Germany; Lt. Gen. Crosbie E. Saint, Col. Tommy R. Franks, and Maj. Alan B. Moon, "Fire Support for Mobile Armored Warfare," *Field Artillery* (June 1988): 12–14, and other articles described and cited in Chapter 2.

6. Interv, Stephen P. Gehring (author), MHO, OSGS, HQ USAREUR/7A, with Gen Crosbie E. Saint, Commander in Chief, USAREUR (CINCUSAREUR), 11 Apr 91, p. 13, tape and transcript in MHO files.

7. These totals included units assigned directly to USAREUR with a personnel strength of about 196,000, plus Army units in Europe that were not directly assigned to USAREUR with personnel strength of approximately 18,000. The non-USAREUR units, including the 5th Signal Command and the 66th Military Intelligence Brigade, generally reported to parent units in the United States, but were also under the operational command and control of the CINCUSAREUR.

Chapter 2

1. Memo, Maj Gen Charles J. Fiala, Chief of Staff (CofS), HQ USAREUR/7A, AEAGX, for United States Commander in Chief, Europe (USCINCEUR), ATTN: ECJ5-P, 1 Apr 88, sub: U.S. Forward Deployed Forces in Europe.

2. *HQ USAREUR/7A Annual Historical Review, 1981*, MHO, OSGS, HQ USAREUR/7A, p. 158, copy in MHO files.

3. G3 Div, HQ USAREUR/7A, *The U.S. Army Task Force in Lebanon*, 1959, pp. 32 and 100–102, copy in MHO files; Lt. Col. Gary H. Wade, *Rapid Deployment Logistics: Lebanon, 1958*, Research Survey no. 3 (Fort Leavenworth, Kans.: Combat Studies Institute, U.S. Army Command and General Staff College, 1984).

4. Gen Glenn K. Otis, CINCUSAREUR, marginal notes on Msg, Headquarters, Department of the Army (HQDA), DAMO-FDP, info to CINCUSAREUR, AEAGC, 131904Z Mar 87, retransmitting Msg, HQDA, DAMO-FDP, to Cdr, U.S. Army Forces Command (FORSCOM), AFOP-F, 091448Z Mar 87, sub: Pershing II (PII) Stationing, copy in MHO files; Memo, Col Joseph H. Lane, Ch, Force Modernization Division (FMD), Office of the Deputy Chief of Staff, Operations, HQ USAREUR/7A, for Assistant Deputy Chief of Staff, Operations (ADCSOPS), HQ USAREUR/7A, 22 Oct 84, sub: Briefings for Dr. DeLauer, USD (R&E); DF, Deputy Chief of Staff, Operations (DCSOPS), USAREUR, to HQ USAREUR/7A staff, 24 Jun 87, sub: Pershing II Backfill Options; Slides drafted by Lt Col Darrell J. Pflaster, Ch, Long-Range Plans Br, Plans Div, ODCSOPS, HQ USAREUR/7A, to respond to taskers of HQDA working group on Representative Force Study III, copies in MHO files.

5. Memo, Maj John M. Nolen, Asst Secretary of the General Staff (SGS), HQ USAREUR/7A, for DCSOPS, USAREUR, 11 May 87, sub: Geneva Negotiating Team; Memo, Maj Gen George A. Joulwan, DCSOPS, USAREUR, for CofS, HQ USAREUR/7A, 13 May 87, sub: Geneva Negotiating Team Meeting at EUCOM [U.S. European Command] on 15 May 1987; Memorandum for Record (MFR), Pflaster, n.d., sub: Visit to Geneva—10 Aug 87; MFR, Pflaster, n.d., sub: Visit of Brig Gen Partlow and Members of the Geneva Negotiation Team—20 August 1987; MFR, Col Joseph B. Goss, Ch, Nuclear-Chemical Div, ODCSOPS, HQ USAREUR/7A, 25 Aug 87, sub: INF [Intermediate-range Nuclear Forces] Representatives Visit; Ltr, Ambassador Maynard W. Glitman, U.S. Negotiator for INF, to Brig Gen Roger K. Bean, Cdr, 56th Field Artillery (FA) Bde, 24 Aug 87; Ltr, Brig Gen Frank A. Partlow, Joint Chiefs of Staff (JCS) Representative for INF, to Bean, 24 Aug 87.

6. Msg, CINCUSAREUR to HQDA, DAMO-FDZ, 310815Z Aug 87, sub: INF and Conventional Force Treaty Impact on Army Force Structure; Msg, CINCUSAREUR, AEAGC-P, to HQDA, DAMO-FDZ, 181314Z Sep 87, sub: INF and Conventional Force Treaty Impact on Army Force Structure; Otis, marginal notes on Msg, Secretary of State to American Embassies (AMEMB), London, Bonn, Paris, Rome, Vienna, USSR, U.S. Mission Vienna, and all Political Advisors (POLADs), 191031Z Sep 87, sub: Withdrawal of Soviet Tank and

Artillery Regiments, copy in MHO files; Memo, Col Frederick H. Borneman, ADCSOPS, HQ USAREUR/7A, for CINCUSAREUR, 30 Sep 87, sub: Withdrawal of Soviet Tank and Artillery Regiments.

7. Memo, Maj C. Lee Smith, Executive Officer (XO), ODCSOPS, HQ USAREUR/7A, for DCINCUSAREUR, 28 Sep 88, sub: 56th Field Artillery Command (56th FA Comd); Interv, author with Maj Gary Swenson, CFE Div, ODCSOPS, HQ USAREUR/7A, 30 Jan 91, pp. 18–20, tape and transcript in MHO files.

8. Memo, Office of the Deputy Chief of Staff, Resource Management (DCSRM), HQ USAREUR/7A, for USAREUR Historian, 18 Oct 95.

9. The details of these developments are documented in HQ USAREUR/7A annual historical reviews (AHR) for the 1970s and 1980s, which are available at the MHO, OSGS, HQ USAREUR/7A.

10. *HQ USAREUR/7A Annual Historical Review, 1987*, pp. 284–88, copy in MHO files.

11. Schubert and Kraus, *The Whirlwind War*, p. 56.

12. Saint, "Foreword," *III Corps Maneuver Book*, pp. 1–3.

13. Draft article, Lt Gen Crosbie E. Saint, United States Army (USA), and Lt Gen Charles J. Cunningham, Jr., United States Air Force (USAF), "Advanced Joint Air Attack Team Tactics," copy in MHO files.

14. Lt. Gen. Crosbie E. Saint and Col. Walter H. Yates, Jr., "Attack Helicopter Operations in the AirLand Battle: Deep Operations," *Military Review* 68 (July 1988): 2–9, as well as related articles by these authors on close and rear operations in the May and June 1988 *Military Review.*

15. Lt. Gen. Crosbie E. Saint, Col. Tommy R. Franks, and Maj. Alan B. Moon, "Fire Support for Mobile Armored Warfare," *Field Artillery* (June 1988): 12–14.

16. Lt. Gen. Crosbie E. Saint and Maj. John T. Nelson, "Destroying Soviet Forward Detachments," *Military Review* 68 (April 1988): 2–11.

17. Ltr, Lt Gen Gerald T. Bartlett, Cdr, U.S. Army Combined Arms Center and Fort Leavenworth, to Lt Gen Crosbie E. Saint, Cdr, III Corps and Fort Hood, 1 Feb 88, no sub.

18. Interv, author with Saint, 12 Dec 90, pp. 1–2, tape and transcript in MHO files.

19. Position Paper, Capt John M. Jones, USA, Regional Negotiations Div, J5, HQ USEUCOM [U.S. European Command], n.d., sub: Conventional Arms Control in Europe (prepared to help brief incoming CINCUSAREUR, Gen Crosbie E. Saint); Interv, author with Swenson, 30 Nov 90, p. 6, tape and transcript in MHO files.

20. Memo, Capt Dwayne Beyer, Asst SGS, HQ USAREUR/7A, for DCSOPS and POLAD, USAREUR, 2 Aug 88, sub: Credible Defense.

21. Memo, Maj Gen Thomas C. Foley, DCSOPS, USAREUR, for CINCUSAREUR, 26 Aug 88, sub: Conventional Stability Talks—CINC's Questions; Briefing Slides, Conventional Stability Talks and Associated Issues, n.d.; MFR, Pflaster, AEAGC-P, n.d. [1988], sub: Meeting With Gen Saint, 31 August 1988, on Conventional Stability Talks; Interv, author with Swenson, 30 Nov 90.

22. Memo, Foley for CINCUSAREUR, 26 Aug 88, sub: Conventional Stability Talks; MFR, Pflaster, Meeting with General Saint, 31 August 1988.

23. Interv, author with Saint, 12 Dec 90, pp. 2–3; Interv, Dr. Charles D. Hendricks with Gen (ret.) Crosbie E. Saint, 7 May 97, tape and transcript in U.S. Army Center of Military History, Washington, D.C.; Interv, author with Swenson, 30 Nov 90, pp. 6–11.

24. Interv, author with Saint, 12 Dec 90, pp. 2–3; Interv, author with Pflaster, Ch, CFE Div, ODCSOPS, HQ USAREUR/7A, 16 Aug 90, pp. 1–2, tape and transcript in MHO files.

25. E-Force (which later developed into the Engineer Restructure Initiative [ERI]) was the reorganization of combat engineers into small, mobile battalions at brigade level with each engineer battalion commander serving also as brigade engineer.

26. Interv, author with Saint, 12 Dec 90.

27. Memo, Col Dennis L. Seiler, Ch, Plans Div, ODCSOPS, for DCSOPS, USAREUR, n.d., sub: Briefing to CINC on CFE Issues, 29 Mar 89, pp. 1–2.

28. Ibid.; Interv, author with Saint, 12 Dec 90.

29. Memo, Seiler for DCSOPS, USAREUR, n.d., sub: Meeting with CINC on 5 June 1989: Summary of His Trip to Washington.

30. Speech, President George Bush, "United States and NATO," in Mainz, Federal Republic of Germany, 31 May 89, in *Vital Speeches of the Day* 55, no. 18 (1 July 1989): 546–49; Interv, author with Swenson, 30 Nov 90, pp. 19–20; Interv, author with Pflaster, 16 Aug 90, p. 5.

31. Interv, author with Swenson, 30 Nov 90, pp. 19–20; Interv, author with Pflaster, 16 Aug 90, p. 5.

32. Interv, author with Col Kenneth G. Carlson, Ch, Doctrine, Concepts, and Analysis (DCA) Div, ODCSOPS, HQ USAREUR/7A, 20 Mar 91, tape, transcript, and attachments in MHO files; Interv, author with Swenson, 30 Nov 90; Interv, author with Pflaster, 14 Nov 90, tape and transcript in MHO files; Interv, author with Saint, 12 Dec 90.

33. Draft memo, unsigned (ODCSOPS) for CINCUSAREUR, n.d., sub: Briefing to GEN Vuono on USAREUR CFE Issues (9 Sep 89), including slides, in MHO files.

34. Interv, author with Carlson, 20 Mar 91, p. 10.

35. Interv, author with Lt Col Kenneth Sharpe, DCA Div, ODCSOPS, 9 Sep 91, tape and transcript in MHO files.

36. Interv, author with Carlson, 20 Mar 91.

37. Ibid., pp. 4–5, including Briefing, DCA Div, ODCSOPS, HQ USAREUR/7A, sub: Times Are Changing: Do We Need a Deployed U.S. Ground Force in Europe. Fall 1989.

38. Interv, author with Carlson, 20 Mar 91.

39. Ibid.

40. Ibid., p. 22; Interv, author with Sharpe, 9 Sep 91, p. 21; MFR, Stephen P. Gehring, MHO, OSGS, HQ USAREUR/7A, 13 Sep 91, sub: LTC Sharpe Interview and Files.

41. *HQ USAREUR/7A Historical Review, 1988–1989*, p. 193, in MHO files.

42. Ibid., pp. 193–94; *HQ USAREUR/7A Historical Review, 1990–1991*, pp. 332–33, 339–40; *HQ USAREUR/7A Annual Historical Review, 1987*, pp. 29–30; USAREUR Regulation 350–1, USAREUR Training Directive, 7 Apr 89, ch 9, sec I; *3d Infantry Division Annual Historical Review, 1990*, pp. 5, 81, copies in MHO files.

43. *2d Corps Support Command Annual Historical Report, 1989*, tab D, encl 3, p. 1, copy in MHO files; Interv, author with Brig Gen Leonard Donald Holder, Deputy CofS (Spt), HQ Central Army Group (CENTAG), 10 Feb 92, p. 3, tape and transcript in MHO files.

44. Interv, author with Carlson, 20 Mar 91, pp. 21–22; *3d Infantry Division Annual Historical Review, 1990*, p. 82.

45. Interv, author with Holder, 10 Feb 92, pp. 3–7.

46. The author makes this statement in the face of broad and weighty opinion to the contrary, including that of General Saint, who told an interviewer from *Jane's Defense Weekly*, "In a sense, we simply turned around REFORGER." Memo, Col Phillip W. Childress, Chief, Public Affairs (CPA), USAREUR, for CINCUSAREUR, 28 Jun 91, sub: CINC Interview, 17 Jun with *Jane's Defense Weekly*, copy on MHO files.

47. Interv, Hendricks with Saint, 7 May 97; *HQ USAREUR/7A Historical Review, 1988–1989*, pp. 180–88; Fact Sheet, Capt P. M. Titorenko, U.S. Air Force (USAF), Warrior Preparation Center (WPC), thru DCSOPS, USAREUR, AEAGC-XO, to MHO, n.d., sub: 1990 USAREUR Annual Historical Review Items.

48. Fact Sheet, Maj Mallicoat, ODCSOPS, HQ USAREUR/7A, AEAGC-EX-C, to MHO, 1 Mar 91, sub: Calendar Year (CY) 1990 Historical Review: V Corps/3AD [3d Armored Division] WARFIGHTER.

49. Fact Sheet, David Spinks, FMD, ODCSOPS, AEAGC-FMD-E, HQ USAREUR/7A, n.d., sub: 1990 Bradley Fieldings in USAREUR; Fact Sheet, Lynn Norman, FMD, ODCSOPS, AEAGC-FMD, HQ USAREUR/7A, n.d., sub: Heavy Expanded Mobility Tactical Truck (HEMTT); Fact Sheet, Maj Varley, FMD, ODCSOPS, AEAGS-FMD-IC, HQ USAREUR/7A, n.d., sub: AH–64/OH–58D Fielding and AH–64 Stationing; Fact Sheet, Maj Craven, FMD, ODCSOPS, AEAGC-FMD-IC, HQ USAREUR/7A, sub: Fielding Army Tactical Missile System (ATACMS) Capable Multiple Launch Rocket System (MLRS) Launchers; Fact Sheet, Maj Varley, FMD, ODCSOPS, AEAGC-FMD-IC, HQ USAREUR/7A, sub: Air-to-Air Stinger (ATAS); Fact Sheet, Capt P. Nelson, FMD, ODCSOPS, AEAGC-FMD-IS, HQ USAREUR/7A, sub: Mg Armored Combat Earthmover (ACE); Fact Sheet, Maj Bideaux, FMD, ODCSOPS, AEAGC-FMD-IS, HQ USAREUR/7A, sub: Improved High Frequency Radio (IHFR) Support to Operation DESERT SHIELD/DESERT STORM; Interv, author with Brig Gen David E. White, Deputy Chief of Staff, Information Management (DCSIM), USAREUR, and Col Dale Fincke, Assistant Deputy Chief of Staff, Information Management (ADCSIM), HQ USAREUR/7A, 6 Feb 91, p. 5, tape and transcript in MHO files; Study, Capt Brian W. Cotter, FMD, ODCSOPS, HQ USAREUR/7A, *Combat Battalions and Separate Companies Fiscal Year (FY) 1980–1991* (Dec 91); Fact

Sheet, Maj Curlee, Office of the Deputy Chief of Staff, Logistics (ODCSLOG), HQ USAREUR/7A, sub: Refuel on the Move (ROM).

50. Interv, author with Brig Gen Walter J. Bryde, Jr., Deputy Chief of Staff, Personnel (DCSPER), USAREUR, 17 Apr 91, tape and transcript in MHO files.

51. Interv, author with Saint, 12 Dec 90.

52. Interv, author with Col Michael F. Kush, Deputy Chief of Staff, Host Nation Activities (DCSHNA), USAREUR, 20 Jun 91, tape and transcript in MHO files.

53. *Stars and Stripes* (Eur ed.), 27 Mar 91, pp. 1, 10.

54. Fact Sheet, Lt Col Ebright, Nuclear/Chemical Div, ODCSOPS, AEAGC-NC-N, HQ USAREUR/7A, n.d., sub: Historical Key Facts for Operation STEEL BOX; Memo, Maj Gen John C. Heldstab, DCSOPS, USAREUR, for USCINCEUR, 9 Dec 90, sub: STEEL BOX European Phase After Action Report; *Stars and Stripes* (Eur ed.), 30 Nov 90, p. 28; Author's discussion of operation with a participant, Matthew P. Caputo, Logistical Staff Off, ODCSLOG, HQ USAREUR/7A.

55. Interv, author with Col Thomas J. McGuire, Deputy Ch, CFE Div, ODC-SOPS, HQ USAREUR/7A, and Team Ch, Air Movements Control Team, Stuttgart, 12 Mar 91, pp. 3–5, tape and transcript in MHO files.

56. Interv, author with Lt Col John Graham, Ch, Policy and Planning Br, CFE Div, ODCSOPS, HQ USAREUR/7A, 1 Nov 90, tape and transcript in MHO files; Intervs, author with Pflaster, 16 Aug 90 and 14 Nov 90; Memo, Maj James F. Dittrich, Asst SGS, HQ USAREUR/7A, to DCSOPS, USAREUR, 10 Apr 90, sub: CINC Notes from March CCC [Component Commanders' Conference]; MFR, Gehring, 31 May 90, sub: CINC Meeting on Force Structure Reduction, copy in MHO files.

57. Fact Sheet, Maj Alvonne M. Steenburn, ODCSLOG, HQ USAREUR/7A, 18 May 91, sub: Equipment Retrograde Under Conventional Forces Europe (CFE) Treaty Limited Equipment (TLE).

58. MFR, Maj Gregory Alderete, ODCSLOG, HQ USAREUR/7A, n.d., sub: Prepositioned Material Configured to Unit Sets, copy in MHO files.

59. Memo, Maj Gen Richard T. Travis, Chief Surgeon (CSURG), USAREUR, for CINCUSAREUR, 30 Jul 90, sub: Termination of Warm Base Hospital Storage Program.

60. *HQ USAREUR/7A Historical Review, 1988–1989,* pp. 128–31; *HQ USAREUR/7A Historical Review, 1990–1991,* p. 271, copy in MHO files.

61. MFRs, Gehring, 24 May 90, sub: CINC Meeting: CFE Data Base for JCS and USEUCOM, and 17 Jul 90, sub: CINC Meeting: BRAC [Base Realignment and Closure] Review at HQDA, copies in MHO files; Tasker, Secretary of the General Staff (SGS), HQ USAREUR/7A, to DCSOPS, USAREUR, 3 Aug 90, sub: ACC Task: Force Posture (with Gen Saint's remarks on enclosed slides); Msg, USCINCEUR to Commander in Chief, U.S. Air Forces in Europe (CINCUSAFE) and CINCUSAREUR, 141405Z Sep 90, sub: European Theater Force Level Planning; Interv, author with Pflaster, 15 Mar 91, p. 7, tape and transcript in MHO files; Slides used to brief Commander in Chief's Commanders' Forum (CCF), 27 Nov 90, CFE Div, ODCSOPS, n.d., sub: USAREUR After the Smoke Clears, copies in MHO files.

62. Memo, HQ USAREUR/7A, AEAGC-P, for Commanders of USAREUR Major and Separate Major Commands, 14 Sep 90, sub: Confidential CIN-CUSAREUR Operation Plan (OPLAN) 4352–90; Note, Pflaster, Jun 92, no sub.

63. Note to author, Pflaster, no sub, n.d., copy in MHO files.

64. *Stars and Stripes* (Eur ed.), 19 Sep 90, pp. 1, 28.

65. Msg, CINCUSAREUR, AEAPA-PP, to AIG [Address Indicating Group] 9075, 271714Z Sep 90, retransmitting Msg, HQDA, SAPA-PP, to AIG 7406, 7405, and Army Staff (ARSTAF) (including CINCUSAREUR), 261630Z Sep 90, sub: USAREUR Force Reductions; Msg, Chairman of the Joint Chiefs of Staff (CJCS) to USCINCEUR, info: CINCUSAREUR and CINCUSAFE, 272311Z Sep 90, sub: Withdrawal of 40,000 Personnel From Europe.

Chapter 3

1. MFR, Gehring, 17 Oct 92, sub: SSI Interview With Gen Saint, 12 Oct 91, copy in MHO files; Interv, author with Saint, 11 Apr 91; Interv, author with Maj Gen John C. Heldstab, DCSOPS, USAREUR, 5 Mar 91, tape and transcript in MHO files; Interv, author with Maj Gen Joseph S. Laposata, Deputy Chief of Staff, Logistics (DCSLOG), USAREUR, 14 Feb 91, tape and transcript in MHO files.

2. Interv, Hendricks with Saint, 7 May 97; Discussion, author with Col (ret.) William D. Chesarek, Apr 97. Chesarek was the assistant DCSOPS during the deployment. He and Saint agree that Colonel Mumby was a major contributor to the effective administration of deployment operations at HQ USAREUR/7A.

3. Interv, author with Heldstab, 5 Mar 91; Interv, Hendricks with Saint, 7 May 97.

4. Interv, author with Maj Gen Cloyd H. Pfister, Deputy Chief of Staff, Intelligence (DCSINT), USAREUR, 20 Aug 91, tape and transcript in MHO files.

5. Ibid.

6. Briefing, Capt Menne, Crisis Action Team (CAT), Current Operations Br, Operations Div, ODCSOPS, HQ USAREUR/7A, 21 May 91.

7. Msg (Personal), Saint to Lt Gen William H. Reno, DA DCSPER, info: Gen Carl Vuono, Chief of Staff, Army (CSA), and Maj Gen Stanley H. Hyman, Cdr, U.S. Army Intelligence and Security Command (INSCOM), 161940Z Aug 90, sub: Operation DESERT SHIELD Effect on USAREUR Manning.

8. Interv, author with Saint, 11 Apr 91; Interv, Hendricks with Saint, 7 May 97. See also Msg, Secretary of State to U.S. Mission, NATO, info: CINCUSAREUR, et al., 161548Z Aug 90, sub: Alliance Consultation on Deployed Forces, no. 3.

9. Msg, USCINCEUR, J3, to CINCUSAREUR, AEAGC-O-CC, 160121Z Aug 90, sub: Operation DESERT SHIELD; Msg, Cdr, 21st Theater Army Area Command (TAACOM), AERSP-O, to Cdr, 70th Trans Bn, info: CINCUSAREUR, 211152Z Aug 90, sub: Aviation Maintenance Support of Operation DESERT SHIELD (DS), FRAGO M 1; Memo, Travis for CofS, DCINC, CINC, 17 Aug 90, sub: MEDEVAC Questions in Support of DESERT SHIELD; Msg, Cdr, 21st TAACOM, to Cdr, 70th Trans Bn, info: CINCUSAREUR, 261130Z Aug 90, sub: Aviation Maintenance Support of Operation DESERT SHIELD (DS) FRAGO M 4; O&I briefing slide, ODCSOPS, AEAGC-O, C + 20, sub: DESERT SHIELD UPDATE: Executing.

10. Msg Cdr, 21st TAACOM, AERSP-O, to Cdr, 70th Trans Bn, info: CINCUSAREUR, 222030Z Aug 90, sub: Aviation Maintenance Support of Operation DESERT STORM, FRAGO M 3; 421st Medical Bn (Evacuation) and 45th Medical Co (Air Ambulance) annual historical reports in *7th Medical Command Annual Historical Review, 1990*, copy in MHO files; *Stars and Stripes* (Eur ed.), 6 Sep 90, p. 2.

11. Facsimile Msg (fax), 7th MEDCOM, AEMPA, Aug 91, sub: 7th MEDCOM Medifacts # 33–91; For example, Msg, USCENTAF TAC to U.S. Central

Command (CENTCOM), USCINCEUR, CINCUSAREUR, et al., 162200Z Aug 90, sub: USCENTCOM Aeromedical Evacuation Concept of Operations for Operation DESERT SHIELD, and Msg, USCINCEUR to Commander in Chief, U.S. Naval Forces, Europe (CINCUSNAVEUR); Ops Support Ctr, Ramstein; CINCUSAREUR; Cdr, 7th MEDCOM, 181600Z Aug 90, sub: Expansion of USEUCOM Hospital Capability in Support of Operation DESERT SHIELD.

12. Memo, DCSOPS, AEAGC-O, for CINCUSAREUR, 24 Sep 90, sub: Deployment of 763d Med Det to DESERT SHIELD; Msg, CINCUSAREUR, AEAGC-CAT, to U.S. Commander in Chief, Central Command (USCINCCENT), CCJ3, CCCC, 281230Z Sep 90, sub: Deployment of the 763d Med Det to DESERT SHIELD; Permanent Orders 150–1, HQ USAREUR/7A, 22 Oct 90.

13. Msg, USCINCEUR, ECPA, to CINCUSAREUR, AEAPA, 060837Z Sep 90, sub: Public Affairs Guidance–Deployment of Elements of 7th Medical Command in Support of DESERT SHIELD; Msg, USCINCEUR, ECMD, to Joint Chiefs of Staff (JCS), J4-LRC, 171708Z Oct 90, sub: MEDSTAT; Msg, CINCUSAREUR Liaison Office (LNO) Bonn, to CINCUSAREUR, AEAGX, 161259Z Oct 90, sub: Medical Support for Operation DESERT SHIELD.

14. Msg, Cdr, V Corps, AETV-CS, to Cdr, 205th MI Bde, et al., 161700Z Aug 90, sub: Warning Order to V Corps OPORD 90–10 (Deployment to DESERT SHIELD); Msg, Cdr, V Corps, AETV-CS, to Cdr, 205th MI Bde, et al., 181530Z Aug 90, sub: Execution Order for V Corps OPORD 90–10 (Deployment to DESERT SHIELD); Interv, author with Pfister, 20 Aug 91; Briefing Slides, Operations Division, ODCSOPS, AEAGC-O, C + 20, sub: DESERT SHIELD Update.

15. Interv, author with Pfister, 20 Aug 91.

16. Msg, USCINCEUR, ECCAT, to CINCUSAREUR, AEAGC-O-CC, 182133Z Aug 90, no sub ("This is a deployment order."); Memo, Heldstab for CINCUSAREUR, 16 Aug 90, sub: NBC [Nuclear, Biological, Chemical] Recon Support for DESERT SHIELD; Memo, Heldstab, for CINCUSAREUR, 23 Aug 90, sub: DESERT SHIELD—NBC Recon Platoon Update; Msgs, Cdr, V Corps, to Cdr, 8th Inf Div, and Cdr, 3d Armd Div, 191951Z Aug 90, sub: NBC Recon Platoon Structure & Training, and 261720Z Aug 90, sub: V Corps OPORD 90–11, Deployment to Saudi Arabia; Msg, Cdr, V Corps, to III German Korps, 071405Z Sep 90, sub: Follow-on Sustainment Training of V (US) Corps NBC Reconnaissance Personnel in Support of Exercise DESERT SHIELD; Memo, Heldstab for CINCUSAREUR, 15 Oct 90, sub: Sustainment of NBC Reconnaissance Platoons; *8th Infantry Division (Mechanized) Annual Historical Review, 1990*, pp. 21–32, copy in MHO files.

17. Memo, Heldstab for CINCUSAREUR, 15 Oct 90, sub: Sustainment of NBC Reconnaissance Platoons; Memo, Heldstab for CINCUSAREUR, 6 Nov 90, sub: Distribution and Deployment of Fox Vehicles.

18. DCA Div, ODCSOPS, HQ USAREUR/7A, *USAREUR Operations DESERT STORM & DESERT SHIELD Theater-Level Observations* (Feb 92), pp. 2–3.

19. Msg, CINCUSAREUR, AEAGC-O, to Cdr, V Corps, et al., 151900Z Aug 90, sub: Deployment Order to Saudi Arabia; Msg, Cdr, V Corps, AETV-CS, to

Cdr, 12th Avn Bde, et al., 211725Z Aug 90, sub: V Corps OPLAN 90–9, Deployment of 12th Avn Brigade to DESERT SHIELD; Msg, Cdr, V Corps, AETV-CS, to Cdr, 12th Avn Bde, et al., 222010Z Aug 90, sub: V Corps Warning Order #12, Deployment of 12th Avn Brigade to DESERT SHIELD.

20. Msg, CINCUSAREUR, AEAGC-O, to Cdr, V Corps, et al., 151900Z Aug 90, sub: Deployment Order to Saudi Arabia; Msg, Cdr, 21st TAACOM, AERSP-O, to Cdr, 60th Ord Gp, 161545Z Aug 90, sub: Operations Order—Operation DESERT SHIELD; Msg, Cdr, V Corps, AETV-GCO, to CINCUSAREUR, AEAGC-O, 170145Z Aug 90, sub: Request Relief From Avn Taskings; Msg, Cdr, V Corps, AETV-GCO, to CINCUSAREUR, AEAGC-O, 170145Z Aug 90, sub: Questions Concerning Deployment of 12th Avn Bde to Saudi Arabia.

21. Quote from Msg, CINCUSAREUR to Cdr, V Corps, et al., 151900Z Aug 90, sub: Deployment Order to Saudi Arabia; Msg, Cdr, V Corps, AETV-CS, 211725Z Aug 90, sub: V Corps OPLAN 90–9; Msg, Cdr, V Corps, AETV-CG, to CINCUSAREUR, AEAGC-O, 211000Z Sep 90, sub: 12th CAB [Combat Aviation Brigade] Deployment Lessons Learned.

22. Msg, CINCUSAREUR, AEAGC-O, to Cdr, V Corps, et al., 151900Z Aug 90, sub: Deployment Order to Saudi Arabia; Msg, Cdr, V Corps, AETV-CS, 211725Z Aug 90, sub: V Corps OPLAN 90–9.

23. Msg, Cdr, V Corps, AETV-CG, to CINCUSAREUR, 281700Z Aug 90, sub: SITREP [Situation Report] 281400Z Aug 1990; Msg, Cdr, V Corps, AETV-GDP, to CINCUSAREUR, AEAGC-O, 271600Z Aug 90, sub: Support for 12th Avn Bde Deployment; Memo, Col J. B. Jenkinson for CINCUSAREUR, 28 Aug 90, sub: 12th Brigade Deployment; Msg, Cdr, U.S. Army Southern European Task Force (USASETAF)/5th TAACOM, to CINCUSAREUR, AEAGC-CAT, 291730Z Aug 90, sub: Support for the 12th Aviation Bde Deployment; Msg, Cdr, V Corps, AETV-GS, to CINCUSAREUR, 311700Z Aug 90, sub: SITREP 311400Z Aug 1990; Msg, Cdr, V Corps, AETV-GS, to CINCUSAREUR, 011945Z Sep 90, sub: DESERT SHIELD Tactical Loading of Ships for Deployment; *Stars and Stripes* (Eur ed.), 31 Aug 91, p. 3.

24. Fact Sheet, Laposata, 27 Aug 90; *Stars and Stripes* (Eur ed.), 31 Aug 91, p. 3; Msg, Cdr, V Corps, to CINCUSAREUR, 011945Z Sep 90, sub: DESERT SHIELD Tactical Loading of Ships for Deployment; Msgs, Cdr, V Corps, to CINCUSAREUR, 311700Z Aug 90, sub: SITREP 311400Z Aug 1990; 031501Z Sep 90, sub: SITREP 031400Z Sep 90; 041930Z Sep 90, sub: SITREP 041400Z Sep 90; 051700Z Sep 90, sub: SITREP 051400Z Sep 1990; 081545Z Sep 90, sub: SITREP 081400Z Sep 90; and 101700Z Sep 90, sub: SITREP 101400Z Sep 90; Memo, Jenkinson for CINCUSAREUR, 28 Aug 90, sub: 12th Brigade Deployment; Msg, Cdr, USASETAF/5th TAACOM, to CINCUSAREUR, 291730Z Aug 90, sub: Support for the 12th Aviation Bde Deployment.

25. Msgs, Cdr, V Corps, to CINCUSAREUR, 131700Z Sep 90, sub: SITREP 131400Z Sep 90; 011745Z Oct 90, sub: SITREP 27 Sep–1 Oct 90; 091240Z Oct 90, sub: SITREP 2 Oct 90–9 Oct 90; and 231420Z Oct 90, sub: SITREP 16–22 Oct 90; Msg, Cdr, XVIII Abn Corps, to Cdr, 101st Abn Div (AASLT), and Cdr, 12th Avn Bde, 190630Z Sep 90, sub: FRAGO #12, Attachment of 12 Avn Bde; Msg,

Cdr, V Corps, to CINCUSAREUR, AEAGC-CAT, 141400Z Sep 90, sub: Shipment of Hellfire Missiles for 12 Avn Bde; Briefing Summary, Maj Thomas Swackhamer, Asst SGS, HQ USAREUR/7A, 13 Oct 90, sub: SWA [Southwest Asia] Sustainment.

26. Msg, Cdr, V Corps, to CINCUSAREUR, 211000Z Sep 90, sub: 12th CAB Deployment Lessons Learned.

27. Msg, Cdr, 5th Sig Cmd, ASQE-OP-WP, to Cdr, 2d and 7th Sig Bde, et al., 181300Z Aug 90, sub: Augmentation for USAISC-CA Operation Desert Shield; Msg, Cdr, 5th Sig Cmd, ASQE-OP-WE, to CINCUSAREUR, AEAGC-CAT, 060200Z Sep 90, sub: 5th Sig Cmd SITREP No 2 as of 051500Z Sep 90.

28. Interv, author with White and Fincke, 6 Feb 91; ODCSPER Briefing Slide, September 1990, sub: Personnel Deployments.

29. Interv, author with White and Fincke, 6 Feb 91; Msg, Cdr, VII Corps, AETSGC-O, to CINCUSAREUR, AEAGC-O, 112300Z Sep 90, sub: Request for Assistance—Desert Shield Communications; Msg, Cdr, V Corps, AETV-IM, to CINCUSAREUR, AEAGC-O, 300900Z Sep 90, sub: Signal Equipment Impact; Memo, DCSIM, USAREUR, for CINCUSAREUR, 4 Oct 90, sub: Communications Support to Operation Desert Shield; Chart, DCA Div, ODCSOPS, HQ USAREUR/7A, *USAREUR Desert Storm and Desert Shield Theater-Level Observations*, Feb 92, p. 4.

30. For Pagonis' and other officers' impressions, see Schubert and Kraus, *The Whirlwind War*, which cites intervs, Lt Col James Ireland, 25 Feb 91, and Lt Col David A. Whaley, Cdr, 7th Trans Gp, 13 Feb 91; Description of phone call in Interv, author with Laposata, 14 Feb 91.

31. Interv, author with Laposata, 14 Feb 91, pp. 3–4.

32. Interv, author with Saint, 11 Apr 91, p. 3.

33. Ibid., p. 10.

34. *HQ USAREUR/7A Annual Historical Review, 1987*, pp. 186–87.

35. Msg, HQDA, DALO-LOC, to CINCUSAREUR, et al., 160009Z Aug 90, sub: Release of Prepositioned War Reserve Materiel Assets and Operational Project Stocks in Support of Desert Shield.

36. Short Note, Laposata to Saint, 16 Aug 90, sub: Release of Forward Positioned Prepositioned War Reserve (FPPWR) Assets in Support of Desert Shield.

37. See Chapter 2 for Saint's policy after December 1989. Msg, HQDA, DALO-SMW, to CINCUSAREUR, AEAGD, 271835Z Aug 90, sub: USAREUR Theater Reserve Availability in Support of Operation Desert Shield; Briefing to Sec Army, 10 Sep 90, sub: Sustaining the SWA Force.

38. Interv, author with Saint, 11 Apr 91.

39. Short Note, DCSLOG, USAREUR, to CINCUSAREUR, 24 Sep 90, sub: Requirements Validation for Desert Shield.

40. Memo, Laposata for CofS, HQ USAREUR/7A, 10 Sep 90, sub: Thoughts on USAREUR as a COMMZ.

41. Marginal notes, Saint, on ibid.

42. Memo, Col J. M. Mabry, ADCSLOG-S, HQ USAREUR/7A, for CINCUSAREUR, 24 Sep 90, sub: EUCOM Visit to CENTCOM.

43. Ibid.; Memo, Mabry for CINCUSAREUR, 25 Sep 90, sub: EUCOM Brief to GEN Galvin on CENTCOM Support.

44. Short Note, Laposata to CINCUSAREUR, 7 Sep 90, sub: Military Tents for Desert Shield.

45. Msg, USCINCEUR, ECJ3-CCD, to USCINCCENT, CCJ3-ALCC, 110913Z Sep 90, sub: OSA Support for USCINCCENT.

46. Slide, HQ USEUCOM, Component Commanders' Conference, 4 Sep 90; Briefing Slides, DCSOPS, USAREUR, AEAGC-CAT, 28 Sep 90, sub: Desert Shield.

47. Msg, Commanding General (CG), U.S. Army, Central Command (ARCENT) Support Command (SUPCOM), Command Group (CMD GP), to USCINCEUR, CINCUSAREUR, et al., 120800Z Sep 90, sub: Critical Equipment Requirements for Operation Desert Shield.

48. Msg, HQDA, DALO-SMW, to CINCUSAREUR, AEAGD-WT, 122225Z Sep 90, sub: USAREUR Theater Reserve Availability in Support of Operation Desert Shield.

49. Briefing Summary, Swackhamer, 12 Sep 90, sub: Support for Desert Shield Long-term.

50. Briefing Summary, Swackhamer, 24 Sep 90, sub: SWA Rotations.

51. Msg, HQDA, DAMO-ZA, to CINCUSAREUR and ARCENT, Fwd, 042355Z Oct 90, sub: Support for Desert Shield.

52. Msg, HQDA, DAMO-ODC-AOC, to CINCUSAREUR, et al., 161901Z Oct 90, sub: Relocation of M1A1 Tanks From USAREUR Stocks; Msg, AMEMB, Bonn, to Secretary of State and CINCUSAREUR, et al., 191745Z Oct 90, sub: FRG Informed of U.S. Decision To Remove Tanks From ATTU [Atlantic to the Urals] To Support Gulf Operations; Msg, HQDA, DAMO-FDD, to COMUSAR-CENT and CINCUSAREUR, 151454Z Oct 90, sub: Modification of M1A1s and IPM1s Deployed to Saudi Arabia; Memos, Laposata for CINCUSAREUR, 19 Oct 90, sub: Retrograde of MlAl Tanks; 1 and 2 Nov 90, sub: Tank Retrograde II; 6 Nov 90, sub: Status of the CAPE MOHICAN; and 11 Nov 90, sub: The Last of the (Cape) Mohican.

53. Msg, HQDA, DAMO-ODO-AOC, to USCINCEUR and CINCUSAREUR, et al., 101520Z Nov 90, sub: Release of M1A1 Tanks From POMCUS [Pre-positioned Organizational Materiel Configured to Unit Sets] in Support of 1MX [1st Inf Div] Deployment to Desert Shield; Interv, author with Pflaster, 14 Nov 90.

54. Msgs, HQDA, DALO-ZC, to USCINCEUR and CINCUSAREUR, 141455Z Sep 90, sub: USAREUR Assets To Support Desert Shield, and 111615Z Oct 90, same sub; Memo, Laposata for CINCUSAREUR, 11 Oct 91, sub: Logistics Support for Desert Shield.

55. Short Note, Laposata to Maj Gen Willard M. Burleson, Jr., CofS, HQ USAREUR/7A, n.d. (logged in CofS office, 27 Aug 91), sub: Missile Resupply for Desert Shield.

56. Briefing Summary, Swackhamer, 30 Aug 91, sub: MLRS/ATACMS Laydown.

57. Memo, Laposata for CINCUSAREUR, sub: Current Update of Logistical Actions for Desert Shield, 2 and 4 October 1990.

58. Msg, Cdr, U.S. Army Depot System Command (DESCOM), to Cdr, Mainz Army Depot (MZAD), 161600Z Aug 90, sub: Activation of MZAD Emergency Operations Center; Short Note, Laposata to CINCUSAREUR, 20 Sep 90, sub: Use of Mainz Army Depot in Support of DESERT SHIELD; Msg, Cdr, U.S. Army Materiel Command (AMC), to CINCUSAREUR, 121430Z Sep 90, sub: Release of Depot Level Reparables Out of Theater; Msg, Cdr, AMC, to Cdr, AMC, Europe, 172100Z Sep 90, sub: Support of DESERT SHIELD Via Mainz Army Depot Repair; Short Note, Brig Gen Carl W. Tipton, ADCSLOG-MRMM, USAREUR, to CINCUSAREUR, 23 Oct 90, sub: Mainz Army Depot (MZAD) Class IX Maintenance Support to DESERT SHIELD; Msg, Cdr, AMC, to CINCUSAREUR, AEAGD, 251515Z Oct 90, sub: Maintenance Support Policy for SWA; Short Note, Laposata to CINCUSAREUR, 31 Oct 90, sub: SWA Retrograde of Reparables to Mainz.

Chapter 4

1. *Crisis in the Persian Gulf Region: U.S. Policy Options and Implications. Hearing Before the Committee on Armed Services*. United States Senate, 101st Cong., 2d sess. (Washington, D.C., 1990), p. 27; Swain, *Lucky War*, pp. 71–85; Schwarzkopf, *It Doesn't Take a Hero*, p. 362.

2. Interv, author with Virginia Jay, CFE Div, ODCSOPS, HQ USAREUR/7A, 20 Nov 90, p. 5, tape and transcript in MHO files; Interv, author with Heldstab, 5 Mar 91, pp. 4–5; Interv, author with Pflaster, 14 Nov 90, p. 3; Briefing to Secretary of the Army, 20 Sep 90, sub: Sustaining the SWA Force: Modernization; Briefing Slide, DAMO-FDD, HQDA, 5 Oct 90, sub: Modernization Synopsis, in Briefing, Director of Force Programs, ODCSOPS, FD, HQDA, 16 Oct 90, sub: Sustaining the Forces in SWA.

3. Interv, author with Saint, 11 Apr 91, p. 1; Interv, Hendricks with Saint, 7 May 97.

4. Interv, author with Graham, 3 Apr 91, pp. 7–8, tape and transcript in MHO files. According to Graham, Saint said, ". . . this list looks an awful lot like a corps . . . why should I send all of this force and not send the corps headquarters. So he tasked us, the DCSOPS, and it fell on me and the folks who work for me, to look at sending a corps to Saudi Arabia to be there in January." Oral history interv, Lt Col Robert Wilson with Gen (ret.) Crosbie E. Saint, Project 1994–3 in the Senior Officer Oral History Program, U.S. Army Military History Institute, 1994. In this interview, General Saint stated that General Vuono called him one day and asked him if he could send a division. Saint says that he responded, "Yes, but I think really based on what I know, what you need is a whole corps." Saint continues that Vuono asked him if he could really send a corps. Saint answered, "Sure, but let me do a little staff work" and call back the next day. Saint says he talked to his deputy, Lt. Gen. John M. Shalikashvili, then answered that USAREUR could provide a corps; Interv, Hendricks with Saint, 7 May 97; Memo, Graham for Ch, DCA Div, ODCSOPS, 21 Mar 91, sub: Why USAREUR Did So Well in SWA.

5. Interv, author with Graham, 3 Apr 91, pp. 7–9; Interv, author with Jay, 20 Nov 90, p. 5.

6. *Stars and Stripes* (Eur ed.), 19 Sep 90, p. 3; Interv, author with Saint, 11 Apr 91; Interv, Hendricks with Saint, 7 May 97.

7. Tasker, Burleson, 4 Sep 90, no sub; Interv, author with Pflaster, 14 Nov 90.

8. Interv, author with Jay, 20 Nov 90; Briefing Slides, CFE Div, ODCSOPS, HQ USAREUR/7A, 12 Sep 90, sub: Force Rotation to Saudi; USAREUR Residual Force Units Only.

9. Briefing Summary, Swackhamer, 12 Sep 90, sub: Support for Desert Shield Long Term.

10. Ibid.; Interv, author with Jay, 20 Nov 90.

11. Faxed copy of Memo, Heldstab for Lt Gen Dennis J. Reimer, DA DCSOPS, 18 Sep 90, sub: USAREUR Support to Saudi Rotations; Interv, author with Jay, 20 Nov 90.

12. Briefing, DA DCSOPS to Secretary of the Army, 20 Sep 90, sub: Sustaining the SWA Force.

13. See Chapter 3 (supported by footnotes 50 and 51).

14. Briefing Summary, Swackhamer, 24 Sep 90, sub: SWA Rotations.

15. Interv, author with Pflaster, 14 Nov 90, p. 4.

16. Interv, author with Graham, 3 Apr 91, pp. 7–9; Intervs, author with Jay, 20 Nov 90 and 15 Apr 91.

17. Briefing Summary, Swackhamer, 13 Oct 90, sub: SWA Sustainment (incl briefing slides).

18. Interv, author with Graham, 3 Apr 91, pp. 7–9. According to Colonel Graham the corps option was discussed several times. These discussions probably involved General Saint and the same people with whom Generals Heldstab and Laposata had worked on 6 October; Briefing Summary, Swackhamer, 13 Oct 90, sub: SWA Sustainment; Interv, author with Saint, 11 Apr 91.

19. Briefing Summary, Swackhamer, 13 Oct 90, sub: SWA Sustainment.

20. Ibid.

21. Ibid.

22. Ibid.; Interv, author with Pflaster, 14 Nov 90.

23. Memo, Heldstab for Burleson, 17 Oct 90, sub: SWA Deployment Order.

24. Ibid.

25. Ibid.

26. Ibid.

27. Copies of slides and reports summarizing their functional assessments are in tabs K, L, M, ML [sic], P, and Q to incl 1 to interv, author with Jay, 20 Nov 90.

28. Ibid.

29. Interv, author with Saint, 11 Apr 91; Interv, author with Heldstab, 5 Mar 91; Interv, author with Graham, 3 Apr 91, pp. 7–9.

30. Interv, author with Saint, 11 Apr 91; Memo, Graham for Ch, DCA Div, 21 Mar 91, sub: Why USAREUR Did So Well in SWA.

31. Jay's list, the CFE Division total rotation requirements list, and the CFE Division list of USAREUR units that could meet these rotation requirements in tabs M (USAREUR Units to SWA), R (Rotation of USAREUR Units to SWA), and S (List of Units by Type Requested) to incl 1 to interv, author with Jay, 20 Nov 90. The lists show 95 units requested, one fewer than Jay stated in the interview.

32. Ibid.; Note, Pflaster to Saint, 24 Oct 90, copy in MHO files.

33. Interv, author with Jay, 20 Nov 90, including CFE Div slides, Rotation of USAREUR Units to SWA, in tab T to incl 1; Briefing Summary, Swackhamer, 27 Oct 90, sub: SWA/CFE Data; Memo, Pflaster for Heldstab, 29 Oct 91, sub: Latest Option(s) for USAREUR Units to SWA. The "sacrosanct" "Tank" is well described in Schwarzkopf, *It Doesn't Take a Hero*, p. 268.

34. Briefing Summary, Swackhamer, 13 Oct 90, sub: SWA Sustainment; Interv, author with Saint, 11 Apr 91.

35. Interv, author with Maj Gen Willard M. Burleson, Jr., CofS, HQ USAREUR/7A, 11 Jan 91, p. 5, tape and transcript in MHO files.

36. Interv, author with Saint, 11 Apr 91.

37. Briefing Summary, Swackhamer, 28 Oct 90, sub: SWA. Participants included General Laposata and Colonel Phillips, ODCSLOG; Colonel Chesarek, ADCSOPS, and Col. Roger L. Mumby, Ch, Ops Div, ODCSOPS, as well as Mr. Pflaster, Colonels McGuire and Graham, and Ms. Jay, CFE Div, ODCSOPS; Colonel Molino, CINC's XO; Colonel Goedcoop, G3 Plans Sec, HQ VII Corps; and Major Thornton, G3 Plans Sec, V Corps.

38. Briefing Slides (incl Saint marginalia and notes), CFE Div, ODCSOPS, 28 Oct 90, no sub; Briefing Summary, Swackhamer, 28 Oct 90, sub: SWA; Memo, Pflaster for Heldstab, 29 Oct 90, sub: Latest Option(s).

39. Interv, author with Saint, 11 Apr 91.

40. Interv, author with Maj. Thomas Swackhamer, Asst SGS, HQ USAREUR/7A, 24 Jan 91, pp. 15–16, tapes and transcript in MHO, OSGS, HQ USAREUR/7A.

41. Briefing Slides (incl Saint marginalia and notes), CFE Div, ODCSOPS, 28 Oct 90, no sub; Briefing Summary, Swackhamer, 28 Oct 90, sub: SWA; Interv, author with Swackhamer, 24 Jan 91; Memo, Pflaster for Heldstab, 29 Oct 90, sub: Latest Option(s).

42. Briefing Slides (incl Saint marginalia and notes), CFE Div, ODCSOPS, 28 Oct 90, no sub; Briefing Summary, Swackhamer, 28 Oct 90, sub: SWA; Memo, Pflaster for Heldstab, 29 Oct 90, sub: Latest Option(s); Lt Gen Frederick M. Franks, Jr., Cdr, VII Corps, 29 May 1991, DESERT SHIELD/DESERT STORM After Action Report. For a good review of the organizational problems faced and solutions found by this deploying support command as well as a description and chart of the enhanced wartime organization, see Brig. Gen. Robert P. McFarlin, "Logistics Command and Control in Southwest Asia," *Army Logistician* (November–December 1992): 11–15.

43. Memo, Pflaster for Heldstab, 29 Oct 90, sub: Latest Option(s); Interv, author with Heldstab, 5 Mar 91.

44. Interv, author with Saint, 11 Apr 91; Interv, Hendricks with Saint, 7 May 97. In the Hendricks interview, Saint stated that he discussed deployment issues with Vuono rather than the vice chief or others.

45. Briefing Slides (incl Saint marginalia and notes), CFE Div, ODCSOPS, 28 Oct 90, no sub; Briefing Summary, Swackhamer, 28 Oct 90, sub: SWA; Memo, Pflaster for Heldstab, 29 Oct 90, sub: Latest Option(s).

46. CFE Div briefing slides, sub: USAREUR Corps to SWA, in tab A to incl 2 to interv, author with Jay, 20 Nov 90.

47. Ibid.

48. Memo, Pflaster for Heldstab, 29 Oct 90, sub: Latest Option(s); Fax, HQ USAREUR/7A (M. Zeller) to Cdr, VII Corps, 29 Oct 90, no sub, including two charts, sub: Why Not 3ID Vice 3AD and Why Not 3ID Vice 3AD HQ?; Lt Col Peter S. Kindsvatter, VII Corps History Ofc, An Initial Overview of the Jayhawk Corps in the 100-Hour War, pp. 2–3; Briefing Summary, Swackhamer, 30 Oct 90, sub: VII Corps.

49. Briefing Summary, Swackhamer, 30 Oct 90, sub: SWA Update; Briefing Notes in tab J to incl 2 to interv, author with Jay, 20 Nov 90.

50. Briefing Summary, Swackhamer, 30 Oct 90, sub: SWA Update; Briefing Notes in tab J to incl 2 to interv, author with Jay, 20 Nov 90.

51. Kindsvatter, An Initial Overview of the Jayhawk Corps in the 100-Hour War, pp. 2–3; Slide, FY [Fiscal Year] 91 Inactivation—Schedule, in CFE Div briefing slides in tab F to incl 2 to interv, author with Jay, 20 Nov 90; Briefing Summary, Swackhamer, 30 Oct 90, sub: SWA Update.

52. Briefing Summary, Swackhamer, 30 Oct 90, sub: SWA Update; Briefing Notes in tab J to incl 2 to interv, author with Jay, 20 Nov 90.

53. Briefing Slides (incl Saint marginalia and notes), CFE Div, ODCSOPS, 28 Oct 90, no sub; Briefing Summary, Swackhamer, 28 Oct 90, sub: SWA.

54. Interv, author with Brig Gen Robert C. Lee, DCSENG, USAREUR, 9 Aug 91, p. 9, tapes and transcript in MHO files; Alan Schlie, "Close Up: Engineer Restructure Initiative," *Engineer* 23 (February 1993): 20–24. General Lee noted, "That [partial implementation of ERI] was done astride the river, though normally you shouldn't be changing horses as you cross the river."

55. Note (with description of options enclosed), Lt Col Daniel E. Gunter, C/G3 Plans, 32d Army Air Defense Command (AADCOM), 30 Oct 90, no sub.

56. Interv, author with Saint, 11 Apr 91.

57. Briefing Slides, sub: USAREUR Units to SWA (incl Jay's notes) in tab M to incl 1 to interv, author with Jay, 20 Nov 90.

58. Interv, author with White and Fincke, 6 Feb 91, p. 9; *The Desert Jayhawk* (Stuttgart: VII Corps Public Affairs Office, 1991), p. 40.

59. Msg, Commander in Chief, Forces Command (CINCFOR), to USCINC-CENT MAIN, COMUSARCENT, USCINCEUR, CINCUSAREUR (AEAMD), et al., 111811Z Nov 90, sub: DEPMEDS [Deployable Medical Systems] POMCUS Hospitals; Memo, Travis for CINCUSAREUR, 5 Nov 90, sub: Release of Hospital Medical Materiel Sets Stored in POMCUS in Support of Operation DESERT SHIELD; *Annual Historical Report/AMMED Activities RCS-MED 41 (R–4), 1 Jan–31 Dec 90*, HQ 7th MEDCOM, para 8.3, copy in MHO files.

60. Msg, CINCUSAREUR, AEADC, to Cdr, V Corps, and Cdr, VII Corps, 231129Z Nov 90, sub: Medical Requirements for Deploying and Residual Forces; Historical Summary, Asst Chief of Staff, Operations (ACSOPS), OCSURG, HQ USAREUR/7A, n.d., sec VIII in *7th MEDCOM AHR, 1991*, copy in MHO files; Msg, CINCFOR to USCINCEUR and CINCUSAREUR, 262232Z Nov 90, sub: RC [Reserve Component] Hospital Units in Support of VII Corps.

61. Interv, author with Heldstab, 5 Mar 91; CFE Div briefing slides, sub: Vilseck and Aschaffenburg Brigade Structure, in tab K to incl 2 to interv, author with Jay, 20 Nov 90.

62. CFE Div briefing slides in tab F to incl 2 to interv, author with Jay, 20 Nov 90.

63. CFE Div briefing slides, 12 Nov 90, in tab B to incl 4 to interv, author with Jay, 20 Nov 90.

64. CFE Div briefing slides in tab C to incl 2 to interv, author with Jay, 20 Nov 90.

65. Memo, Graham for Ch, DCA Div, 21 Mar 91, sub: Why USAREUR Did So Well in SWA.

66. Interv, Hendricks with Saint, 7 May 97; interv, author with McGuire, 12 Mar 91.

67. Interv, author with Saint, 11 Apr 91, p. 2; Commander in Chief's Calendar, Thursday, 1 November 1990, HQ USAREUR/7A; Schubert and Kraus, *The Whirlwind War*, p. 111.

68. Fax Transmittal Header Sheet, Col J. F. Coughlin, Ch, J5 War Plans Div, ARCENT Rear, to Pflaster, 7 Nov 90, no sub, containing ARCENT slides, in tab E to incl 4 to interv, author with Jay, 20 Nov 90; Memo, Coughlin for Pflaster, et al., 7 Nov 90, sub: Reinforcement TPFDD [Time-phased Force Deployment Data].

69. Memo, Graham for Ch, DCA Div, 21 Mar 91, sub: Why USAREUR Did So Well in SWA.

70. MFR, Pflaster, n.d., sub: Nov 8, 1990 Meeting on Sending Corps to SWA.

71. Msg, Secretary of Defense to AIG 8798 and 8799 for Public Affairs Officers, 090030Z Nov 90, sub: News Briefing by Secretary of Defense Dick Cheney and Chairman of the Joint Chiefs of Staff, General Colin Powell, at the Pentagon, on Thursday, November 8, 1990, at 4:45 p.m.; Memo, Graham for Ch, DCA Div, 21 Mar 91, sub: Why USAREUR Did So Well in SWA.

72. Interv, author with Holder, 10 Feb 92; Maj. Roger King, *Second Armored Division (-) Annual Historical Report, Calendar Year 1991*, ch 1, p. 4, copy in MHO files.

73. Msg, CINCUSAREUR to Cdr, VII Corps, et al., 091023Z Nov 90, sub: USAREUR DESERT SHIELD Deployment Order 21; Memo, Heldstab for Reimer, 3 Nov 90, sub: USAREUR Deploying Force Structure.

74. Verbal inquiry, author to Jay, 7 Feb 92; Interv, author with Pflaster, 14 Nov 90.

75. CINCUSAREUR Deployment Order 22, Deployment of VII Corps to SWA, 10 Nov 90, which is included as Appendix C to this study.

76. Interv, author with Burleson, 11 Jan 91; Interv, author with Saint, 11 Apr 91.

77. Interv, author with Saint, 11 Apr 91.

78. Draft msg, Saint to Gen Gordon R. Sullivan, VCSA, n.d. (Nov 90), sub: USAREUR Force Reduction Update, copy in MHO files.

Chapter 5

1. Interv, author with Maj Stephen Howard, Plans Div, ODCSLOG, HQ USAREUR/7A, 14 Mar 91, tape and transcript in MHO files; Interv, author with Laposata, 14 Feb 91.

2. Interv, author with Saint, 11 Apr 91; Slides in tab B to incl 2 to interv, author with Jay, 20 Nov 90.

3. Briefing Slides (incl Saint marginalia and notes), CFE Div, ODCSOPS, HQ USAREUR/7A, 28 Oct 90, no sub; Briefing Summary, Swackhamer, 28 Oct 90, sub: SWA; Interv, author with Saint, 11 Apr 91; Slides in tab B to incl 2 to interv, author with Jay, 20 Nov 90.

4. Interv, author with Laposata, 14 Feb 91, p. 12.

5. Ibid., p. 8.

6. Interv, author with Howard, 14 Mar 91.

7. Interv, author with Burleson, 11 Jan 91.

8. Facsimile Msg, Coughlin to Pflaster, 7 Nov 90, sub: Reinforcement TPFDD; Memo, Graham for Ch, DCA, 21 Mar 91, sub: Why USAREUR Did So Well in SWA; Briefing Slides, ODCSOPS, n.d. (first week of Nov 90), sub: Time Phased Force Deployment Data (TPFDD); Briefing Summary, Swackhamer, 15 Nov 90, sub: 151630 Update; Draft Msg (Personal), CINCUSAREUR (Saint) to HQDA (Sullivan), n.d., sub: Air Movement of VII Corps Soldiers.

9. Major Dittrich quotes General Laposata in Briefing Summary, Dittrich, 30 Oct 90, sub: AUSA/SWA Support; DCSLOG Slides in tab I to incl 4 to interv, author with Jay, 14 Feb 91.

10. Briefing Slides, ODCSLOG, sub: Movements Concept, n.d., in tab J to incl 4 to interv, author with Jay, 20 Nov 90. Deployment Process Chart taken from this briefing; MFR, Pflaster, n.d., sub: Nov 8, 1990 Meeting on Sending Corps to SWA; USAREUR Deployment Order 22, 10 Nov 90.

11. Briefing Slides (incl Saint marginalia and notes), CFE Div, ODCSOPS, 28 Oct 90, no sub; Briefing Summary, Swackhamer, 28 Oct 90, sub: SWA; Memo, Pflaster for Heldstab, 29 Mar 92, sub: Latest Option(s).

12. Interv, author with Laposata, 14 Feb 91; Interv, author with Howard, 14 Mar 91.

13. Msg (Personal), Saint for Reimer, Gen Robert W. RisCassi, Gen Edwin H. Burba, Jr., Gen John W. Foss, and Gen William G. T. Tuttle, Jr., 121600Z Nov 90, sub: Enhanced Force Policy; Memo, Laposata for CINCUSAREUR, 10 Nov 90, sub: Status of Desert Battle Dress Uniform.

14. Note, Laposata to Saint, 3 Jan 91, sub: Status of VII Corps Cots; Memo, Col Joel S. Levanson, Cdr, U.S. Army Contracting Command, Europe (USAC-CE), 2 Jan 91, sub: Cot Procurements in Support of DESERT SHIELD.

15. Msg, CINCUSAREUR, AEAGD, to Cdr, VII Corps, 21st TAACOM, et al., 142200Z Nov 90, sub: Change 4 to CINCUSAREUR Deployment Order 22.

16. Interv, author with Saint, 11 Apr 91, p. 5; Msg, CINCUSAREUR, AEAGC, to HQDA, DAMO-FDZ/DAMO-AOC, et al., 101300Z Nov 90, sub:

Tactical Wheeled Vehicles for Operation DESERT SHIELD; Msg, CINCUSAREUR, AEAGC-O/CAT, to HQDA, DAMO-AOC, USCINCCENT, USCINCEUR, Cdrs, V and VII Corps, et al., 190640Z Nov 90, sub: USAREUR SITREP #84; Lt. Col. Peter S. Kindsvatter, "VII Corps in the Gulf War: Deployment," *Military Review* 72 (January 1992), pp. 7–8.

17. Interv, author with Pfister, 20 Aug 91.

18. Msg, CINCUSAREUR to Cdrs, V and VII Corps, et al., 221357Z Nov 90, sub: DESERT SHIELD Taskings/Information.

19. Interv, author with White and Fincke, 6 Feb 91.

20. For example: Memo, Laposata for CINCUSAREUR, 20 Nov 90, sub: Use of Local Purchase to Support DESERT SHIELD Deployments; Msg, HQDA, DAMO-ODO-AOC, to CINCUSAREUR, AEAGD-SM-EOC, 170711Z Jan 91, sub: Withdrawal of Theater Reserves/POMCUS Assets in Support of Operation DESERT SHIELD; Info Note, Laposata to Saint, 4 Jan 91, sub: Swap-out of Non-repairable Equipment for 12th and 54th Engineers; Info Note, Laposata to Saint, 7 Dec 90, sub: Commissary Support of DESERT SHIELD; Msg, Cdr, V Corps, AETV-GD, to CINCUSAREUR, et al., 291300Z Nov 90, sub: Update of Logistical Support for VII Corps Units.

21. Msg, Cdr, VII Corps, to CINCUSAREUR, AEAGD-CAT-LOG, 152250Z Nov 90, sub: VII Corps Critical Shortages; Msg, Cdr, V Corps, to Cdrs, 3d Armd Div and 8th Inf Div, et al., 181900Z Nov 90, sub: Equipment Transfer Guidance for Announced CFE Units.

22. Msg (Personal), Saint for Reimer, RisCassi, Burba, Foss, and Tuttle, 121600Z Nov 90, sub: Enhanced Force Policy.

23. Interv, author with Laposata, 14 Feb 91, pp. 2–3.

24. Ibid., p. 6.

25. Ibid., p. 22.

26. Ibid.

27. Briefing Slides, 3d Armored Division Profile and 3d Infantry Division Profile, in tab G to incl 4 to interv, author with Jay, 20 Nov 90.

28. Kindsvatter, "VII Corps in the Gulf War: Deployment," p. 5.

29. Interv, author with Holder, 10 Feb 92, pp. 3–7.

30. Interv, author with Pfister, 20 Aug 91, p. 14.

31. Interv, author with Lee, 9 Aug 91, pp. 10–11; Memo, Lee for CINCUSAREUR, 5 Dec 90, sub: Preparing USAREUR Engineer Units for Deployment to SWA.

32. Msg, Cdr, 7th MEDCOM, AEMPO-T, to AIG 0803, 151700Z Nov 90, sub: Commanding General 7th MEDCOM Training Guidance in Support of Operation DESERT SHIELD.

33. Memo, Brig Gen Richard E. Davis, Asst Deputy Chief of Staff, Operations—Training (ADCSOPS-T), for Heldstab, 20 Nov 90, sub: Target Lifters for VII Corps Deployment.

34. Memo, Maj Gen Ronald E. Brooks, DCSPER, USAREUR, for CINCUSAREUR, 14 Aug 90, sub: Deletion of Soldiers on Orders for USAREUR Units.

35. Msg (Personal), Saint for Reno, info: Vuono and Hyman, 161940Z Aug 90, sub: Operation DESERT SHIELD Effect on USAREUR Manning.

36. Interv, author with Brig Gen Mary C. Willis, Cdr, 1st Personnel Command (PERSCOM), 11 Jun 91, pp. 3–4, tape and transcript in MHO files.

37. Chart and aggregate strength figures taken from tab B (USAREUR Personnel Status) to incl 2 to interv, author with Jay, 20 Nov 90.

38. Interv, author with Willis, 11 Jun 91, p. 7.

39. Chart and aggregate strength figures taken from tab B to incl 2 to interv, author with Jay, 20 Nov 90.

40. Memo, Bryde for CINCUSAREUR, 9 Nov 90, sub: Designating USAREUR in Direct Support of SWA (Stop Loss).

41. Msg, CINCUSAREUR, AEAGA-M, to AIG 8858 and others, 101430Z Nov 90, sub: Stop Loss in USAREUR.

42. Msg (Personal), Saint to Reimer, RisCassi, Burba, Foss, and Tuttle, 121600Z Nov 90, sub: Enhanced Force Policy.

43. Msg, CINCUSAREUR, AEAGA-M, to Cdrs, USAREUR maj comds, 061230Z Dec 90, sub: Enhanced Force Policy in USAREUR; Interv, author with Bryde, 17 Apr 91, pp. 10–11.

44. Interv, author with Bryde, 17 Apr 91, p. 11.

45. Ibid.; Interv, author with Willis, 11 Jun 91, p. 6.

46. Interv, author with Willis, 11 Jun 91, p. 5; Interv, author with Bryde, 17 Apr 91; Note, Bryde to CINCUSAREUR, 13 Nov 90, no sub.

47. Interv, author with Willis, 11 Jun 91, p. 5.

48. Memo, Willis for CINCUSAREUR, 8 Jan 91, sub: Assigned and Attached Personnel for VII Corps Deployment.

49. Interv, author with Willis, 11 Jun 91, p. 5.

50. Note, Bryde to CINCUSAREUR, 13 Nov 90, no sub; Msg, CINCUSAREUR, AEAGA-M, to AIG 9848, 121548Z Nov 90, sub: Cross-Level Priorities To Fill DESERT SHIELD Deploying Units; Msg, CINCUSAREUR, AEAGA-M, to AIG 9848, 161250Z Nov 90, sub: Revised Cross-Level Priorities To Fill Units Deploying to DESERT SHIELD and Changes to USAREUR Stop Loss Policy.

51. Memo, Bryde for CINCUSAREUR, 15 Nov 90, sub: Cross-leveling Priorities and USAREUR Stop Loss; Interv, author with Bryde, 17 Apr 91, p. 3; Interv, author with Willis, 11 Jun 91, pp. 7–8.

52. Msg, CINCUSAREUR to Cdr, VII Corps, 101500Z Dec 90, sub: Personnel Status; Interv, author with Bryde, 17 Apr 91, pp. 5–6.

53. Ibid.

54. Msg, CINCUSAREUR, AEAGA-M, to AIG 7533, et al., 092030Z Nov 90, sub: Family Care Plan Execution for DESERT SHIELD Deployment; Interv, author with Bryde, 17 Apr 91, p. 5.

55. Interv, author with Bryde, 17 Apr 91, p. 7; Memo, Willis for CINCUSAREUR, 2 Apr 91, sub: Deployability; and incl H to interv, author with Willis, 11 Jun 91.

56. Memo, Col Thomas M. Crean, Judge Advocate (JA), USAREUR, for CINCUSAREUR, 28 Mar 90, sub: Missed Movement.

57. Interv, author with Bryde, 17 Apr 91, p. 7.

58. Msg, Cdr, 7th Pers Gp, to V Corps, VII Corps, et al., 111200Z Dec 90, sub: Operation Desert Storm Replacement System for VII Corps; Msg (incl Saint marginalia), Cdr, VII Corps, AETS-X-GH, to CINCUSAREUR, AEAGC-O, 281936Z Jan 91, sub: VII Corps Base SITREP #13.

59. Interv, author with Lt Gen John M. Shalikashvili, DCINCUSAREUR, 19 Mar 91; Interv, Hendricks with Saint, 7 May 97; Interv, author with Saint, 11 Apr 91; Interv, author with Burleson, 11 Jan 91; Interv, author with Laposata, 14 Feb 91; MFR, Bruce H. Siemon, Ch, MHO, OSGS, HQ USAREUR/7A, n.d., sub: Notes From Meeting With Col Kindsvatter, VII Corps DS/DS Historian. Other examples in Msg, Cdr, VII Corps, to Cdr, 11th Avn Bde, 141040Z Nov 90, sub: VII Corps FRAGO 31–90, Attachment of 3–58th ATC (-) to 11th Avn Bde; Msg, Cdr, 1st Armd Div, to Cdr, VII Corps, 121000Z Nov 90, sub: Activation of 312th Support Center, or Msg, Cdr, VII Corps, to CINCUSAREUR, 150840Z Nov 90, sub: Activation of 244 Corps Support Center (USAR); Msg, Cdr, VII Corps, to Cdr, 1st Armd Div, et al., 131320Z Nov 90, sub: VII Corps Taskings vs Real World Situation; Msg, USCINCEUR to Cdr, 1st Armd Div, et al., 111103Z Nov 90, sub: Disposition of USCINCEUR Positive Control Material.

60. Interv, author with Holder, 10 Feb 92.

61. Interv, author with Laposata, 14 Feb 91, p. 15.

62. Ibid.

63. Interv, author with Burleson, p. 6.

64. Msg, USCINCEUR, Battle Staff, to CINCUSAREUR, et al., 101400Z Nov 90, transmitting Msg, USCINCCENT to USCINCEUR, et al., 101730Z Nov 90, sub: Force Deployment Planning TPFDD Guidance; Msg, COMUSARCENT Main, G4, to Cdr, VII Corps, CINCUSAREUR, et al., 141320Z Nov 90, sub: Logistic Support Concept for Receipt of Additional Forces; Interv, Hendricks with Saint, 7 May 1997.

65. Listing taken from DCA Div, ODCSOPS, HQ USAREUR/7A, *USAREUR Desert Storm and Desert Shield Theater-Level Observations*, Feb 92.

66. CFE Div list, VII Corps Unit Deployment Sequence, in tab ML to incl 4 to interv, author with Jay, 20 Nov 90.

67. Fold-out deployment chart, DCA Div, ODCSOPS, HQ USAREUR/7A, *USAREUR Desert Storm and Desert Shield Theater-Level Observations*, Feb 92; Msg, Cdr, MTMC, Europe, MTEUREOC, to CINCUSAREUR, et al., 151900Z Nov 90, sub: Desert Shield Port Call #4; Info Note, Heldstab to CINCUSAREUR, 14 Nov 90; Msg, Cdr, VII Corps, AETSCG, to Cdr, 1AD, and other deploying units, 190010Z Nov 90, sub: Deployment Execution Order No. 3 — Movement to Seaports.

68. Msg, CINCUSAREUR to Cdr, 21st TAACOM, 192100Z Nov 90, sub: VII Corps Convoy to SPOEs.

69. Interv, author with White and Fincke, 6 Feb 91, p. 3.

70. See Charles E. White, Historian, 21st TAACOM, *First in Support: The 21st Theater Army Area Command in Support of Operation Desert Shield, 17 August*

1990–31 March 1991, June 1991. Dr. White provides a concise description of 21st TAACOM's massive support of the deployment.

71. *Stars and Stripes* (Eur ed.), 12 Dec 90, pp. 13–15; Msg, Cdr, 21st TAA-COM, to Cdr, 3d Inf Div, 020945Z Jan 91, sub: Port Support Personnel; *History of the 1st Infantry Division Forward, April 1970–August 1991*, p. 58, in MHO files; Memo, Kush for CINCUSAREUR, 19 Nov 90, sub: Host Nation Support (HNS) in the Netherlands, Belgium, and Germany.

72. Interv, author with Laposata, 14 Feb 91.

73. Interv, author with Burleson, 11 Jan 91, p. 6.

74. Interv, author with Laposata, 14 Feb 91, p. 17; Briefing Summary, Dittrich, 30 Oct 90, sub: AUSA/SWA Support.

75. Interv, author with Laposata, 14 Feb 91; Interv, author with Howard, 14 Mar 91.

76. Press Release, Deutsche Bundesbahn, Frankfurt/Main, "Desert Shield and Granby: Militaertransporte zu den Nordseehaefen," 15 Nov 90.

77. *Stars and Stripes* (Eur ed.), 30 Nov 90, p. 2.

78. Interv, author with Laposata, 14 Feb 91; Interv, author with Howard, 14 Mar 91.

79. Msg, American Consulate (AMCONSUL), Stuttgart, to Secretary of State, et al., 071300Z Dec 90, sub: Adding VII Corps to Desert Shield.

80. Briefing Summary, Dittrich, 25 Oct 90, sub: 21st TAACOM CARC Painting.

81. Info Note, Laposata to CINCUSAREUR, 8 Jan 91, sub: CARC Paint.

82. Interv, author with Saint, 11 Apr 91, p. 7; *Stars and Stripes* (Eur ed.), p. 2; Memo, Bryde for CINCUSAREUR, 13 Dec 90, sub: Vehicle Accidents During Convoy Operations.

83. Briefing Summary, Swackhamer, 30 Nov 90, sub: 0730 O&I.

84. Msg, Cdr, VII Corps, to DCINCUSAREUR, 170815Z Nov 90, sub: Use of Sea/Land Containers—VII Corps Deployment.

85. Briefing Summaries, Swackhamer, 23 Nov 90, subs: O&I and 1630 Update; Interv, author with Laposata, 14 Feb 91; Interv, author with Howard, 14 Mar 91.

86. Memo, Maj Gen Wilson A. Shoffner, Cdr, 3d Inf Div, for Saint, 22 Nov 90, no sub.

87. Msg, Cdr, Military Traffic Management Command (MTMC), Eur, to Cdr, MTMC, 242000Z Nov 90, sub: Additional Port in NOREUR [Northern Europe].

88. Briefing Summary, Swackhamer, 27 Nov 90, sub: O&I.

89. Msg, USCINCEUR to USCINCCENT, 061624Z Dec 90, sub: Desert Shield Movement Coordination.

90. Note, DCINCUSAREUR to CINCUSAREUR, 19 Dec 90, no sub.

91. Memo, Col James E. Callahan, Ch, USAREUR Liaison Team to ARCENT, for CofS, HQ USAREUR/7A, 20 Dec 90, sub: Trip Report.

92. Ibid., pp. 3–4; MFR, author, SSI Interv.

93. Interv, author with Burleson, 11 Jan 91, p. 9.

94. For example, Msg, Cdr, MTMC, Eur, to Cdr, VII Corps, 250100Z Nov 90, sub: Desert Shield—Port Call & Performance.

95. Info Note, Laposata to CINCUSAREUR, 27 Nov 90, no sub.

96. Msg, Cdr, VII Corps, to deploying units, 300315Z Nov 90, sub: LNO Responsibilities.

97. Briefing Slides (incl Saint marginalia), ODCSLOG, HQ USAREUR/7A, 12 Mar 91, sub: VII Corps Deployment Profile.

98. Interv, author with Howard, 14 Mar 91, p. 14.

99. Msg, CINCUSAREUR, AEAGD-T, to AIG 0873, 6774, 7533, 9073, and 9848; Cdr, 2d Armd Div; Cdr, 18th Engr Bde; Cdr, 32d AADCOM; Cdr, 200th Theater Army Materiel Management Center (TAMMC), Cdr, MTMC-Eur, 152120Z Nov 90, sub: Uploading of .50 Cal and Below Small Arms Ammo; Interv, author with Laposata, 14 Feb 91, p. 24.

100. Msg (Personal), Saint to Vuono and Gen John Galvin, USCINCEUR, 161030Z Nov 90, sub: USAREUR Deployment Update.

101. Msg, Cdr, V Corps, AETV-GC, to Cdr, 3d Armd Div, et al., 291430Z Nov 90, sub: Combat Loading of Vehicles Deploying To SWA Amended.

102. *NRC Handelsblad*, 26 Nov 90; Memo, ODCINC for DCINC, 27 Nov 90, sub: Waiver for Barges.

103. Msg, USCINCEUR to USCINCCENT, 061624Z Dec 90, sub: DESERT SHIELD Movement Coordination; Briefing Summary, Swackhamer, 25 Nov 90, sub: O&I; Interv, author with Saint, 11 Apr 91, p. 9.

104. Interv, author with Saint, 11 Apr 91, p. 9.

105. Memo, Brig Gen J. R. Landry, CofS, HQ VII Corps, for Burleson, 22 Nov 90, sub: DESERT SHIELD Issues; Briefing Summary, Dittrich, 24 Nov 90, sub: Morning O&I; *History of the 1st Infantry Division Forward*, pp. 59–62.

106. Interv, author with Shalikashvili, 19 Mar 91, p. 8; Interv, author with Heldstab, 5 Mar 91, p. 8; Interv, author with McGuire, 12 Mar 91, p. 7; Briefing Summary, Swackhamer, 26 Nov 90, sub: 0730 O&I.

107. Interv, author with Heldstab, 14 Feb 91, p. 8; Interv, author with McGuire, 12 Mar 91, p. 8.

108. Msg, MACCAT, retransmitted in Msg, 322 ALD ALCC, Ramstein Air Base (AB), to USAREUR MACLO Det 1, 201631Z Nov 90, sub: European APOEs [air ports of embarkation] for DESERT SHIELD II Deployment.

109. Interv, author with McGuire, 12 Mar 91, p. 10.

110. Interv, author with Holder, 10 Feb 92.

111. Interv, author with McGuire, 12 Mar 91; Memo, Heldstab, n.d., sub: USAREUR AMCC [Air Movement Control Cell]: Executive Overview; Interv, Hendricks with Saint, 7 May 97.

112. Msg (Personal), Saint for Galvin, 281120Z Nov 90, sub: Airlift Allocation.

113. Interv, author with McGuire, 12 Mar 91, p. 9.

114. Msg, CINCUSAREUR, AEAGC-O-CAT, to Cdrs, VII Corps, 21st TAA-COM, et al., 251405Z Nov 90, sub: Change 7 to CINCUSAREUR Deployment Order 22, 10 Nov 90; Kindsvatter, "VII Corps in the Gulf War: Deployment."

115. Msg, Cdr, 21st TAACOM, to CINCUSAREUR, et al., 201145Z Dec 90, sub: Closure of CSC/RON [Remain Over Night] Sites; Msg, Cdr, 21st TAACOM,

to AIG 858 and 879, 210001Z Dec 90, sub: Reduce Manning for Tactical Operations Centers.

116. Msg, Cdr, 21st TAACOM, to Cdr, 3d Inf Div, 020945Z Jan 91, sub: Port Support Personnel.

117. Msg, COMUSARCENT MAIN to CINCUSAREUR, 200936Z Jan 91, sub: Redeployment of 4–16 Inf and 3–34 AR.

118. Memo, Heldstab, n.d., sub: USAREUR AMCC: Executive Overview.

119. DCA Div, ODCSOPS, HQ USAREUR/7A, *USAREUR DESERT STORM and DESERT SHIELD Theater-Level Observations*, Feb 92; Briefing Slides (incl Saint marginalia), ODCSLOG, HQ USAREUR/7A, 12 Mar 91, sub: VII Corps Deployment Profile; Briefing Slides, Maj Pruitt, Operations Div, ODCSOPS, HQ USAREUR/7A, 16 Jun 91, sub: SWA Deployment; Msg (Personal), Saint to Powell, 040953Z Jan 91, sub: USAREUR Deployment. While the figure of 75,500 USAREUR troops deployed to Southwest Asia given in the DCA Division study has been widely accepted, calculations of personnel deployed in various elements and time periods yield sums between 78,000 and 79,250.

120. Interv, author with Saint, 11 Apr 91; Memo, Heldstab for CINCUSAREUR, 22 Jul 91, sub: Philosophical Thoughts About Residual Force Deployment—Operational and Strategic Movement; DCA Div, ODCSOPS, HQ USAREUR/7A, *USAREUR DESERT STORM and DESERT SHIELD Theater-Level Observations*, Feb 92; Briefing Slides (incl Saint marginalia), ODCSLOG, HQ USAREUR/7A, 12 Mar 91, sub: VII Corps Deployment Profile; Briefing Slides, Pruitt, 16 Jun 91, sub: SWA Deployment; Msg (Personal), Saint to Powell, 040953Z Jan 91, sub: USAREUR Deployment.

Chapter 6

1. For further information, see Msg, HQDA, DAMO-ZA, to CINCUSAREUR, 021420Z Nov 90, sub: CINCCENT Force Requirements, incl Saint marginalia; Msg, HQDA, DAMO-ZA, to Cdr, FORSCOM, info: CINCUSAREUR, 021430Z Nov 90, sub: CINCCENT Force Requirements, incl Saint marginalia; Msg, CINCFOR, FCJ6, to COMUSARCENT Main, info: CINCUSAREUR, 162130Z Nov 90, sub: DESERT SHIELD Enhanced TPFDD Requirements; Msg, HQDA, DAMO-FDZ, to CINCUSAREUR, AEAGC-FMD, 201300Z Nov 90, sub: ARCENT Force Structure Shortfalls; Msg (Personal), Saint to Reimer, 040830Z Dec 90, sub: CINCCENT Force Requirements; Table of Organization and Equipment 11–305J, 1 October 1982, pp. I–1, I–2; Slides from Decision Brief, n.d., sub: DESERT SHIELD Enhanced Force "FORSCOM Wish List," in tab Q to incl 4, interv, author with Jay, 20 Nov 90; Msg (Personal), Saint to Vuono and Galvin, 300830Z Jan 91, sub: Where We Stand.

2. Msg, Secretary of State to all Diplomatic and Consular Posts, 022333Z Jan 91, sub: Department Press Briefing Transcript, Wednesday, January 2, 1990; Memo, Heldstab for CINCUSAREUR, 8 Jan 91, sub: USAREUR Commitment to ACE Mobile Force Land (AMF[L]).

3. Msg, USCINCEUR, ECJ3, to CINCUSAREUR, AEAGC, 231243Z Dec 90, sub: Operation PROVEN FORCE; Msg, CINCUSAREUR to Cdr, 21st TAACOM; Cdr, Special Operation Support Command Theater Army (SOSCTA), et al., 130630Z Jan 91, sub: Deployment Order for Operation ELUSIVE CONCEPT; Briefing Summary, Capt J. Carabeau, Asst SGS, HQ USAREUR/7A, 8 Jan 91, sub: ELUSIVE CONCEPT; HQ, U.S. Air Forces in Europe (USAFE), *USAFE and the Gulf Crisis: A Chronology of United States Air Forces in Europe's Participation in* DESERT SHIELD, DESERT STORM, PROVEN FORCE, *and* PROVIDE COMFORT, *JULY 1990–DEC 1991*, pp. xviii–xxi.

4. Msg, USCINCEUR, ECJ3, to CINCUSAREUR, AEAGC, 231243Z Dec 90, sub: Operation PROVEN FORCE; Msg, CINCUSAREUR to Cdr, 21st TAA-COM, Cdr, SOSCTA, et al., 1306307Z Jan 91, sub: Deployment Order for Operation ELUSIVE CONCEPT; Briefing Summary, Carabeau, 8 Jan 91, sub: ELUSIVE CONCEPT; Briefing, Operations Div, ODCSOPS, HQ USAREUR/7A, 21 May 91, sub: United States Army, Europe, Contributions to the Victory in the Gulf.

5. See Msg, USCINCEUR to CINCUSAREUR, 130647Z Jan 91, transmitting Msg, JCS to USCINCEUR, 122200Z Jan 91, sub: PROVEN FORCE Patriot Support.

6. Briefing Summary, Capt Joann Webber, Asst SGS, HQ USAREUR/7A, 16 Jan 91, sub: O&I; Fold-out Chart, DCA Div, ODCSOPS, HQ USAREUR/7A, *USAREUR* DESERT STORM *and* DESERT SHIELD *Theater-Level Observations*, Feb 92.

7. Briefing Slide, ODCSOPS, n.d., sub: USAREUR Patriot Battalions, in Briefing Summary, Webber, 28 Jan 91, sub: O&I; Msg, Cdr, 32d AADCOM, to CINCUSAREUR, 131200Z Dec 90, sub: Request for Advice and Assistance

Concerning Unit Deployment; Briefing Summary, Webber, 4 Feb 91, sub: 32d AADCOM; Marginal Notes, Saint, on Msg, HQDA, 151548Z Dec 90, sub: CINCCENT Force Requirements.

8. Memo, Heldstab for CINCUSAREUR, 23 Oct 90, sub: Update on Patriot Deployment.

9. Marginal Note, Saint, on Msg, COMUSARCENT to Cdr, USAREUR, 121330Z Dec 90, sub: Response on Class IX Support for Patriot Request; Marginal Note, Saint, on Msg, COMUSARCENT Main to AIG 11747, 152000Z Dec 90, sub: LOGSTAT Report No. 101.

10. Briefing Summary, Swackhamer, 2 Jan 91, sub: O&I; Msg, Cdr, 32d AADCOM, to Cdr, 69th Air Defense Artillery (ADA) Bde, et al., 022100Z Jan 91, sub: Warning Order 1–91.

11. Memo, Shalikashvili for DCSOPS, USAREUR, 3 Jan 91, no sub.

12. Interv, author with Shalikashvili, 19 Mar 91, p. 11.

13. Interv, author with Saint, 11 Apr 91, p. 8.

14. Ibid.; Memo, Heldstab for CINCUSAREUR, 18 Jan 91, sub: Patriot.

15. Msg (Info), USCINCEUR to CINCUSAREUR, 180750Z Jan 91, retransmitting Msg, CJCS to CINCFOR, info: USCINCEUR, et al., 180350Z Jan 91, sub: Patriot Requirements; Memo, Heldstab for CINCUSAREUR, 18 Jan 91, sub: Patriot.

16. Msg (Info), USCINCEUR to CINCUSAREUR and Cdr, 32d AADCOM, 200135Z Jan 91, retransmitting Msg, CJCS to USCINCEUR, et al., 192340Z Jan 91, sub: Patriots for Israel. This is the only order deploying a Patriot battalion to Israel that is available at HQ USAREUR/7A. It was issued after the first USAREUR Patriots were already operational in Israel. It modifies its references that also were issued after the Patriot battalion was on its way to Israel. The original orders were probably either TOP SECRET and destroyed or made by telephone.

17. Interv, author with Shalikashvili, 19 Mar 91, p. 12; Msg, CINCUSAREUR to HQDA, DACS-ZA, 210600Z Jan 91, sub: Deployment of Patriot to Israel/Turkey; Briefing Slide, OCINC, HQ USAREUR/7A, n.d., no sub; Msg, CINCUSAREUR to Cdr, VII Corps, et al., 210600Z Jan 91, sub: USAREUR SITREP #147 as of 210600Z Jan 91.

18. Msg (Info), USCINCEUR to CINCUSAREUR and Cdr, 32d AADCOM, 200135Z Jan 91, retransmitting Msg, CJCS to USCINCEUR, et al., 192340Z Jan 91, sub: Patriots for Israel; Msg, CINCUSAREUR to Cdr, 32d AADCOM, 221000Z Jan 91, sub: C2 Responsibilities; Msg, USCINCEUR to HQ USAREUR, AEAGC/AEAPA, 201637Z Jan 91, sub: Public Affairs Guidance—Deployment of Patriot to Israel.

19. Msg (Info), USCINCEUR to CINCUSAREUR, 180750Z Jan 91, retransmitting Msg, CJCS to CINCFOR, info: USCINCEUR, et al., 180350Z Jan 91, sub: Patriot Requirements; Briefing Summaries, Webber, 16 Jan 91, 18 Jan 91, 21 Jan 91, 28 Jan 91, and 4 Feb 91, sub: O&I; Msg, USCINCEUR, to AIG 824, 190703Z Jan 91, sub: USEUCOM SITREP, 19 Jan 91; Msg, USCINCEUR to CINCUSAREUR, 250143Z Jan 91, sub: Deployment Order; Msg (Personal), Saint to Vuono and Galvin, 300830Z Jan 91, sub: Where We Stand.

20. Memo, Maj Diane L. Berard, Asst SGS, HQ USAREUR/7A, for DCSOPS, USAREUR, 7 Jan 91, sub: Topics/Subjects for Mondays O&I; Briefing Summary, Swackhamer, 8 Jan 91, sub: O&I.

21. Msg, CINCUSAREUR to Cdr, V Corps, et al., 112300Z Jan 91, sub: Operation Order—Individual and Crew Replacements for ARCENT.

22. Briefing Slide, Operations Div, ODCSOPS, HQ USAREUR/7A, 21 May 91; Memo, Lt Gen David M. Maddox, Cdr, V Corps, for Saint, 14 Jan 91, sub: Corps Mission. For additional info, see Msg, CINCUSAREUR to Cdr, V Corps, 282032Z Jan 91, sub: Crew Replacement to SWA.

23. Msg (Personal), Saint to Vuono and Galvin, 300830Z Jan 91, sub: Where We Stand.

24. Briefing Slide, Operations Div, ODCSOPS, HQ USAREUR/7A, 21 May 91.

25. Memo, Heldstab for CINCUSAREUR, 24 Jun 91, sub: Individual/Crew Replacement Lessons Learned DESERT SHIELD/STORM; Interv, author with Bryde, 17 Apr 91; Msg, Cdr, 3d Inf Div, to Cdr, 1st Bde, et al., 161045Z Jan 91, sub: Operation Order 2–91.

26. Memo, Laposata for CINCUSAREUR, 24 Oct 90, sub: Arty Ammo for DESERT SHIELD; Memo, Laposata for CINCUSAREUR, 10 Nov 90, sub: Update on Movement of 55,560 STONS of Ammunition to Support DESERT SHIELD; Msg, Cdr, 200th TAMMC, to CINCUSAREUR, et al., 151400Z Nov 90, sub: Ammunition Support for DESERT SHIELD.

27. Msg, HQDA, DAMO-ODO-AOC, to CINCUSAREUR, et al., 172015Z Nov 90, sub: Munition Requirements, Operation DESERT SHIELD; Msg, HQDA, DAMO-ODO-AOC, to CINCUSAREUR, et al., 212350Z Nov 90, sub: Additional Class V Requirements for Operation DESERT SHIELD.

28. Memo, Laposata for CINCUSAREUR, 28 Dec 90, sub: Additional Sustainment Ammo for DESERT SHIELD; Msg (Personal), Saint to F. Franks, 311424Z Dec 90, sub: Request for Water Distribution Equipment and Training Ammunition; Msgs, Cdr, MTMC, Eur, to CINCUSAREUR, et al., 141326Z Jan 91 and 171335Z Jan 91, sub: Ammunition Outload; Briefing Summaries, Dittrich, 3 Jan 91, sub: Log; 10 Jan 91, sub: D.S. Sustainment Ammo Program; 17 Jan 91, sub: DESERT STORM Sustainment Ammo; and 28 Jan 91, sub: Ammo Update; Msg, Cdr, MTMC, Eur, to Cdr, 200th TAMMC, et al., 010900Z Feb 91, sub: Ammunition Status.

29. Briefing Summaries, Dittrich, 1 Feb 91, sub: Ammo Update, and 7 Feb 91, sub: Ammo Laydown.

30. Msg, Cdr, 200th TAMMC, AEAGD-MMC-C, to USEUCOM, USCENT-COM, CINCUSAREUR, et al., 191900Z Feb 91, sub: Sustainment Ammunition Schedule; Msg, CINCUSAREUR, AEAGC-O-CAT, to Cdr, VII Corps, Cdr, ARCENT, et al., 260600Z Feb 91, sub: USAREUR SITREP #183 as of 160600Z Feb 91; Msg, Cdr, AMC, AMCOC-AMO, to Cdr, 200th TAMMC, 072045Z Mar 91, sub: Class V Shipments.

31. *HQ USAREUR/7A Historical Review, 1 Jan 90–31 Dec 91*, pp. 269–70.

32. Memo, Webber for DCSOPS, 4 Feb 91, sub: O&I Card.

33. Memo, Charles Yasi, Principal Assistant Responsible for Contracting (PARC), HQ USAREUR/7A, thru Levanson, for Head of Contracting Activity, USAREUR, 31 Dec 90, sub: Request for Review and Authorization for Use of a Letter Contract; Msg, HQDA, SARD-ZCS, to CINCUSAREUR, et al., 192115Z Jan 91, sub: Heavy Equipment Transporters for Operation Desert Shield.

34. Memo, Levanson, 2 Jan 91, sub: Cot Procurements in Support of Desert Shield.

35. Msg, USCINCEUR, ECJ4-TLCC, to CINCUSAREUR, et al., 182020Z Dec 90, transmitting Msg, Cdr, AMC, AMCOC-SM, to AIG 12113, 081444Z Dec 90, sub: European Desert Express Implementation Procedures.

36. Briefing Slide, 7th MEDCOM, n.d. (Oct 90), sub: Corps Medical Support Imperatives; Briefing Slides, 7th MEDCOM, n.d., sub: Deploying Medical Force; Discussion, author with Barbara Slifer, Public Affairs Officer (PAO), 7th MEDCOM, 3 Apr 92. These plans included 7th MEDCOM Operations Plan 1001–90 and draft 7th MEDCOM Operations Plan 1002–90; USAREUR Air Movement Control Cell, *After Action Report: VII Corps Deployment to Operation Desert Shield*, Annex T, "7th Medical Command's Support of Operation Desert Shield."

37. Memo, Travis for CINCUSAREUR, 24 Aug 90, sub: Medical Plan for SWA.

38. Msg (Personal), Shalikashvili to Lt Gen Edwin S. Leland, Jr., CofS, USEU-COM, 160425Z Nov 90, sub: Casualty Reception at Nuernberg Airport.

39. Briefing Slides, Cdr, 7th MEDCOM, n.d., sub: Deploying Medical Force; Briefing Slide, 7th MEDCOM, n.d. (Oct 90), sub: Corps Medical Support Imperatives.

40. Msg, CINCUSAREUR, AEAMD-PA, to AIG 9075, et al., 181623Z Dec 90, sub: Command Information EURRELEASE: Medical Reserves Arrive; Msg, CIN-CUSAREUR, AEAGA-O-CAT, to HQDA, DAMO-ODO-AOC/DASG-HCO, and Cdr, FORSCOM, 090720Z Jan 91, sub: Overview of USAREUR Medical Augmentation.

41. Msg, CINCFOR, FCJ5, to CINCUSAREUR, AEAGC, 221818Z Nov 90, sub: USAREUR Medical Support Requirements for Operation Desert Shield and VII Corps Deployment; Msg, CINCUSAREUR, AEAMD-PA, to AIG 9075, et al., 181623Z Dec 90, sub: Command Information EURRELEASE: Medical Reserves Arrive; Msg, CINCUSAREUR, AEAGA-O-CAT, to HQDA, DAMO-ODO-AOC/DASG-HCO, and Cdr, FORSCOM, 090720Z Jan 91, sub: Overview of USAREUR Medical Augmentation.

42. Msg, CINCUSAREUR, AEAMD-PA, to AIG 9075, et al., 181623Z Dec 90, sub: Command Information EURRELEASE: Medical Reserves Arrive; Maps entitled "Medical reservists served in five countries," provided by Barbara Slifer, PAO, 7th MEDCOM, 28 Apr 92, in MHO files; Msg, CINCUSAREUR, AEAGA-O-CAT, to HQDA, DAMO-ODO-AOC/DASG-HCO, and Cdr, FORSCOM, 090720Z Jan 91, sub: Overview of USAREUR Medical Augmentation.

43. Msg, CINCUSAREUR, AEAMD-PA, to AIG 9075, et al., 181623Z Dec 90, sub: Command Information EURRELEASE: Medical Reserves Arrive.

44. Msg, HQ 7th MEDCOM to MEDDAC, Augsburg, et al., 221214Z Jan 91, sub: Public Affairs Guidance: Hospital Expansion for USAREUR Personnel MEDEVACED From SWA; Memo, Maj Gen Michael J. Scotti, Jr., CSURG, for DCINCUSAREUR, 7 Jan 90, sub: Contingency Hospitals; Memo, Scotti for CofS and DCINCUSAREUR, 4 Jan 91, sub: SWA MEDEVAC; Msgs, USCINCEUR to CINCUSAREUR, 111528Z Jan 91, sub: Aeromedical Evac Equipment and Supply Requirements to Support DESERT SHIELD, and 111738Z Jan 91, sub: DESERT SHIELD Aeromedical Evacuation and Medical Planning Factors. Saint's note appears on the latter message.

45. Msg, CINCUSAREUR, AEAGA-O-CAT, to HQDA, DAMO-ODO-AOC/DASG-HCO, and Cdr, FORSCOM, 090720Z Jan 91, sub: Overview of USAREUR Medical Augmentation; Memo, Scotti for CINCUSAREUR, n.d. (last week of Jan), sub: Overview of USAREUR Medical Support; Msg, CINCUSAREUR to Cdr, V Corps, et al., 172010Z Dec 90, sub: Inactive Contingency Hospitals; Memo, Cdr, 7th MEDCOM, for CINCUSAREUR, ATTN: AEAPA-PP, 7 Jan 91, sub: Public Affairs Augmentation in Wartime; Memo, Scotti for CofS and DCINCUSAREUR, 31 Dec 90, sub: EUCOM Hospitalization Reception Capability for Operation DESERT SHIELD; Briefing Summary, Dittrich, 16 Dec 90, sub: CSURG Update.

46. Cdr, 7th MEDCOM, Aug 91, 7th MEDCOM Medifacts #33–91: DESERT STORM Patient Tracking Report; Chart, Slifer, PAO, n.d.; Discussion, author with Slifer, 3 Apr 92; Memo, Col David H. Hicks, ADCSPER, through Bryde for CofS, HQ USAREUR/7A, 20 Feb 91, sub: Movement Policy for Family Members of USAREUR Soldiers Wounded/Injured and Medically Evacuated to CONUS or KIA [Killed in Action].

47. Msg, USCINCEUR to CINCUSAREUR, 231839Z Aug 90, transmitting Msg, Cdr, PERSCOM, to USEUCOM, Cdr, 7th MEDCOM, and Cdr, 1st PERSCOM, 221200Z Aug 90, sub: Casualty Operations in Support of Operation DESERT SHIELD; Fax, Willis to Burleson, 10 Aug 90, sub: Casualty Reporting for U.S. Personnel in Saudi Arabia; Note, Burleson to Willis, 15 Aug 90, no sub.

48. Briefing Summary, Maj Dan K. Anderson, Asst SGS, HQ USAREUR/7A, 30 Nov 90, sub: Casualty Management.

49. Interv, author with Willis, 11 Jun 91, pp. 9–10.

50. Ibid.; Briefing Summary, Anderson, 4 Dec 90, sub: Mass Casualty/Fatality Operations; Memo, Bryde for CINCUSAREUR, 1 Mar 91, sub: Community Casualty Assistance Planning.

51. Memo, Bryde for CINCUSAREUR, 17 Jan 91, sub: Family Member Visits to Europe During Gulf Hostilities; Memo, Col T. Scofield, Asst CSURG, Spt Svcs, for CofS, HQ USAREUR/7A, 28 Dec 90, sub: Family Member Visits to Europe During Gulf Hostilities; Memo, Bryde for CINCUSAREUR, 31 Jan 91, sub: Request for Special Airline Rates; Msg, Cdr, 21st TAACOM, to Cdrs, 7th MEDCOM and 21st TAACOM, and U.S. Military Community Activities (USMCA), 261715Z Feb 91, sub: Invitational Travel Orders (ITO) for Family Members; Msg, Cdr, VII Corps, AETSD-X-GA-M, to Cdr, USMCA, Nuremberg, 011600Z Mar 91, sub: Airport Processing for PNOK [Patient Next of Kin] of DESERT STORM Casualties.

52. Msg, CINCUSAREUR, AEAPA-PP, to AIG 0803 and 9075, 241830Z Jan 91, sub: PA Plan for Support to Desert Storm Patients; Msg, USCINCEUR, ECDC, to CINCUSAREUR, 011347Z Jan 91, sub: Public Affairs Plan— USCINCEUR Medical Regulating and Evacuation CONOPS—Operation Desert Storm; Memo, Childress for CINCUSAREUR, 22 Jan 91, sub: PA Plan for Treatment of Desert Storm Casualties; Briefing Summary, Webber, 23 Jan 91, sub: O&I.

53. Briefing Summary, Webber, 15 Feb 91, sub: O&I.

54. Schubert and Kraus, *The Whirlwind War*, pp. 153 and 167–70; Swain, *Lucky War*, p. 176; U.S. Department of Defense, *Conduct of the Persian Gulf War: Final Report to Congress* (April 1992), p. 129.

55. Although VII Corps' campaign in the desert still awaits definitive narrative examination, a number of currently available studies are very valuable. (1) The official VII Corps after action report is available at the Center for Army Lessons Learned (CALL), Fort Leavenworth, Kansas 66027–1327 (Memo, Lt Gen Frederick M. Franks, Jr., Cdr, VII Corps, for Commander, U.S. Army, Central Command, ATTN: AFRD-DPT-AAR, 29 May 91, sub: Desert Shield/Desert Storm After Action Report. (2) Lt. Col. Peter S. Kindsvatter, the VII Corps historian during the Gulf War, covers the highlights of VII Corps' combat role in *Military Review* 72 (1992), nos. 1, 2, and 6. (3) Brig. Gen. Robert H. Scales, Jr., director of the Desert Storm Study Project created by the Army chief of staff, presented his team's detailed study of the U.S. forces' ground campaign in Scales, *Certain Victory*. (4) Swain, *Lucky War*, covers VII Corps accomplishments, issues, and problems from the Third Army perspective.

56. Scales, *Certain Victory*, pp. 216–20; Schubert and Kraus, *The Whirlwind War*, pp. 173–83 and 187–88.

57. Scales, *Certain Victory*, pp. 223–53 and 261–70, with the quoted words on p. 270; Schubert and Kraus, *The Whirlwind War*, pp. 177–79, 183–86, and 188–92.

58. Michael R. Gordon and Bernard E. Trainor, *The Generals' War: The Inside Story of the Conflict in the Gulf* (Boston: Little, Brown, and Company, 1995), pp. 355–74; Rick Atkinson, *Crusade: The Untold Story of the Persian Gulf War* (Boston: Houghton Mifflin Company, 1993), pp. 458–61; and Schubert and Kraus, *The Whirlwind War*, pp. 192 and 197.

59. Scales, *Certain Victory*, pp. 291–316.

60. Schubert and Kraus, *The Whirlwind War*, pp. 202–03, and U.S. Department of Defense, *Persian Gulf War: Final Report*, p. 408.

61. Data Card For CINCUSAREUR, 13 Jun 91, sub: USAREUR Deaths in SWA, as of 2400; Briefing Summary, Webber, 20 Mar 91, sub: O&I.

62. The controversy over Franks' and Schwarzkopf's generalship is discussed in Atkinson, *Crusade*, pp. 405–07, 421–28, 440–41, and 469–76; and in Gordon and Trainor, *The Generals' War*, pp. 379–82 and 427–32. A critical article by James G. Burton, "Pushing Them Out the Back Door," *U.S. Naval Institute Proceedings* 119, no. 6 (June 1993): 37–42, was answered by Steve E. Dietrich, "From Valhalla with Pride"; Richard M. Swain, "Compounding the Error"; and

Ronald H. Griffith, "Mission Accomplished—In Full," in *U.S. Naval Institute Proceedings* 119, no. 8 (August 1993): 59–60, 61–62, and 63–64, respectively. Swain, "Reflections on the Revisionist Critique," *Army* 8 (August 1996): 24–31, recently presented a thoughtful and wide-ranging reappraisal of the issues raised in the debate.

63. Briefing Summary, Webber, 1 Mar 91, sub: O&I.

Chapter 7

1. Note, Bryde, on Memo, Willis, thru DCSPER, for CINCUSAREUR, 9 Jan 91, sub: DS Families Leaving USAREUR.

2. Briefing Slides, CFE Div, ODCSOPS, HQ USAREUR/7A, 12 Nov 90, subs: VII Corps Personnel Profile and Ghost MILCOMs, in tab B to incl 4 to interv, author with Jay, 20 Nov 90.

3. Msg, CINCUSAREUR to AIGs 9848 and 7533, 141520Z Nov 90, sub: CINCUSAREUR's Message to Families of Soldiers Deploying on Desert Shield; Memo, Anderson for DCSPER, USAREUR, 14 Nov 90, sub: CINC Message to Families.

4. ODCSPER, HQ USAREUR/7A, *Family Support Task Force Issue Book*, sec IV, Miscellaneous (briefing slides), 8 Feb 91.

5. Msg, Cdr, 1st PERSCOM, to AIG 9848, 211530Z Aug 90, sub: Advance Return of Family Members to CONUS [Continental United States].

6. Msg, CINCUSAREUR, AEAGA-M, to AIG 7533, 8858, 9848, and 11718, 101630Z Nov 90, sub: Movement of Family Members Due to Deployment of USAREUR Units to Desert Shield; Msg, CINCUSAREUR, AEAGA-M, to AIG 7533, 8858, 9848, and 11718, 291409Z Nov 90, sub: Delegation of Authority To Approve Advance Return of Dependents and Escort Travel.

7. Msg, CINCUSAREUR, AEAGA-M, to AIG 7533, 8858, 11718, and 9848, 101630Z Nov 90, sub: Movement of Family Members Due to Deployment of USAREUR Units to Desert Shield; Memo, Anderson for DCSPER, USAREUR, 22 Jan 91, sub: D.S. Demographics.

8. Msg, CINCUSAREUR to AIG 9848 and 7533, 141520Z Nov 90, sub: CINCUSAREUR's Message to Families of Soldiers Deploying on Desert Shield; Memo, Anderson for DCSPER, USAREUR, 14 Nov 90, sub: CINC Message to Families.

9. Briefing Slide, ODCSPER, HQ USAREUR/7A, in Briefing Summary, Webber, 1 Mar 91, sub: O&I.

10. Memo, Bryde for CINCUSAREUR, 7 Jan 91, sub: USCINCEUR Congressional Testimony; Msg, HQDA, DAPE-MPE-DR, to Cdr, PERSCOM, et al., 111717Z Jan 91, sub: Early Return of Dependents From Europe.

11. Msg, CINCUSAREUR to Cdr, VII Corps, et al., 270850Z Nov 90, sub: Command and Control Realignment Post VII Corps Deployment; Msg, CINCUSAREUR to Cdr, V and VII Corps, 21st TAACOM, 56th FA Comd, 7th Army Training Command (7ATC), and USASETAF, 031200Z Dec 90, sub: Community Organization Plans for Desert Shield; Memo, Hicks for CofS, HQ USAREUR/7A, 5 Dec 90, sub: Flattening VII Corps Position Structure. See also Chapter 1 on the restructuring of USAREUR's military community organization.

12. Msg, CINCUSAREUR to Cdr, V and VII Corps, 21st TAACOM, 56th FA Comd, 7ATC, and USASETAF, 031200Z Dec 90, sub: Community Organization Plans for Desert Shield; Memo, Bryde for CINCUSAREUR, 1 Dec 90, sub:

CINC Guidance for Community Organization— DESERT SHIELD; General Officer Steering Committee, DESERT STORM Special Study Project, 9 Jul 91; USAREUR and 7th Army IG, Special Inspection: Key Post-Deployment Operations, Report no. 91–4, n.d. [1991]; Interv, Hendricks with Saint, 7 May 97. The Army and USAREUR responded to this lesson learned—as they did to many other lessons of Operations DESERT SHIELD and DESERT STORM—by increasing emphasis on selection, training, and performance of rear detachment commanders in future deployments. USAREUR, for example, instituted a thorough rear detachment commander's course for prospective rear detachment commanders before and during the deployment to Bosnia.

13. Msg, CINCUSAREUR to Cdr, V and VII Corps, 21st TAACOM, 56th FA Comd, and 7ATC, 141530Z Nov 90, sub: Community Organization Plans for DESERT SHIELD.

14. Msg, CINCUSAREUR, AEAGA-HS, to Cdr, V and VII Corps, 21st TAA-COM, 56th FA Comd, 7ATC, and USASETAF, 170630Z Nov 90, sub: Support for Families During DESERT SHIELD; Interv, author with Saint, 11 Apr 91, pp. 8–9.

15. Msg, CINCUSAREUR, AEAGA-HS, to Cdr, V and VII Corps, 21st TAA-COM, 56th FA Comd, 7th ATC, and USASETAF, 170630Z Nov 90, sub: Support for Families During DESERT SHIELD.

16. Msg, CINCUSAREUR, AEAGA-HS, to Cdr, V and VII Corps, 21st TAA-COM, 56th FA Comd, 7ATC, and USASETAF, 031200Z Dec 90, sub: Community Organization Plans for DESERT SHIELD.

17. Memo, Saint for Distribution A (company level), 3 Dec 90, sub: Family Support Groups and Community Mayors During DESERT SHIELD Deployment. See also AR 608–1, *Army Community Service Program*, 30 October 1990.

18. Msg, CINCUSAREUR, AEAGA-HS, to Cdr, V and VII Corps, 21st TAA-COM, 56th FA Comd, 7ATC, USASETAF, 26th Spt Gp, and U.S. Army, Berlin (USAB), 040700Z Dec 90, sub: HQ USAREUR DESERT SHIELD Family Support Telephone Line.

19. Quotation from Msg, CINCUSAREUR, AEAGA-HS, to Cdr, V and VII Corps, 21st TAACOM, 56th FA Comd, 7ATC, and USASETAF, 170630Z Nov 90, sub: Support for Families During DESERT SHIELD; Msg, CINCUSAREUR, AEAPA-CI, to AIG 9075, info: HQDA, SAPA-CI, DACS-AELO, USCINCEUR, CINCUSAFE, Armed Force Network Europe (AFNE), *Stars and Stripes*, and USASETAF, PAO, 290932Z Nov 90, sub: Command Information EUR-RELEASE 91–38: Family Support Groups; Computer Printouts, ODCSPER, HQ USAREUR/7A, 18 Jan 91 and 5 Feb 91, sub: Community Support for DESERT STORM Families, in MHO files.

20. Msg, CINCUSAREUR, AEAGA-HS, to Cdr, V and VII Corps, et al., 181600Z Dec 90, sub: Support to Family Support Groups (FSG); USAREUR Pamphlet 600–2, USAREUR Personnel Opinion Survey 1991—General Findings Report, vol. 1, Family, 13 Jun 91, pp. 19–21; Inspector General Report no. 91–4, Special Inspection: Key Post Deployment Operations, pp. A–6, A–8; Memo, Burleson for CINCUSAREUR, 28 Dec 90, sub: Wincup Visit.

21. Faxes, Cdr, VII Corps Base, to CINCUSAREUR, 24 Jan 91 and 22 Mar 91, sub: SITREP, VII Corps Base; CPA, USAREUR, AEAPA-CI, "Command Information EUR-RELEASE 91–77—CINC Conducts AFN Interview."

22. Msg, CINCUSAREUR, AEAGA-HS, to Cdr, V and VII Corps, 21st TAA-COM, 56th FA Comd, 7ATC, and USASETAF, 170630Z Nov 90, sub: Support for Families During Desert Shield; Computer Printouts, ODCSPER, HQ USAREUR/7A, 18 Jan 91 and 5 Feb 91, sub: Community Support for Desert Storm Families; USAREUR Pamphlet 600–2, USAREUR Personnel Opinion Survey 1991—General Findings Report, vol. 1, Family, 13 Jun 91, pp. 19–21; Inspector General Report no. 91–4, Special Inspection: Key Post Deployment Operations, pp. A–6, A–7, A–8.

23. Msg, CINCUSAREUR, AEAGA-HS, to Cdr, V and VII Corps, 21st TAA-COM, 56th FA Comd, 7ATC, and USASETAF, 170630Z Nov 90, sub: Support for Families During Desert Shield; Computer Printouts, ODCSPER, HQ USAREUR/7A, 18 Jan 91 and 5 Feb 91, sub: Community Support for Desert Storm Families; AR 608–1 and DA Pam 608–47.

24. Computer Printouts, ODCSPER, HQ USAREUR/7A, 18 Jan 91 and 5 Feb 91, sub: Community Support for Desert Storm Families; USAREUR Pamphlet 600–2, USAREUR Personnel Opinion Survey 1991—General Findings Report, vol. 1, Family, 13 Jun 91, pp. 19–21; Inspector General Report no. 91–4, Special Inspection: Key Post Deployment Operations, pp. A–6, A–7, A–8.

25. USAREUR Pamphlet 600–2, USAREUR Personnel Opinion Survey 1991—General Findings Report, vol. 1, Family, 13 Jun 91, pp. 21–28.

26. Msg, Cdr, 5th Sig Comd, to AIG 11728, 031700Z Dec 90, sub: The "Helpful One" Telephone Support; Msg, CINCUSAREUR, AEAPA-CI, to AIG 9075, 191900Z Dec 90, sub: Command Information EUR-RELEASE 91–50: HELPFUL 1 Update; Computer Printouts, ODCSPER, HQ USAREUR/7A, 18 Jan 91 and 5 Feb 91, sub: Community Support for Desert Storm Families; USAREUR Pamphlet 600–2, USAREUR Personnel Opinion Survey 1991—General Findings Report, vol. 1, Family, 13 Jun 91, pp. 19–21; Inspector General Report no. 91–4, Special Inspection: Key Post Deployment Operations, pp. A–6, A–7, A–8.

27. Msg, CINCUSAREUR, AEAGA-HL, to AIG 9069, 0884, and 7533, 260830Z Dec 90, sub: Use of Alcohol and Drug Abuse Prevention and Control Program (ADAPCP) Counselors During Desert Shield Deployment.

28. Interv, author with Willis, 11 Jun 91, pp. 12–13; 1st PERSCOM, Lessons Learned, Operation Desert Shield/Storm, Issues: Force Structure—Postal Company, Equipment Shortfall on Postal Company TOE, Contingency Plans for Mail Support, and Assignment of APO Numbers for Deploying Units; Memo, Willis for CINCUSAREUR, 6 Dec 90, sub: Streamlining of Postal Operations; ODCSPER, *Family Support Task Force Issue Book*, 8 Feb 91, p. 20.

29. Msg, CINCUSAREUR, AEUPE-P, to AIG 9848, 7533, et al., 171700Z Jan 91, sub: Moratorium on Mailing Parcels; Msg, HQ, Military Airlift Command (MAC), to USCINCEUR, et al., 251430Z Jan 91, sub: Mail Security Procedures.

30. Interv, author with White and Fincke, 6 Feb 91, pp. 13–15; Interv, author with Willis, 11 Jun 91, p. 12; ODCSPER, *Family Support Task Force Issue Book*, 8 Feb 91, pp. 15, 20; Msg, CINCUSAREUR to Cdr, V and VII Corps, et al., 150312Z Dec 90, sub: DESERT FAX; Msg, CINCUSAREUR to Cdr, 7ATC, Berlin Bde, 21st TAACOM, 29th Sig Bde, USMCA, Karlsruhe and Baumholder, 7th Army Combined Arms Training Center (CATC), 22d ASG, et al., 150853Z Feb 91, sub : AT&T DESERT FAX Administrative Instructions; Memo, Crean for CINCUSAREUR, 9 Jan 91, sub: Solicitation of Services from AT&T; Msg, CINCUSAREUR, AEAPA-CI, to AIG 9075, et al., 221513Z Jan 91, sub: Command Information EUR-RELEASE 91–65: DESERT FAX.

31. Msg, CINCUSAREUR, AEAGA-HC, to Cdr, V and VII Corps, 21st TAACOM, Berlin Bde, 7ATC, USASETAF, and 26th Spt Gp, 150900Z Jan 91, sub: Child Care Priority for Children of Deployed DESERT SHIELD Soldiers.

32. ODCSPER, *Family Support Task Force Issue Book*, 8 Feb 91, pp. 2, 5; Msg, CINCUSAREUR, AEAGA-M, to AIG 9848 and 7533, info: USCINCEUR, 080800Z Dec 90, sub: Operation DESERT SHIELD Family Support.

33. Msg, CINCUSAREUR, AEAGA-M, to AIG 9848 and 7533, info: USCINCEUR, 080800Z Dec 90, sub: Operation DESERT SHIELD Family Support; Memos, Kush for CINCUSAREUR, 4 Jan 91, sub: Support From Local German Communities on Project Friendship, and 22 Feb 91, sub: Thank You Letters for Free Transportation; Memos, Bryde for CINCUSAREUR, 4 Feb 91 and 21 Feb 91, sub: Daimler Benz Project Friendship Initiative; Memo, Bryde for CINCUSAREUR, 11 Apr 91, sub: CSA/VCSA Summary Thank You Letters; Memo, Bryde for CINCUSAREUR, 9 Oct 91, sub: Update on Donated Vehicles.

34. Msg, CINCUSAREUR, AEAPA-CI, to AIG 9075, 301400Z Nov 90, sub: Command Information EUR-RELEASE 91–39: USAREUR Housing Policy for DESERT SHIELD Deployment; Msg, CINCUSAREUR, AEAEN-HG, to AIG 7530, 211153Z Nov 90, sub: USAREUR Housing Policy Guidance No. 2, DESERT SHIELD; *Stars and Stripes* (Eur ed.), 7 Dec 90, p. 2.

35. *Stars and Stripes* (Eur ed.), 14 Dec 90, pp. 1, 28; Msg, Cdr, AMC, to Cdr, AMC, Europe, 142059Z Dec 90, sub: Unaccompanied Dependent Space Available Travel; Msg, HQ MAC, to AIG 8521 and 8314, et al., 182040Z Dec 90, sub: Unaccompanied Dependent Space Available Travel; ODCSPER, *Family Support Task Force Issue Book*, 8 Feb 91, p. 3.

36. ODCSPER, *Family Support Task Force Issue Book*, 8 Feb 91, p. 1.

37. Memo, G. Kim Wincup, Asst Sec Army, Manpower and Reserve Affairs, for CINCUSAREUR, 17 Jan 91, sub: Family Support Requirements.

38. Briefing Summary, Swackhamer, 5 Dec 90, sub: ACES [Army Continuing Education System] Family Member Support; Msgs, CINCUSAREUR, AEAGC-T-ACES, to Cdr, V and VII Corps, 21st TAACOM, USASETAF, USAB, 7ATC, and AIG 7533, 101620Z Dec 90, sub: Education Support for Spouses of Deployed Soldiers, and 111625Z Dec 90, sub: Education Support for Spouses of Deployed Soldiers II; Memos, Davis for CINCUSAREUR, 24 Jan 91, sub: ACES Interest Survey of Family Members, and 1 Mar 91, sub: Spouse Scholarship Program.

39. Msgs, Dir, Department of Defense Dependents Schools–Germany, DODDS-G, to CINCUSAREUR, Cdr, V and VII Corps, 21st TAACOM, USAB, 7ATC, and 26th Spt Gp, 110915Z Dec 90, and to USCINCEUR and AIG 9848 and 7533, 071601Z Dec 90, sub: DESERT SHIELD Support; Ofc of the Dir, DODDS-G, briefing booklet and slides, in Briefing Summary, Dittrich, 8 Jan 91, sub: Ms. Woods Briefings.

40. Fact Sheet, Army Community Service (ACS), Coleman Kaserne, Gelnhausen, n.d. (Jan), sub: Army Community Service Family Support Programs.

41. Msgs, CINCUSAREUR, AEAGA-HS, to Cdr, V and VII Corps, 21st TAA-COM, 56th FA Comd, 7ATC, 26th Spt Gp, et al., 081640Z Dec 90, 190850Z Dec 90, 111130Z Jan 91, and 201510Z Mar 91, sub: Good Ideas for DESERT SHIELD Family Support, Nos. 2 thru 5.

42. Memo, Bryde for CINCUSAREUR, 4 Mar 91, sub: Berchtesgaden R&R; Msg (Personal), CINCUSAREUR for Reno, et al., 220715Z Mar 91, sub: USAREUR Soldier's Recreation Center, Berchtesgaden; Memos, Bryde for CIN-CUSAREUR, 5 Apr 91, sub: USAREUR Soldiers Recreation Center, Berchtesgaden; 17 Apr 91, sub: Berchtesgaden Reward Program; and 16 May 91, sub: USAREUR Soldiers Recreation Center Berchtesgaden (USRCB) Update.

43. Memo, Maj Dittrich, 30 Nov 90, sub: Project Friendship; Note, Burleson for DCSHNA, USAREUR, 30 Nov 90, no sub; Memo, Kush for CINCUSAREUR, 27 Nov 90, sub: Project Friendship; Msg, AMEMB, Bonn, to CINCUSAREUR, et al., 292005Z Nov 90, sub: Bundeswehr "Project Friendship" To Aid Military Families Affected by DESERT SHIELD Deployment; Der Bundesminister der Verteidigunginformations- und Pressestab, Mitteilungen an die Presse: Die Bundeswehr hilft XXVII/78, Bonn, 28 Nov 90; Msg, CINCUSAREUR, AEAHN-GR, to Cdr, V and VII Corps and 21st TAACOM, 071200Z Dec 90, sub: Project Friendship; Memo, Kush for CINCUSAREUR, 1 Feb 91, sub: Update on "Project Friendship."

44. Memo, Kush for CINCUSAREUR, 2 Jan 91, sub: USFLO Flash Reports (MP Wagner letters to officials); Memo, Col Walter A. Bawell, CINCUSAREUR Liaison Officer, AMEMB, Bonn, for CINCUSAREUR, 3 Dec 90, sub: Activities Report for the Period 1–30 November 1990.

45. Interv, author with Kush, 20 Jun 91, p. 9; U.S. Statutes, 104: 872–74; Msg (Personal), Saint to Sullivan, 040900Z Jan 91, sub: Approval Authority for Gifts/Donations in Support of DESERT SHIELD; Memo, Bryde for CINCUSAREUR, 25 Jan 91, sub: Donations.

46. Memo, Col Quentin W. Richardson, Actg JA, USAREUR, to CIN-CUSAREUR, 21 Dec 90, sub: Gifts and Donations in Support of DESERT SHIELD; Msg (Personal), Saint to Sullivan, 040900Z Jan 91, sub: Approval Authority for Gifts/Donations in Support of DESERT SHIELD; Memo, Bryde for CINCUSAREUR, 25 Jan 91, sub: Donations; Msg, CINCUSAREUR to Cdr, V and VII Corps, 21st TAACOM, 7ATC, 26th Spt Gp, USMCA, Berlin, and USASETAF, 251950Z Jan 91, sub: Accepting Gifts and Donations in Support of DESERT STORM.

47. The following provide examples: Memo, Pfister for CINCUSAREUR, 10 Sep 90, sub: Trash Flyer; Msg, Cdr, Det 5, 527th MI Bn, to CINCUSAREUR, et

al., 061030Z Nov 90, sub: Proposed Meeting To Promote Conscientious Objector Status; Rpt, PAO, HQ V Corps, 28 Nov 90, sub: Daily Press Review; Msg, Cdr, Det 6, 527th MI Bn, to CINCUSAREUR, et al., 301407Z Nov 90, sub: DESERT SHIELD (Support) Activity Report; *Stars and Stripes* (Eur ed.), 8 Dec 90, p. 2; Msg, Cdr, Det 2, Co A, 527th MI Bn, to CINCUSAREUR, et al., 030900Z Dec 90, sub: DESERT SHIELD Activity Report; Interv, author with Kush, 20 Jun 91.

48. Interv, author with Kush, 20 Jun 91.

49. Interv, author with Pfister, 20 Aug 91; Memo, Heldstab for CIN-CUSAREUR, 14 Jan 91, sub: Antiterrorism Plans.

50. Interv, author with Pfister, 20 Aug 91, pp. 14–16; Memo, Heldstab for CINCUSAREUR, 14 Jan 91, sub: Antiterrorism Plans.

51. Msgs, CINCUSAREUR to Cdr, V and VII Corps, 21st TAACOM, et al., 101700Z Nov 90 and 151415Z Nov 90, sub: USAREUR Force Protection Planning in Support of DESERT SHIELD; Memo, Heldstab for CINCUSAREUR, 14 Jan 91, sub: Antiterrorism Plans; Msg, CINCUSAREUR to Cdr, VII Corps, 241230Z Dec 90, sub: Civilian Guard Augmentation Resulting from Deployments in Support of Operation DESERT SHIELD; Msg, CINCUSAREUR to Cdr, 42d MP Gp, 121715Z Jan 90, sub: MP Reaction Force Tasking.

52. Briefing Summary, Berard, 12 Dec 90, sub: U/R Force Protection DS Impact; Memo, Heldstab for CINCUSAREUR, 13 Dec 90, sub: Force Protection Contingency Message.

53. Msg, HQDA, DAMI-CIC, to UDITD, USAREUR, 142300Z Jan 91, transmitting Msg, Joint Staff, 120356Z Jan 91, transmitting Msg, Secretary of State to all diplomatic and consular posts, 120255Z Jan 91, sub: Terrorist Threat Advisory; Msg, CINCFOR, FCJ3-CAT, to AIG 12126, et al., 191230Z Dec 90, sub: FORSCOM Force Protection Advisory: Update No. 4; Msg, 66th MI Bde to CINCUSAREUR, et al., 171500Z Jan 91, sub: IIR 2 212 7076 91/Weekly Summary on Terrorist Related Info: DESERT SHIELD; Memo, Heldstab for CIN-CUSAREUR, 13 Dec 90, sub: Force Protection Contingency Message; Briefing Summary, Berard, 15 Jan 91, sub: Force Protection Plan.

54. Msg, CINCUSAREUR to Cdr, V and VII Corps, et al., 170230Z Jan 91, sub: THREATCON [threat condition] Change; Discussion Paper, Phil McWilliams, ECJ1-SA, HQ USEUCOM, 18 Jan 91, sub: Terrorist Actions in EUCOM; Msg, Cdr, VII Corps, AETS-X-GH, to CINCUSAREUR, et al., 171740Z Jan 91, sub: VII Corps Base SITREP #2 as of 171600Z Jan 91; Msg, Cdr, V Corps, to Cdr, 3d Inf Div, et al., 170029Z Jan 91, sub: V Corps Force Protection Message #91–002 (Execute STOPWATCH); Msg, Cdr, V Corps, to Cdr, 3d Inf Div, et al., 282000Z Feb 91, sub: V Corps Force Protection Missions. Col. Donald G. Goff, Chief, PLEX Division, ODCSOPS, HQ USAREUR/7A, who was the operations officer at HQ, V Corps, during the Gulf War, noted that USAREUR needed to employ 23,000 personnel daily to meet THREATCON CHARLIE security requirements throughout USAREUR; Author discussion with Goff, 11 Mar 97.

55. Fact Sheet, Mr. Paul Gehman, ODCSINT, HQ USAREUR/7A, 21 Jan 91, sub: Current Assessment of Terrorist Threat to USAREUR; Msg, Cdr, VII Corps,

to CINCUSAREUR, 211700Z Dec 90, sub: Security of U.S. Installations; Memo, Brig Gen Salvatore P. Chidichimo, Provost Marshal, USAREUR, for CofS, HQ USAREUR/7A, 5 Feb 91, sub: Bundeswehr Security Support; Memo, Kush for CINCUSAREUR, 8 Feb 91, sub: Bundeswehr Security Support.

56. Memo, Chidichimo for CINCUSAREUR, 22 Jan 91, sub: THREATCON; Memo, Heldstab for CINCUSAREUR, 24 Jan 91, sub: THREATCON; Msg, Cdr, 7ATC, to CINCUSAREUR, 041600Z Mar 91, sub: 7th ATC THREATCON Status; Msg, Cdr, V Corps, to Cdr, 3d Inf Div, et al., 141028Z Mar 91, sub: THREATCON Level; Msg, CINCUSAREUR to Cdr, V and VII Corps, et al., 151404Z Mar 91, sub: USAREUR THREATCON Status; Msg, Cdr, V Corps, to Cdr, 3d Inf Div, et al., 151813Z Mar 91, sub: USAREUR THREATCON Status; Msg, Cdr, V Corps, to Cdr, 3d Inf Div, et al., 191200Z Mar 91, sub: USAREUR THREATCON Status; Memo, Webber for DCSINT, USAREUR, 5 Mar 91, sub: Threat Assessment.

57. Interv, author with Heldstab, 5 Mar 91, p. 8.

58. Interv, author with Saint, 11 Apr 91, p. 10; Msg, CINCUSAREUR to Cdr, V Corps, et al., 131200Z Dec 90, sub: CINCUSAREUR Concept Plan 4285–90.

59. Msgs, CINCUSAREUR, AEAGC-O-CAT, to Cdr, V and VII Corps, et al., 200610Z Nov 90 and 270850Z Nov 90, sub: C2 Realignments—Post VII Corps Deployment; Permanent Orders 181–1, 181–2, 181–4, 181–5, 181–6, 181–7, 181–8, and 181–9, 21 Dec 90, and 11–1, 18 Jan 91, HQ USAREUR/7A, attached residual VII Corps units to V Corps, effective 15 Dec 90.

60. Msg, HQDA, DAMO-ZA, to CINCFORSCOM, CINCUSAREUR, Cdr, Eighth Army, and HQDA, NGB-ARZ-ARR and DAAR-FMF, 031345Z Dec 90, sub: Scheduled Unit Inactivations and DESERT SHIELD.

61. Memo, Col John P. J. Dussich, Senior USAR Adviser, HQ USAREUR/7A, for ODCSOPS, AEAGC-XO, 8 Mar 91, sub: Annual Historical Review, CY 90; Msg, CINCUSAREUR, AEAMD-PA, to AIG 9075 and USCINCEUR, ECPAO, et al., 181623Z Dec 90, sub: Command Information EURRELEASE: Medical Reserves Arrive; Briefing Summary, Swackhamer, 7 Dec 90, sub: 0730 O&I.

62. Msg, CINCUSAREUR, AEAGC-CAT, to Cdr, V and VII Corps, 21st TAA-COM, 1st PERSCOM, 4th ASG, Burtonwood, et al., 220935Z Feb 91, sub: Clarification of Support Requirements and Funding for Reservists Backfilling Deployed USAREUR Forces; Msg, CINCUSAREUR, AEAGC-O-CAT, to AIG 9848, et al., 061201Z Dec 90, sub: Logistic Support for Reservists.

63. Memo, Dussich for ODCSOPS, HQ USAREUR/7A, AEAGC-XO, 8 Mar 91, sub: Annual Historical Review, CY 90; 1st end, AEUR-O (AEAGS-H/8 Feb 91) (870–5), Maj Lippmann, n.d., sub: Annual Historical Review; O&I Slides, Current Operations Br, Operations Div, ODCSOPS, HQ USAREUR/7A, 8 Mar 91, sub: IRR [Individual Ready Reserve] Deployment as of 071800 Mar.

64. Memos, Shoffner for DCSOPS, USAREUR, 20 Nov 90, sub: CINC Visit to 3ID, and 19 Nov and 24 Nov 90, sub: Reorganization of 3ID; Briefing Summary, Swackhamer, 5 Dec 90, sub: 3ID.

65. Briefing Summary, Swackhamer, 5 Dec 90, sub: 3ID. The first of the ODCSOPS slides stated the objective as: "GOAL: Ready to Deploy."

66. *Annual Historical Review 1991, 8th Infantry Division (Mechanized)*, p. 9–4; Msg, Cdr, 8th Inf Div, AETV-THZ, to Cdr, V Corps, AETV-CG, 271300Z Nov 90, sub: Force Modernization Impacts of DESERT SHIELD.

67. Memo, Maddox for Saint, 14 Jan 91, sub: Corps Mission; Msg (Personal), Saint to Vuono and Galvin, 300830Z Jan 91, sub: Where We Stand.

68. Msg (Personal), Saint to Vuono and Galvin, 110600Z Jan 91, sub: USAREUR Status After DESERT SHIELD Phase II; Memo, Col William D. Chesarek, ADCSOPS, for CINCUSAREUR, 2 Feb 91, sub: Readiness of 3 ID (-), 1/1 AD.

69. Memo, Tipton, Cdr, 200th TAMMC, for CINCUSAREUR, 28 Dec 90, sub: Operation CLEAN-UP. General Saint approved the "operation" and each initiative in marginal notes on General Tipton's memorandum, copy in MHO files.

70. Memo, Heldstab for CINCUSAREUR, 24 Jan 91, sub: Priority of Fill for Residual Force; Memo, DCSOPS for DCSLOG, 29 Jan 91, same sub.

71. Memo, Burleson for Cdr, 21st TAACOM, 200th TAMMC, and ODC-SOPS, ODCSLOG, ODCSENGR, ODCSHNA, and ODCSRM, HQ USAREUR/7A, 7 Jan 91, sub: Planning Force Structure for Theater Reserve (TR) and POMCUS.

Chapter 8

1. Msg, CINCUSAREUR to Cdr, V and VII Corps, et al., 081030Z Feb [apparently March] 91, sub: USAREUR "Desert Farewell" Redeployment/Reception Order #1; Ann D to CINCUSAREUR Redeployment/Reception Order #1, Logistics, 18 Apr 96.

2. Msg, CINCUSAREUR to Cdr, V and VII Corps, et al., 081030Z Feb [Mar] 91, sub: USAREUR "Desert Farewell" Redeployment/Reception Order #1; Ann D to CINCUSAREUR Redeployment/Reception Order #1, Logistics, 18 Apr 91; Slides, no proponent (probably DCSOPS/DCSLOG), n.d. (CINCUSAREUR approved 6 Mar 91), no sub; Memo, Brig Gen John G. Coburn, DCSLOG, USAREUR, for CINCUSAREUR, 2 Aug 91, sub: Reserve Component Support for Return of Equipment from SWA.

3. Msg, USCINCEUR to CINCUSAFE and CINCUSAREUR, 141405Z Sep 90, sub: European Theater Force Level Planning; Msg, HQDA, DAMO-ZA, to CINCFORSCOM, CINCUSAREUR, et al., 031345Z Dec 90, sub: Scheduled Unit Inactivations and DESERT SHIELD; Slides used to brief CCF, 27 Nov 90, CFE Div, ODCSOPS, n.d., sub: USAREUR After the Smoke Clears; MFR, Gehring, 4 Dec 90, sub: CINC Meeting on Relationship of CFE and DESERT SHIELD; Memo, Pflaster, n.d., sub: Trip Report to DA, 8–11 January 1991; MFR, Gehring, 25 Jan 91, sub: Pflaster Trip to DA, Jan 91, and First Agreement on European End-state Numbers; MFR, Gehring, 5 Feb 91, sub: CINC Meeting on 92.2K; Interv, author with Pflaster, 15 Mar 91, p. 7.

4. Draft Msg, Stu Drury, CFE Div, ODCSOPS, HQ USAREUR/7A, Nov 90, sub: USAREUR Force Reduction Update, in tab E to incl 5 to interv, author with Jay, 20 Nov 90; Slides used to brief CCF, 27 Nov 90, CFE Div, ODCSOPS, n.d., sub: USAREUR After the Smoke Clears; MFR, Gehring, 4 Dec 90, sub: CINC Meeting on Relationship of CFE and DESERT SHIELD.

5. Msg, HQDA, DAMO-ZA, to CINCFORSCOM, CINCUSAREUR, Cdr, Eighth Army, and HQDA, NGB-ARZ-ARR and DAAR-FMF, 031345Z Dec 90, sub: Scheduled Unit Inactivations and DESERT SHIELD; Msg, Cdr, VII Corps, to Cdr, 3d Inf Div, et al., 041400Z Dec 90, sub: Update of Status of Operation HOMEWARD BOUND Units and Effect on Units Deploying to SWA; MFR, Gehring, 4 Dec 90, sub: CINC Meeting on Relationship of CFE and DESERT SHIELD.

6. Fax, Heldstab to Maj Gen Harold T. Fields, Jr., DA ADCSOPS, 15 Dec 90, no sub, transmitting Memo, Heldstab for Fields, n.d., sub: SWA/USAREUR Unit Retrograde. Information on Saint's position on numbers that could be drawn down and the DA response are taken from MFR, Gehring, 4 Dec 90, sub: CINC Meeting on Relationship of CFE and DESERT SHIELD, and Interv, author with Pflaster, 15 Mar 91, p. 4.

7. Briefing Summary, Webber, 19 Feb 91, sub: Return of Forces From SWA; Interv, author with Pflaster, 15 Mar 91; Interv, author with Graham, 25 Jun 92.

8. Interv, author with Saint, 11 Apr 91, p. 12; Interv, author with Pflaster, 5 Mar 91, p. 4; Briefing Summary, Webber, 15 Mar 91, sub: Col McGuire—SWA.

9. Interv, author with McGuire, 12 Mar 91, pp. 12–14; Msg, Cdr, USAR-CENT Main, AFRD-DT, to AIG 11743, 281130Z Feb 91, sub: Major Subordinate Command (MSC) Redeployment Priorities.

10. Interv, author with McGuire, 12 Mar 91, p. 12–14.

11. Ibid., pp. 14–15.

12. Note, Burleson to Saint, 4 Mar 91, no sub; Briefing Summary, Webber, 15 Mar 91, sub: Col McGuire—SWA.

13. Memo, Shalikashvili thru Burleson for Saint, 4 Mar 91, no sub; Interv, author with McGuire, 12 Mar 91, pp. 12–13.

14. Note, Burleson to Saint, 4 Mar 91, no sub; Briefing Summary, Webber, 15 Mar 91, sub: Col McGuire—SWA.

15. Briefing Summary, Maj P. Phillips, Asst SGS, HQ USAREUR/7A, 5 Apr 91, sub: Redeployment from SWA.

16. Briefing Summary, Webber, 15 Mar 91, sub: Col McGuire—SWA; Interv, author with McGuire, 17 May 91, pp. 1–9, tape and transcript in MHO files.

17. Briefing Summary, Webber, 15 Mar 91, sub: Col McGuire—SWA; Interv, author with McGuire, 17 May 91, pp. 1–9.

18. Memo, Pflaster for CINCUSAREUR, 10 Apr 91, sub: Latest VII Corps TPFD; Msg, Cdr, VII Corps, to CINCUSAREUR, 220811Z Mar 91, sub: Redeployment of Medical Units and Personnel to USAREUR.

19. Msg, HQ USCINCCENT, CCPM, to USCINCEUR, info: USAREUR DCSOPS, 081600Z Mar 91, sub: USAREUR Support for Military Customs Inspection (MCI); Msg, Cdr, V Corps, to Cdr, 3d Inf Div, et al., 081239Z Mar 91, sub: FRAGO 57 to V Corps OPORD 913; Msg, COMUSARCENT Main, G3, to CINCUSAREUR, 131200Z Mar 91, sub: Theater Clearance for USAREUR Redeployment Support; Msg, Cdr, V Corps, to Cdr, 3d Inf Div, et al., 260936Z Mar 91, sub: FRAGO #1 to OPORD 91–9; Msg, HQDA, DAMO-OD-AOC, to CINCUSAREUR, et al., 171931Z May 91, sub: Residual Force Structure Requirements for ARCENT; Briefing Summary, Phillips, 5 Apr 91, sub: O&I; Briefing Summaries, Capt James D. Campbell, Asst SGS, HQ USAREUR/7A, 24 Jun 91 and 1 Jul 91, sub: O&I; Briefing Summary, Webber, 26 Jun 91, sub: CSA Briefings; O&I slide, Current Operations Br, Operations Div, ODCSOPS, 25 Sep 91, sub: USAREUR Personnel Deployed in Support of PROVIDE COMFORT.

20. Memo, Col Thurman R. Smith, Acting CofS, HQ VII Corps, for Commander, USARCENT, n.d., sub: DESERT SHIELD/DESERT STORM Redeployment After Action Report.

21. Memo, Shalikashvili for Saint, 4 Mar 91, no sub; Msg, Cdr, VII Corps, to CINCUSAREUR, 052043Z Mar 91, sub: Early Redeployment of VII Corps Soldiers; Msg, CINCUSAREUR, AEAGC-O-CAT, to Cdr, V and VII Corps, et al., 110600Z Mar 91, sub: USAREUR SITREP #196 as of 110600Z Mar 91; ODC-SOPS, USAREUR, USAREUR Operation DESERT FAREWELL Redeployment and Demobilization After Action Report (Sep 91), p. 2.

22. Msg, CINCUSAREUR to Cdr, V and VII Corps, 290730Z Mar 91, sub: USAREUR SITREP #213 as of 290730Z Mar 91; Briefing Summary, Phillips, 1 Apr 91, sub: O&I; Msg, CINCUSAREUR to Cdr, V and VII Corps, et al.,

271350Z Apr 91, sub: USAREUR SITREP; Briefing Summaries, Webber, 15 May 91, 29 May 91, 3 Jun 91, 31 Jul 91, and 30 Aug 91, sub: O&I; Memo, Coburn to CINCUSAREUR, 2 Aug 91, sub: Reserve Component Support for Return of Equipment from SWA; Msg, CINCUSAREUR, AEAGC-O-CAT, to Cdr, V and VII Corps, et al., 180730Z Oct 91, sub: USAREUR SITREP #313 as of 180730Z Oct 91; USAREUR Operation DESERT FAREWELL Redeployment and Demobilization After Action Report, DCSOPS, USAREUR (Sep 91), p. 1; Memo, Col John Costello, CofS, 32d AADCOM, 24 Sep 91, sub: After Action Report (AAR) on Redeployment from Operation DESERT STORM.

23. Interv, author with McGuire, 17 May 91, pp. 1–9; Memo, Laposata for CINCUSAREUR, 10 May 91, sub: DESERT FAREWELL/PROVIDE COMFORT Logistics Update #3.

24. Interv, author with McGuire, 17 May 91, pp. 1–9; Memo, Laposata for CINCUSAREUR, 10 May 91, sub: DESERT FAREWELL/PROVIDE COMFORT Logistics Update #3; Msg, USCINCEUR, ECJ4, to CINCUSAREUR, et al., 021054Z Apr 91, sub: Disposition of Foreign Equipment; Msg, COMUSARCENT Main, G3/G4, to Cdr, VII Corps, info: CINCUSAREUR, 310656Z Mar 91, sub: Equipment Redistribution for Saudi POMCUS; Msg, Cdr, AMC, to CINCUSAREUR, et al., 042136Z Mar 91, sub: Drawdown of USAREUR Stocks CTG 25MM HEI-T M792 for USMC [U.S. Marine Corps] Support in SWA; Ann D to CINCUSAREUR Redeployment/ Reception Order #1, Logistics, 18 Apr 96.

25. Memo, Coburn for CINCUSAREUR, 7 Aug 91, sub: SWA Redeployment Ship Status; Msg, Cdr, V Corps, to CINCUSAREUR, et al., 151615Z Oct 91, sub: Condition of Unit Equipment Returning From SWA; Msg, Cdr, AMC, to Cdr, 200th TAMMC, 191734Z Aug 91, sub: SWA Retrograde to USAREUR; Memo, Tipton for CINCUSAREUR, 5 Apr 91, sub: 12th Avn Bde Aircraft Redeployment.

26. *1st Armored Division Annual Historical Review, 1 Jan 91–31 Dec 91*, Part One, Chap IV, sec VI and VII, copy in MHO files.

27. Ibid., section VIII; Part Two, Chap I and II; and Part Three, Chap I and II; *3d Infantry Division Historical Summary, 1991*, pp. 33–36 and 41–42, copy in MHO files.

28. *1st Armored Division Annual Historical Review, 1 Jan 91–31 Dec 91*, Part Two, Chap I and II; Part Three, Chap I and II; and Postscript; Permanent Orders 97–20, HQ USAREUR/7A, 18 Jun 91, and 61–2, HQ, V Corps, 22 Apr 92.

29. O&I Briefing Slides, Current Operations Br, Operations Div, ODCSOPS, 8 Mar 91, sub: IRR Redeployment; Msg, CINCUSAREUR, AEAGC-O-CAT, to Augsburg MEDDAC, et al., 091400Z Mar 91, sub: Redeployment of USAREUR Medical Augmentation Units to CONUS; Msg, Cdr, PERSCOM, to CINCUSAREUR, et al., 130900Z Mar 91, sub: Release of DESERT STORM Temporary Tours of Active Duty (TTAD) Volunteers; Briefing Summary, Phillips, 19 Jun 91, sub: O&I; Briefing Summary, Campbell, 21 Jun 91, sub: O&I; Msg, Cdr, VII Corps, to CINCUSAREUR, 220811Z Mar 91, sub: Redeployment of Medical Units and Personnel to USAREUR; Msg, CINCUSAREUR to Cdr, V and VII Corps, et al., 271350Z Apr 91, sub: USAREUR SITREP; Memo, Col Roger W. Ahrens, Cdr,

266th Theater Finance Command, for DCSOPS, USAREUR, AEAGC-DCA, 4 Oct 91, sub: Submission of After-Action Reports for Redeployment and Demobilization Phases of Operations DESERT SHIELD and DESERT STORM.

30. Msgs, CINCUSAREUR to AIG 12368, et al., 121000Z Mar 91, 140535Z Mar 91, and 031500Z Apr 91, sub: Release of Soldiers From Active Duty (Stop-Loss Demobilization); Msg, CINCUSAREUR, AEAGA-M, to AIG 9848, et al., 201000Z Mar 91, sub: Return of Cross-Leveled Soldiers to Parent Unit; Msg, CINCUSAREUR, AEAGA-M, to AIG 9848, et al., 191321Z Apr 91, sub: Termination of Involuntary Foreign Service Tour Extension (FSTE) in USAREUR—DEROS [Date Eligible for Rotation From Overseas] Adjustment.

31. Interv, author with Jay, 29 Jan 92, tape and transcript in MHO files; Memo, Webber for DCSOPS, USAREUR, 27 Mar 91, sub: SWA CSS [Combat Service Support] Units to CONUS. For further information, see Msg, HQDA, DAMO-ZA, to Cdr, FORSCOM, Cdr, U.S. Army Training and Doctrine Command (TRADOC), CINCUSAREUR, et al., 041916Z Jun 91, sub: Enhancing CONUS Contingency Capability (EC3), incl facsimile msg, Col T. D. Barcellos, HQDA, ODCSOPS, DAMO-FDO, to Pflaster, 27 Mar 91, no sub.

32. Memo, Childress for CINCUSAREUR, n.d., sub: Announcement of USAREUR Units Identified To Enhance CONUS Contingency Capabilities; Interv, author with Jay, 29 Jan 92.

33. Interv, author with Jay, 29 Jan 92.

34. Msg, USCINCEUR to AIG 824, et al., 170703Z Mar 91, sub: USEUCOM SITREP 17 Mar 91; Briefing Summary, Phillips, 1 Apr 91, sub: O&I; Briefing Summary, Webber, 1 May 91, sub: O&I; Msg, CINCUSAREUR, AEAGC-O-CAT, to Cdr, V and VII Corps, et al., 180730Z Oct 91, sub: USAREUR SITREP #313 as of 180730Z Oct 91.

35. Briefing Summary, Phillips, 1 Apr 91, sub: O&I; Briefing Summary, Webber, 15 Apr 91, sub: O&I.

36. General information on Operation PROVIDE COMFORT and Joint Task Force–Bravo (JTF-B) taken from Lt Col Gordon W. Rudd, draft monograph, "Operation PROVIDE COMFORT, One More Tile on the Mosaic, 6 April to 15 Jul 91," n.d.; Briefing Summaries, Webber, 15 Apr 91 and 29 May 91, and Campbell, 31 Jul 91 and 30 Aug 91, sub: O&I; O&I slide, Current Operations Br, Operations Div, ODCSOPS, 25 Sep 91, sub: USAREUR Personnel Deployed in Support of PROVIDE COMFORT; Msg, CINCUSAREUR, AEAGC-O-CAT, to Cdr, V and VII Corps, et al., 180730Z Oct 91, sub: USAREUR SITREP #313 as of 180730Z Oct 91.

37. Memo (Personal), Maj Gen Roger K. Bean, Cdr, VII Corps Base, for Saint, 30 Apr 91, sub: SITREP, VII Corps Base; Msg, CINCUSAREUR to Cdr, VII Corps, et al., 170730Z Jun 91, sub: USAREUR SITREP #281 as of 170730Z Jun 91; Memo, Heldstab for CINCUSAREUR, 6 Jun 91, sub: Wives' Letter; *8th Infantry Division (Mechanized) Annual Historical Review, 1991*, pp. 16–1, 16–2, 16–10, 16–11, 16–14, 16–15, 16–19, 23–6, and 23–7.

38. Msg, Cdr, AMC, to AIG 12636, et al., 161900Z Jun 91, sub: AMC-SWA SITREP #281, 16 June 1991; Fax, Cdr, 11th Armored Cavalry Regiment (ACR),

to CINCUSAREUR, Jul 91, sub: SITREP; Msg, USCINCEUR to CINCUSAREUR, 121613Z Aug 91, sub: 11th ACR; Msg, USCINCCENT to Secretary of Defense, CJCS, Secretary of State, USCINCEUR, CINCUSAREUR, et al., 261520Z Nov 91, sub: Proposed Public Affairs Guidance—Redeployment of Battalion Task Force.

39. *32d Army Air Defense Command Annual Historical Review, 1 Jan 91 to 31 Dec 91*, p. 1–6–4; Msg, CINCUSAREUR, AEAGC-O-CAT, to Cdr, V and VII Corps, et al., 180730Z Oct 91, sub: USAREUR SITREP #313 as of 180730Z Oct 91; O&I Slide, Current Operations Br, Operations Div, ODCSOPS, 25 Sep 91, sub: USAREUR Personnel Deployed in Support of Provide Comfort.

40. Msgs, CINCUSAREUR to Cdr, V and VII Corps, et al., 291209Z Apr 91 and 020857Z May 91, sub: Command and Control in USAREUR During and Post-Redeployment From SWA; Msg, Cdr, V Corps, to Cdr, 3d Inf Div, et al., 100800Z May 91, sub: Instructions for Post SWA Command and Control Realignment.

41. Memo, DCSOPS, AEAGC-CFE, no sig block (Pflaster, C/CFE Div, ODC-SOPS), for CINCUSAREUR (initialed by Saint, 1 Apr 91), sub: Changing the Flow of Units Returning Without Equipment; Briefing Summary, Phillips, 5 Apr 91, sub: Redeployment from SWA (incl stationing plans and community support, briefed to Shalikashvili); In-process review slides, CFE Div, 10 Apr 91, sub: Redeployment & Drawdown Supportability??? [sic]; Memo, Brig Gen Richard E. Davis, DCSOPS, USAREUR, for CINCUSAREUR, 24 Oct 91, sub: Accelerated Drawdown. See also memo, Richard Cheney, Secretary of Defense, for CJCS, 21 Jun 91, sub: FY 1992 European Realignment Execution Directive.

Glossary

AADCOM	army air defense command
AB	air base
ACE	Allied Command, Europe
ACQ	acquisition
ACR	armored cavalry regiment
AD	armored division
ADA	air defense artillery
AFN	American Forces Network
AFRTS	armed forces radio and television system
AG	adjutant general
AH–64	Apache combat helicopter
ALO	authorized levels of organization
AMC	U.S. Army Materiel Command
Amb	ambulance
AMMED	Army Medical Department
Ammo	ammunition
AOR	area of responsibility
APO	Army post office
APOE	aerial port of embarkation
AR	Army Regulation/armor/armored
ARCENT	U.S. Army Central Command
Arty	artillery
ASL	authorized stockage list
ASLT	assault
ATC	army training command
ATE	automatic test equipment
ATMCT	air terminal movements control team
AV	aviation
AVIM	aviation intermediate maintenance
BB&T	blocking, bracing, and tie-down equipment
Bde	brigade
BDO	battle dress overgarment

BDU	battle dress uniform
Bn	battalion
BTRY	battery
C-Day	commitment day
CAC	casualty area command
Cav	cavalry
CEOI	communications-electronics operating instruction
CEWI	combat electronic warfare intelligence
CFE	conventional forces, Europe
CH–47	Chinook transport helicopter
CID	U.S. Army Criminal Investigation Command
CIDS	counterintelligence daily summary
CINCUSAREUR	commander in chief, United States Army, Europe
CL IX	CLASS IX (repair parts)
CM	chemical
Co	company
CONUS	continental United States
CMBT	combat
Cmd	command
Comp	composite
CONEX	container express
COSCOM	corps support command
CP	command post
CPO	chemical protective overgarment
CS	combat support
CSE	combat support equipment
CTA	common table of allowances
Ctl	control
DA	Department of the Army
DAC	Department of the Army civilian
DACG	departure airfield control group
DCG	deputy commanding general
DCPC	direct combat probability coding
DCSLOG	deputy chief of staff, logistics
DCSOPS	deputy chief of staff, operations
DCSPER	deputy chief of staff, personnel
Decon	decontamination
DEPMEDS	deployable medical systems

Det	detachment
DISCOM	division support command
Div	division
DM	Deutsche Marks
DS	direct support
DSU	direct support unit
EAC	echelon-above-corps
EN	engineer
EOD	explosive ordnance disposal
Equip	equipment
Evac	evacuation
(F)	(Forward)
FA	field artillery
FACOM	field artillery command
FCP	family care plans
Fin	finance
Fld	field
FSB	forward support battalion
FWD	forward
GDR	girder bridge
Gp	group
GS	general support
HELO	helicopter
HEMTT	heavy expanded mobility tactical truck
HET	heavy equipment tractor
HHB	headquarters and headquarters battery
HHC	headquarters and headquarters company
HHD	headquarters and headquarters detachment
HMMWV	high mobility multipurpose wheeled vehicle
HQ	headquarters
HQDA	Headquarters, Department of the Army
Hvy	heavy
I&A	imagery and analysis
IAW	in accordance with
ICW	in coordination with
ID	infantry division
IN	infantry

INTSUM	intelligence summary
JCS	joint chiefs of staff
JFC-E	Joint Forces Command East
JFC-N	Joint Forces Command North
JOPES	joint operations planning execution system
JTF	joint task force
LEMCO	light equipment maintenance company
Log	logistics
LOG CAT	Office of the Deputy Chief of Staff, Logistics, Crisis Action Team
LOGMARS	logistics application of automated marking and reading symbols
Lt	light
M1	Abrams tank
M2 and M3	Bradley fighting vehicles
Maint	maintenance
MARCENT	U.S. Marine Central Command
MBT	main battle tank
MCC	movements control center
Mech	mechanized
Med	medical
MEDCOM	medical command
MEDSOM	medical supply, optical, and maintenance
Mdm	medium
MI	military intelligence
MILCOM	military community
MILPER	U.S. Army Military Personnel Center
MLRS	multiple launch rocket system
MMC	materiel management center
MOS	military occupational specialty
MP	military police
MPRJ	military personnel records jacket or file
MPSA	Military Postal Service Agency
MRE	meals, ready to eat
MSB	main support battalion
MSC	major subordinate command
MSG	message
MSL	missile
MTMC-Eur	Military Traffic Management Center, Europe

Mvmt	movement
MWR	morale, welfare, and recreation
NA	not available
NATO	North Atlantic Treaty Organization
NBC	nuclear, biological, and chemical defense
NCO	noncommissioned officer
NCOER	noncommissioned officer efficiency report
NET	new equipment training
NLT	not later than
O&I	operations and intelligence
OCIE	organizational clothing and individual equipment
ODCSOPS	Office of the Deputy Chief of Staff, Operations
ODCSPER	Office of the Deputy Chief of Staff, Personnel
OER	officer efficiency report
OH–58	Kiowa scout helicopter
OPCON	operational control
Ord	ordnance
ORF	operational readiness float
Pers	personnel
PERSCOM	United States Army Personnel Command
PLL	prescribed load list
POC	personnel operations centers
POE	port of embarkation
POL	petroleum, oils, and lubricants
POMCUS	pre-positioned organizational materiel configured in unit sets
POR	preparation of replacements for overseas movement
Proc	processing
Reforger	Return of Forces to Germany
ROWPU	reverse osmosis water purification unit
S&S	supply and service
SETAF	Southern European Task Force
SGS	secretary of the general staff
SIDPERS	Standard Installation/Division Personnel System

Sig	signal
SITREP	situation report
SMC	USAREUR separate major command, reporting to the deputy commander in chief, USAREUR
SPOE	seaport of embarkation
Sqdn	squadron
Spt	support
SSSC	self-service supply center
STU-II	secure telephone unit
Sup	supply/support
Svc	service
SWA	Southwest Asia
TAACOM	theater area army command
TBD	to be determined
TC ACCIS	transportation coordinator's automated command and control information system
TF	task force
TMCA	transportation movement control agency
TAMMC	theater army materiel management center
TFC	theater finance command
THREATCON	threat condition
TOPO	topographic
TPFDD	time-phased force deployment data
TPU	tank and pump unit
Trans	transportation
TRITAC	tri-service tactical communications system
UBL	unit basic load
UH–60	Black Hawk utility helicopter
UIC	unit identification code
UMC	USAREUR major command, reporting to the commander in chief, USAREUR
USAF	United States Air Force
USAFE	United States Air Forces in Europe
USAPGE	United States Army Postal Group, Europe
USAREUR	United States Army, Europe
USAREUR/7A	United States Army, Europe, and Seventh Army
USCENTCOM	United States Central Command
USCINCEUR	United States commander in chief, Europe

USEUCOM   United States European Command
USPS   United States Postal Service
USTRANSCOM   United States Transportation Command

V/S   Vulcan/Stinger

Wea   weather
WWMCCS   worldwide military command and control
                            system

Bibliographical Note

The records of Headquarters, United States Army, Europe, have since 1987 normally been processed in accordance with the policies and procedures contained in Army Regulation 25–400–2, *The Modern Army Recordkeeping System (MARKS)*. Upon retirement from active office files, unclassified records are held temporarily at a Records Holding Area in Darmstadt, Germany, and classified records at the Washington National Records Center in Suitland, Maryland. From these locations records that will be permanently retained are ultimately shipped to the National Archives.

Much of the information in this study on the planning both of USAREUR support to Operation DESERT SHIELD and of the drawdown and restructuring of U.S. Army forces in Europe derived from documents found in the then-active files of the Conventional Forces in Europe Division of the Office of the Deputy Chief of Staff, Operations, HQ USAREUR/7A, under the office symbol "AEAGC-CFE." Other information about HQ USAREUR/7A actions was found in the files of the proponent staff office named in the citation, particularly those of the Deputy Chief of Staff, Personnel (AEAGA), for personnel policy and general home-front issues; Deputy Chief of Staff, Operations (AEAGC), for planning, operational, and training issues; and Deputy Chief of Staff, Logistics (AEAGD), for logistical matters. The records of the Office of the Chief Surgeon, USAREUR, and Headquarters, 7th Medical Command, should be consulted for medical issues and those of Headquarters, 1st Personnel Command, for personnel procedures.

Many other sources used for this study will not be found in these files because normal files maintenance and retirement procedures were not followed for many documents relating to the drawdown and deployment. This study was researched late in 1990 and throughout 1991 and written in 1991 and the first months of 1992, starting early in the drawdown and restructuring process and continuing through the deployment of USAREUR personnel and equipment to Southwest Asia until shortly after the last USAREUR personnel returned to Europe. At that time most information about the drawdown was not only classified SECRET, according to the definitions and the classification and declassification procedures in Army Regulation 380–5, but was also designated CLOSE-HOLD, which limited its dissemination to a small group designated by the USAREUR commander as "trusted agents." Trusted agents avoided as much as possible putting this sensitive drawdown information on paper and saving it and, when it was necessary to create documents, retained them in unique office files or even personal files rather than standard office files. No provisions were made for ever withdrawing the CLOSE-HOLD designation and releasing the information outside this small, but expanding, circle. Since the deployment from Europe to Saudi Arabia was closely bound up with the drawdown—and planned largely by the same offices and people—many deployment documents were also tightly restricted, unavailable, and possibly destroyed, forgotten, or lost in special office or personal files.

Fortunately, some of the CLOSEHOLD files thus created have been preserved. Among these are personal collections of documents related to both the drawdown and deployment retained by Darrell Pflaster, Chief, CFE Division, and Virginia Jay, a member and later chief of CFE's Plans and Policy Branch. Both Mr. Pflaster and Ms. Jay worked closely with the USAREUR Military History Office to ensure that these records were saved, and documents copied and retained in their collections are cited extensively in this study. The USAREUR Military History Office and Mr. Pflaster are now working with the U.S. Army Military History Institute to establish at the latter's Carlisle Barracks, Pennsylvania, repository a collection of Pflaster's personal papers, including all his computer disks relating to long-range planning, the elimination of intermediate-range nuclear forces, the implementation of arms control agreements, force reductions, and deployments between 1987 and 1995. Pflaster's files contain much of the material cited as tabs and enclosures to the Jay interviews. These documents should also be found in the retired files of the Office of the Deputy Chief of Staff, Operations, HQ USAREUR/7A.

Copies of the principal documents on which this study relies have been retained as back-up source material in the historians' background material files (870–5d) of the USAREUR Military History Office. The USAREUR Military History Office organizational history file (870–5a) also contains a set of outgoing HQ USAREUR/7A Crisis Action Team messages from November 1990 through August 1991 related to Operations DESERT SHIELD and DESERT STORM and related operations and task forces. Both of these sets of files will eventually be transferred to the National Archives.

As a result of the exceptional security protecting early drawdown and deployment planning, this study, and particularly its first two chapters, relies more heavily than is typical on recorded oral history inter-

views rather than on memorandums, correspondence, and other docu-
ments. The recorded tapes and final draft transcripts of these interviews
are maintained in the Military History Office, HQ USAREUR/7A.
Transcripts of some of the interviews, including those of Generals Saint,
Shalikashvili, Burleson, Heldstab, and Laposata, will be provided to the
U.S. Army Center of Military History and the U.S. Army Military History
Institute.

Index

AADCOM, 32d. *See* Army Air Defense Command (AADCOM), 32d.
Abrams tanks. *See* M1; M1A1.
ACE. *See* Allied Command, Europe (ACE).
ACE Mobile Force, 164–65
Ad Dammam, 155, 243, 247
AH–64. *See* Apache, AH–64.
Air ambulance units, 11, 55–56, 106, 180–81, 247
Air Defense Artillery Brigades
  10th, 168
  11th, 166, 169
  94th, 259
Air Defense Artillery units (battalion level)
  3d Air Defense Artillery, 4th Battalion, 145
  3d Air Defense Artillery, 5th Battalion, 111
  5th Air Defense Artillery, 3d Battalion, 111
  7th Air Defense Artillery, 1st Battalion, 169–70, 259
  7th Air Defense Artillery, 2d Battalion, 166
  7th Air Defense Artillery, 4th Battalion, 165, 259
  7th Air Defense Artillery, 5th Battalion, 259
  43d Air Defense Artillery, 2d Battalion, 166
  43d Air Defense Artillery, 3d Battalion, 166
  43d Air Defense Artillery, 4th Battalion, 168
  43d Air Defense Artillery, 8th Battalion, 166
Air defense artillery units, use of, 60, 62, 89, 97, 104–05, 110–12, 164–70, 248, 256, 259

Air Force, Ninth, 4. *See also* United States Air Force.
Airborne Corps, XVIII, 4, 56, 81–82, 112, 186, 188–91, 193, 248
Airborne Division
  82d, 67–68, 155
  101st (Air Assault), 4, 65
AirLand Battle, 5, 8–9, 20, 24–26, 34, 95, 97, 261
AirLand Battle Future, Nonlinear, 34
Airlift, 60–62, 65, 68, 91, 117, 144–45, 155–60, 168–70, 247–48, 252, 262
Al Busayyah, 190
Al Jubayl, 155, 247
Allied Command, Europe (ACE), 46, 164–65
Allied Forces, Central Europe, 18, 24
Amberg, 108
American Forces Network–Europe, 111, 248
American Shanti, 174
Ammunition, 13, 46, 62, 69, 71–72, 74, 78–79, 91–92, 122, 150–51, 153, 159, 172–76, 250
Amsterdam, 37, 253
Andrew, Col. Gary, 173–74
Ansbach, 167, 253
Antwerp, 38, 91–92, 118, 122, 150, 153, 160, 237, 253
Apache, AH–64, 19, 21, 24–25, 39, 54, 60–61, 64, 125
Arabian Peninsula, 4, 87
ARCENT. *See* United States Army Central Command (ARCENT).
Area Support Group
  29th, 156
  80th, 145
  543d, 145
Armor units (battalion level). *See also* Cavalry units (battalion level), 8th Cavalry, 3d Battalion.